D1216541

THE GOOD LIFE

ALSO BY LOREN BARITZ

The Servants of Power: A History of the Use of Social Science in American Industry (1960)

City on a Hill: A History of Ideas and Myths in America (1964)

Backfire: A History of How American Culture Led Us into Vietnam and Made Us Fight the Way We Did (1985)

EDITOR OF:

Sources of the American Mind (1966)

John Taylor's *An Inquiry into the Principles and Policy of the Government of the United States* (1969)

The Culture of the Twenties (1970)

The American Left: Radical Political Thought in the Twentieth Century (1971)

THE GOOD LIFE

*The Meaning of Success for the
American Middle Class*

BY
LOREN BARITZ

Harper & Row, Publishers, New York
Grand Rapids, Philadelphia, St. Louis, San Francisco
London, Singapore, Sydney, Tokyo, Toronto

This book was originally published in hardcover in 1989 by Alfred A. Knopf, Inc. It is reprinted by arrangement with Alfred A. Knopf, Inc.

THE GOOD LIFE. Copyright © 1982 by Loren Baritz. All rights reserved. Printed in the United States of America. No part of this book may be used or reproduced in any manner what-soever without written permission except in the case of brief quotations embodied in critical articles and reviews. For infor-mation address Harper & Row, Publishers, Inc., 10 East 53rd Street, New York, N.Y. 10022.

First PERENNIAL LIBRARY edition published 1990.

Library of Congress Cataloging-in-Publication Data
Baritz, Loren.
    The good life: the meaning of success for the American middle class / Loren Baritz.
        p.   cm.
    Reprint. Originally published: New York : Knopf, 1989.
    Includes bibliographical references.
    ISBN 0-06-097275-0
    1. Middle classes—United States—History—20th century.
2. Success—United States—History—20th century. 3. United States—Social life and customs—20th century.   I. Title.
    HT690.U6B37   1990   89-45625
    305.5′.5′0973—dc20

90 91 92 93 94 FG 10 9 8 7 6 5 4 3 2 1

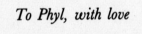
To Phyl, with love

Contents

Acknowledgments ix

Introduction xi

1. Assaying the Golden Land 3

2. The Wonderful World of Dissatisfaction 56

3. The Triumph of the Middle Class 105

4. Costs of the Dream 166

5. Culture War 225

6. Freedom from Love 289

Notes 319

Index 347

Acknowledgments

I am obliged to friends and colleagues for reading this manuscript, telling me what was wrong, how it could be improved, and offering moral support. I am especially grateful to Christopher Lasch, Lawrence Levine, Bruce Laurie, Milton Cantor, Murray Schwartz, Gerard McCauley, and Ashbel Green. Harriet Sigerman began as my research assistant and quickly became a colleague who participated fully in every phase of the evolution of this book. Phyllis Baritz, as usual, read and improved the manuscript while enduring one's obsessions, almost always with loving good cheer.

L.B.

Introduction

Searching for the American middle class is a little like looking for air. It is everywhere, invisible, and taken for granted. The middle class, however, can be found if it is defined beforehand, for then it is possible to track the qualities identified as significant. This, of course, is a form of deduction, more acceptable to Sherlock Holmes than to modern science, but necessary if we are to give shape and substance to air.

In a land where poverty and injustice have proved ineradicable, where economic busts as well as booms seem inevitable, it is wrong to say that the middle class was or is the whole American story—aside, of course, from the obvious fact that it is hardly unique to America. Appearing throughout commercial Europe in the seventeenth century, and in pockets even earlier, the class of merchants, clerks, and ministers began to think differently about themselves and their families.[1] And yet, given that the American middle class does share values and habits with its counterparts of other times and places, it is in many respects distinctive and *sui generis*. Widespread economic opportunity and, especially, immigration have unquestionably made the American story different.

Most important, America's spirit and tone, its historical mythology and official aspirations, political bent, educational arrangements, the centrality of business enterprise, as well as the dreams of the vast majority of its people, derive from the psychology of the great imperial middle. Although by no means have all Americans been middle-class, that is what most have wanted to be, and they have conducted themselves in ways acceptable to the norm before they have had or even after they have lost the price of admission. Americans, especially, have blurred strictly economic class boundaries by reason of their hopes, not necessarily their wealth. The widely perceived class *un*consciousness of the American people is a consequence of a class psychology characteristic not only of actual members of the middle class but of aspirants to that status, and overall, therefore, of the great majority of the nation.

There are two different ways to define class, both sensible, but leading to different results. Many analysts, following Marx, define this shaggy beast by its "objective" condition, that is, by what it owns and how much money it has accumulated, and by its opposition to people who have less. These scholars seek statistical measurements of income by generation, education, occupation, and region. One of my major purposes in the present work is to show that such apparent precision does not adequately illuminate what has happened in America.

For I believe that class, especially in America, is a state of mind, defying useful measurement, allergic to the supposed charms of the inchworm. This conception, more in the tradition of Flaubert than of Marx, stresses detail, vignettes, argument, and tone—a focus on the individual—not calculation. It seeks to locate private life, especially intensely personal desires, as the stuff of middle-class existence, nowhere shown better than in *Madame Bovary*. This way to attack the problem assumes the necessary economic context for its subjects, and occasionally even attempts to make connections between psychological and economic realities; but it focuses on the everyday life of its subjects, not only on their wallets. Of course, money is no mere detail, and the attitude of the middle class toward it is a major piece of business, as Flaubert understood better than anyone. A full definition of the subjective middle class is spread throughout this book.

America seemed made to order for the fullest expression and deepest satisfaction of people who wished on their own to remake, not the world, but their own lives and those of their children. If the world was remade in the process, and the middle class hoped it would be in its own image, that would be a fine if peripheral consequence. For the people of the middle, life was personal, not historic, to be measured most accurately by the neighbor, not the philosopher, cleric, or politician: private lives in privately owned space, with individuals separately exploring the meaning of the good life. For more people than ever before in the history of the world, a middle-class personality eventually emerged. That is what this book is about.

It is because class membership is so largely a matter of perception that the middle class has withstood every challenge, at least in America in the twentieth century. The middle class absorbed or dismissed its many critics, often changing its collective mind a bit in the process, but never abandoning its dream, its plans for the children's future, its faith in the nation's fundamental soundness. It was no use for intellectuals on the left or moralists on the right to lecture middle-class Americans about how they were acting against what others perceived to be their own best interests. They knew what they were interested in, and would not be dissuaded by the logic or disapproval of others.

To discuss what they were interested in, I have tried to focus this book on what they, not others, were hoping, thinking, and doing. But how is it possible to get under such a collective skin? I have generally excluded high culture or literature—not often experienced by middle-class Americans—as a key to the middle class; and, in any case, America has not yet found its Flaubert or Thomas Mann. After too many false starts, my criterion for judging what should be excluded finally became clear: if the middle class was uninterested in an event, person, or institution, I followed its lead. I tried to focus on habits of living and working, on assumptions about value, on desires and goals, and not on great institutions, from which middle-class Americans usually recoil. To sneak up on private life, I have used census materials, polls, popular magazines, and memoirs, along with a large and excellent body of scholarship. I needed to understand the details of domesticity, as sometimes revealed in advertising, radio, movies, fashions, television, the constant redefinition of sex and sex roles, marriage, work, and raising children.

An important theme of *The Good Life* concerns the eventual deformation of the American male, starting during World War II, and the evolution of the ideal woman, from being strong in the 1930s to being good during the forties and fifties, martyred in the sixties, and an equal person thereafter. Aside from the content of such concerns, this raises the question about whether cultural history should be written by decades. It must seem an arbitrary way to analyze the evolution of a class. It is true that such an emphasis on decades is not only arbitrary but misleading. People normally don't lead their lives, or change their beliefs, in so mindless a response to the calendar. Yet, in America, three decades—the roaring twenties, the Great Depression, and the furious sixties—were distinct cultural moments whose peculiarities profoundly influenced masses of people, sometimes permanently. Having to treat each of these decades as authentically unique may give this book the feel of mechanical organization. Despite my strong desire to avoid this, I finally decided that it was better to surrender to the record. I suppose that is what any member of the prudent middle class would do.

THE GOOD LIFE

I

ASSAYING
THE GOLDEN LAND

Pious Protestants once prepared themselves to welcome their eternal fate naked and alone, with terrifying honesty before a furious God. The great Protestant reformers of the sixteenth century taught their followers that to obey their God they must abandon the ancient institutions which codified truth and power. The Reformation dared men to think for themselves, risk all for the good of their souls. The self had to be thrown against human history, in opposition to respectable opinion and institutions that had once seemed eternal and universal.

In time, a tiny band of true believers in England concluded that they must quarantine themselves by departing custom and country for a virgin place where they could restart their lives free from the outrages and temptations of their damned neighbors. The Puritans who sailed to the new world had not been persecuted; they were all at least comfortable in England, and some were wealthy. But they feared the apocalypse they thought was coming. They knew their middle-class sufficiency made them unlikely pioneers, but such a worry was merely of the flesh, whose mortification, they believed, was good for the spirit. They sailed under the winds of inspiration, not seeking perfection, not hiding from the civilized world, but to improve their lot with a God whose anger was infinite. They resettled to save themselves and teach others—the world, if it would listen—how to walk on God's straight path. They abandoned family and hearth so that on the Day of Awe they could each, alone and pathetic, face the music of thundering cymbals, not murmuring harps.

The fervor of the first generation was not sustainable, and only a few American settlers, especially in areas other than New England, were inebriated with the Lord. Shortly, almost all of the voluntary newcomers arrived in search of what the first Puritans had abandoned: the good things of life, an opportunity to ease the burdens of the flesh. These were the pioneers for whom the munificence of nature's American bounty was ground for hope, justification for present privation in the expectation of progress. Exchanging the old country's encrusted class relationships for the new world's social fluidity, the pioneers came to plant the seeds of a free life that offered a chance to begin anew, to wrest food and shelter from opportunity, and, reversing Kafka, to begin to metamorphose from an insignificant beetle in the old world into a free man in the new.

Nonetheless, in outlook and motivation these less-pious pioneers had much in common with the Puritans. Both groups conceived of individual improvement as a project so transcendent that it organized their lives. The Puritans unwillingly stressed individualism—one sinner before God, no institutional or priestly intercessors, no Virgin Mary, to smooth things over—even while they strove to create tightly knit communities. While defending their own nonconformity, the Puritans despised and punished dissidents who lived amongst them. They believed that salvation lay in each individual's heart and soul, but that there were rules to follow. Others rejected such rules as inconsistent with the individuality of true religious devotion. Such individualism was implicit in the very foundation of the Reformation and in thousands of subsequent sermons and tracts. The Reformation created an irresistible centrifugal spin, first into an uncontrollable number of sects, and then inevitably into individuals. In New England, this spin created dissenters dangerous to Puritan orthodoxy, including Roger Williams and Anne Hutchinson, and, in time, backsliding merchants, whores, and revolutionaries.

The ambitious, more secular pioneer workers in what temporarily passed for a vineyard had also fled the emotional bonds of home to hazard a new world on their own, less tightly tied to churches that were not established or a state that was at most tenuous, challenging fate with their individual strength and will. To the pioneers, individualism was a fact of life, not a prejudgment or a theory. Whereas for the Puritans individualism was a postulate deduced from their theology, for the pioneers it was a position induced from their daily experience. Living in perhaps dangerous isolation, threatened with destruction if he stepped wrong, the pioneer, whether he flourished or failed, had only himself to thank or blame. For him, success came from self-reliance and independence was proof of virtue.

The future American middle class grew from the twin roots of the Puritans' unendurable moral system and the pioneers' difficult success. The Puritans tirelessly taught that worldly success might be a hint of God's mysterious favor. The pioneers daily lived amidst such practical favor. The Puritans and their successors advocated the moral discipline necessary to gain wealth; the rigors of their lives taught the pioneers the same lessons. In America, work, diligence, perseverance, sobriety, and thrift paid off. To Americans and others who knew what was happening, it seemed like a miracle, as if God had hidden America until He had located worthy people, Protestants, who merited the world's second garden.

The American nation was shaped by the collision of cultures. Its growth from wilderness to farms, to counting houses and

trade, and then to an industrial civilization, required a continuing infusion of new people whose fate depended upon their
ability to conform to the new world's demands. Most came for
economic opportunity, and their success or failure depended
on the mixture of their native attitudes and habits with those
of the people who had arrived earlier. This rude and sometimes
shocking encounter revealed what migrating people expected
and were able to perform, as it also disclosed what Americans
desired and were willing to tolerate. As immigrants were forced
to adapt to their new country, their presence compelled Americans, often unwittingly and resentfully, to accommodate to
them, and neither party emerged unscathed. Immigrants expected somehow to fit in, probably not as real Yankees, about
whom they knew precious little, but as productive workers and
useful citizens. Throughout the centuries they faced the same
questions: What does America want from us? Are we prepared
to change? Will survival require that we abandon our values
and customs? If we do, who will we be?

America wanted men and women to do the work that those
already present had come to disdain. Colonial America needed
agricultural labor, servants, factory hands and clerks, positions
filled by black slaves in the South. Those regions where the sea
could be made to supplement the farm sought sailors, fisher-
men, and shipbuilders. The appetite for inexpensive laborers
who in an emergency could function as part-time soldiers became increasingly voracious. The freedom and comparative
prosperity of the already-settled Anglo-Saxons rested on the
willingness of a growing number of other Europeans to emigrate, to come and assist in the great enterprise of taming and
building the new world.

From the very beginning of American life, wealth offered an
alternative to inherited privilege. Among Americans, hierarchical European institutions, especially nobility, were most
alien. What then was to prevent a man, however humble upon
arrival in the new land, from dreaming and planning for his
very own ascent into becoming a true American, independent,

proud, able to care for his family and to provide his children a more advantageous start in their own lives? Colonial life, the attitudes necessary to survival and progress, gave birth to the values—prudence, order, ambition, industry, and optimism— of a nascent middle class. Obviously neither slaves nor the hopelessly poor could dream so sweetly.

Opportunities for wealth were everywhere in nature's peculiar American abundance. In time, the early settlers of Virginia discovered the generosity of the southern land, the basis of the region's wealth for centuries to come. The fertility of the land, almost everywhere but New England, seemed to challenge farmers to find ways to fail. Even incompetent or profligate farmers might make progress. Nature's bounty allowed one colonial farmer to recommend cutting down the tree as the best method for harvesting hickory nuts. Recent immigrants, especially Germans, were offended by the wasteful and destructive farming habits of their American neighbors.

The potential fluidity of status in the new world was not welcomed by those who were already powerful, firmly middleclass in comfort and outlook before they emigrated. John Winthrop, son of a lawyer and grandson of a cloth merchant, the first governor of Massachusetts Bay colony, explained to his Puritan followers that it was God's eternal design that some should be rich and others poor, some dignified, others mean. A community could be forged between these extremes, he said, only if all of its members were motivated by Christian love, rather than by avarice, envy, or competitive ambition. But in communities of more tepid believers, even including some in the morally ambitious Bay colony, imperatives other than love had to be invoked to secure public order: law, punishment, and intimidation. So Nathaniel Hawthorne mused that the first tasks of a people wanting to establish a civilized life in a wilderness were to build a graveyard and a gallows.

The economic growth of the colonies created the need for more of everything—raw materials, people, wealth, and power. Local leaders, now comfortable by American if not European standards, naturally were determined to persevere, despite assorted calamities, including epidemic disease and conflict with Indians. However harmful to business enterprise, such misfortunes could be overcome. But these men already viewed deliberate interference in their affairs as an unwarranted threat to continuing prosperity.

When the British drew a line beyond which land speculators could not do business, when they closed the port of Boston to its thriving commerce in the world's oceans, they struck at the essence of American life, infuriating northerners and southerners alike. The American revolution was fought over tax policy, the rights of property, and the idea that lawful institutions— crown and parliament—became unlawful when either or both took without consent what men had legally earned. Freedom meant the right to go about one's business, to be left alone within the rightful law—"the laws of nature and nature's God," Jefferson explained—to which consent had been freely given. When Britain interfered with the Americans' rights of property, it deflected the pursuit of happiness.

The American revolution was led by middle-class lawyers, merchants, and plantation owners to protect what they had enjoyed for a century and a half, while other wealthy Americans, supporters of the crown, fled the country. Only a handful of radicals, such as Samuel Adams and Thomas Paine, favored a more egalitarian revolution. The men who led the colonies into nationhood and crafted the Constitution were propertied, respectable, and prudent. The leading soldiers and revolutionaries were more than solid citizens. Their wealth gave them standing and authority, as John Adams, a mere provincial lawyer, envious and resentful over the unearned wealth of others, understood: "Would Washington have ever been commander of the revolutionary army or president of the United States, if he had not married the rich widow of Mr. Custis? Would Jefferson ever have been president . . . if he had not married the daughter of Mr. Wales?"[1]

Poor Americans failed to resist a constitution drafted by and for men of substance because they were unable to act in concert, and because so many were recent immigrants who were unsure of themselves and, more important, aspired to the prosperity currently enjoyed by others.[2] However poor they were in reality, many, perhaps most, immigrants had middle-class aspirations that functioned as a conservative force throughout the democratic upheavals of the nation's history.

If immigrants came with money, training appropriate to the new environment, and habits consistent with living on their own, their adjustment was relatively smooth. The more they resembled the acclimated Anglo-Saxons, the easier life was for them. Of course they were expected to work, accept and value what they found, reject old world hierarchies, be respectable, and within a reasonable period accumulate wealth.

Until World War I, the Germans were widely accepted by Americans as ideal candidates for citizenship in the nation and full participants in American life. In fact, many recently arrived Germans were more deeply devoted to a work ethic than native-born pathfinders, vagrants, and brawlers. Above all, the Germans were superior farmers, understood the economics of family agriculture, and did not constantly pull up stakes, like many American farmers, to find greener grass. Their rootedness helped stabilize the communities in which they settled. Many Americans were grateful, for even if the Germans spoke the wrong language at least most were Protestant.

By the revolution, Germans were the largest ethnic minority in the colonies, about 120,000 having settled in Pennsylvania alone, where they comprised about one-third of the population. As usual, then and since, people decided to go to America in response to deteriorating economic conditions in the home country, as well as reports of opportunities in the new world. The number of emigrants who left because of political or religious motives was always comparatively small. Only when old-world chances for economic improvement or even stability diminished, when letters from America glowed with promise, did people consider the arduous and sometimes dangerous Atlantic crossing. Whenever America's economy stumbled, the number of emigrants shrank.

By the eighteenth century the Pennsylvania Germans, called "Dutch," already included prosperous farmers, as well as a continuing flow of newcomers, many of whom had been middle-class in the old country. Skilled workers, professionals, including doctors and ministers, as well as the stray and straitened aristocrat, began to appear in Germantown. Others recognized that the Germans were energetic, frugal, honest, and diligent. They were perceived to mind their own business, were respectable, and contributed to the nation's progress, ideal candidates for advancement into valued middle-class status.[3]

In appearance and productivity the Germans' farms, especially the stone barns and fat livestock, impressed everyone else, except that, as was often noticed, the barns were better than the houses, and the animals more carefully tended than their large families. Family members, rather than hired hands or slaves, slavery being an institution the Germans detested, worked the land, tended animals, pruned orchards, and repaired fences. Relatively uneducated and superstitious, deeply attached to the land, these Protestants created a patrimony that could be transmitted through the generations, and built a way of life that would be independent and permanent. A secure middle class arose on the foundation of the great barns.

The clannish solidarity and obvious property lust of the Germans did not endear them to all of their neighbors. Benjamin Franklin, often unhappy with them, observed that the energy and industry of the English seemed to flag in America, "but it is not so with the German laborers; they retain their habitual industry and frugality they bring with them, and, receiving higher wages, an accumulation arises that makes them all rich." English-speaking farmers, more interested in commercial agriculture, less diversified, anxious to sell their holdings to Germans, referred to them as "the dumb Dutch."[4]

• • •

The German devotion to farming, and to ultimate dispersion throughout the United States, conformed to the young nation's sense of itself. The great and unifying myth of the nineteenth century centered on the farmer, on the West. James Fenimore Cooper told the story of the explorers and pathfinders in the tales of Leatherstocking's adventures with the true children of the forest, the Indians. This would seem to be the stuff of epic national legends, but it was not to be for the Americans. They required the legend of quieter people, like themselves, who followed in the tracks of the explorer. They needed a song of the farmer.

The idea of the self-reliant, virtuous, and necessarily democratic farmer was widely shared by the men of the revolution, although the more commercial New Englanders were occasionally a little rude about it. But Washington and Jefferson, along with many others, insisted that political intelligence, public morality, and national prosperity depended on the continued dominance of pastoral America, secure in its republican virtue. For them, the abundance of land and the political qualities of the American farmer would prevent the growth of great cities, which bred a kind of poverty, including helpless starvation, unknown in agrarian societies and inconsistent with the values of a democratic and self-sufficient people. These Americans looked upon Europe's class divisions as a model to avoid assiduously. Thus, for most of the Founding Fathers, America could safeguard its uniqueness, its civic virtue, only by maintaining eternal vigilance against fawning city people, whose decadence would destroy the republic. Manliness was the American answer to the mincing courtiers of the Continent, and the farmer, secure in his strength, instinct, and virtue, epitomized a new and better man than Europe had seen since Rome fell.

The westward movement of the nineteenth century was an astounding achievement. What the first explorers made possible was secured not by them, but by the people who came to settle, to clear the forest, till the fields, and raise their children.

The plowman, not the scout in deerskin, symbolized the age. The trailblazer showed the way, of course, but his life in the forests was anarchic. In contrast, plowmen were builders whose determination and dreams formed the foundation of a new democratic society in whose prosperity all who were willing to work could share. The historian Henry Nash Smith described what they accomplished: "They plowed the virgin land and put in crops, and the great Interior Valley was transformed into a garden: for the imagination, the Garden of the World."[5]

It was widely believed that, along with the plowmen's seeds, America's virtuous and democratic future was germinating in this garden. Here, as Walt Whitman and a thousand others proclaimed, was the authenic America. (The myth persists. Most Americans still assume that life on a farm is "more honest and moral," a belief that inspired the *New York Times* to declare that nothing in the nation's history has "succeeded in erasing that pastoral America . . . [and] never will."[6])

Germans continued to arrive throughout the nineteenth century, with over eight million reported in the census of 1910. They disembarked at every American port, filled out such cities as Cincinnati and Milwaukee, and sought homesteads in the Midwest. In 1850, when Germans constituted over a quarter of America's foreign-born population, land in the Mississippi Valley sold for $2 an acre, houses cost $30, and a newcomer could begin farming, livestock included, for a total outlay of about $150. In an already familiar pattern, Germans often bought farms that had been cleared by native-born Americans, who seemed more interested in starting a farm than in continuing to improve the land. The German preference was just the opposite. As a German farmer in Missouri wrote to his family in the old country: "There is scarcely a farm that is not for sale, for the American farmer has no love for home, such as the German has."[7]

The failed revolutions of 1848, and the repression that followed, changed the nature of the exodus to America. Among the one million Germans who arrived during the 1850s, there were now, for the first time, political refugees, along with a much larger but less influential number of workers, craftsmen, and farmers. The political Forty-eighters, as they were called, were generally well educated, broadly cultured and often free-thinking, propertied, with high status in the German middle class, and they tended to settle in cities, where they thought that some measure of sustaining culture might be possible. Their number included artists, doctors, lawyers, merchants, journalists, and educators. Disdainful of what they considered the boorishness of American life in general, especially of farmers, and in particular of the earlier German arrivals, the Forty-eighters were determined to press the revolution in America until such time as the states of Germany came to their senses, on which happy day they intended to repatriate. Scornful of American schooling, appalled by slavery and corruption, sectarian and rigid sabbaths, and the temperance movement, the political refugees frightened the already established German communities, which feared that Americans would condemn all Germans as rude, ungrateful, and arrogant. And the settled Germans, including Catholics alongside the Pietists and Lutherans, were offended by the newcomers' anticlericalism.

Vastly confident of their own identity, the political refugees had no intention of adapting to the young nation; rather, with their firm belief in their own superiority, they understood their mission to be the enlightenment of others to follow their lead. The German community was thus split between an acclimated, agrarian middle class and the zealous Forty-eighters, who not only claimed leadership but, like Carl Schurz, earned it by working as journalists. Even before the political exodus, Germans had been unhappy with the undignified American press. A German writer concluded that in America men preferred to become professionals or merchants, but, "failing in this, one becomes a newspaper man and publishes a newspaper with seventeen columns of advertising and three columns of slander against the government.''[8]

German communities across the nation responded enthusiastically to the lectures, exhibits, and celebrations—such as the centennial of Schiller's birth in 1859—the Forty-eighters brought to them. Unlike most other immigrant groups, the Germans imported their leaders, rather than waiting upon evolutionary processes to raise them from the lower class. The youth, insecurity, and acknowledged deficiencies of American culture compelled many already established Americans to affirm the Germans' superiority and their great contributions, especially those of the élite refugees, some of whom were on the Harvard faculty. Anonymous farmers and artisans were also praised for their more modest accomplishments. It was they who converted the celebration of Christmas from a national riot to a spiritual rite.[9]

The Irish experience was entirely different from that of the Germans. Although the members of neither group behaved uniformly, it is possible to generalize. The Germans, many of whom were prepared for life in the new world because of their experience and attitudes in the old, dispersed throughout the country, became successful farmers, were predominantly Protestant, and were welcomed. In contrast, the migrating Irish, especially after the potato famine, were peasants unequipped for life in America, who huddled together in the cities of the eastern seaboard and were predominantly Catholic, and despised. The Germans had followed the American prescription for immigrants' adjustment to the new land; the Irish, despite the fact that many (though far from all) spoke English, seemed more foreign, less assimilable, and threatened both the agrarian ideal and the middle-class aspirations of the nation. They were impoverished when they came and it seemed they would remain destitute forever.

Less than half-a-million Irish had emigrated before the American revolution, most of them relatively comfortable Ulster Protestants. But even then Catholic girls were valued as domestic servants, and the indenturing system made their transportation and servitude possible. They had, as they put it, "emigrated for nothing." An uneven influx to America continued until all the potatoes, their sole diet except for milk, rotted in the fields in 1845 and throughout the next decade, resulting in a million deaths, an equal number of evictions, and the emigration of almost two million. This was a flight in panic, not an organized social movement. The Irish Emigrant Society of New York repeatedly warned new arrivals to disperse throughout the nation and particularly to avoid the cities of the East Coast, an impossible goal for masses who arrived prepared only to beg. They were probably worse off than any other European immigrant group. Whatever the advice they received, their poverty rooted them where they landed, so that the Irish population of Boston trebled in mid-century. Work on canals, roads, and railroad tracks took Irish laborers into the West, where some stayed. The great majority, however, were immobilized in port cities, in an environment of hatred and enduring poverty. To make matters worse, for reasons of controlling the flock, the Catholic Church preferred its parishioners concentrated, and opposed an Irish movement into the country.[10]

With the famine in Ireland came rising rents charged by absentee English landlords, foreclosures that increased whenever times were hard, increasing taxes, a spreading conviction among peasants and cottiers that life was against them, and that starvation was the inevitable lot of those too demoralized or weak to move. But they believed that somewhere it must be possible to live, perhaps not in comfort, but at least to live. Despite the ostensible promise of America, these people remained largely pessimistic in outlook, overwhelmed by feelings of powerlessness, of being buffeted by dark and uncontrollable forces. They were passive, feared change, opposed individuality, accepted the authority of the Church, and were wedded to Ireland, the family, and the community—traits not conducive to adjustment to the fluidity and individualism of their adopted nation. "Famine emigrants," one scholar wrote, "seemed oblivious, even antagonistic, to bourgeois ideals and leadership."[11] Involuntary emigrants, they felt like exiles from a beloved land that had destroyed their hopes and almost killed them. Many blamed the hated English overlords, whose kinsmen the Irish now encountered everywhere in America.

From 1851 to 1921 almost four million Irish immigrants settled in the United States. The great majority were Catholics whose primary language was Irish. Isolated within the provincial confines of Gaelic culture, they were more desperate and less skilled than their predecessors before the famine. Compared to the earlier arrivals, the immigrants after the famine were younger and more likely to be unmarried. Now half of all immigrants were female. In 1880, 85 percent of the immigrants were listed as common laborers, farm workers, and servants, somewhat reduced from the percentage for the previous twenty years; in 1900 it rose to over 90 percent.

Because it was peculiarly intense and especially unwelcome, the movement of Irish immigrants into Boston differed from that into other locations. The newly arrived famine immigrants were among the poorest peasants of the South and West of the old country. In 1840, the population of Boston proper was just over 61,000; by 1855, after the famine, it had more than doubled, with much of the increase caused by the Irish influx. Some 50,000 Irish struggled to survive in Boston, while the number of other foreign-born people remained small, with only some 2,000 Germans in residence.

The commercial nature of Boston's economy meant that there were few unskilled industrial jobs waiting for untrained newcomers. Some jobs were available in the cloth mills in the countryside, where Irish men and women eventually found work, replacing the mill girls who left for marriage and because the Irish would work for less. But in Boston town, the rule was clear: the better the job, the fewer Irish employed. The majority struggled on as casual day laborers, that is, were unemployed most of the time, while for their mothers and sisters jobs as menial servants were easier to find. Irishmen might wash dishes or clean stables, but more skilled occupations, such as barbering, were reserved for blacks, who, in most respects, were preferred to the Irish. Only the shanty Irish were segregated in the city.

Because most recent Irish immigrants were too poor to leave Boston, and too despised to be offered work, Boston developed what was extraordinary in America—a surplus labor pool. Bosses in search of brawn for digging and carrying were drawn to Boston as a national reservoir of starving Irishmen, who were transported throughout America and Canada for work on water projects and railroads. Exploited and cheated, these laborers usually returned to their families within a year, as poor as they had been before they left. At the expense of the Irish, along with other despised foreigners, especially Asians on the West Coast, the nation was being built.

The energy of the Irish and the profits that flowed from starvation wages built Boston's industry. In the two decades after the famine, the number of industrial workers in Boston, now the nation's fourth-largest industrial city, rose from about 10,000 to 40,000. Factory workers in New York then received $8 to $10 a week; in Boston they earned only half as much. But what the Irish built for the huge profit of others eventually created more work and thus provided even this pariah people the beginning of a way out, a way up.

This enormous Catholic and proletarian presence in the midst of Protestant and mercantile Boston, a town grown increasingly self-satisfied with its middle-class rationality, optimism, and general prosperity, along with its literary culture, was a soul-shaking perturbation. The civilized cosmopolitanism of Boston's cultural élite, for whom England was the mother country, was more favorably disposed to tolerate abstractions than real and different people. The collision between the complacent middle class and the desperate, fatalistic Irish peasant—allergic to the idea of progress—created hatred on both sides. By 1845, local newspaper advertisements for jobs already declared: "None need apply but Americans." Cosmopolitan Boston reserved its bile especially for the swarming Irish, with other nationalities and local blacks faring far better.

Feeling threatened, Boston's élite responded by hunkering down into its sense of superiority and higher civilization. Embedded in English social reflexes, the circle of gentlemen in Boston grew tighter, more exclusive, and increasingly complacent. It was not merely that the Irish would not be allowed to penetrate this fortress, but that historical credentials—pedigree, of all things under the American sun—were now a prerequisite simply for membership, let alone fair treatment. Thus emerged the true Boston Brahmin, who, as Oliver Wendell Holmes explained, must derive from "four or five generations of gentlemen and gentlewomen."

Only the Irish in Boston created independent institutions to protect themselves from hatred and nourish their dark cultural assumptions. In reaction, natives complained about their clannishness, proof that the Irish, in contrast to the Germans, were unwilling and unable to become Americans. The Irish clung to their Church, which became increasingly militant. It denounced what it viewed as the moral corrosion of public education, a function it insisted was the obligation of family and church, not state. The profound conservatism of the Irish and their opposition to reform of every kind—feminism, temperance, the abolition of slavery—separated them from everyone else, the Germans, the French, the handful of Jews, and the natives. The Church's opposition to intermarriage, and the disdain of others for the Irish, resulted in fewer cross-cultural marriages than for any other group, including blacks, 12 percent of whom were married to whites.

The Irish turned to political activity as another line of defense. Their group solidarity against a hostile and brutal world and their religious cohesion led them, during the decade of famine in Ireland, to become naturalized citizens and obediently to vote in steadily increasing numbers, and, because of their bloc politics, with disproportionate influence. They eventually seized the balance of political power, to the disgust of the native gentlemen with their grand genealogies. When the Irish discovered their local political muscle, and their ability to frustrate every reform measure, Boston's famous tolerance shattered. Xenophobic, anti-Catholic politics became the norm in Boston, through the Civil War, when the Irish supported the Union but not emancipation of the slaves.

In postwar Boston, Brahmin sniffishness, the progress of crude Yankee industrialists, and the electoral activity of the Irish led to a temporary and superficial armistice. The Brahmins retreated from the odors of an increasingly industrialized town, newly rich Yankees were glad of continued cheap Irish labor, and some of the second-generation Irish began to progress toward a slightly improved future.[12]

Outside of Boston, many former peasants left the Church when they left the Emerald Isle. Half of the common laborers in New York's Irish Sixth Ward rarely if ever attended mass. But instead of accepting secular authority as a substitute for their supposed respect for the Church, these young workers, suspicious of strangers and resentful of employers, sought refuge and power in their own semi-secret societies, such as the Molly Maguires, rather than trust in the politics of the respectable middle class. These were the men of the New York draft riots during the Civil War, who stormed the streets to oppose conscription, express their bigotry against blacks, and destroy the symbols of "property, propriety, and Protestantism." Not only did they neglect their Church, they distrusted all authority, save that of the community of their brothers in suffering. They would become tough-minded union members.

By the 1870s, the Irish had, almost alone among immigrant groups, concentrated in cities, where, because of their numbers and needs, they exercised astonishing political power, and not only in Boston and Tammany Hall. They had neglected what native Americans assumed was the necessary and purging pioneer phase of the American experience. According to the values of the guardians of American virtue at the turn of the century, that was what was wrong with the Irish, an omen of the disdain that later urban immigrants would face.

E. A. Ross, a midwestern sociologist, was among the most splenetic spokesmen for the necessity of a western experience to convert impoverished Europeans into acceptable candidates for the American middle class. For him, immigration's most significant and pernicious contribution to American life had been to hand over the northern cities to the Irish. Unlike the earlier Germans and the Scandinavians, the Irish "never got their feet upon the land . . . but remained huddled in cities." As a result, the Irish had not become American enough: "The Hibernian domination has given our cities genial officials, brave policemen, and gallant fire-fighters. It has also given them the name of being the worst-governed cities in the civilized world." According to Ross, the Irish ward boss quickly discovered that immigrants were ignorant and helpless and that he could provide them services—a job, bail money, or a fix at city hall—in exchange for their vote. "So the ward politicians became pioneers in social work," and created a tribal politics that put personal loyalty and kinship above the Constitution.[13]

Partly weaned by experience from the old-world reflexes of their parents, but never freed from memory, some of the younger Irish generation were beginning to emerge from degradation. They succeeded best away from the East Coast, and struggled most in Boston. By the early twentieth century, a higher proportion of Irish than Anglo-Protestant students attended college, often at Catholic institutions. (Native-born rural Americans did not yet need college to support their hopes.) Other and newer immigrant groups were replacing the Irish as fuel for America's roaring factories. With this hard-won upward mobility, the Irish, like other immigrants, faced a pivotal question, posed in 1872 by the Irish nationalist Patrick Ford: "How shall we preserve our identity?"[14]

• • •

In the 1880s, as is well known, the sources of immigration shifted away from the blonds to the brunets, from the North Europeans to those from the South and East. In 1905, for instance, 27 percent of the immigrants came from northwestern Europe while 73 percent came from the South and the East. Those figures would have been reversed only twenty years earlier. Before the eighties, more than 95 percent of all immigrants had come from northwestern Europe.[15] Now people swarmed from Poland, Czechoslovakia, Austria, Hungary, Yugoslavia, Russia, Lithuania, Finland, Rumania, Bulgaria, Turkey, Greece, Italy, Spain, and Portugal. The English language was native to none, and Protestantism was foreign to most.

Although the country of the immigrants' dreams had changed, the dreams had not. To millions of immigrants America was still the land of promise, perhaps not quite the promised land, but a place where a man could support his family, where no one had to bow, and where soldiers would not kill citizens because of religion. Yet most of them, like the earlier Germans and Irish, came to America not out of hatred or fear of the political systems of their native lands, not because of their admiration for American life, but because of economic deterioration at home.

Beginning in the 1880s, despite occasional busts, the American industrial boom was a magnet powerful enough to attract people from the Apennines to the Urals. The great American industrial belly was spreading, and its capacity to gorge on increasing numbers of cheap laborers seemed limitless. The city, not the farm, was already the repository for the wealth accumulated by the industrial Robber Barons, who, for all the complaining about their rapacity, were America's newest heroes.

The dramatic acceleration of American industry depended on the availability of inexpensive labor, and the more eager, perhaps even desperate, such workers were, the better. The absolute need of new immigrants to find work quickly benefited employers whose dreams of a golden future were threatened by the absence of enough hands. However onerous and unrewarding the work, this was a bargain that satisfied both parties, at least at first.

Like the Germans and Irish, the newer immigrants came in two waves. The first was comparatively small, composed of relatively comfortable craftsmen and small farmers. They left the ancestral home to avoid a further erosion of their status, traveled with their families, and came with some money. This group was most welcomed by Americans, moved easily into the middle class, and in time became the leaders of their ethnic groups in the new country. By contrast, the second and much larger group of immigrants was younger, poorer, owned no land, and could not hope to do so. They left to get a start that was impossible at home. Those in this group traveled as individuals rather than as families, and many came to America in the hope of earning enough money to return home and buy land. Both groups knew what they were doing, could not accommodate themselves to the economic conditions at home, and were determined to find a way to survive, even if that required leaving the familiar hills of home.[16]

Concern, if not hysteria, about this new immigration was understandable. Approximately 20 million people immigrated to the United States before 1900, the largest population transfer in history. The increases among each ethnic group were astounding. For example, while 3,000 Italians and one Russian, perhaps a Jew, entered the new country in 1870, 270,000 Italians came in the eighties; 600,000 in the nineties; and 2 million arrived between 1900 and 1910. Because of World War I, the number dropped to 1.25 million in the next decade. The first 23 Jews had arrived in North America in 1654. By the Revolution they numbered about 2,500, and a steady trickle continued until, as with the Italians, a true exodus formed. Then, some 160,000 Jews came to America in the 1880s; 344,000 in the nineties; 1 million from 1900 to 1910; and, before World War I shut down the flow of people, another half million reached America's shores. Two million Jews had come by 1920, comprising about 3.5 percent of America's total population.[17]

Neither paranoia nor simple-mindedness was necessary to conclude that so vast a resettlement would change America. Not only were the new immigrants different, but some natives thought that their sheer numbers alone might prove too much for the still-young nation to absorb. When the Statue of Liberty was given a one-hundredth birthday party in 1986, the immigrants who had come through New York and their descendants constituted 40 percent of the American people.

The American myth of the immigrant is out of focus. Assumptions about American superiority led the cultural custodians of the time to devalue people who behaved differently, dressed out of local fashion, and spoke with an accent. Emma Lazarus, the author of the famous sonnet affixed to the Statue of Liberty, personified this American arrogance. From a wealthy Jewish family whose ancestors had come to America in the seventeenth century, she was thoroughly assimilated, preferring Emerson's universalism to the quaint and antiquated rituals of her forebears. When Abraham Cahan, a Russian immigrant and future leader of the Jewish community, arrived in America, he was greeted by an immigration committee that included Lazarus, a "wealthy young Jewish lady," he wrote, "who belonged to the cream of the monied aristocracy." At first, she and other upper-class American Jews opposed the immigration of the pathetic eastern European Jews, but the intensity of Russian persecution in the 1880s and the sad state of those who arrived touched her.[18] And so she wrote of "The wretched refuse of your teeming shore." For all the afflictions the immigrants suffered, it is not likely that many felt like wretched refuse. What they did feel like was poor— not the same thing, except to Americans who equated culture with money.

Senator Daniel Patrick Moynihan set matters right in 1986 when he said these people "were not the wretched refuse of anybody's shores. They were an extraordinary, enterprising, and self-sufficient folk who knew exactly what they were doing, and doing it quite on their own, thank you very much." Warming to the point, the Senator added: "Put plain, the immigrants of the second half of the nineteenth century came from societies more civilized than ours."[19] Many immigrants but few Americans understood this at the time. The travelers were trading their cultures, often more religious and idealistic, for economic opportunity. Whether the trade was worth it depended on how much money could be made how soon, and whether what they considered to be American vulgarity would require too much cultural sacrifice.

Reacting to the deluge of new people, Senator Henry Cabot Lodge of Massachusetts, at the time, expressed the characteristic American dislike for the East Europeans; to him, they were "appalling in quality." He assumed that the Italians were not so bad because at least they were part of western civilization and many had an "infusion of Germanic blood," but those from eastern Europe were "utterly alien to us, not only ethnically, but in civilization, tradition, and habits of thought." Composed of "an enormous percentage of wholly uneducated persons," they might be swallowed by America, he said, but they could never be digested. The Senator demanded a way to bar the hordes of bizarre, unassimilable, and dangerous aliens so that the American "race" would not be polluted beyond reclaim.[20]

Lodge, along with other northeasterners in the circle of Henry Adams, was offended by the great unwashed as well as by the vulgarity of new money emanating from gigantic businesses in oil and steel. Disdainful of the coming democratic disorder, they embraced American imperialism as a way to control the future (and provide raw materials for the capitalists they despised). Along with the agrarian Populists, the northeastern gentlemen saw clearly that industrialism and urbanism, in both of which immigrants were essential, were creating new social arrangements in which their privileges and power would become anachronistic and then vestigial, and eventually vanish. The Populists fortified themselves for a struggle against what they considered to be maniacal bankers, while their peculiar allies, the refined reformers, carefully planned how they could persuade others to stand against the future—mechanization, cultural democracy, an economy of consumption, and fortunes in the hands of ill-trained people.[21]

Others shouted that these strangers—"Polacks, hunkies, dagoes, and kikes"—would steal jobs away from natives, swamp political institutions, pollute education, support corrupt urban bosses, introduce an alien radicalism, and, as hyphenated Americans, prove to be only tepid patriots. John R. Commons, a distinguished labor scholar at the University of Wisconsin and a political Progressive, believed that America was committing "race suicide" by failing to exclude "the flood of races from Southeastern Europe." Religion was part of the problem: "The church to which he [the southern immigrant] gives allegiance is the Roman Catholic, and, however much the Catholic Church may do for the ignorant peasant in his European home, such instruction as the priest gives is likely to tend toward an acceptance of their subservient position on the part of the working-men."[22]

For Commons, basic Americanism meant carrying out Lincoln's vision of a democratic government of, by, and for the people. But, he assumed, the fidelity demanded by the Catholic Church encouraged cultural resignation—an acceptance of one's place within a hierarchy—which destroyed the self-reliance required by American democracy and, as his view implied, the ambition demanded of the middle class.

Comparing the immigrants to the "typical" American, a midwestern professor asserted that the fathers of the immigrant families were not real men. "Natural selection, frontier life, and the example of the red man produced in America a type of great physical self-control, gritty, uncomplaining, merciless to the body through fear of becoming 'soft.' " For this observer, the contrast between Daniel Boone and the flaccid men of the ghetto was laughable. He thought that it would be a very long time before the immigrants' offspring could "produce the stoical type who blithely fares forth into the wilderness, portaging his canoe, poling it against the current, wading in the torrents, living on bacon and beans, and sleeping on the ground, all for 'fun' or to 'keep hard.' "[23]

Some greenhorns would have shuddered at the suggestion of what for them was a sacrilegious diet. Many of them felt that they had fared forth into the wilderness just by coming to America. They had crossed an ocean, not a stream, had already slept on the floor, and thought that their lives were hard enough without trying to emulate boy-men who liked to play in the woods. The cultural values of nineteenth-century Protestant America did not speak to the lives of people who were concerned with streetcars, not canoes. To their way of thinking, Daniel Boone would have been better off if he had gone to college.

America was rapidly moving away from the attitudes and behavior appropriate to the Garden of the World, and not many of the established, middle-class natives approved. Though they were not farmers themselves, they wanted others on the land, away from the politics and corruption of the city. In 1904, Frank Sargent, the commissioner-general of immigration, urged urban immigrants to move to the valleys of Colorado and Utah and grow beets.[24] Élites feared that they would lose control. Economic interests, especially organized labor, feared competition. And the spiritual guardians of the republic were horrified at the prospect of losing America.

To gain America the immigrants had to pass a gauntlet first at Castle Garden at the foot of Manhattan and later in the cavernous red-brick shed on Ellis Island. New York City was not the only American port of entry, but it came close. In 1907, for example, 1,285,000 immigrants arrived in America; 1,000,000 went to New York while the rest were distributed among the ports of Boston, Philadelphia, Baltimore, San Francisco, and others. Ellis Island was the central gateway to the immigrants' future. They could be denied their dream and sent back if they had a contagious disease or if they were likely to become a public burden because they lacked enough money to get started or a relative or friend to care for them. There were other restrictions, but these were the two that affected the most people, even if they rarely knew about them before a doctor mysteriously peeled back an eyelid, or an official made them count out their money before him. In the first decade of this century the Italians brought an average of $19.45 with them; Jews had $29.09.[25]

After passing inspection, the newcomers gravitated to the big cities, although by 1920 they could be found in almost every section of the nation. Of the 10 million people who entered the country in the first decade of the century, almost one-third settled in New York, mostly in New York City, 18 percent in Pennsylvania, and 7.5 percent each in Illinois and Massachusetts. Of the 2 million Italians entering in this same period, about half went to New York and one-quarter to Pennsylvania. Seventy percent of the 1 million Jews went to New York. Most of the 1 million Poles along with most of the Hungarians, Croatians, and Slovenes went to Pennsylvania, often to find work in heavy industry and the mines. From 1890 to 1920, the population of many American cities at least doubled in size, including New York, Chicago, Los Angeles (increased tenfold), Detroit (almost fivefold), Houston, Dallas (fourfold), Washington, D.C., Cleveland, Indianapolis, Milwaukee, San Antonio (fourfold), and Memphis.[26]

By 1890 New York City's population had grown to about 1.5 million people, of whom over 40 percent were foreign-born; if their American-born children were counted, the foreign "stock" was almost 80 percent. By 1900 six other cities had a foreign-stock population of over 70 percent: Boston, Buffalo, Chicago, Cleveland, Detroit, and Milwaukee. In 1920, the Census Bureau announced that for the first time most Americans lived in cities.[27]

For the defenders of nineteenth-century Yankee conventions, the power of the immigrants' urban numbers and the corruption of urban politics did not by themselves tell the whole sorry story. Nativists insisted that the immigrants created what was for America a new form of squalor. They inhabited what many Americans called "colonies" within the cities, enclaves of the mother tongue, where Poles, Italians, or Jews congregated with their own kind. Everyone learned to call these colonies ghettos, although more accurately they were slums of fellow nationals living next to other nationals. However much this separatism worried the defenders of the American faith, it offered obvious advantages to the greenhorns: emotional support and familiarity in a strange place; time to learn English while daily life was conducted in the old language; conveniently located churches and synagogues; and familiar food, newspapers in the native language, opportunities for socializing with countrymen, and acceptable funeral arrangements. The colonies also protected the newcomers from the face-to-face bigotry of the natives. Living apart with their countrymen softened the culture shock, held the new nation at arm's length, and gave the immigrants time.

The nativist slandered the immigrants when he accused them of creating slums because they did not know better. Except for the Boston Irish, there had been no ghettos for the earlier immigrants from northern Europe, not because they were more fastidious, but because when they arrived urban employment was found in small, dispersed shops, and available housing was scattered throughout the town. More important, most of them headed out for the land, to the pleasure of the cultural custodians. By the time the Poles, Italians, and Jews arrived, economic forces had created specialized economic zones in the developed American city. Residential segregation occurred only when urban industries became concentrated. Poor people who could not afford the expense of traveling distances to their jobs had no choice but to live close to their work.

The defenders of the true faith, the cityphobes and nativists, usually overlooked a parallel urban migration from American villages and farms almost as great as that from the old world. From 1880 to 1910, over 11 million native Americans moved from the countryside to the cities, always to find work.[28] American life was dramatically changing, and in precisely the direction that the singers of America's most cherished myths had warned against.

The custodians of America's destiny were especially worried about the Italians. By World War I they made up the largest percentage of all new immigrants and seemed uniquely ignorant, superstitious, clannish, criminal, violent, and transient. They were offered the former jobs of Irishmen, the heaviest, most dangerous, and lowest-paying work, whether in New York's Little Italy or in the coal mines of Iowa. They also absorbed the brunt of much of the bigotry and violence earlier aimed at the Irish. In the 1890s Colorado miners murdered six Italian workers who may or may not have been connected to the death of an American saloonkeeper; three Italians were dragged from the jail of a Louisiana town and lynched. And in New Orleans a mob headed by the district attorney hanged eleven Sicilians.[29]

It was widely held that Italians, while contributing little to America, were "birds of passage," who would return to the beloved gardens of their native villages as soon as they saved a little money. Of all the immigrant groups, the Italians were perceived as least able to relinquish their nostalgia for the hills of home, and therefore as least appreciative of America. The self-appointed Italian-watchers reacted according to a formula: they resented the many Italians who went back, and suspected that those who stayed wanted to leave and would do so when they could.

Stefano Miele stayed, but his heart remained in his parents' village. Raised in a middle-class home in a town near Naples, he decided to join the exodus to America after seeing how much money former Italian emigrants brought back from "La Merica."

> If I am to be frank, then I shall say that I left Italy and came to America for the sole purpose of making money. . . . If I could have worked my way up in my chosen profession in Italy, I would have stayed in Italy. But repeated efforts showed me that I could not. America was the land of opportunity, and so I came, intending to make some money and then return to Italy. This is true of most Italian emigrants to America.[30]

Miele worked for an Italian religious newspaper in New York and attended law school at night. After five years he was admitted to the New York bar and enjoyed greater success than he had ever imagined. So, for him, "America has proved itself . . . the land of opportunity, but I have not forgotten Italy—it is foolish to tell any Italian to forget Italy." Italy meant the family and the communal life of the village. As he saw it, the Anglo-Saxon American was basically a businessman who did not know how to laugh, while the Italian understood how to make life worth living. Nonetheless, Miele did not return to the ancestral hills.[31]

Yet great numbers of Italians did return. In the mid-nineties, over 40 percent of new arrivals went back to the old country. In 1910 the Italian reflux approached 75 percent of the number of new immigrants. In contrast, Jewish repatriation was then running at less than 1 percent, not only because they had nowhere to go but because entire families had come over (some 43 percent of Jewish immigrants were female and about 25 percent were under fourteen), while Italian immigrants were mostly (about 80 percent) young, single male farm laborers from southern Italy.[32]

Ethnic theater disclosed the differences between Italian and Jewish attitudes toward their new American home. While local Jewish playwrights wrote about life in the Lower East Side, the Italians imported their theater from the old country. The

Yiddish theater was detailed, specific, and realistic, while the Italian stage was characterized by universal passion, sentimentality, or farce. One critic accounted for this difference: "The Yiddish community have become once for all identified with New York and are undergoing changes . . . incident to a genuine life here; but the Italians remain Italians, dreaming of sunny Naples."[33]

In time, of course, the Italians' nostalgia faded, just like that of every other immigrant whose standard of living was improving. A theater critic in the 1920s concluded that "the Jews . . . keep up the living tradition of their tongue by sheer force of intellect, whereas the Italians seem bent upon forgetting whatever culture they bring along."[34] Forgetting through time or a new generation was central to becoming an American, for while memory was green it collided with the new world.

Like other immigrants, Italians had to adjust to specific aspects of American culture. A countryman advised them to mind their own business, to curb their supposedly natural impulses toward helping others as well as their inherent curiosity. He explained that it was crucial for Italians to learn that freedom did not mean they could ignore authority, as they had in the old country. Recently arrived Italians, he noted, were amazed that a traffic officer's signal could halt hundreds of automobiles without protest from the drivers. Finally, he admonished his fellow immigrants that all Americans were required to profess some religion, however mildly, but that on the other hand the doctrinal conflicts familiar in Europe were not acceptable in America.[35]

The Italians were widely blamed for saving their money and not investing to improve their living standard. Even when their incomes improved, they continued to live as if they had just stepped off the boat. That this habit gave stability to *la famiglia* was not appreciated by their American observers: "Unless they have enough to purchase a plot of ground—and to be a landholder is their highest ambition—they will secrete their savings without any effort to place them where they will bring in a return." Consequently, they were "slow to profit by their own increasing prosperity."[36] Some Americans were annoyed because the Italians who were prospering did not play their role correctly—they were criticized for not displaying their material progress into the middle class.

America's message to greenhorns was clear: they should "assimilate," that is, "melt" into the mainstream of American life, learn to think and act like everybody else (though, of course, Americans were themselves fractured in a hundred different ways), and forget their pasts as they became indistinguishable from whoever was giving this advice. It was on such cultural ground that the immigrants encountered Anglo-Saxon, Protestant America. This encounter produced hatred as well as better understanding, and not only native rejection of the upstarts, but also disdain by transplanted Europeans for uncultured Americans.

While the American context into which immigrants came was significant in shaping their lives, the cultural baggage they brought was at least as important. The old-world heritage, religion, secular rituals, and habits of these usually proud people could not be immediately dissolved by the pressures and customs of America. This heritage was a source of self-esteem and a bulwark against uncontrolled change. For many, living decently with self-respect required the retention of the old ways, maladjustment in a sense, a partly deliberate distance between themselves and what they saw as the money-grubbing nature of life in the new world. They would adjust in order to make a living, and when possible buy American clothes as protective coloration. But not many adults were willing to trade their traditional way of life for what they considered the largely unsatisfactory lives of Americans. Once in a rare while, an American acknowledged that, perhaps, the new immigrants had something of value besides sweat to contribute. One author not only defended the immigrants but was willing to question what he acknowledged to be his own stuffy Anglo-Saxon heritage: "We know little of the joy of living. We take our holidays sadly, and laugh with mental reservations."[37]

Indeed, many of the newcomers were convinced that their way of life was superior to the perceived coarseness and rudeness of Americans, even while the vast majority realized that their new freedom permitted them to make economic progress. Many immigrants resented and rejected America's demand to forget their pasts even as they hurried to learn English and appear as "real Americans" to the outer world. Each immigrant group had to decide whether to slough off a bit of the past, a bit of their lives, to ease the transition into American life. Many were willing to pay almost any price, including heroic self-sacrifice, to safeguard the future and reach out to the American cornucopia—except to become "just like them." Their children, however, were likely to resemble "them," and their grandchildren were likely to become "them." And yet not always, and not everywhere. Some who had moved into the wider American world would return on holidays or the sabbath to the ghetto or neighborhood for a periodic cultural booster shot.

The self-esteem of each immigrant group was uniquely challenged in the process of adjusting to America. On the West Coast, Japanese domestic servants were affronted by the ignorant American housewives they served. One young man heard a policeman refer to him as a "Jap." "Fancy," he reacted, "the Californian translation for 'Great Nippon' is 'Japs'! It gave away 100% of dignity." The Japanese mistook salt for sugar, did not know how to hold a knife, thought cheese that smelled was rotten, and found the beds too soft. Japanese women had special difficulties: "Wearing Western-style underwear for the first time, I would forget to take it down when I went to the toilet."[38] Above all, the Japanese encountered American racism, an experience unknown to the Europeans, who were discriminated against for other reasons.

Racism was endemic on the West Coast, especially in California, where violent anti-Asian bigotry had first erupted before the Civil War. In the 1880s, Congress excluded the Chinese from entering the country. But certain Chinese were exempted from the law and welcomed: merchants, teachers, ministers, students, and tourists, that is, the middle class.[39] While a penniless mass of unskilled and uneducated laborers, like the earlier Irish, frightened the settled Americans, class similarities compensated for the wrong birthplace, skin color, religion, and language.

The immigrants' misperception of America was usually more harmless than the Americans' misunderstanding of them. For example, on a newcomer's first trip to Milwaukee's downtown, he had trouble crossing a street because of the throngs of shoppers. Though he did not make it across the street, he was impressed with the seeming religiosity of Americans, because in his native village such crowds assembled only to make a pilgrimage to a shrine. "And I was told that there is no religion in America. Even on Corpus Christi we didn't have such processions in Slovenia."[40]

The self-aggrandizing puffery of Americans, and the demurrers of the ignorant greenhorns, began where appropriate, with the heralded magnificence of New York City. One sociologist, an expert on "Americanization," reflected the local chauvinism in his conclusion that "on arrival, the newcomer to our land is dazzled by the splendor of America." However, M. E. Ravage, a Rumanian immigrant, and an expert on not very much, was not overwhelmed by his first sight of the New York skyline, thinking it rather like other cities in Europe through which he had traveled. And an Italian boy said to himself on arrival: "I do not see how the people can think to compare the American city with the beauty of Rome, or Venice, or Naples."[41]

Although natives and immigrants were ambivalent and confused about each other, the immigrants were almost always grateful for better economic opportunity and, in the case of persecuted peoples, for political freedom. But many others were occasionally explicit about the irrelevance of America's political system. For example, an Italian's decision to emigrate was motivated exclusively by the desire to make money: "Neither the laws of Italy nor the laws of America . . . influenced me in any way. I suffered no political oppression in Italy. I was not seeking political ideals: as a matter of fact, I was quite satisfied with those of my native land." Similarly, a Serb blurted out that he would flee if he was expected to become an American and abandon his native allegiances: "My mother, my native village, my Serbian orthodox faith, and my Serbian language and the people who speak it are my Serbian notions, and one might as well expect me to give up the breath of life as to give up my Serbian notions." Many Mexicans' love of their native country was too strong to permit them to become American citizens.[42]

In general, greenhorns were neither blank slates on which Americans could write as they pleased nor disoriented and overly suggestible. They did not want to change in ways they thought necessary to become more fully American. Disdaining the aggressiveness of American women, a man from Syria longed for the submissive women of the old country: "I say, give me Syria, the mother of mankind!"[43] Their native cultures gave the immigrants identity, a hold on reality, and a way to fend off the more corrosive elements of American life. It is a pity that Emma Lazarus and her transfixed readers could not understand.

Yet some immigrants *were* "uprooted" in the classic sense of disorientation and paranoia. According to historian Oscar Handlin, "the immigrants lived in crisis because they were uprooted." He added, "The immigrants existed in an extreme situation. The shock, and the effects of the shock, persisted for many years."[44] This is a fair enough description of some of the newcomers. But it does not capture fundamental nuances. For instance, it does not describe a nineteen-year-old Russian, Isaac Don Levine, who arrived in Boston in 1914. He boarded a train heading west, not to a farm, as the guardians of tradition advised, but to Kansas City. Like so many others he bought American clothes as soon as possible, finding them comfortable but lacking in grace or elegance. The collar, however, made him "curse the twentieth-century civilization."

Wherever Levine turned in his new setting, he encountered bizarre customs. He was bewildered by the way men hitched up their pants legs when they sat down, by the fact that Americans never finished a sentence, by rocking chairs and enormous beds, absolutely oval eggs, food that was rarely fresh, ubiquitous toothpicks and mustard, the absence of good strong vodka, and the presence of a great number of saloons. He learned that the natives' peculiar mouth problem was only a local rite known as gum-chewing. He discovered that a theater building was marvelous, but that the music performed within "was much worse than that of a very mediocre theater at home," while the play offered good scenery but bad acting. Americans preferred moving pictures anyway. Most of all, he learned that big businessmen ruled the golden land as kings, wielding more influence over public opinion than even the czars back home. "It is business that can be called the god of this country, and in all the schools business and not labor is pointed out as the ideal occupation."

Obviously such an immigrant, not typical but also not unique, did not arrive in America with an empty head. He had standards and made comparisons. He loved his new nation, but was not willing to blink at its defects. He felt that Americans who despised the immigrants were inferior in taste and culture to the impoverished greenhorns huddling in Kansas City's ghetto. He was not psychologically or culturally uprooted, or panting to become just like the natives. Rather, he hoped that the Italians and the Russians could add civilization to America's obsession with business, to leaven what he perceived to be the monomania of America's middle class.[45]

The cultural cost of improved economic opportunity was a constant immigrant refrain. An Italian thought he had discovered the true meaning of America when he observed: "It become more pleasure to work than to take the leisure."[46] A Dane who originally planned to make money in America and return home was so successful at his business that he stayed, became wealthy, and dreamed of what might have been. Traveling the world in search of adventure, he attempted to inject some sparkle into his life. He was grateful for the money and the freedom it bought, but:

> I had to put aside all those things that represent the finer ideals of life, music, art, and literature. I had expected that I would have to give up for a time my writing and poetry; but I had not expected to find my life stripped so thoroughly bare of even a reference to these things—the talk around the shop and outside was mostly about baseball and prizefights—so different from what I had been accustomed to in Denmark.[47]

An accomplished writer and Russian-Jewish immigrant, Anzia Yezierska, spun out the psychological consequences of America's coldness. "I'm afraid of my heart," one of her fictional immigrant women lamented. "I'm burning to get calm and sensible like born Americans. But how can I help it? My heart flies away from me like a wild bird." Her "born American" friend knew better: "But I don't want you to get down on earth like the Americans. That is just the beauty and wonder of you. We Americans are too much on earth; we need more of your power to fly."[48]

Immigrants were not so green and disoriented that they felt unmixed gratitude to the nation that offered a chance to earn more money, what in the old country would be a fortune. Repeatedly they complained that America was a gigantic and heartless money-making machine. To make money was, of course, what most of them had come for in the first place. But some believed there were limits, that if their new country could not order its priorities better it would deform its people. The government itself provided evidence that the home of the brave was also the home of the new golden calf. When an immigrant

applied for the first papers required for citizenship, he received
from the Bureau of Naturalization a letter explaining why becoming a citizen was important; four times the letter men-
tioned that citizenship would result in "a better position that
pays you more money," and no other reason was given. One
Jew concluded that for his coreligionists the new nation "is the
land of bluff, that religion, morality, politics and learning are
a sham and the only thing of value in this country is almighty
Mammon." A Croatian physician in Pittsburgh wrote in similar bitterness: "Everybody who gets Americanized becomes a
good citizen, i.e., a shrewd business man . . . who knows how
to outwit the intricacies of the law, and how to be ashamed of
his origin, his name and his religion." His experience taught
him that Americans were dishonest.[49]

Naturally, immigrants were enraged by Americans who were
condescending or hostile. Complaining about his new country,
a Russian worker in Ohio wrote that the basic difficulty was
that "we have here too many Americans . . . and they look
upon you as if you were a low thing and they were great men.
I hate them!"[50] A Welshman working at a West Virginia coal
mine in 1895 had similar feelings. He perceived that civilization
was not advanced by such workers:

> The white man of this state and adjoining states is about
> the most contemptible person on the face of God's earth.
> He is unbearably ignorant and does not know it. He has
> generally been brought up on the mountains, hog fashion,
> and when they come to the mines and earn a lot of money,
> they swell out and don't know themselves. . . . These de-
> testable cranks seem to think that the poor niggar [sic] was
> made to receive their insults and brutality.[51]

However poor, the Europeans often felt they could not talk
to the "born Americans," not only because of language problems but because the Americans "are common boors, so-called
'American sports.' " It was no different for women. An immigrant milliner attempted to organize a union among the

native-born Americans, but she soon gave up: "It's no use trying to organize the American women. They don't care about
anything but making dates. It's all men and dances."[52]

Intellectuals, professionals, and political activists were most
critical of their adopted middle-class culture, while the mass of
immigrants were, of course, not of one mind. The demanding
claims of the old and the new culture created not only ambivalence but pain, especially when children embraced a different
balance than their parents. Orthodox religious leaders were
obliged to warn their flocks away from America's secularism
and materialism, with results about which we can only speculate. Like anyone else, an insulted greenhorn would consider
the source. There were reasons, after all, why the foreign-born
comprised such large percentages of organized and radical labor organizations. But the self-hate on which theories of radical
disorientation and culture shock implicitly rest has been exaggerated. Adult immigrants were clearly eager to become American, earn money, and buy new clothes. They were not,
however, straining to abandon their culture, their sense of self.
The greenhorns were not "refuse," deformed, or eager to cut
out their cultural hearts. They were, however, determined to
make money. That is what they came for. That is what the
natives, by example and sermon, reinforced.

As in the old world, the institution to which every immigrant
group was most tightly attached was the family, the domain of
the wife and mother and the force that gave meaning and coherence to life. Unskilled workers found their way to America
and into the American economy with the advice and support
of family and friends. The family, not the individual, ordered
the lives of these millions. By binding its members to the habits
of memory, the old-world communal culture as remembered
by the parents operated as an effective brake on individual
ambition and restlessness.[53]

The greatest threat to the integrity of the family was the

education of the children. Catholics supported parochial schools partly for religious reasons, but, equally important, to keep the family's culture and language alive, protect parental authority, and harbor the children a safe distance away from America. Jews attempted the same maneuver with Hebrew schools, but these did not replace secular education. In any case, the great, democratic American school system seemed deliberately targeted against the dignity of the father, the sanctity of tradition, and the human warmth of the family. Therefore, the schools threatened the security of the parents in their old age when, of course they had always assumed, their children would care for them. Unless, in the meantime, the children had become modern, disrespectful, and American.

On the other hand, the schools taught the children English and in other ways helped them to acquire the skills needed to succeed. However hard the parents struggled, they knew that the schools offered their children the best opportunities for bettering themselves. Pulled between their allegiance to their culture and their material aspirations, parents were often obliged to sacrifice the children's loyalty to ensure that the children's progress into the middle class would not be frustrated. Consequently, as the youngsters acclimated, making strange friends and learning not only formal English but street slang, becoming, as was said millions of times, "wild" and unmanageable, the old-world culture inevitably lost. In a 1908 letter to her sister in Poland, Helena Dabrowskis lamented that her adaptive children "will not listen to their mother. . . . But no, they wish only to run everywhere about the world, and I am ashamed before people that they are so bad. . . . They were good in the beginning but now they know how to speak English, and their goodness is lost." Or else, when the children abandoned the old-world traditions of their parents, an inversion occurred. These children, the family's first Americans, became, in Erik Erikson's phrase, "their parents' cultural parents," criticizing the parents for failing to learn proper English and middle-class manners.[54]

Regardless of the precise mixture of old and new cultural loyalties, the old-world family was not necessarily the repository of wisdom and warmth, since it could also, and perhaps more frequently, remain a blatant tyranny organized to exploit the children and constrain the wife. Immigrant parents invented a domestic ritual designed to compel working children to fidelity: handing over the unopened pay envelope. In retaliation against rigid parents who refused to return an allowance, a few youngsters steamed open their envelopes and gave their parents amended sums. But most honored the domestic drill out of a variable mixture of love and fear. Grasping parents, according to Jane Addams of Chicago's Hull House, created delinquents. She reported a survey of two hundred working girls among whom 62 percent turned over to the mother the sealed envelope with every cent they earned.[55]

Some of those children who spurned familial culture raised themselves. Freed from their awkward and ineffectual parents and therefore also from the past, they could concentrate on themselves, nurture their individual dreams and ambitions, and make plans that would frighten or devastate parents. The resulting conflict between the generations could be heartbreaking. For example, in 1917, an old Jew sold cookies on the street to scratch out a living, despite having fairly prosperous children. Why did he not live with them?

I cannot live among machines. I am a live man and have a soul, despite my age. They are machines. They work all day and come home at night. . . . During supper they talk about everything in the world—friends, clothes, money, wages, and all sorts of gossip. After supper they dress up and go out. . . . They have all been to school—educated people; but just try, for the fun of it, and ask them if they ever read a book. Not on your life. Books have nothing in common with them; Judaism has nothing in common with them; Jewish troubles have nothing in common with them; the whole world has nothing in common with them. . . . They make money and live for that purpose. When I grasped this situation a terror possessed me and I did not believe these were my children. I could not stand it to be there; I was being choked; I could not tolerate their behavior and I went away.[56]

Such middle-class children were, of course, the future, adjusted to the American market, fulfilling the economic aspirations of their parents, betraying the values in which they had been reared.

America entered the twentieth century through a paradox. It moved toward an increasingly urban, secular, and industrial culture by absorbing millions of immigrants who were mostly rural, comparatively religious, and lacking industrial skills. It is striking how often the new immigrants described their previous lives as medieval. Because most were unequipped for industrial life, they fell neatly into their unskilled slots in the new economic order, which depended on their muscle to operate the nation's industrial plant.

For the flood of immigrants, the peasants and town dwellers, the process of crossing centuries of social and economic development as well as oceans could be simultaneously exhilarating and frightening. By their numbers and their tenacious hold on their own traditions, these waves of people undermined certain traditional American attitudes. Because they brought more Catholicism and Judaism to America, they helped to dilute the Protestant hold on the national spirit. Because they became city people, they helped to weaken, but not uproot, the myth of the farmer.

From the conventional American viewpoint, it was the "Hebrew race" that was the most exotic. At first, Jews had no native defenders willing to state their case in public. After the European revolutions of 1848, significant numbers of German Jews had migrated to America and dispersed throughout the nation, but they were not at all certain that an inundation of Jews from Russia and the Pale would be desirable. Would the new Jews "fit in"? Would they embarrass the assimilated German Jews—Reformed, not either Orthodox or freethinkers, like the newcomers—who worried that Christian Americans would react to the deluge with a sweeping anti-Semitism that would engulf them as well as the greenhorns? After the turn of the century, however, the German Jews, despite their condescension to the uneducated, unrefined, and discomfiting ragpickers, recognized their solidarity with the eastern Jews, organized charities on their behalf, and quietly resisted attempts to restrict additional immigration.

Most new immigrants were peasants for whom city life was a new experience. For them everything about America was new, especially the adjustment to living in the ghetto. The Jews were the exception. Forbidden to own land or work as farm laborers, forced to move to the towns of the Pale after 1882, many of them were familiar with both the ghetto and the town. By converging on the Lower East Side, Jews were also responding to their ancient need for community to pray, buy kosher food, and live a fully Jewish life. A Yiddish playwright, for example, conveyed this message through an atypical character, a Jewish farmer: "In the country if a Jew wants to be a Jew, he can't. . . . The town Jew is really a Jew. He can exchange a few words with a rabbi, attend synagogue when he's supposed to, and he can donate to charity."[57] The Lower East Side warrants a closer look because it illuminates the experience of most immigrants, Jewish or not.

About a third of eastern Europe's Jews made the difficult decision to go to America, to risk everything for an unknown fate in a distant land that they knew of only from letters from *landsleyt* who had already emigrated, from the hustling hype of steamship agents, from gossip and rumors, and perhaps from the hope that somewhere life had to be better. The vast majority were poor and simple people who shared a vibrant religious and communal culture, whose political fears were realistic, and whose chance to earn a living in the old country was slim and diminishing. More than other immigrant groups the Jews emigrated as families, although many traveled in sequences, with the father or son coming first to earn passage money for the rest. With these masses, as Irving Howe described them, came the "obsolete artisans, socialist firebrands, bewildered wives, religious fanatics, virtuosos of the violin, illiterate butchers, scribblers of poetry, cobblers, [and] students." The practical side of this collective leap toward America was that for these beleaguered people America would become, as so many Jews had fervently imagined, the *"goldeneh medina,"* the golden land.[58]

Initially, their "golden land" was the Lower East Side, the American ghetto whose pulse was driven by hope alone. On arrival some felt their dreams collapse in the noise and filth of New York, and, inevitably, second thoughts and homesickness set in for the old world they had not been able to endure. The Lower East Side, which surpassed the slums of Bombay in population density, was a bedlam that could make a greenhorn panic. In this slum the old world could seem relatively ordered, with familiar horizons, cherished family memories, and acceptable Jewish behavior. As one of the characters in a novel about the immigrants expressed it, "One enjoys life in Russia better than here. . . . There is too much materialism here, too much hurry and too much prose—and yes, too much machinery."[59]

On the whole, the immigrant Jews were more highly skilled than other immigrant groups. Because their work in Europe had been restricted in kind and location, many had worked as tailors, furriers, or leather workers. They were skilled at the commercial use of the scissors and sewing machine. And so they heaped themselves on top of each other in the most notorious slum of the time, later idealized as "colorful" and "quaint."

Unlike other immigrants, the Jews at least did not have to learn how to live as an outcast minority. Centuries of European persecution had forced them to acquire the indispensable skills of the pariah. They were wary of others, alert to social cues, and quick to decipher their new cultural ecology. They were deeply aware of the need to create a home that was an emotional refuge, a place to catch the breath and recover spent energies from the clawing demanded by earning a living in America. But this home could not function properly when its members each scattered in a different direction and time of day for the sweatshop or pushcart, or when the children learned to be ashamed of their parents' broken English and old-country customs. How difficult to remain a good Jew in this new Babylon. But for most, *Yiddishkeit,* the cultural rather than religious traditions, would see them through, not always sweating and crying, but also dreaming and laughing, not only in the intimacy of the family, but in the larger community of struggling Jews.

This, then, was the key to their experience: the attempt to re-create their old-world community in a new-world setting, to take what they wanted, especially an opportunity to ascend into the middle class, while retaining what they valued in their own family customs and national traditions. They all prayed that the retention of their distinctive cultures would not interfere with their economic ambitions, and although some were willing to pay even this price, most were not. It is true that those least willing or able to change had fewer economic opportunities, so their material aspirations came to rest on their children, sometimes as integral members of the family or, most difficult of all, as individuals who would make their way on the outside, forming their own separate families, probably neglecting parents and history—that is, as Americans.

The earlier-arriving German Jews had generally sought assimilation—into Christian Germany before their arrival and Christian America after it—and represented to the less-educated and less-affluent eastern Jews a fawning religious betrayal. Moreover, the German Jews, in spreading themselves across the United States, could not have created a cohesive and compelling culture even if they had wanted to, as they did not. The two groups found antagonism more natural than co-operation. The easterners desired to create a cultural center; the Yiddish language, not often spoken by the Germans, was their means, and poverty was the motive. This resulted in an organized immigration—profoundly different from that of the Irish—that, according to one scholar, "was neither atomized nor chaotic." These Jews created mutual-aid societies, unions, fraternal organizations, educational institutions, a dizzying array of cultural centers, including theater and reading clubs, and, of course, synagogues by the hundreds. Intertwined in such cultural roots, the strong family, for better or worse, was central. Therefore, if the East European Jews were "up-rooted" at all, it was temporary; living in this tightly knit ghetto, they were not yet in America.[60] They were sheltered by what they knew and loved, which many of the young were determined to leave.

Like the Irish, Jews knew their migration was permanent, that there was no turning back, and that somehow, someday they had to learn to tolerate America. Orthodox Jews, how-ever—the scholars and the rabbis—could never adjust to what seemed like the overwhelming pressures of secular America. Organizing one's day by the movement of a clock instead of what seemed like the vaguer movement of the sun was itself symptomatic of the relentless routine of American life, what a *landsman* described as too much prose. The most hateful aspect of America for traditional Jews was the realization that "all of the people of this country worship the Golden Calf."[61] The frenzied way Americans chased money was disgusting, but ap-parently necessary, because everything was so expensive, es-pecially rents. Those who could not adjust would not become Americans. A poor but learned man, revered in the old coun-try, was pathetic in the new. The great majority who could adapt became Americans who were on their way to an im-proved standard of living, to a foothold on the edge of the American middle class.

Over and over Jews complained that something terrible was happening. They were becoming coarse, like Americans. They were losing their history and had become slaves to a clock, a machine, and a boss. It was true that some were spitting blood, but thousands more were choking on the golden land itself. (This was also true for the Christian immigrants, many of whom, however, could go back if they wished. Of the thirteen million immigrants of all nationalities and religions who arrived between 1900 and World War I, four million returned to Europe within five years.[62])

Learning English was the first necessary step into American life, even while the old language continued to protect dignity and perhaps sanity. Learning to read English was like regaining lost eyesight or entering adulthood a second time. For one immigrant woman, deciphering the street signs on Delancey Street meant regained competence and dignity: "I can . . . be a lady and walk without having to beg people to show me the way." The free public libraries helped thousands of newcomers, but night school was a better path to the language of the future. What immigrants were taught always reflected how they were viewed by teachers and school boards. For example, a manual for English teachers in night school suggested that immigrant men and immigrant women required different vocabularies. Men should know how to read "EXIT" and "FIRE ALARM" signs; women were drilled to understand "BARGAIN SALE" and "REDUCED."[63]

Upon arrival, Jewish greenhorns were faced with an economic choice. They could become peddlers (like the earlier German Jews, some of whom now owned stores specializing in soft goods) or clothiers. The peddler either had no other skills or wanted to avoid the sweatshops, or both. Hawking his bits of thread or tin cups or anything else he could carry in his pushcart or up and down the tenement stairs, he risked losing his dignity as a person, and sometimes more. In 1906 a woman described a bit of this life:

My husband became a peddler. The "pleasure" of knock-
ing on doors . . . cannot be known by anyone but a peddler. If anyone does buy anything "on time," a lot of the
money is lost, because there are some people who never
intend to pay. In addition, my husband has trouble because he has a beard, and because of the beard he gets
beaten up by the hoodlums.[64]

The peddler had to yell louder and wheedle more cleverly
than his competitor—usually another Jew, and perhaps even a
landsman—undersell him if possible, give more credit, take less
profit, and pray that at day's end he had something to show
for his humiliation. He dreamed that after he had sold enough
fish he might someday, with luck and avoiding the evil eye,
open his own store.

In the early waves of Jewish immigration, garment workers
made up about half of those who worked in industry. The
garment industry was rapidly expanding when the East European Jews began to arrive. They all became instant proletari-
ans, and were exploited by the boss, frequently another Jew
(at first a German but later one of their own, a *landsman* from
eastern Europe) who was himself struggling to make a living
by seeking additional ways to cut costs and increase sales. The
class struggle in the needle trades was fought between Jews.

Jews became tailors for a number of reasons: some had actually worked in the Russian garment industry, and the needle
trades in New York were located where a greenhorn without
English, right off the boat, could find them. Moreover, many
of the industry's employers were themselves Jews, and let their
employees observe the Sabbath and work on Sunday. Finally,
as Irving Howe explains, these Jewish employers were naturally "inclined to hire greenhorns whom they could exploit
with familial rapacity."[65]

Laborers in a shop usually worked sixty hours a week, while
those who worked at home put in about eighty-four hours.
Both also worked "overtime." Child labor in the tenements

was the rule, and grandparents in their seventies learned how to use an iron. Many of the shop workers took garments home, often toiling past midnight. The young Jews who were trying to earn passage money for their families waiting in the old country wanted to make and save as much as they could. They were self-exploiters with a mission, and therefore unlikely supporters of the new labor unions. The radical intellectuals and agitators had their work cut out for them because, as more Jews arrived, wages declined. There were hundreds of Jews ready to take the place of a slow, contentious, or sickly worker. Tuberculosis became known as a peculiarly Jewish affliction.[66]

The politics of Jewish immigrants derived from their European experiences and American realities. Some had been socialists in the old country, preferred the "refined" Russian language to Yiddish, the "crude" language of the ghetto, and were thoroughly secular. Of course, national differences created sub-groups within the Jewish fold. For example, one Rumanian East Sider noticed that, "unlike the other groups of the Ghetto, the Rumanian is a *bon vivant* and a pleasure lover; therefore he did not long delay to establish the pastry-shop (while his Russian neighbor was establishing the lecture platform)."[67] The Russian radicals took upon themselves the mission of awakening Jewish workers to the causes of their suffering and the action necessary to force employers to make improvements. These ideologues were passionate orators, perfervid in their denunciations of American (and Russian) exploitation, full of the emotional juices that could flood over their audiences while ensuring that sectarian differences could never be resolved. Socialists led most of the trade unions and the dominant Yiddish press.

Abraham Cahan, the founding editor of the socialist *Jewish Daily Forward* (1897), was a local treasure. He came to America as an anarchist, but converted to socialism when he realized that a disciplined organization was essential if the workers were ever to stand up to the bosses. Cahan found American politics to be "cheap, vulgar, double-faced, or just plain crazy . . .

nauseating hypocrisy.''[68] He realized that the despised Yiddish was the language of the people he hoped to stir. Gaining local fame for his ability to speak to the people in their own language, he made the *Forward* a voice for Yiddish-speaking Jews by giving advice to the lovelorn as well as by reporting on the state of the East Side and the city, the nation, the world, the Jews, and occasionally the cosmos.

To step out of the ghetto was to step closer to America, perhaps even to associate with Christians, with the risks implied by such fraternizing. When a Jew could afford to leave the supposed charms of the Lower East Side, he left. In the early nineties, three-quarters of New York's Jews lived on the Lower East Side; by 1903 the percentage had dropped to half; by 1916 it was less than a quarter.[69] But when they left the ghetto they congregated elsewhere with other Jews, not to create new ghettos but, because they now had a little money, to create Jewish ''neighborhoods.''

When the conditions were right and the move was made, perhaps by lugging their possessions on the city's new subway, the Jews began to develop their own middle class and to start up the American ladder. Heading out one family at a time, they moved to the new neighborhoods with hope that their next apartment, rarely a private house, would be the first of many, each reflecting their growing ability to live in America. They usually retained their sense of belonging to the spiritual or cultural community of Jews, but now they had moved somewhat closer to a more atomized life than Jews had ever known— closer, that is, to mainstream, individualistic, middle-class America, facing the immigrant's perennial question of whether economic progress would destroy cultural identity. It was, however, already settled that they would remain people of the city. Former Catholic peasants, also accumulating some wealth, faced similar experiences: from the ghetto to the neighborhood, from the known to the less known, into an America that for all was always problematic.

For immigrants who were politically or economically ambitious, success depended on their acceptance by others. Such ambitions fostered acquiescence in the American way. The ethnic leadership achieved by the immigrant middle class inevitably led it to urge its followers to submit and conform: if Japanese, to remain deferential; if German, to live together and avoid socialists; if Irish, to preserve family roles; if Italian, to avoid regional rivalries; if Yugoslav, to accept business values; if Jewish, to foster cooperation between the Germans and the Easterners; and if Mexican, to cooperate with business management. Everywhere, middle-class immigrants urged their poorer cousins to work hard, be thrifty, and stay out of trouble.[70] They were internal boosters of the idea of a superior America, of the inherent rights of the individual beyond his family's wishes or needs. And yet, even these ethnic agents of modernization rarely broke completely with their own pasts. That task was later undertaken by their children.

World War I intensified Americans' suspicion of the "hyphenated Americans," who were presumably guilty of split loyalties. The heated nationalism of war provided nativists with a stage from which to thunder at the aliens, whom they had detested all along. How ironic that of all immigrant groups the Germans should now become the target. They had usually been praised as model immigrants, the most assimilated and successful. Now, however, army units in the Midwest prepared for an armed insurrection by German-Americans; Delaware, Iowa, and Montana prohibited teaching German in the schools; and German music was booed off the stage. Individual Germans were forced by local vigilantes to change their names or to kiss the flag; some were flogged or smeared with tar and feathers. One group of miners in southern Illinois lynched a German alien. Theodore Roosevelt, who had opposed immigration in the 1890s, took the lead in denouncing as "moral treason" the supposed split allegiance of the German-Americans. Woodrow Wilson declared that he did not want the vote of any "hyphenate." The Chicago *Tribune* called for a more passionate nationalism and argued that restricting immigration was now necessary for national defense.

After generations of being accepted by America, the Germans suddenly found themselves treated as enemy agents. Everything they had built, all the improvements they had contributed, including the diverse work of the estimable Forty-eighters, was now suspect. Nativist bigotry destroyed the seeming sincerity of America's previous invitation to aliens to come, work hard, integrate into the middle class, and find happiness through acceptance. Now such openness seemed empty and hypocritical. After the war, some of the Germans' cultural cohesion revived, but the prewar German esprit did not recover.[71]

Most of the other immigrant groups were generally not attacked, so long as they did not overtly disturb the conformity that was everywhere smothering not only dissent but difference. A leader of the xenophobic Native Sons of the Golden West summarized the national mood: every alien "must live for the United States, and grow an American soul inside of him, or get out of the country."[72]

By launching an ambitious national campaign of "Americanization," natives sought to foster the growth of this soul in all immigrants. In Detroit, which proclaimed itself the "most American city," three out of four residents were of foreign stock. The growing automobile industry had attracted waves of Italians, Hungarians, Rumanians, Greeks, Armenians, and Poles. An observer concluded that "the mills which made Detroit great in size . . . threatened to destroy its Americanism." The local Chamber of Commerce, with the cooperation of Detroit's manufacturers, decided that ignorance of English prevented immigrants from holding steady jobs and becoming authentic Americans. Indeed, the problem became so acute that one plant was "forced to employ Negroes because of the scarcity in Detroit of white workmen who speak English." English classes in night schools soon opened all over the city.

The Packard Motor Car Company found one way to motivate its immigrant workers. Under the slogan of "Americans first," it announced that after January 1916 "promotions to positions of importance . . . will be given only to those who are native born or naturalized citizens," as well as to aliens who had taken out their first papers for citizenship. An English school opened inside the Ford plant instructing the students to "walk to the American blackboard, take a piece of American chalk, and explain how the American workman walks to his American home and sits down with his American family to their good American dinner." With the official blessing of the Secretary of the Interior, other cities "also became aroused to the importance of being American, and have taken steps to hurry the process of digesting the foreign lumps in their midst."[73]

Of course, some immigrants resented this lurching toward Americanization. A Czechoslovakian-born attorney advised that the first step in a sensible program would be for Americans to learn to respect the immigrants. He contended that the greatest need was to "teach the American-born children to treat the others as their equals." His daughter had once asked him, "Daddy, why does Jennie call me a hunkie?" An Austrian explained to Americans that "if you practice democracy Americanization will come of itself." Similarly, a Czech newspaper in St. Louis argued that Americanization would easily succeed when exploitation stopped, "when the American standard of living will go hand in hand with the American form of just, lawful government." The editor of a Hungarian newspaper lamented that the immigrant too often was made to feel "that he is not a white man as he used to be on the other side."[74] This man's racism, however, revealed that he had already made a key adjustment to the new land.

Just as the calamitous forces of World War I began to crash on Europe, Walter Weyl, a well-known economist and social critic, tried to understand what had happened to the United

States. He was perceptive enough to avoid the American fixation on its episodic and superficial middle-class politics. Instead, he focused on the immigrants who unknowingly created a new national environment. Weyl realized that the immigrant "forces the native American to change, to change that he may feel at home in his own home."

Comparing his America to an earlier time, Weyl concluded that it had become much more wealthy while now it also included increasing numbers of poor people. "We are massing in our cities armies of the poor to take the place of country ne'er-do-wells and village hangers-on." The founding fathers' dour predictions of the economic consequences of urbanization turned out to be accurate. The arrival of so many strangers with their own traditions precluded any consensus about a usable past or conventional habits. Far from offering such stability, America had already become too diverse, urban, literate, traveled, restless, sophisticated, extravagant, competitive, and middle-class.

The former peasants and shtetlers living in America's cities had also changed. Because Weyl appreciated city life in ways that would have been inconceivable to the pioneers and their latter-day cheerleaders, he recognized that the culture of the city would change, just as the millions who lived there would. The city was home for money, education, high culture, social interaction, and crime, the preeminent place of power, the home for the middle class. This meant that the characteristic Yankee farmer, however comfortable, and whether he liked it or not, was losing his favored place in the sun. "The immigrant," Weyl wrote, "even in the gutter of the city, is often nearer to the main currents of our national life than is the average resident of the country." The nation's center of gravity had shifted, from the land to the city, from a mythical and powerful sense of homogeneity to a bewildering diversity. As a result, the "children [of immigrants] are more literate, more restless, more wide-awake."[75] Where now was a national standard against which to judge behavior? Where now was the nation itself?

Old Henry Adams, offended by the modern world and Jews, fascinated by power, which he could merely observe, was an authentic voice of an anachronistic meritocracy that could not survive, as he knew, under the iron discipline of the new market. Some of the old men like him were admirable, of course, like darkly varnished paintings best stored in museums. But now it seemed time to get on with it, to sort out who was to get what, and how to rid the masses of people of the moral ideas inherited from the Protestant past. The lessons of the old Puritans were irrelevant to the emerging world of employees who worked in skyscrapers.

The little man's day in the city was finally coming. Under the market's discipline the urban middle class would learn to consume as never before. It was in the driver's seat. But the yokels and rural boobs, as Mencken called them, were awake to their danger, poised to reclaim their prior privileged standing, to roll back the chaos and reclaim, if they could, the nation they believed was rightfully theirs.

2

THE WONDERFUL WORLD
OF DISSATISFACTION

The gentlemanly amateurs in business, finance, and the profes-
sions had been losing status ever since the affairs they managed
became too technical for them to understand. In their place a
new breed of trained professionals, with better grades than the
former gentleman's C, emerged to do the new work demanded
by the magnitude of the mass market and the spread of technology and specialization. For decades, schooling had been replacing breeding, with deeply democratic implications. This
change gave the urban middle class, including the college-
bound children of immigrants, an identity card and work
permit.

Everywhere it appeared, the middle class irrevocably bound
itself to facts about the market, customers, suppliers, laws,
trends, schedules, timetables, statistics, grades, actuarial ta-
bles, blood-pressure readings, interest rates, profit margins,
and, in America during the 1920s, bridge scores. This is what
Nietzsche meant when he observed that for the middle class
the newspaper replaced the prayer book. Wanting to be "realistic," aspiring or assimilated members of the middle class, in
order to master the present, sought freedom from the irrelevant

assumptions of the past. Anachronistic ways of thinking, especially idealism, were dangerous, not merely pointless. Its embrace of facticity buried the middle class in its immediate affairs and present desires, made itself its standard of value and conduct, partly immunized against art and literature, and created a class astigmatism that blurred the continuity of life, while obscuring pleasure and solace once available. It was truly on its own, just where it wanted to be.

Becoming middle class required some accumulation of goods and resources, of course. But an altered frame of reference was even more important. Having worked their way out of poverty, millions of native-born Americans and immigrants, all protective of their own distinctiveness, had already passed the threshold that divided socially incompetent greenhorns from acculturated Americans. The material improvement in their lives permitted them to move to a new social setting, more restrained, less emotional, more calculating, less familial, more individualistic. Believing that respectability was essential to their increasing prosperity, they wanted to polish their manners in order to conform to people they admired and whose approval they sought. They feared convulsive social change that could thwart their plans and thus rejected radical ideas as perverse and pointless.

The middle class accepted the political and economic status quo, which, after all, had permitted it to hope and flourish. It wanted the future to resemble the present, only more so. Many of its members probably attributed their success to their own apparently effective personalities and beliefs, perhaps not realizing that they would then have to blame themselves in the unlikely event of a fall. Most of all, they wanted to be left alone, especially by government, to live privately in their private quest. If disruption by others could be restrained, they believed there was no end to the future success they and their children would enjoy. They were optimists so long as others would not be given license to disturb their peace.

This demand for privacy, usually equated to freedom, led

the middle class inward, to concentrate on the welfare of individuals in the immediate family, not on affairs of state or the demands of others—the poor—for a fuller measure of justice. Initially wanting to be left alone for economic reasons, the middle class began to focus on the psychology of the self as the foundation of everything it hoped to build. Such an imperial and allegedly autonomous self not only obliterated the past, it replaced the world.

In the years just before World War I, a relatively small but audible number of social rebels happily rejected the increasingly middle-class nature of American life. These were young intellectuals, advocates of free love, atheists, radical political theorists, poets, painters, and assorted fans, many of whom migrated to Greenwich Village, a mecca for bohemians, while others were scattered across the nation. Everywhere they called for smashing conventions in the name of greater personal freedom. They eagerly condemned the idea of Anglo-Saxon superiority, believing that "the only hope for American culture lay in the influx of cheerful Italians and soulful Slavs."[1] This bohemianism flaunted its differences from what it perceived to be the constricted and joyless qualities of middle-class culture. By turns playful and grim, the prewar radicals drew up a comprehensive bill of particulars against American materialism, conformity, smugness, vulgarity, and personal repression.

This suggests that the war alone did not produce the pervasive wave of social criticism that characterized the 1920s. But the twenties *were* different. The war, flawed peace, and affluence made the difference. The disillusionment of the twenties was different from prewar bohemianism because it put personality at the center of social change. Postwar rebels concluded that human fallibility was to blame for the lamentable state of the world, that deformed personality, not external force, enabled technology and industry to dominate culture and politics, and public life to degenerate into an intrinsically foolish as well as dangerous game. What was different about the rebellion of the twenties was that it was modern in all the ways that would mark the rest of the twentieth century. The sophisticated post-war rebels, unlike most of their predecessors, had no specific cause or grievance. Rather, their revolt was cosmic. They protested the human and cultural condition whose most favored beneficiaries they were.

Thinking of the twenties, F. Scott Fitzgerald later remembered that "life . . . was largely a personal matter." He baptized those years "The Jazz Age." And Gertrude Stein, following a lead given her by the manager of a garage in Paris, told Hemingway: "All of you young people who served in the war, you are a lost generation."[2] This uneasy but potentially liberating sense of a culture fracturing, of an individual's freedom to chart a personal course presumably unshaped by the demands of family or convention, marked this decade in unique ways. Intellectuals were more deeply affected than others, but a change pulsed throughout American culture, leading some to cling even more tightly to old and tested ways, others to experiment with what they considered unique freedoms, and a minority of free spirits who could afford it to flee the country. It was a time to think about what America meant, what it was for.

Of course, not everyone who fought in the war was lost. Most came home in relatively good shape, neither maimed nor bereft of life's purpose. The sharpest pain of the war was reserved for those who mourned the death of a loved soldier, for the badly wounded, and for the idealists, such as President Woodrow Wilson, who had nursed romantic hopes for the peace. Some of the young men who fought what was supposed to be the world's last war came home tougher, more cynical, gagging on the contradictions between their innocent intentions and the horrifying realities of trench warfare and mustard gas. When the grotesque peace was revealed in Versailles's aptly named Hall of Mirrors, there were no longer acceptable reasons for the mutilations and deaths. In the end, Wilson had bargained his ideals away and the Senate rejected the League of Nations. For the most idealistic and well-educated recruits the war turned out to be fraudulent. For the majority—the Johnnys who came marching home again, who were less self-conscious, less disillusioned for having had fewer illusions—the war was just a war, a horror perhaps, but not a betrayal of civilization itself.

Middle-class young people, however, recoiled from the traditions of the most culturally conservative Americans, who had been eager to go to war to protect what they assumed were the nation's core values. While an unsupported war turned the young into skeptics of establishment culture, a cynical peace made them enemies. World War I, like the future war in Vietnam, created a cultural solvent that weakened the bonds between generations, as well as those between the young and establishment culture.

One of the "wild young people" spoke for his tribe: "The older generation had certainly pretty well ruined this world before passing it on to us. They gave us this Thing, knocked to pieces, leaky, red-hot, threatening to blow up; and then they are surprised that we don't accept it with the same attitude of pretty, decorous enthusiasm with which they received it, way back in the eighteen-nineties."[3] The culture against which these young people rebelled was shaped by suffocating assumptions about the perfectibility of man, the angelic nature of woman, the power of right over might, "of flannels, tennis, bicycles, Tennyson, Browning, and the Blue Danube waltz." In place of this mannered and self-hypnotic world, the young were "forced to become realists overnight, instead of idealists, as was our birthright." Henceforth, if the older generation wished to spill blood for what it believed, but the young did not, let it shed its own.[4]

Insulted from the left by young rebels, the middle class was besieged from the right by small-town America, which, with allies even in major cities, fought ferociously to protect a way of life that had built the nation while sustaining the people's spirit throughout the nineteenth century. Provincial and urban America held conflicting assumptions and contradictory values: change was on the side of the urban middle class and recent urban immigrants; tradition was on the side of the villagers and the children of the earlier, agricultural immigrants. The less-Protestant cities were set upon by the more-Protestant hinterland. For villagers, the painful but liberating disillusion of the cultural élite was anti-American, foreign to what was most precious in the nation's heritage. But they were also obliged to acknowledge that, thanks to immigration, most Americans now lived in cities, the source of the nation's debilitating cynicism.

Most immigrants had not intended to change America. But their diversity and great numbers ensured that a consensus would not again dominate American life. Their hopes diverged from the American dream of an earlier era. Their plans did not center on perfecting a new polity or acquiring land to work. Mostly, they focused on the economic benefits of acculturation and education, so as to become full participants in the middle class. The booming economy of the 1920s supported such aspirations across the nation, but mostly in cities, where immigrants and their children lived.

The tenacity of the past, even in an individual who created vast changes in the world, is illustrated in the life of Henry Ford. Perhaps no one did more than he to shape the early twentieth century. Yet in his values and vision he represented an earlier era. He believed in self-reliance, thrift, sobriety, efficiency, America, Christianity, and the healing influences of nature. He believed in facts and courage. Contemplating the achievements of his life, he also believed in himself.

After a few failures, Ford had gone off on his own in 1903 to form his famous automobile company. He applied the revolutionary assembly line to manufacturing and five years later unveiled the universally known Model T, the Tin Lizzie.

The world has not been the same since. He was making his dream real:

> I will build a motor car for the great multitude. It will be large enough for the family but small enough for the individual to run and care for. It will be constructed of the best materials, by the best men to be hired, after the simplest designs that modern engineering can devise. But it will be so low in price that no man making a good salary will be unable to own one—and enjoy with his family the blessing of hours of pleasure in God's great open spaces.[5]

This last phrase, for him, was not empty rhetoric. He seriously believed that one major purpose of the new machine was to take masses of people back to nature, to get them out of the cities where they were denied light and air, and where, without his flivver, they were trapped.

His hatred of the "pestiferous" city was a steady drumbeat: "The City concentrates within its limits the essence of all that is wrong, artificial, wayward and unjust in our social life." It was "where the internal social impurities break out in a festering sore." His solution to this deplorable problem was eminently simple: "the abolition of the City, its abandonment as a blunder." The Model T would bring about a wholesale exodus to the suburbs. Before his car was available, only the rich could escape from the concrete, but "now the working man finds it not only possible but advantageous to live in the country, and thousands of them are doing it even while they work in the City." He urged workers to live in small communities "where a man knows his neighbor, where there is a commonality of interest, [and] where life is not artificial." The small town lived in sympathetic response to the changing seasons, without extreme wealth or poverty, and with "none of the violent plagues of upheaval and unrest" (such as strikes) that necessarily afflicted the great urban coagulation.[6]

For Ford, the problem was that the cities were bloated with the wrong kind of people: "The custom of immigrants settling in the cities should be so regulated as practically to be stopped." He praised the earlier pioneers who tamed the wilderness, but warned that "not all modern immigrants are of pioneer quality." Never having been baptized in the Mississippi, the new immigrants, some of whom had never been baptized anywhere, were bringing "destructive ideas" along with various other bundles. These new hordes were dangerous "because they run contrary to the spirit of America."[7]

Ford hated Jews as the most dangerous of the new city people. He contended that America had been built by the "Anglo-Saxon-Celtic race," which had been "chosen throughout the centuries to Master the world . . . [as] the Ruling People." Then along came the Jews, "a people that has no civilization to point to, no aspiring religion, no universal speech, no great achievement in any realm but the realm of 'get,' cast out of every land that gave them hospitality, and these people endeavor to tell the Sons of the Saxons what is needed to make the world what it ought to be!" Formulating a new law of social development, his newspaper, the *Dearborn Independent,* asserted that the Jews were responsible for the world's evil because "there must be some foundation of truth in a conviction that lasts for centuries." For over seven years he carried on an anti-Semitic crusade to ensure that America would remain Christian, rural, and unresponsive to the needs and opportunities of the modern world.[8]

This tawdry exhibition of bile reverberated with implications that went far beyond Ford's purely personal limitations. It revealed that he did not understand, and certainly did not like, much that was central to the modern economy that he had helped to invent. He did not like modern capitalism, which, in a familiar stereotype, he associated with "the international Jewish financier." He rejected internationalism, and he hated debt and banks. He despised bureaucracy and did not want strangers controlling any part of his operations. As a natural result, the new General Motors Corporation, thoroughly uninterested in antiquated pioneer values and irrational social attitudes, eventually took most of the automobile business away from him.

Not even Henry Ford could prevent the continuing flood of social change. He relied on the sound engineering and low price of the standardized black Model T. He had obviously made a good product, and assumed that sensible buyers would not have to be prodded or fooled into purchasing his cars. He detested marketing, merchandising, and advertising, and refused to compromise the integrity of his machine with useless gimcrackery merely to attract irrational buyers.

In contrast, from 1919 to 1925, General Motors was redefining modern business. It created the General Motors Acceptance Corporation to provide financing for retail customers so they could buy on credit. No longer did people need to save before enjoying a product, and this was as revolutionary as the assembly line. Giving credit to strangers made it possible for the mass to consume mass-produced goods. GM then redesigned its products so that, in its language, it could offer "a car for every purse and purpose," from the expensive Cadillac to the popular Chevrolet, in a full array of colors. It made the important decision to change some aspect of the styling of its cars every year, thereby unleashing entire industries whose purpose was to persuade the American buyer that newer was better, that his neighbor had the latest shade of blue, and that he would feel better if he had it too.

While Ford relied on sound engineering and the putative commonsense of the traditional American, GM counted on engineering, glitter, and the pliability of the mass market. In 1921, Ford commanded slightly over 55 percent of the market, while GM had only 13 percent. Then retail credit, colored paint, annual style changes, decentralized management, and engineering innovation all began to flow from GM. Henry Ford fought a mulish rearguard action by clinging to the Model T until 1927, when he finally shut down to retool for a new model. In the same year, perhaps in reaction to lawsuits and not wishing to diminish unnecessarily the number of potential buyers,

Ford publicly apologized to American Jews for his slanders. By then his entire achievement was in jeopardy and his share of the market was down to 25 percent. In another ten years it fell to 19 percent, behind Chrysler.[9]

Henry Ford was out of place in the urbanized and culturally diverse twentieth century. He had succeeded brilliantly when he applied himself to certain mechanical problems, but lost the competitive struggle to management teams, designers, and financial wizards, and to what became modern American advertising. Most of all, he was overtaken by businessmen who understood that America was changing in ways he loathed. These Protestant businessmen may have hated it too, but they adapted, and had no sympathy for Ford's nostalgia for an earlier time when social values superseded profits.

Millions of Americans admired Henry Ford, even to the point of supporting a presidential boomlet for him in the early 1920s. His mechanical genius and great wealth accounted in part for this adulation. But there was another dimension, which *The New Republic* identified: the average American saw Ford "as a sort of enlarged crayon portrait of himself; the man who . . . has achieved enormous riches, fame and power without departing from the pioneer-and-homespun tradition."[10]

It is ironic, then, that Henry Ford led the charge to mass production—that is, production for a mass society he himself could not countenance. He was a better master of the inanimate world of car parts than of the animate world of customers on whose response his own fortune would finally depend. Embodying the values of the past, he was composed of provincial emotions.

Throughout the twenties, rural America fought to retain its national ascendancy. Villagers resented the snickering of intellectuals, feared the immigrant swarm, condemned the great cities as evil, and chastised the middle class for its shocking and profligate behavior. Henry Ford and others who feared and fought the twentieth century, sometimes while hurrying it along, personified what had been the nation's most fundamental and authentic cultural values. Politically strong in the past, they would not, of course, willingly relinquish their status.

Hardly the pathetic fool of H. L. Mencken's diatribes, the villager had a full and lethal arsenal, and won almost every political battle he entered, including the election of the decade's three presidents. Herbert Hoover was fortunate enough to run against a Catholic from the streets of New York. Small-town America controlled the country's public life during the twenties, which is why its critics despaired. The critics could plan for a world liberated from their nightmare of provincial myopia and paranoia, but the villagers' strength made success unlikely. Though Zenith, as Sinclair Lewis called his small town, would be attacked by desperate farmers on the one side and disillusioned intellectuals on the other, it could rely on enough support in all quarters to ensure victory. Part of its power rested on the inertia of state and national legislatures, whose districts were drawn in the previous century or, less innocently, gerrymandered more recently with a sharp eye to the interests of Mencken's boobocracy.

The "boobs'" political power drove Mencken into a froth: "Our laws are invented, in the main, by frauds and fanatics, and put upon the statute books by poltroons and scoundrels." The cultural rebels assumed that everyone who was anyone knew the feed salesmen and village boosters were powerful and ridiculous, and that finally it was time to say so.[11]

Yet the battle lines were drawn not just between opposing politics but between opposing cultures. Both armies, one determined to hang on, the other eager to let go, realized that they were fighting for the nation's soul. Even the ratification in 1920 of a constitutional amendment giving women the vote was not at the heart of the conflict. Woman suffrage was a carefully controlled single-issue crusade based on a contradiction: the idea that women were equal to men, on the one hand, but were at the same time morally superior, and would, as a consequence, purify politics. In 1915, the dominant national mood toward female suffrage was apathy. It was different in the South, where opposition to votes for women was passionate because this issue necessarily raised again the question of disenfranchised blacks. The greatest enthusiasm was in the West, while the Northeast and the Midwest were reportedly cynical, believing that women voters would not change, much less improve, the nation's politics.[12] Generally, women's enfranchisement was not seen as a threat to the family or the stability of the republic. That is why it passed. The cultural rebels recognized, as did the provincials, that even such a major political reform was not central to the great struggle between the party of tradition and that of individual freedom.

The villagers' goal was to put into practice President Harding's memorable pronouncement: "not heroics but healing; not nostrums but normalcy; not revolution but restoration." While intellectuals rejected the war because the peace had not gone far enough, many provincial Americans grew restive because it had gone so far as to threaten national sovereignty, as in the proposed League of Nations. The public policy demanded by the villager and his occasional urban ally was designed to protect a familiar but threatened America: "normalcy . . . restoration." They sought to conserve a more congenial culture in which values had been clear, religion secure, intellectuals knew their place, and the fields of God's Country purified men to honor and love their nation.

The plight of the American farmer during most of the decade lent even more urgency to the villager's battle. Not only had farm prices collapsed in 1921, but the mechanization of agriculture displaced hundreds of thousands of farm workers. Almost twenty million Americans left the farms for the big cities, the largest flight from the farm in the nation's history. The cultural guardians who had insisted that new immigrants shun the cities for clean rural life, were, by now, merely relics. Perhaps memories of Paree made it difficult to keep 'em down on the farm, but the economic crunch made it impossible.

The new burst of urban growth could not be attributed to immigration, which restrictive legislation in the mid-twenties reduced by 70 percent. The immigration law of 1924 imposed national quotas that favored immigrants from the nations of North and West Europe (the nations where the forebears of the villagers originated) and discriminated against Catholics, Jews, and Asians. Also, not surprisingly, closing the doors to foreigners made it necessary to offer unskilled industrial work to blacks, who thereby benefited from the new xenophobia. From 1915 to 1928 over one million southern rural blacks moved north. They found jobs in the automobile plants of Detroit, as well as in the metal and meat industries, and joined with the industrially unskilled white farmers to form a fresh supply of inexpensive labor. Just as earlier immigrants had diversified the labor force, so now this movement of native-born blacks and whites partly re-Americanized the factory.[13]

The key to provincial fears and power was Prohibition, the most culturally revealing struggle of the twenties. This "noble experiment" was preeminently the creation of provincial, Protestant, white Americans. The pattern of voting on the Eighteenth Amendment in the House of Representatives is indicative: of the 197 representatives who supported the amendment, 129 came from towns of less than 10,000 people and 64 came from villages smaller than 2,500; in contrast, out of 190 representatives who opposed the amendment, 109 came from cities of over 25,000 people. "In fact," as a historian of Prohibition concluded, "national prohibition was a measure passed by village America against urban America."[14] Nonetheless, middle-class urbanites could always get liquor, if they were willing to make a contribution to the criminal bootleggers, many of whom were aliens or recent Americans, thereby confirming the dry villagers in their suspicions about urban corruption and the foreign menace.

The struggle against the city and what it implied was shared by the revived Ku Klux Klan, whose membership rose to about four million in the twenties. The Klan's leader regarded his organization as the only effective means of subduing culturally subversive blacks, Catholics, and Jews. He said that Klansmen "have enlisted our racial instincts for the work of preserving and developing our American traditions and customs." Central to this task was a full-scale offensive against the results of the "melting pot," which the Klan considered "a ghastly failure," whose "very name was coined by a member of one of the races—the Jews—which most determinedly refuses to melt." To purge America of its rot the Klan broke with what it understood to be "liberalism" because it "had provided no defense against the alien invasion, but instead had excused it— even defended it against Americanism."[15]

The provincial aversion to strangers fed into the Red Scare of 1919 and the early twenties. A. Mitchell Palmer, the Attorney General, did not create the fear of alien radicals or the desire to send them back to where they came from. He himself embodied Zenith and was vulnerable to its pressures. Sharing a growing national belief that recent immigrants were plotting revolution, Palmer once gave this description of the aliens he swept up in one of his raids: "Out of the sly and crafty eyes of many of them leap cupidity, cruelty, insanity, and crime; from their lopsided faces, sloping brows, and misshapen features may be recognized the unmistakable criminal types."[16] He saw New York's Lower East Side as the favored lair of the criminal reds. That was where Leon Bronstein, later known as Trotsky, had hidden out while biding his time. Unleashed, such sociopaths would overthrow the real America.

On January 2, 1920, the Palmer raids began, with over six thousand people taken into custody in the following weeks.[17] If the alien could be deported, as legislation of May 1920 made possible, or prevented from entering, as new immigration laws provided, or sentenced to die, as Sacco and Vanzetti would be, the vigilant old-stock American could at last sleep easily, free of fears that in the dead of night strangers would steal his land, wife, and blue-eyed daughters.

Religious fundamentalism was Zenith's central reflex; it held together Prohibition, the Klan, and nativism. Billy Sunday's "booze sermon" demanded more than abstinence; he called for the deportation of foreigners involved in bootlegging as well as of anyone who refused to kiss the flag. Members of the middle-class smart set sneered at the evangelists who wrapped the cross in the flag, baptized by the thousands, and attacked booze, anarchy, and Darwin in the same long breath. Villagers responded that clever city people could chirp all they liked, but too much education and genuine piety were incompatible. They dismissed their critics as not religious and therefore not patriotic enough to represent the nation. The critics dismissed them as fools.[18]

Fundamentalism's best champion was William Jennings Bryan, the voice of the village, frequent candidate for President, teetotaling Secretary of State, and a sworn enemy of what he thought of as Darwin's ancestral ape. He chose to joust against modern science, thus against most of the middle class, in Dayton, Tennessee. The Scopes trial, with Bryan facing the urbane Clarence Darrow of Chicago, turned on whether it was a punishable crime to teach evolution in the public schools. Bryan had protested against the theory of evolution since the turn of the century, but, because of accelerating social change, village fears overheated in the twenties and convinced him that the time had come to act.

He accused the generation of the Jazz Age of "mind-worship—a worship as destructive as any other form of idolatry."[19] For him, America's head and heart were at war, which meant that its authentic folk religion was under attack by dark international forces gathering strength in the un-American metropolis. Among these forces, he singled out science: "A scientific soviet is attempting to dictate what shall be taught in our schools and, in so doing, is attempting to mold the religion of the nation. It is the smallest, the most impudent, and the most tyrannical oligarchy that ever attempted to exercise arbitrary power."[20]

Mencken chortled, and Darrow ridiculed such "fool ideas,"

and both simply dismissed the organizing values and customs of a large part of the nation. Naturally, the villagers fought back, regarding their opponents as not merely arrogant but traitors. The urban middle class considered this struggle a partly diverting sideshow, not a threat, not important enough to deflect it from its own business.

The middle class displayed a similar lack of concern about public affairs in general. Political considerations had become static in the good life. Concerns about the Klan, Prohibition, religious fundamentalism, immigration restriction, evolution, and xenophobia continued to interest the wider public as phases in the war over the nation's culture, but the deepest and bitterest quarrels flared outside of politics. The economic boom made this possible, as it permitted President Coolidge to announce that America's business was business.

And for many, business was good. From 1914 to 1926 real wages increased by almost 30 percent, and one historian calculated that, though there was a growing number of very wealthy Americans, the condition of the poor also improved (the data on which he based his conclusion were, to put it gently, imperfect). But the purchasing power of one hour of a worker's labor grew by 50 percent, more than the increase in wages because prices of key products, including cars, were falling. Although the coal and textile industries and agriculture floundered, industrial productivity increased by 40 percent, and the work week was shortened. The net increase in the value of real estate showed the largest gain, followed by consumer goods and automobiles. Already the United States was consuming half of the world's energy.[21] Because of prosperity, along with some owners' strident anti-union campaigns, union membership declined from year to year. It was "the new era," the time when urban middle-class Americans were supposedly being freed from financial insecurity. For the first time, tens of thousands of middle-class Americans began to participate in the stock market, buying shares on margins of up to 90 percent and purchasing houses, cars, and radios on credit. This apparent democracy of consumption seemed endless.

Because adjustment to the emerging economy implied a new, more accepting attitude toward debt, unassimilated immigrants and culture-bound natives continued to practice old-fashioned thrift, of which the most startling evidence was the purchase of a private house. As early as 1907 immigrants were buying houses at about the same rate as native-born Americans (16 to 18 percent of the families in each group). By the end of the twenties, first-generation immigrant families who were home owners rose to over 40 percent, an almost inconceivable increase. While the numbers varied among specific ethnic groups, the overall percentage of first-generation immigrant home owners far surpassed that of native-born Americans. For instance, by the decade's end, immigrant Polish families who owned houses rose to almost 50 percent; the rate for Italians was 40 percent, for Czechs 54 percent, and Lithuanians 45 percent. In contrast, only 19 percent of native-born American families owned homes (a rate not significantly changed from that of twenty years earlier), and 29 percent of native-born children of immigrants.[22] Buying a house seemed motivated by cultural insecurity. The more at home people felt in America, the less driven they were to own a home.

Before World War I, the conventions of the real-estate market required a buyer to pay in full for a house before moving in. In the 1920s, however, houses became more expensive and more consumers already were in debt for other installment purchases, so a mortgage became the accepted instrument to finance the purchase of a house. The usual length of a mortgage extended from five to ten years, although the loan was often not completely paid at the end of the period, when buyers became vulnerable to the money market's volatility. Because ethnic groups supported their own building and loan associations to lend mortgage money, usually for longer periods and at lower interest rates than mainline banks, it was sometimes cheaper for immigrants to finance a home. By 1916, there were already seventy-four Polish associations in Chicago.[23]

Many immigrant families bought houses even while they were fighting poverty. They, as well as their slightly better-off fellow nationals, managed this by combining the salaries of several family members, and by taking in lodgers, usually countrymen. Economically mobile immigrant workers bought more houses than workers who were locked into manual jobs. In Cleveland, for example, as many as 60 percent of blue-collar Italians and Slovaks owned their own homes, while families who were moving into the middle class became home owners at the rate of 69 percent for the Italians and an astonishing 80 percent for the Slovaks.[24]

Aside from the wages of the head of the family, every immigrant group depended most on the labor of children to help acquire a house. Child labor contributed 22 percent of the total family income for immigrant families, 20 percent for second-generation families, and 17 percent for those born of American parents. Working wives brought in much less income, about 3 percent in each of the three groups.[25]

The parents' sometimes monomaniacal drive to acquire a house was, of course, hard on some of the children. That was as the parents and perhaps the children expected. Jane Addams of Hull House observed that four-fifths of the youngsters brought before the juvenile court were the children of foreigners. Most were Germans, and next were the Poles. "Do their children suffer," she asked, "from the excess of virtue in those parents so eager to own a house and lot?"[26] To draft a fourteen-year-old and commandeer all of his wages for the greater and future good of the family made economic sense, but it also speeded the process by which the second generation turned against the parental code.

After the house was purchased, and the family's income improved somewhat, the number of working children declined, partly because their income became less crucial, and also because families began to recognize the economic advantages of education. By 1930, for every group including blacks, the percentage of children attending school rose from a range of 50 to 80 percent to over 90 percent.

The economics of attending school conflicted with the immigrants' desire to transmit their culture intact and unpolluted by America. One solution was parochial education, which each Catholic ethnic group devised separately since the goal was to maintain ethnic culture as well as religious tradition. A Polish writer declared that "a Pole who says he is a Catholic but who is ashamed of or neglects the Polish language, is not a Catholic." Most immigrants demanded that the children learn the native language and culture. In Chicago, for example, the more recent immigrants followed the earlier example of the Germans and Irish, each of whom had built their own churches and schools; by 1930, twenty Irish and thirty-three German schools were operating. Czechs and Poles (Chicago had the world's largest Polish parish) constructed their own ethnic institutions to safeguard the children. Only the Italians, more deeply conditioned to expect children to work by age fourteen, and most suspicious of the damage education might do to parental, and especially paternal, authority, refrained from building their own churches and schools. For them, education was the business of the family, not outsiders. But by the twenties even the slowly acclimatizing Italians were more inclined to send their children to school.[27]

For ethnic as well as native-born Americans, home ownership was the fulfillment of a dream, not only a place but a life to call your own. Relatively poor workers universally thought of their own house not only as a cultural refuge, which it was, but a sanctuary for old age, a potential source of income in hard times, and a source of pride. Many of the propertied ethnics remained workers throughout their lives, were not motivated by any belief in their own eventual climb into the middle class, and accepted the reality that where they were was where they and their children were going to be. They aspired to security, not a steadily increasing income. They were not middle-class in their work or hopes.

Nonetheless, the fact of home ownership made propertied workers susceptible to middle-class preoccupations. They hungered for order and regularity, for the security of an ethnically homogeneous neighborhood. The reality of their lives made them seem likely participants in radical resistance to the injustices of America's economic system; but their commitment to their neighborhoods, to the protection of their castles, made them politically conservative and placed them at the service of the middle class, so long as it did not change the rules that these propertied workers assumed were necessary to safeguard their property—their security and pride.

It was different for the Jews, especially in New York. After the war, they began to form their own construction companies to build apartments especially for Jews, with the result that building increased by over 200 percent from the previous decade. These builders also made higher-status housing accessible to renters, people who could not afford to buy or who wished to invest their money in business, not housing. This was an "ethnic version of the American dream."[28]

A reflection of their deeply urban instincts, apartment living signified that for the Jews a place to live was a secular object easily replaced, not a deeply felt cultural necessity to keep outsiders at bay. There were not many outsiders where they lived, and, unlike other ethnic groups who owned houses, they expected to move as their income permitted. The New York Jews occupied apartments on the great boulevards, while their gentile neighbors resided on the side streets in private brick houses. The Jews' deeper interest was in the return on business investment, the sort of personal property they could take with them. Perhaps because historical experience had led Jews to value mobility, the very rootedness of a private house seemed not to meet their needs. They were protected by the neighborhoods, and thereby became more, not less, visible.

In short, like many others, the Jews wanted it both ways, more like jugglers than schizophrenics: ethnic stability and middle-class progress, identity and change. And they succeeded, at least until their more acculturated children resolved to voyage to that other planet, the expansive and exciting world of the gentile. Like the ambitious children of every white ethnic group, ethnic identity for the young Jews was a memory, perhaps strong and compelling, but not the center of life. Unlike the parents, the children had to make a conscious decision about what their ethnicity meant, if anything.

The material progress of the middle class led to its political quiescence. Why rock the political boat when it seemed to be sailing toward the pot of gold? It was recognized at the time that the public was losing its political existence because it was unable or reluctant to identify with other people's problems. The increasing complexity of life created a crippling discrepancy between current political needs and the traditional political machinery, making politics increasingly irrelevant to what the middle class cared most about. Political life degenerated into a mere reflex. The 50 percent who voted seemed to sleepwalk through the political routine, their minds on other matters, more important, more personal, more focused on the cultural icons that fascinated everyone.[29]

The new icons consisted of either new technology available to individuals, such as cars and kitchen appliances, or other individuals who stood out from the anonymous, democratic mass, such as Rudolph Valentino, Al Capone, and Charles Lindbergh. Their fame was utterly dependent on technology. What would Valentino have been without the movies? How would Capone have managed without his cars and trucks? Was Lindbergh the hero or his airplane?

Middle-class fascination with technology reflected its excitement over wealth and the future. New products promised opportunity for new enterprise, while their acquisition indicated social status. The dissemination of new technologies seemed to show that the education and direction of the nation were sound. The mass consumption of automobiles, radios, and movies disclosed the world's highest standard of living, the most modern people, and speed. Leaders of the American middle class thought of themselves as nimble, poised to exploit new chances. The spread of technological innovation in the twenties showed that it was an exciting time to be alive. And some of the new technology was at work bringing new celebrities into the local movie house or over the parlor radio.

National interest in such technology and preoccupation with such "personalities" was forming a mass culture. This was the emergence of a specific national culture based on artifacts, news of the latest style of rumble seat or shade of lipstick or the most up-to-date bulletin on the consuming preferences of celebrities.

Radio greatly facilitated this preoccupation with gadgets and glamour. Within its first eight years, it had become a $500 million industry comprising five hundred local stations. By 1928, there were fifty radios for every thousand people (compared to thirty-seven in Great Britain and twenty-two in Germany), and there were approximately seventy-five million listeners around the world. The idealistic hopes that radio would contribute to world peace, improve democracy, advance education and high culture, and bring religion's good news to the millions were squeezed out by the interests of the middle class and advertising.[30] On a much smaller scale, mail-order catalogues also brought the news of products to the nation. The new gospel of pleasure through acquisition was heard in city and province alike.

At the same time advertising took a new and psychologically important direction. Now ads focused not on the engineering of the product, or on what it could do, and certainly not on Henry Ford's benighted social values, but on the consumer's personal deficiencies, which the product was supposed to correct. Aside from sucking up dirt, a vacuum cleaner had another purpose:

I was the woman whose husband gave her each Christmas
some pretty trinket. The woman whose youth was slipping
away from her too fast. The woman whose cleaning burdens were too heavy. . . . In one short year I have discovered that youth need not go swiftly—that cleaning
duties need not be burdensome. For last Christmas my
husband did give me a *Hoover*. [31]

This dream machine simultaneously eliminated filth and age—
apparently the same thing.

The new ads encouraged the notion that correct consumption habits would lead to the fulfillment of the potential buyer's
fantasies by motivating her—usually her—to correct the little
embarrassing secret she had worried about since puberty. The
product would clean up, smooth down, or eliminate this defect,
and then she could hold up her head as she moved along the
path toward personal fulfillment. Advertising understood that
its function was partly to sell products, of course, but it was
now also in the more important business of creating consumers. The solution to their problems and anxieties was the immediate purchase of the offered products. Thus: "He was
conscious that something stood between him and greater business success—between him and greater popularity. Some subtle something he couldn't lay his hands on." [32] Shh. Bad breath.
LISTERINE. Quick.

Two propositions informed the views of the advertising industry. The trade magazine *Printers' Ink* explicated the first:
"The proper study of mankind is *man* . . . but the proper study
of markets is *woman*." The second theorem was widely discussed. An ad-agency representative explained that "what we
are really saying is the great bulk of people are stupid." Another agency lectured the industry about the "shallow brain-
pans" of people "in the mass." [33] In short, an effective ad
campaign would be geared to emotional, even frenzied, retarded women with grotesque tastes.

The most thoughtful proponents of advertising realized they

had become a new priesthood. Their gospel of good news preached that almost anyone could live an abundant and better life *now*. The ads of the twenties translated this revelation into a partly confused creed about who was leading whom. If the ministers of the good life could determine what people were thinking, the ads would succeed. On the basis of hunches and intuitions, neither science nor a diabolical capitalistic conspiracy, they prepared messages to tell people what it was thought they wanted to hear. It was not very subtle. In the words of *Printers' Ink,* it is "wholesome to live and enjoy abundantly . . . happiness in the hand is in itself like money in the bank. . . . To live and to enjoy—that is the basis of modern economics."[34]

The good life now rested on the mass acquisition of things that would make life easier and more pleasant for millions. This gospel promised and delivered hundreds of thousands of jobs, lifted the economy, and helped to realize the dream of a better life, better, that is, to the extent that material objects could provide. For the housewife an electric washing machine, a modern iron, and a vacuum cleaner not only saved her back but also introduced her to the promised benefits of more technology. She was urged to keep a sharp eye out for additional machines to ease her load, create more leisure, impress her friends and neighbors, and discuss with the repairman.

By spreading the gospel of consumption, the new ministers redefined sin in ways thoroughly compatible with middle-class assumptions. Nineteenth-century Protestant values impeded the full flowering of the new ethic, which was based on pleasure, not work; spending on the installment plan, not thrift; and a generalized dissatisfaction with what one already had, not contentment. The admen did not invent this. They reflected what their potential customers already took as gospel. At a sales convention in 1929, a General Motors executive told the plain truth: advertising's goal was to encourage as many people as possible to be "healthily dissatisfied with what they now have in favor of something better. The old factors of wear and tear can no longer be depended upon to create a demand. They are too slow.''[35]

The new gospel therefore rested on an interesting proposition: contentment prevented happiness. One adman explained that contentment was in fact subversive of the American way: "An absolute resignation to things as they are is found among the fatalistic inhabitants of India and China." But in America, happily, advertising "helps to keep the masses dissatisfied with their present mode of life.''[36] Based on the optimistic middle-class assumption that living would continue to improve, that the present was less desirable than the future, this mass grumpiness, not invented but echoed and amplified by the ad agencies, was the single most powerful engine of economic growth the world had ever known.

At its height, it helped to usher millions of mostly middle-class consumers into the new world of installment spending. Toward the end of the decade, about $6 billion worth of consumer goods were bought on credit: 85 percent of furniture sales, 80 percent of phonographs, 75 percent of electric washing machines, and most of the vacuum cleaners, pianos, sewing machines, radios, and electric refrigerators. Bankers eventually accommodated themselves to installment buying and referred to debt as the "new thrift.''[37] What had once been the scandal of indebtedness died with the birth of the mass market, absolutely dependent on credit to create enough consumers to absorb the inventory.

Two major themes emerged in the advertising art of the twenties. The first depicted the middle-class American family at home, and the second emphasized the overwhelming importance of romantic love. The home was a place where the family played house: the woman happily played in the kitchen, while the men played with radios, boys, and dogs. No one was guilty of exertion, and everyone belonged to a family. Single adults, presumably requiring fewer products, did not exist.

Romantic love, with or without children, was the very center of existence. The failure to enjoy the adolescent's conception of true love was to miss the meaning of life, and the pathetic soul who lacked this profound source of the only genuine happiness had only herself to blame. She—almost exclusively "she"—had done something wrong: she had failed to purchase the products that would have kept her young, her skin smooth, her breasts the correct size and shape, her body antiseptic, white, perfumed, polished, plucked, and pure. She would never know the mysteries of sex because, without love and youth, sex was unthinkable. "Some women age so young and fade out—constipated." "Look like a schoolgirl all your life; use Palmolive for your skin." This view of pubescent love depended on wealth and the leisure required to shop correctly, to attend the right parties in the right dress, to participate in the right sports with the right costume and equipment, to take the right vacations using the right luggage tucked neatly away in the trunk of the right car. Such love was unavailable to the poor, certain unmentioned dark-skinned races, people who sweated, and apartment-dwellers who did not own a dog.[38] Admen were not writing off a large part of their potential market; they were appealing to the middle-class desire to become like the fortunate few depicted in the ads.

A third recurrent image, in a tirelessly repetitious cliché of capitalist realism, showed Mr. Consumer in a setting designed to capture the hearts and wallets of the middle class. The Man at Work invariably occupied an impressive office, with a telephone at his fingertips, and behind his imposing, uncluttered desk there was a huge window for surveying the world at his feet. Early in the decade, when he looked out his window he viewed the world of the factory he apparently owned, but later in the decade the vista became that of the modern city. His was the highest vantage point, although an occasional airplane or dirigible was a little higher. This thoroughly modern man, the ideal toward which it was assumed everyone aspired, evolved from the mere boss of the factory to the master of all he surveyed, dominating the city, the world, the future.[39]

No product summarized this newest version of the good life

better than the automobile. The car ads no longer described its features, as in the Model T ads. Instead they described a way of life: free, young, smiling, in tune with nature, and essential if the reader was to join that fraternity of Americans who understood how to live. The silent message was obvious: if you love what is best about your country, buy a Chevy.

Consumers reacted as the ads intended, and the automobile industry invested more heavily in advertising than any other. In 1910, about 180,000 cars were produced; in 1924, production reached an astonishing 4 million. By 1927, 20 million cars had been manufactured, half of them Model Ts, and three-quarters of the sales were made on credit. The average wholesale price of a car in 1910 was $2,000; six years later, it had fallen to $900. In its early years the price of the Model T was $950; by 1924 it sold for $290. In the later twenties, the industry spent $60 million a year on advertising. Standardization, economy of scale, and accounting controls were both cause and effect of the campaign of national advertising.[40]

But, naturally, Henry Ford disapproved of seducing sensible Americans into purchasing products whose cost would be increased by the effort to persuade them to buy. It violated his version of common sense: "Cut it all out; it's an economic waste and I never did believe in it." With the stinging success of General Motors, however, Ford was obliged to unveil his new Model A and hire the N. W. Ayer and Son advertising agency to hawk his snazzy new product. An ad for the Model A showed it parked before an elegant house, with a maid and chauffeur hovering. The text began: "Women's eyes are quick to note and appreciate the trim, graceful lines of the new Ford, its exquisite two-tone color harmonies, the rich simplicity and quiet good taste reflected in every least little detail of finish and appointment." Still, though Henry Ford was forced to adapt, he was not required to like it: "We are no longer in the automobile but in the millinery business."[41] The Ayer people understood that they were appealing to the urban middle class, not to the self-sufficient, virile, hardscrabble farmer, so admired by the boss, who could not aspire to the sissified comforts Ford was now marketing.

Technology and the absorption in celebrities' lives and buying habits had created a national middle-class community of interest based on consumption, not citizenship. For those who could afford it, and some who could not, shopping was rapidly becoming their major cultural activity. The architecture of the newly organized kitchen—divided cupboard space, the exciting new breakfast nook, and cooking with gas[42]—along with redesigned vacuum cleaners and washing machines, not to mention the exquisite suspense about whether Henry Ford would replace the Tin Lizzie, were matters of national attention, even passion.

Great significance, in particular, was attached to the newly electrified kitchen, which, it was argued, would liberate the housewife from drudgery so that she could freely express her creativity, indeed, her very personality. Unlike most provincial village wives, the urban, middle-class woman was released from the need to produce clothing or bread. She was now free to become the ideal American woman devoted to the emotional stability of her family, an expert in homemaking with the requisite skills in color coordination and subtle flavorings, the nation's chief purchasing agent, and, most important of all, a model mother who could give her complete attention to her children. Young women used to learn to make things; their modern middle-class counterparts learned how to service people. The *Ladies' Home Journal* thrilled to the possibility that postwar American children would be the world's first generation to be raised exclusively by their mothers.[43] On the favored children would be lavished a single-minded attention, to a degree previously unknown.

But the supposed freedom of the American woman left her working at least as hard as her mother, and with less time for herself. New gadgets did their job, but new and more exacting

definitions of cleanliness required even more energy. No previous generation of women had spent so much time shopping
and operating the conveniences designed to save time. This
liberation was a trap made expressly for the middle class, but
one whose appeal was universal. For women it was difficult to
see whether there could ever be a way out.

The immediate solutions for some middle-class women included higher education, jobs, somewhat relaxed sexual codes,
fewer children, and more divorce. The small family led Theodore Roosevelt to rant about "race suicide," but a historian
explained that what T.R. really meant was "class suicide."
For it was the middle-class women who practiced birth control,
got divorces, or did not marry in the first place. The divorce
rate in 1910 amounted to about nine divorces for every hundred
marriages, a rate that increased to about thirteen in 1920, and
almost seventeen in 1929. Equally important, divorce was becoming less scandalous. The only study of the subject conducted in the decade reported that about 25 percent of the
married men and almost as many married women admitted to
adultery.[44] All was not well in the American home, but the
problems were not yet fully acknowledged, especially not by
people in pain.

Ideal sexuality for the middle class was consistent with its
other values: respectability, orderliness, modernity, and safety.
The young had to be allowed to romp, of course, but not so
much as to damage their otherwise promising futures. They
could learn to be rational about sex, avoid accidental pregnancies and venereal disease. Young women were expected to be
more responsible than their partners, not because of some inherent and overpowering glandular hypertrophy in males, but
because women had more to lose: virginity, reputation, and
marriageability—the future.

Sex roles were equally framed by middle-class aspirations.
In his possessions, Father was to exude as much success as he
could afford, and the family was his most important possession.
Mother was to invest her time and taste in the emotional equi-

librium of her husband and their children. It was an arrangement designed to show each other and the world that the family had imposed rational order on itself, and was, as a consequence, reliable, nice, and prepared to move further up.

For the middle class, conflict between the generations disrupted domestic harmony and in acute cases shattered dreams about the future. The cultural tragedy of the immigrant family's loss of its children to the great and anonymous American mass also played a central role in generational recriminations.

When, because of the perceived callousness of the old, young people with deep conviction and passion and in sufficient numbers became cultural guerrillas, it was inevitable that the original goals of their revolt would expand. What was at issue, according to a young woman, was a frontal attack on superannuated authority, an essential step in "the eternal struggle of mankind for freedom."[45] The generational hissing was precisely over whether the young could be free, or freer, from cultural constraints without endangering the republic, world peace, or their eternal destination in the economy of heaven. For them, sexual rights became a touchstone of emancipation in this crusade, compelling them in turn to assault the interdictions of conventional religion, the arbitrary constraints imposed on women, and the hypocrisies of public life in general, nowhere better evidenced than in the frivolity of prohibition. Gin became the lubricant of a generation and, in an instant, the twenties' Flaming Youth appeared.

It was recognized at the time that the rebellion of the young was different from the ordinary difficulties the generations always had with each other. The difference lay precisely in the seriousness of what was now being attempted, not merely freedom to try one's wings, but a challenge to the right of the older generation to continue doing business as it wished. Again, the difference was middle-class affluence, as Judge Ben Lindsey of Colorado, a friend of the young, explained:

In the past the revolt of youth always turned out to be a futile gesture. It never brought much change. But now the gun's loaded. These boys and girls can do what boys and girls never were able to do in the past. They can live up to their manifesto, and nothing can prevent them. The external restraints, economic restraints that were once so potent, have gone never to return.[46]

A common argument was that the revolt of the twenties was unique because it was ill-mannered. This was because, from an upper-class viewpoint, the badly reared daughters of vulgar middle-class mothers were now swarming over the college campuses, overwhelming traditional courtesy by their numbers. As one woman insisted, "the sex manners of the large majority of uncultivated and uncritical people have become the manners for all, because they have prospered, they are getting educated, and there are so many of them." Some of the coeds' mothers lived vicariously in the partying and other, more clandestine activities of their daughters, encouraging them to be as popular as possible so as to snag a husband. If popularity required bad manners or something worse, so be it. This same commentator, a self-appointed social arbiter, lamented that all social classes now wanted the same things for their daughters—security through sexual popularity. She traced the decline of American civilization to the acquisition by the unprepared, unmannerly new middle class of more money and education than its members, especially the crude mothers and vulgar daughters, knew what to do with.[47] Because the new middle class was not confident about the social skills required higher up the ladder, questions of decorum came to be anxiously discussed. Emily Post's *Etiquette* became, in the phrase coined at the time, a "best seller."

The public's obsession with the young was, according to a young woman, "nothing more nor less than a preoccupation with the nature of that generation's sex life." Mass culture, especially the movies, poured oil on the flames, but there is no doubt that the generation that made a war was now revolted by the sight of a woman's knee. Of course, some middle-class mothers caught their daughter's fevers, and life became inverted: "A girl may be a bad influence for her mother."[48]

In time, some members of the older generation, usually women, expressed sympathy for the aspirations of the young. One woman, for example, understood and approved the seriousness of the change: "The young people—and the young women, I believe, are, however unwilling and unconscious, the leaders in this—are setting out *together* on the search for standards of right and wrong that may be valid for them."[49] The fire and foreboding of the Chicago *Tribune,* however, was more characteristic: "A generation of young people are passing through the nervous excitations of our luxurious, high-geared, speed-loving time and at the same time are deprived of many of the restraints and safeguards of the past. Can the results be other than unfortunate and in some cases tragic?"[50]

Most Americans lived somewhere between the country village and Greenwich Village. Relatively affluent during the twenties and unchallenged by the poor, urban middle-class Americans were the bridge between the little old lady in Dubuque and the literary exiles in Paris. These Americans in the middle underpinned the world of the Jazz Age, the flapper, and the speakeasy. Many young people, thoroughly respectable, wanted to experiment a bit with what for them were new freedoms, but only up to a point, to avoid a pain in the head or heart in the morning. In *Our Dancing Daughters,* Joan Crawford played a tantalizing flirt who finally, however, stopped short because she could not ignore her mother's vague moral code.

Within this ambivalent context, somewhat freed from traditional sexual restraints but still susceptible to a binding conventionality, middle-class urban Americans tolerated the fashions of the flapper, a name coined by H. L. Mencken in 1915 to describe the shameless hobble-skirted woman whose ankles were on view, tame in comparison to the scandal that was coming. The flapper's style in the twenties was a point-by-point repudiation of the Gibson girl, the late-Victorian image of femininity. Miss Gibson had long, upswept hair while Miss Flapper bobbed hers. The Gibson girl demurely concealed her legs beneath voluminous skirts; the flapper raised her hem above her knees and rolled her stockings below them. Shoulders, breasts, and hips were emphasized in 1900; the flapper bound her breasts flat and wore loosely fitted blouses. The Duchess of Windsor, whose waistline was perhaps not what she would have wished, informed the waiting world that the desirable measurements for the ideal woman were 30-30-30. Another, much more precise adviser to the young declared that a woman of 5 feet 3 inches should weigh about 119 pounds and measure 28.8(*sic*)-24.7-35.2.[51] Emphasizing youth, the flapper was horrified by the slightest hint of fat—her tubular dress would naturally hang from any protuberance, such as an unfortunately generous bust, making her appear, she thought, like the trunk of a mature sugar maple. Gibson was the picture of maternity in either fact or prospect. The flapper was free and prepubescent.

The contradiction in this retooling of the young, middleclass woman was her short hair. The flapper's studied naïveté, her boyish asexuality on the one hand and innocent, little girl's short skirt on the other, contrasted with the fact that her short hair—like cosmetics, drinking, and smoking—had been a cultural symbol of the whore or the Greenwich Village radical. It was the hair, apparently also boyish, that was the flapper's erotic display, an obvious renunciation of long girlish tresses and a newly possible proclamation of her sexuality. Because long hair worn loose was acknowledged to be appropriate only for preteens, slightly older women were required to spend much time fixing it so that it would not swing loose, producing an effect that struck the new generation as unapproachable and prim. Bobbed hair was widely attacked as an explicit sexual invitation. The shorn women defended it on the grounds of liberation.[52]

By following the shifting erogenous zones of female fashion, the flapper proved to the interested world that she could play, smoke if she dared, do the Charleston and the shimmy, and could run as fast as possible. She was made to order for and by the salivating advertisers. Could she be persuaded to start smoking or would she have to settle for murmuring, as the ads instructed, "Blow some my way"? Deprived of breasts and hips but with legs all over the place, she dressed for fun and teenage gamboling. She represented the culture's first mass-produced ideal of youth, most effectively depicted in the movies. It was entirely appropriate that F. Scott Fitzgerald, among others, recognized the psychological costs of what became a national hymn to the teenager as a standard of beauty, one he had helped to insinuate into the imagination of the middle class, his readers. He was not pleased with himself: "If I had anything to do with creating the manners of the contemporary American girl I certainly made a botch of the job." The obsession with youth, slimness, and chronic gaiety could not, of course, be sustained. The ideal flapper could not survive, as Fitzgerald understood. "I think the faces of most American women over thirty are relief maps of petulant and bewildered unhappiness."[53]

The question that agitated the decade was whether the external behavior of the younger generation indicated a decline in morality. While the Pope decried "the present immodesty and extravagance in women's dresses," newspapers and magazines had a field day. *The Literary Digest* surveyed opinion to answer the question "Is the younger generation in peril?" The answers were divided, as expected, and predictably the responses dealt almost entirely with women. The men apparently were less threatened or less interesting.

Most is known about middle-class college students because they seemed to be the agents of sexual experimentation, were easiest to study, or most willing to talk. Coeds transfixed the nation, eliciting an interest that seems prurient even from sexual researchers. The studies done at the time imply that the sexual code was changing in the embraces of young middle-class Americans who lived away from home and could afford the auxiliary equipment thought necessary to petting parties—cars, fashionable clothing, music, and gin. Here were located the flaming youth who changed the rules of sexual play and entertained or scandalized the nation.

The young were greatly amused as the older generation mourned over the decline of civilization: "Are we as bad as we're painted? We are." Churchly and parental taboos were bent or broken, as the young transformed the moral problem of sex into a matter of personal need and desire. The new outlook collided directly with the Victorian double standard, especially in regard to women. The young rebels demanded greater female sexual independence and overthrew the custom of courtship, with its implied commitment to marriage, in favor of dating as many men or women as possible. In fact, wholesale popularity—pairing without promises—supplanted the delimited intensity of spooning in the swing on the young woman's front porch. The sexuality that the young accepted included what they called necking or petting, which, while definitions varied across the country, always meant every form of sexual play except intercourse. One study found that over 90 percent of the coeds petted, often in petting parties that were designed precisely to enforce the code against intercourse, rather than being the mad orgies the public loved to whisper about. The young themselves ostracized their peers who "went too far." But intercourse was acceptable for an engaged couple, although many women remained anxious about the future implications of their lost virginity. Nonetheless, deep love made deep sex permissible, a pleasure experienced by almost half of all college women, of whom more than half did so with a partner they intended to marry.[54]

Female dancing and dressing hypnotized the nation. The Episcopal Church mounted a national campaign to teach girls to "uphold standards." The Catholic archbishop of the Ohio diocese warned against the shimmy and "bare female shoulders.'' The New York legislature gave the commissioner of licenses power to censor dances. In Utah, a woman whose skirt was more than three inches above the ankle could be punished by a fine and jail sentence. In Philadelphia, clergymen conducted a "scientific survey" to design a "moral gown" and, averaging all the responses, concluded that seven and a half inches was enough "see level." Virginia and Ohio both debated the depth of necklines and the dangers of "diaphanous material." Seventeen states concerned themselves with the maximum amount of visible female skin that the conventional public morality of the exposed women and stimulated men could withstand. Or was it stimulated women and exposed men?

Dozens of college newspaper editors despaired for the nation's future because of the outrageous new dances performed by these women whose bodies, tightly clutched by their partners, were clearly on view. The Hobart College *Herald* claimed that "American morals have undoubtedly degenerated with the dance." Such decadence proved contagious as it spread from overheated dancing to everyday life. A musician at the University of Illinois refused to play at dances because the girls, some of them "like Madonnas . . . dance by me with their eyes closed, their cheeks inflamed, a little line of passion across their brows." The daily *Nebraskan* described its campus as immunized against "the Eastern dances" but knee-length skirts had already arrived from the wicked city. A mass meeting of students supported "simple dress" to help the nation "return to normalcy." It was shocking to learn that some mothers not only failed to disapprove of their daughters' misconduct but even flapped themselves. The catalogue of catastrophe was endless, so much so that the Smith College *Monthly* finally decided that "the poor, shocked middle-aged of the world have made themselves so absurd!"[55]

The militant flappers refused to surrender. A small-town working girl was annoyed: "Why should the fact that a girl has legs arouse the wrong kind of impulses in a man? Does he think we travel on wheels?'' If the male's glands were working too hard, he should learn to control his emotions, just as women had always been forced to do. If men truly disapproved of the flapper, she wondered, why was she constantly surrounded by them? An editorial in the Boston *Herald* agreed that male vulnerability was not the problem:

> How many of [the men] really want the world made safe for masculinity? Do they not, in their secret souls, relish a world where danger greets them on every hand? If they, poor souls, really do pine in secret for the ''good, old-fashioned girl,'' in place of the perfumed, gauzy creature they pretend to like, they can easily get her.[56]

A popular historian who witnessed the decade's cultural evolution understood the seriousness behind the flapper's antics. He suggested that the characteristic young woman of the twenties in effect said to her men: ''You are tired and disillusioned, you do not want the cares of a family or the companionship of mature wisdom, you want exciting play, you want the thrills of sex without their fruition, and I will give them to you.'' She then whispered to herself: ''But I will be free.''[57]

Yet, behind her masks, Miss Flapper was difficult to identify. She occasionally spoke as if she understood some aspects of the meaning of freedom, then had a fit over the color of her mascara. ''She will vote and hold a job,'' reported one man who had hoped for better, ''but only if she may continue to look like a Cleopatra.'' She would accept a clerical job on condition that she be permitted to wear ''a costume which suggests that her real ambition is to loll among the expensive pillows of a modern harem.'' For him, the flapper was exposed as a fake, not a progressive, merely a ''jazz baby.'' On the other hand, a letter to the *Daily Illini* in 1922 explained that ''the flapper is the girl who is responsible for the advancement of woman's condition in the world.''[58] There is something in both views.

The transformation began when girls realized that they did

not want to emulate their mothers. Some of the accumulated wisdom of age became either pointless or oppressive. Mother might be a better cook, "but who wants to cook? Better seamstress—but who wants to sew? Have a keener eye for spots on the wallpaper or more accurately distinguish veal from lamb." Revealing the middle-class affluence and superficial education of the flapper, one girl responded, "You can hire a good Swede to do all that!"[59]

Although the flapper wanted more than anything else to marry and settle down, but not in her mother's fashion, she was part of what was an unintentional vanguard for future generations of feminists. Her enemy was the intimidating and seemingly impervious fortress of Victorian paternalism. If such battlements could be scaled, however cautiously or playfully, if even a small vulnerability could be demonstrated, the way would be opened for her more determined daughters and granddaughters. Concentrating on the apparently trivial rights of style, and her obviously significant rights as an adult with her own sexuality, the flapper indisputably enjoyed merely shocking the custodians of culture. Her descendants would not be so easily amused.

It was important that women had already been given the vote. It was more significant that, in opposition to polite opinion, they used rouge, shortened their skirts, drank gin when they wished, smoked in public, had affairs, and in other ways thumbed their noses at the restricted and corseted world approved by their loving and bewildered fathers. In raising their battle flags for the right to flirt and dance the Charleston, young middle-class women opened some distance between themselves and the formidable social authority of centuries.[60] The more serious feminists who struggled in the future would necessarily repudiate the coquettishness and political immaturity of the seemingly juvenile flapper, while failing to credit her as a brave and effective, if unconscious, trailblazer.

• • •

Like the ubiquitous image of the flapper, the idea of celebrity arose almost naturally from the technologies—improved printing presses for the tabloid newspapers, radio, and movies—that made mass communication possible. It is likely that Charlie Chaplin was then the most widely recognized human being in history. After spending a few years elsewhere in the country, Chaplin came to New York during World War I. One newspaper headlined the grand event: "HE'S HERE." Additional explanation was unnecessary.

Its need for respectability and approval led the middle class to conform to currently fashionable opinion. It was horrified by eccentricity in its own ranks, but entertained by it in the very rich or poor, as well as in the otherwise well-bred foreigner. Designating wealth as the universal measure, middle-class Americans lionized wealthy strangers whose lives were riskier, more glamorous, and sexier. Ordinary middle-class women might even emulate a celebrity's surface style, while enjoying gossip about his or her immorality.

By definition, a celebrity represented a break from conformity—adventure and warmer blood than would be tolerable at home or in the office. While members of the middle class might flee from celebrity for themselves, unless great wealth could be guaranteed in advance, they were mesmerized by it as a release from the constraints on their own lives, which they had worked so hard to enforce. They used the celebrity as the basis for fantasy, of course, but not as an antidote to lives that they believed were good.

A celebrity is a darling plucked from the crowd by the gods, usually heaped with worldly treasure, pampered, applauded, sent away to a distant Hollywood, an isolated and magical kingdom where the sun always shines, where equally blessed beauties could splash and dine and giggle with each other and, because of distance and money, remain safe from the drooling mass of worshippers.

These birds of paradise were given almost everything the American dream could offer—fame, fortune, success without effort. Power, however, was reserved for some vague background presence called a producer, who made arrangements, signed checks and contracts, and made adult decisions beyond the ken or control of the gorgeous children. They were all children, or childlike, in their dependence on Daddy. But the question of who was in charge was usually an internal matter of little consequence to star-struck fans.

During the war the discovery was made that these golden creatures could persuade vast audiences to buy war bonds, that celebrity was not limited to a single field of endeavor. The halo threw its light everywhere. When stars spoke about world affairs or selected a breakfast cereal, their fans responded. The cause or product absorbed the glamour of the star. The plumed children could bless or heal or manipulate the multitudes not by a laying on of hands but by smiling. There was great profit in the lesson that a celebrity was not just a person well known for some achievement—the old-fashioned idea of mere fame—but someone to be adored and actually emulated, even if only so far as wearing earrings like Joan Crawford.

At first, the darlings had to follow certain rules, lest the wrath of provincial America return them to obscurity. Rural Methodists and urban Catholics had already been clucking about the stars' indecencies of dress and decorum. After a particularly lurid sex-and-murder scandal involving the comedian Fatty Arbuckle, the movie producers' association appointed Will Hays, a Postmaster General, to censor the movies. It was as though the mostly Jewish producers had entrusted this squinting Protestant to guard the nation against themselves. Censorship was not actually imposed during the twenties, but the threat seemed to work. Such serpents as there were in the Garden of Hollywood learned to slither more discreetly.[61]

The tabloid press (along with the press photographers) and movies came of age at the same time in the twenties. They happily fed off each other as both spooned up tidbits of delicious and carefully managed gossip about the darlings, who was rising and who crashing in dreamland, and who was being naughty with whom. Because of the maturation, if that can be the right word, of the techniques of mass communication the idea of celebrity originated in this decade, as did the new industry of public relations. The lessons being learned concerned the techniques by which it was possible to talk to a huge society, to reflect and confirm what masses of people wanted. Nor was the other lesson ignored: great fortunes could be made by mastering the arts of mass communication.

The twenties were the golden age of the silent movies, and, in terms of public consumption, Hollywood's utopia. The weekly attendance at the movies in 1929 was greater than ever before or since—over 100 million went to the Bijous and Palaces every week.[62] Nothing in the history of mass entertainment had equaled this fascination and even addiction of every stratum of the consuming public. Here were glamour, sex, adventure, laughter, and tears with unprecedented accessibility and impact. Hollywood successfully strove to discover the formulas that would appeal to the widest number of ticket buyers, as Cecil B. DeMille repeatedly revealed in his sexy Bible stories. For the young, the movies were a social classroom, a deliberate portrayal of the good life available to people who would take the trouble to become rich enough to consume wisely. The old were offered nostalgia and the spice that enlivened rainy evenings and, the producers hoped, rainy lives. For everyone, the movies represented the new, the thrill of modern living, what it meant to live in the greatest nation on earth. Now, just what were contending politicians so exercised about?

The movies of the twenties were preeminently concerned with the changing behavior of young women—they were called "new women"—portrayed by actresses such as Clara Bow, Joan Crawford, and Gloria Swanson, "the moderns." They began to supplant Lillian Gish and Mary Pickford, the previous female leads, who had specialized in female sacrifice, submissiveness, and virginity. The new woman revealed more skin, exulted in her appetite for life, especially sex, and exhibited irrepressible physical freedom. Determined to sate their ambitions, the moderns happily relied on their sex to make their way in the world of money. Nonetheless, they remained virginal in their hearts, a condition most managed to protect until marriage. The sexual behavior the movies depicted was eroticism without intercourse.

The erotic rested instead on consumer goods—cosmetics, jewelry, and clothes—rather than on the body's juices. While sex was constrained, acquisitiveness was not. Entire movies—*Charge It, Ladies Must Dress,* and, best of all, *Gimme*—showed the liberation supposedly inherent in furs and lace. One De Mille movie, *Why Change Your Wife?* (1920), demonstrated how a frumpy matron (Gloria Swanson) lost her husband to a glamorous, properly dressed, and perfumed vamp. At first, the deserted wife vows to be done with it because, she said, she "hates men and clothes." Quickly regaining her senses, she acquires a "sleeveless, backless, transparent, indecent" wardrobe. Arrayed in feathers and gold lamé, she naturally recaptures her stunningly stupid husband.

Many movies probed the modern woman's anxiety that marriage might not meet her deeper needs. Almost three hundred movies pretended to explore adultery, as a way to titillate audiences. But, even while concentrating on the adventure and pleasure of an illicit rendezvous, they necessarily communicated the message that, at their very best, men were untrustworthy. When Gloria Swanson dressed up, or down, to recapture her husband, her thought flashed on the screen: "The more I see of men the better I like dogs."[63] Whether marriage could do more than solve the young woman's economic puzzle was, in the movies of the twenties, less a question than a joke.

As for the movies, the exploitation of sex created a profitable urban market for confession and picture magazines. Obviously, sex for profit was hardly new to the world, and sex-oriented movies were popular before the twenties. But the mass production of titillation was a sure sign of advertising's success and self-consciousness. The ability to profit from the weaknesses of the buyer opened exciting vistas to the market's newest manipulators. At first, they had to guard against excess lest they stir the cultural custodians into retributive action. Partly out of deference to the custodians, and partly out of their own sense of decorum, and often out of undiluted cynicism, the vanguard of titillation always retained something of the past. Much of the Protestant garden was being paved, but its standards would not so easily disappear. A letter of instruction written by a sex-magazine editor to his authors illustrates the contortions of which the human mind is capable:

> I intend to keep—a sex magazine, but sex need not necessarily mean dirt. I want to stick to elementals, sex-elementals—the things closest to the heart of the average woman or girl, whatever her ignorance or sophistication. Above all, I mean to lift the moral tone of the magazine. I believe that to treat sex trivially is to diminish its dramatic value, while sober treatment enhances it. Characters may do anything they please but they must do it from some lofty, or apparently lofty, motive. If a girl falls, she must fall *upward*. [64]

Zenith, casting its shadows in both directions, to Hollywood and New York, would not be vanquished yet. One civilized man, struggling to keep his spirit alive while teaching at Ohio State, encountered only the stereotypes of the villager: "thin-lipped, embittered by the poisons that unnatural repression breeds, with a curious flatness about the temples, with often, among the older men, a wiry, belligerent beard." He watched them with their ladies, "shallow-bosomed, ill-favored wives—stern advocates of virtue—walking on Sunday self-consciously to church."[65]

For the prospering urban middle class, the anxieties of cultural conflict and the spiritual anguish of the lost generation could be shunted aside in the bubbly ambience of the Jazz Age. Affluent and politically indifferent, many city people embarked on Fitzgerald's quest for cash and success. The flapper and her boyfriend, along with the literary exiles, turned away from society in their respective celebrations of the inviolate individual. None of them could find a usable social past. For them, history began with puberty.

The search not for a usable past but for an alternative to the past was a symptom of modernity. The European masters of abstract art had accomplished a revolution in perception by overturning an esthetic that with significant variations was ancient. At first the liberated middle class had detested their art. Their bourgeois outrage had nourished the modernist avant garde. But now part of the middle class was itself in rebellion, a cultural phenomenon that was to grow in importance throughout the twentieth century. The middle class no longer could be moved by the symbolic outrages of artists, or, indeed, by anyone else's battles. It was becoming self-consumed. And its golden children were struggling to be freer than their parents, with their constricting cultural memories.

The conflict of generations consoled one disillusioned intellectual: "The most hopeful thing of intellectual promise in America today is the contempt of the younger people for their elders; they are restless, uneasy, disaffected." From this clash, the young would "attempt to create a way of life free from the bondage of an authority that has lost all meaning, even to those who wield it."[66]

Investing such hope in the children echoed a prewar dream, one that had been particularly important to Randolph Bourne, a skeptical essayist whose hatred of adult hypocrisy turned him toward youth as humanity's only meager chance. The twenties, however, gave a new intensity to the paean to immature innocence, and not only because modern advertising was now singing the same song. The children of postwar sophistication felt that because standards were changing they could newly chart the future, not the world's future, but, more importantly, their own. Yet, some realized, those guideposts had once kept even the young from getting hopelessly lost. Restraints could

bestow a certain security. They once had signified that part of
the world was known. The elimination of conventional interdictions was liberating, of course. It could also be frightening.

Disbelief was a complex freedom. In the twenties, masses of
people found authoritative belief untenable. Irreligion's struggle against the older interdictions was often successful. Yet, to
avoid self-recrimination, the delicious taste of new freedoms
had to be approached with care. Inevitably, there would be a
morning after. Did this mean that individual conscience had
replaced social conventionality as the monitor of behavior? As
a matter of course, the answer was yes and no, for some and
not for others, some of the time but not always. The most
effective rebels could no more wipe the slate clean than the
cultural custodians could prevent any new markings on it.
Walter Lippmann portrayed these ambiguities in the specific
context of the decade:

> The evidences of these greater difficulties lie all about us:
> in the brave and brilliant atheists who have defied the
> Methodist God, and have become very nervous; in the
> women who have emancipated themselves from the tyr-
> anny of fathers, husbands, and homes, and with the in-
> termittent but expensive help of a psychoanalyst, are now
> enduring liberty as interior decorators; in the young men
> and women who are world-weary at twenty-two; in the
> multitudes who drug themselves with pleasure . . . who
> have made moving pictures and the popular newspapers
> what they are.[67]

The distinguishing characteristic of the modernizing youth
of the middle class was not the fact of rebellion but their disillusionment with their own rebellion. The middle-class young,
free and alone at last, did not have a job to do or a place to go
or a dream to reach. Lippmann's contemporary description
cannot be improved:

They have seen through the religion of beauty because, for one thing, they are too much oppressed by the ugliness of Main Street. . . . They cannot . . . make a religion of patriotism, because they have just been demobilized . . . and the religion of humanity is utterly unacceptable to those who have to ride the subways during the rush hours.[68]

Many middle-class young people retreated inward to explore the increasingly fascinating universe of the ego. Having just learned of Freud, memorizing a few catch phrases good for parlor games, they learned that there were things about themselves they had not suspected. Freud showed why the rejection of the parental code was essential to health. The parent embodied the past, the child the future. Such personifications revealed that the individual replaced the world. His own moods and motives, preferences and aversions, were far more interesting than the antics of villagers, and more important than maintaining constant vigilance against an older generation that was too preoccupied with making money and winning approval to fight back. Personal rather than social history became central and psychoanalysis was one way to make the past usable, the past of the individual. Memory replaced history. Sherwood Anderson caught the mood: "If there is anything you do not understand in human life consult the works of Dr. Freud."[69] Or, more accurately, consult the Freudian slogans you heard at the new and fashionable preening ritual: the cocktail party.

Even while experiencing personal success, some of the children of the middle class joined the intellectuals in thinking that the idea of social progress was among the fatalities of the war, the peace, and Freudianism. Émile Coué recited his supposedly energizing incantation: "Day by day in every way I am getting better and better," while Edison and Ford led the world to a celebration of technological progress, but the war showed that humanity was not necessarily well served as a result. Who finally would win in the struggle for survival between Darwin and Bryan? Social theories might grow increasingly clever, but the political and economic masters of the earth seemed also to have something to say about how the world would be ruled, who would rule, and the staying power of the past. The American economy, part of it at least, could boom along, but even the usually sanguine John Dewey concluded that "we have harnessed this power to the dollar rather than to liberation and enrichment of human life."[70] The immigrants' complaint that America was a market, not a culture, now echoed in more respectable quarters.

With the crash of the stock market, the decade's literary finale came appropriately in 1929, in a humane, gentle, and anguished lament by Columbia professor Joseph Wood Krutch. *The Modern Temper* summarized the difficulties of being alive and aware during the twenties. It was a lamentation over a suppurating spiritual crisis created because the material conditions of life for the middle class were improving, enabling its satisfied beneficiaries to define the good life as their very own, fiercely but implicitly challenging other lives of spirit and mind, not of the past alone, but of the calamitous present and therefore the unwelcome future.

Krutch feared that the scientists and industrialists who were satisfied with what they had wrought necessarily suffered a coarsening of the spirit. He assumed they would prove to be the fittest in the struggle for survival, and that they would survive to rule. Others, more sensitively tuned, had seized on a superannuated humanism, trying desperately to ignore their own growing disbelief. The proposed retreat into self, into imagination perhaps, depended on irony, an attitude Krutch realized was appropriate to proponents of lost causes. Power ignored humanity, and humanism was out of touch with everything, even with itself: "Both our practical morality and our emotional lives are adjusted to a world which no longer exists. In so far as we adhere to a code of conduct,'' Krutch explained,

> we do so largely because certain habits still persist, not because we can give any logical reason for preferring them, and in so far as we indulge ourselves in the primitive emotional satisfactions—romantic love, patriotism, zeal for justice, and so forth—our satisfaction is the result merely of the temporary suspension of our disbelief in the mythology upon which they are founded.[71]

Deracination was the major characteristic of modernity, not for the allegedly uprooted immigrants, but for the educated and privileged intellectuals who were wrestling with what it all meant, with what living in the twenties in America required.

The urban middle class, however, was neither anguished nor sinking into irony. It exulted in its success, perceived the republic as sound, and assumed it was nicely adjusted to the realities of modernity, which after all had made its progress possible. Elegies were misplaced, not for America. But as Krutch saw it, the self-satisfaction of the middle class was central to the decade's anguish. He believed that the people of his time had to work harder than earlier Americans to adjust to living. He recognized that learning to live with ambiguity, with unprecedented uncertainty, was now more important than ever. Science, far from providing answers, was also part of the problem. With growing and spreading freedom, the reasons why freedom once seemed important were no longer clear.[72]

The modern mood as it came through the filter of Krutch's critical intelligence was rootless and aimless, disillusioned with everything including disillusion, and secure in the knowledge that knowledge would not help. In command of language, Krutch told of its meaninglessness. He described the need somehow to act for goals no longer believed worthy, to which, however, the booming middle class subscribed without question. Above all, Krutch's modern man was exhausted, not from a particular exertion, but chronically so, while middle-class

Americans were energetic and eager to continue striving toward the good life, as they defined it. For Krutch, the burden of asking not why, but how, to endure was too much. That was not a vital question for the men and women who had come to believe that their futures were guaranteed by the rewards of living in a country that permitted them to enjoy the fruits of their labor, it was hoped, forever.

look back after 2016
· define middle class
· Socialism in sout? : FDR, Hoover
· Unions AFC & CFO
· stock market
· jobs, strikes, riots, unemployment
· immigrants + 1nd generation kids
· prejudices - kkk

3

THE TRIUMPH
OF THE MIDDLE CLASS

Late in the depression Americans were asked in a Gallup poll
what "social class" they belonged to. Almost all respondents
(88 percent) said the middle class. When asked what their "income class" was, 31 percent said lower, 68 percent chose the
middle, and 1 percent identified themselves as upper class.[1] That
20 percent of the people demoted themselves when the question
turned from social to income class illustrated how they thought.
Where one belonged on the American pyramid depended on
money, of course, a reasonably objective marker. But it also
reflected attitudes and values. If poverty was perceived to be
temporary, if one's dreams reflected expectations of economic
mobility, and if the values of the middle class, however vaguely
understood, were embraced, Americans thought of themselves
as poor but middle-class.

Middle-class Americans were often afraid but rarely angry.
Having invested their dreams in the promises of the economy
as it was, in American institutions as they found them, they
could not rebel against the system without abandoning their
hopes, which were inextricable from the fate of the nation.
Hypnotized by property, they feared the marketplace, which

created their wealth, and the competition of others. They feared government, international conflict, and organized labor as uncontrollable forces that might retard accumulation. They feared the poor as a reminder of where they had come from and as a potential threat to order. Although they were envious, they did not fear the greater wealth of others. They knew anecdotes about people just like themselves who had become millionaires overnight. Henry Ford and Samuel Goldwyn—a farm boy and a semiliterate immigrant glove salesman—had good ideas and good luck and had come from backgrounds every bit as dull as anyone's. What was to prevent others from doing the same? Even though they had not reached the level of the giants, an extraordinary number of Americans had enjoyed an improvement in their standard of living.

The articles of middle-class faith were wonderfully imprecise. The root assumption was that personal progress was an inspired and irrevocable law. Progress toward wealth might be slowed but could never be stopped. Yet it was necessary to cooperate with the inevitable, to prepare for wealth. Education was a necessary path on the way to the bank, but this education required learning middle-class manners, speech, and the catechism of its economic faith, all more important than formal study. Finally, optimism made it possible for the heart to beat in rhythm with like-minded people, so that everyone who was respectable could assume that life not only could but would be beautiful, soon.

The goal at the end of the rainbow was ownership of property on an ascending scale of expense: first, clothing and cosmetics required by the community for the mate hunt, then a car, a house, its appropriate furnishing and accouterments, then college for the kids, and finally surplus cash. At each step, ownership of property revealed a successful personality to oneself and others. The consequence of success was perceived independence: stand on your own feet in your own house and you will live the American dream. Because you believe you made it on your own you have a right to your rewards. Your knowledge, gained the hard way, and your personality, formed by what you assume is clever observation of the way the world really works, a belief validated by success, are responsible for what you are worth in money and as a person.

The peculiar American vulnerability to public opinion had been observed since before the American Revolution and throughout the nineteenth century. But the twentieth century's susceptibility to opinion resulted from economic success, as fact or hope. This was also present much earlier, but it now supplanted other causes for the drive to conform. Worrying that their imperfect English and unfashionable clothing would prevent them from finding work, immigrants necessarily developed very sensitive antennae to detect the moods of the natives. Moreover, they were living in someone else's country, as they first conceived of themselves, and it was essential to behave properly in their host's house—his opinion, after all, could affect their lives beyond their power to resist.

In the twenties, as immigrants and native-born Americans adapted to the mass market, improved their standard of living, and expanded their expectations, it was natural that they should become increasingly responsive to the manners and opinions of already established middle-class Americans. Because success required people to fit in, to alter behavior to match that of others, those others became appropriate judges of success or failure. Their opinions became pivotal to self-esteem. Downward mobility did not require adaptation, because in such a case it was essential to retain the middle-class code to prove to yourself as much as to others that you were superior to your fate, which was, as all could see, inappropriate and temporary.

Some critics on the political left now argued that because increasing numbers of middle-class Americans were unemployed or becoming poorer, their "objective condition" had thrown them into the proletariat. They owned little or nothing, were exploited not exploiters, and were no longer members of their former class. A Marxist political theorist admitted that "there is still an ideological barrier, but the economic barrier

exists no longer."[2] For him, Americans' stubborn and irrational commitment to middle-class values prevented them from
recognizing their need to support radical change. Yet he was
certain that the "reality" of the depression would finally impose upon the slipping middle class the realization that its "liberation" depended on meshing its psychology with its thinning
or empty wallet.

But Americans were unwilling to align self-perception with
their deteriorating economic reality. To do so would have been
a surrender, an abandonment of self-esteem and hope, of faith
in America. Of those whose income placed them in the middle
class, close to 90 percent said that was where they belonged.
Yet 70 percent of poor Americans, and 75 percent of the rich,
also identified themselves as middle-class. The exception was
in the old South, where lived the greatest proportion of people
(17 percent) who thought they were upper-class. Blacks seemed
to characterize themselves by their own standards, not by those
of whites. Consequently 16 percent of blacks designated themselves upper-class; 36 percent, middle-; and 26, lower- (22 percent did not know).[3]

As economically mobile workers moved into the middle class
during the 1920s, they adapted to more polite culture, became
more reasonable than they had been, less resentful, better educated, richer, and more secular. Of course, they were conscious of the relatively sudden improvement of their status and
were absolutely determined to make more progress.[4] Continuing a long-term trend, a fluid social hierarchy based on personal wealth was expanding to include many more people than
ever before. This was the meaning of American freedom and
opportunity.

Defining progress as the accumulation of wealth, middle-
class Americans wanted orderly progress, not stability. To
them, economic growth seemed a phenomenon of nature. Their
solution to inadequate domestic budgets was to increase incomes, not to cut expenditures or reduce desires. In the middle

of the depression a sociologist observed that for the middle class to think otherwise "feels too much like a denial of one's heritage as an American and the admission of personal defeat."[5] The middle class therefore assumed that economic collapse was artificial, a consequence of unnatural greed, including its own. The depression threatened not only the livelihoods of millions of people, it assaulted the purpose of life. The conclusion was inescapable: if personal worth is measured in dollars, so is personal worthlessness. Such an attitude was devastating, especially for individualistic, middle-class Americans with inadequate psychological buffers against a cruel world.

Obviously, immigrants and their children were equally vulnerable. Through Americanization, especially among members of the second generation, who had departed from parental values, the emotional security of the family was abandoned for the financial opportunities of the broader world. These ambitious people understood that there was not much to break their fall, but they never expected to fall. For them, nature's own law proclaimed that the economic street was one way—upward.

From the Great Depression's low ground, the 1920s seemed frivolous and self-indulgent. The experience of massive unemployment and almost universal anxiety made many Americans wince at the memory of the Jazz Age. To drink deeply from the American cup, one and a half million of them had invested their futures in the stock market. They were now embarrassed by their former pursuit of folly, their naïve dreams about the wealth they had planned to win.

Most Americans, however, had not invested their money or their sweet dreams in the market. Some were gratified that the high rollers with their short skirts and disdain for the traditional conventions of American life had finally got what was coming to them. Many believed, perhaps a little too eagerly, that those destroyed by the crash were proof of the wages of sin. From this perspective the crash would purge the republic of Wall Street's power and bloat, its pernicious manipulation of Main Street and of the lives of little guys trying only to feed their families. The trouble was that punishment now was inflicted on everyone, the decent as well as the guilty.

This was not the Red Decade. Revolution was not in the air. A writer who traveled across the nation to learn what people were thinking concluded, "Only lawyers and bankers talk revolution." Those who would lose from radical social change, of course, feared that it was coming; those who might gain wanted to become like those who had something to lose. Moreover, the reforming impulses of the New Deal helped to suffocate whatever revolutionary zeal might otherwise have surfaced. Earl Browder, then the head of the American Communist party, reminisced about the depression: "No mass discontent with the economic system existed except such as provides the basis for *reform* movements." Neither capitalism nor the rights of property owners were seriously attacked; instead, from every corner of the nation came a grimly serious defense.[6] Personal aspirations continued to override economic circumstances. The fundamental perception of these hard times was that everything comes to him who waits. This was the triumph of the middle class. A small number of Americans held radical ideas, some compelling, some bizarre, but they could not claim the decade as their own. If the decade of the 1930s is to have a color it must be gray, befitting the fear, acquiescence, and impotence of the mass of the American people, middle-class in every way but income.

Although the political attention span of citizens in the republic of hope almost never extended beyond an occasional half hour, the majority of those Americans who bothered to vote in 1932 declared themselves opposed to President Hoover. His opponent seemed like a pleasant man who had campaigned by making only the usual vague promises. Rumors circulated that he was crippled and some sort of an aristocrat, but anyone would be better than the pinched president whose cheerful assurances had become a joke.

Yet Americans were happily surprised when they listened on their radios to Franklin Roosevelt's inaugural speech. He seemed different not only from Mr. Hoover but from all conventional politicians. His voice was strong, his language direct and clear, and he seemed to know what he was talking about. He declared that the basic values and institutions of the nation were intact, that America was still as vibrant as ever. The only problem that could defeat his effort to end the depression was psychological: "The only thing we have to fear is fear itself."[7] He was not afraid, rather just the opposite, almost cocky. FDR had introduced the nation to his radio magic. From photographs and newsreels people began to notice the set of his jaw, the tilt of the cigarette holder, his engaging smile. Was it possible that the four-year game of electoral blindman's bluff had actually stumbled onto a leader?

The new President asserted that money was not life's most important value (who among the frustrated middle-class consumers really believed this?), that political democracy required economic democracy, that government had to act forcefully because depression was an emergency like war, and that he would immediately close all the banks for a forced holiday, and not reopen questionable banks before they were audited. With great skill he used the radio to communicate with the nation, not as an abstract mass audience, but, it seemed, with each person individually. The microphone was his friend. He seemed exciting, sympathetic, and commanding. Perhaps, Americans hoped, he would actually do some good.

What could be expected of him? In the first hundred days of his administration he extracted unprecedented executive power from Congress. It was acknowledged that he could have nationalized the collapsed banking system. But that would have fallen beyond FDR's purview. In what has since become a

famous dialogue, the President answered a young reporter's
silly questions with typically superficial responses:

> Mr. Roosevelt, are you a Communist?
> No.
> Are you a capitalist?
> No.
> Are you a Socialist?
> No.
> Well, what is your philosophy then?
> Philosophy? I am a Christian and a Democrat—
> that's all.[8]

This President, absolutely committed to freedom, including
free enterprise, was no closet ideologue dreaming of radical
alternatives to the traditional American way. His "ideology"
consisted of his own imprecise and conventional values, which
he held out as a model for the nation to follow. But he was
sufficiently flexible—unprincipled, his enemies charged—to try
novel programs. Determined to use government to help the
needy and keep the nation steady, he stole the thunder from
true believers on both the left and the right, who demanded
more fundamental change than he could stomach. He protected his country for the middle class and for those who aspired to become middle-class.

Frances Perkins, the Secretary of Labor and an old friend
of the President, summed it up: "Roosevelt took the status quo
in our economic system as much for granted as his family."[9]
His plan was to save capitalism from the stupidity and greed
of its star players. He would accomplish this through his appeal
to the new urban masses, a political coalition of the "forgotten
men" comprised of the jobless, ethnic groups, labor, blacks,
and especially the insecure but voting members of the middle
class, most but not all of whom supported him. His sympathy
for the plight of the depression's victims helped to persuade
them that he was not only their President, but also their friend

and protector, a living father of his country. Soon enough the spokesmen for business learned to hate his guts.

The important (and elusive) facts about the depression concern the ways Americans survived. It marked people in ways more significant than saving bits of string and a broken comb in a kitchen drawer. How people lived through hard times shaped their politics and sense of the future. It determined their attitudes toward family, neighbors, and nation. This story must be deduced from what they did at work, at home, and at leisure.

This depression was different because its misery was unusually tenacious. For a while, before it was entirely clear that the market crash would lead to general deflation, some people assumed that the economy would soon improve: on a sunny day not far off, a corner would be turned, the President would do something. But hope could not be sustained forever. A year became two became a decade and more. The corner seemed to recede as you approached, and the reward for endurance was the need for more endurance.

The Roaring Twenties' illusion of easy money had intoxicated the nation, and its binge had driven stock prices through the roof. Soon even the inexperienced and naïve had been captivated by the clicking of the great American wheel of fortune. The upward pressures had continued to build until late October 1929, when the bubble burst on Black Thursday. One share of Montgomery Ward in early September of 1929 cost $138; three years later it was worth $4. The *New York Times* industrial average collapsed from 452 to 58. Within three years the skid destroyed 75 percent, or $90 billion, of the value of the nation's securities.[10]

The contagion spread throughout the economy. Steel production, for example, fell to 12 percent of capacity,[11] banks failed across the nation, new orders for goods were canceled, wages

were savaged, prices collapsed, millions of American workers
were fired. The mass society had failed. Mass production depended on mass marketing and a mass culture to create mass
consumption. When any one of these activities faltered or failed
the rest would follow straight into the bog.

Although the depression was worldwide, it was worse in the
United States than in most other nations. Hunger was less
threatening even on marginal farmland in Italy or Poland. For
every new immigrant who entered the golden land in 1932,
more than three left for the greater security of the old country.
Edmund Wilson reported: "Mrs. Dimiceli says that the Italians who come to America and go in for racketeering have
wonderful opportunities, but that there is no place for a skilled
machinist." In 1931, 100,000 Americans from almost every part
of the country applied for 6,000 jobs in the Soviet Union.[12]

While many Americans thought it only fair that the market
gamblers had been humbled, many intellectuals were delighted
that the depression had revealed the incompetence of America's business leadership. They had groaned when President
Coolidge announced that America's business was business, and
when industrialists piously commended harder work to workers
who were already working hard. In his own way, Henry Ford
had explained that "the very poor are recruited almost solely
from the people who refuse to think and therefore refuse to
work diligently." And when the spokesmen for consumption
had described a shining new era waiting for those who understood the uses of debt, many intellectuals had recognized that
the republic of consumption was not their country. They had
argued eloquently and perceptively against a culture dominated by the values of the balance sheet, although they realized
that precious few out there were listening. But the depression
raised their spirits—finally they could point to the terrible reality of hunger and unemployment as evidence of the stupidity
or crookedness of the nation's business leaders.[13]

• • •

The number of people without work was stunning. About 8 million Americans were jobless in 1931; 13 million in December of the following year; and when FDR took his oath of office in March 1933, 15 million Americans—almost one out of three workers—were unemployed. That was the low point. Then the number of jobs began to rise slowly until another drop in 1938, after which it climbed again. The hardest-hit industries were construction and manufacturing of durable goods. Unskilled workers were fired faster than skilled, often because skilled workers were demoted to take their jobs. Unemployment for black skilled workers was approximately double the rate for whites.[14]

Women, frequently forced into the labor market by the unemployment of their fathers or husbands, often had better chances for employment than men, and were jobless for shorter periods. But female employment collided with the attitude that the male who was not a breadwinner was less than a man. Opinion polls revealed that three-quarters of the women and 80 percent of the men did not approve of employment for a married woman whose husband was capable of supporting her, for fear that she would displace a man and because, of course, her place was in the home. When married men were asked whether they would approve of their wives working at salaries of up to $25 a week, almost three-quarters said no; but if a wife were offered $50, fewer men would let their pride stand in the way.[15]

Because the cost of living in the early depression dropped by almost 16 percent, wage cuts of 20 percent in manufacturing industries were gouging. A non-unionized coal miner's wage cut of 23 percent was extreme, especially because his pay was already low before the collapse. The rates of deprivation varied from industry to industry: railway workers' wages, for example, were cut by a rate lower than the decline in the cost of living, as were those of utility and retail-trade workers. Industry paid its workers an average annual wage of $1,543 in

1929, a sum that dropped a third by 1933, similar to the fate of miners and domestic help; wages of construction workers were cut almost in half; but salaries of federal government employees declined by only 13 percent.[16]

How much was needed to live? In the middle of the depression the poorest families spent $250 a year on food, while those making more than $3,000 a year spent four times as much. An item of food that cost $1.32 at the end of a 1929 fell to 82 cents in 1932, and rose to $1.03 at the end of 1937. Food consumption did not significantly drop on a per capita basis during the depression (though people ate more citrus fruit and shelled peanuts but less ice cream), but these average figures fail to show that for certain groups hunger was a daily reality. A government study found that more than 25 percent of American families were not getting adequate nutrition.[17]

Never before had so many Americans been in such trouble. With the possible exception of certain areas of the South in the Civil War, the Americans, even in their wars, had never faced a cataclysm that shook every household, whose tenacity made it impossible to predict when or even if it would finally end. No amount of official optimism could reassure the nation. President Hoover's famous and fatuous lullabies contributed to his defeat. The people understood that the depression was a time for reality, not manipulating images. At least they knew where they stood with Governor Talmadge of Georgia, whose solution for the millions of jobless was to "let 'em starve."[18] The people realized—how could they not?—that the issue now was survival.

To view the depression from a variety of perspectives—middle-class, midwestern farmers, hungry city people, industrial workers, Kentucky coal miners, southern blacks, and the businessmen and workers of a small city in Indiana—leads to the conclusion that even this devastating emergency could not destroy hope. For almost everyone, shrinking resources seemed irrelevant to class affiliation. New flexibility and adaptability were necessary, but most people clung tightly to conventionality as a way to survive in dangerous times. Voices of radical dissent were heard but not heeded. Patriotism and a sense of national community deepened. People knew that the way out of the depression would have to be national, that government was the key—a recognizable American government, perhaps more intelligent and vigorous than its predecessors, but not revolutionary. Americans wanted change that would not threaten individual opportunity, their definition of the good life as Americans, the only way to ensure success.

The middle class demanded that the world work in orderly, not mysterious ways. Allergic to excess and intensity in the personalities and politics of others, it felt an abiding respect for the authority of opinion and institutions, if not of leaders and officials. It revered the rules of the game. It carried its politics in its hope and preferred not to become politically exercised. As usual, it continued to wish to be left alone to conduct business, raise the children, tend the lawn, socialize with nice neighbors, and worship or not as the spirit and community inclined. It wished on its own terms to live and let live, but, first of all, it wished to be allowed to live.

In 1932, Gerald Johnson, a newspaperman with the Baltimore *Sun*, described the impact of hard times on the "average Americans" who lived on his street. His neighbors were "ordinary people," including a junior officer in a bank, a carpenter, an insurance salesman, clerks, and others. Mr. Johnson believed that his street was "a representative cross-section of the American middle class." The depression did not find this street until 1931:

Frankly, we are scared. However, we had seen it coming and had had time to brace ourselves, so that we are not exactly stampeded. We are somewhat resentful because we think the depression has been made worse than it need have been by the stupidity of our rulers; but we know very

well that Mr. Hoover did not create the panic. We are to
a certain extent gloomy, but we are by no means in despair. . . . We are persuaded that we are going to have to
sweat for the next six months, but we do not believe for
a moment that the hard times are going to continue for
the next six years. And perhaps the most remarkable effect
of all is that we are very tired of humbug.[19]

Johnson was impressed by the "relative tranquillity" with
which his neighbors accepted the depression while the rest of
the world was engulfed in revolutions. They were not obsessed
by a Communist threat, because American "Reds" had nothing to offer. He wrote approvingly that "to date the capitalistic
system seems to be as firmly entrenched in America as the
Republic itself." These middle-class Americans and, he added,
millions of others like them, in the $2,500 to $25,000 income
brackets, were disillusioned with capitalists, not capitalism.
They were afraid but did not express social resentments or
political anger. Instead, they were willing to be patient, to remain passive, but they would not endure more political and
economic lies by the masters of money who had dictated to the
1920s. The dream of the twenties was "all illusion." Now that
these ordinary Americans had lived through the great American treasure hunt, they would abide no more national con
games or promises of magic. They were discovering reality and
it frightened them. But, claimed Johnson, they were not
beaten.[20] They were still Americans, living on hope, believing
that this too would pass—otherwise America would not be
America—and for them to fail the nation must fail. They were
as secure as the nation, even as they were sinking.

Some midwestern farmers were not passive. When falling farm
prices eroded or obliterated their incomes, they were in debt
for everything: taxes and mortgages on land and buildings,
seed, fertilizer, equipment, and even groceries. Committees

spontaneously arose to fight foreclosure sales. Across the agricultural heartland the agents of banks and insurance companies
were threatened with violence if they executed a sale. In Kansas the body of a murdered agent was found shortly after he
had foreclosed a farm. In Ohio a farmer swung a noose from
his barn to help a sales agent more fully appreciate the drama
of the moment. Talk of the "revolution of the farmers" was
everywhere, except among farmers.

Furious over the prospect of losing their land and their way
of life, these farmers, squeezed throughout the twenties, became enforcers of their own law. They threatened or committed violence to protect their homes and defend their property
rights as Americans. Like Gerald Johnson's neighbors, they
condemned individual capitalists who, in their view, were un-
dermining capitalism and the nation that they and their pioneer forefathers had built and always honored. They thought
of themselves as patriots, not revolutionaries. The traitors were
the bankers and the sheriffs, agents for a heartless, distant city
power, probably dominated by foreigners, who seemed resolved to profit from the destruction of the truest Americans.
Thus a foreclosure riot in Iowa ended only when a deputy
sheriff acceded to the demand of the infuriated farmers, got on
his knees, and kissed the flag.[21]

The individualism and independence of farmers, traditionally opposed to the wicked ways of the city, occasionally degenerated into moral callousness. When asked what to do about
the hundreds of thousands of able-bodied people who would
never again find work, more than 25 percent of rural Americans, as compared to only 9 percent of urban respondents,
answered that they should shift for themselves. Rural areas still
dominated state legislatures, especially in the Midwest. In Ohio
and Illinois, for example, rural legislators voted against tax
increases to feed people starving in the cities at a time when
one out of six families in Pittsburgh was on relief or employed
by the WPA, one out of five in Chicago, one out of four in
Akron and Detroit, one out of three in Cleveland, and half the

families in Flint. Governor Henry Horner of Illinois carefully analyzed the emergency: "We can't keep feeding these bums forever."[22]

Violence sparked by evictions also occurred in cities, but without the farmers' weapons or angry patriotism. The great black and white migrations from the farms to the cities made masses of people vulnerable to real danger. During the 1930s, 136,000 blacks moved to New York State, and 50,000 each to the District of Columbia and Illinois. Altogether, black and white, native and foreign-born, almost 400,000 people migrated to New York during the depression, and almost 1 million to California, mainly Okies, refugees from the Midwest's dust storms.[23] The Okies did not head for the cities, but many depression migrants did. And, as always, the cities bred an alien sense of dependency. People had to rely on others to do what they had done for themselves before. Where does the garbage go? Where does the water come from? Having left your family, where do you go for help? In a community of strangers, who mourns the dead?

A 1931 census of New York's Lower East side found about 15,000 homeless men and women attempting to survive through the facilities of various religious missions, flophouses, the Salvation Army, municipal lodging houses, speakeasies, and the nickel subway. One mission, a former Chinese theater, where, it was said, whites and Chinese had once gone to smoke opium, still attracted busloads of well-dressed tourists, who gawked at the homeless people sleeping there. New York, said a social worker, had become a "school for bums."

Further uptown a group of wealthy women opened a free lunch counter, serving three cheese and mustard sandwiches and coffee to each diner. Crowds stared through the window at the people eating. Outside one day two men argued: "That's to keep 'em from riotin'; it's to keep 'em quiet that they're feedin' 'em." His companion disagreed: "Har! Ye talk like a radical. . . . That's fir hadvertising that they're feedin' 'em, them's society girls in there." The first speaker was more worried. If the homeless were not fed, they would go on a rampage. "An' what's to prevent 'em from takin' what they want? They's a million of 'em in the city; if they was to march they'd make a procession!"[24]

There was a "procession" of 10,000 blacks in Harlem in 1935. About half of Harlem's families barely survived on inadequate relief, and others were often supported by the women of the household because no one would hire the men. As customary, unions refused to enroll black workers. A riot began when a Puerto Rican boy stole a pocket knife from a dime store and assaulted the store's workers, who then beat him. The news that a black boy was being beaten to death spread everywhere and the black shoppers in the store attacked the white employees. Crowds massed, the police charged, Communists distributed leaflets, and people pulsed through the streets, smashed windows in over 200 stores, threw bricks at the mounted police, and looted. Three blacks were killed, hundreds were wounded, and about 100 were arrested. But this was merely an explosion, not a sustained protest. It was the most that these impoverished, densely packed (233 persons per acre in Harlem), diseased, and hungry people of the metropolis could manage.[25] And they paid for it not only in broken heads but in the diminution of retail services. As a matter of course, much of the city press blamed it on Communists.

Urban poverty led to disillusionment, to dispiritedness, to panhandling, and standing in interminable lines for food that never tasted right and that never seemed to last. It led to defeat and futility. It did not lead to organized protest or political action. If the city was a "school for bums," the main lesson seemed to be to look out for oneself, to get in line early, to drift through days and perhaps years of hopelessness, and death. Political romantics who expected the urban poor to seize the moment, to lead the nation in political reconstruction, did not understand the psychology of city poverty. It finally destroyed the human will.

This could not be said of the industrial workers who fought the bosses' efforts to protect their firms by demanding more work for less pay. When politicians, press, and police cooperated, there were ways to deal with radicals. If they were aliens, the Immigration Service would do its duty. The Boston *Herald* ran an editorial quoting with approval the anti-union sentiments of American presidents, Catholic bishops, a Protestant clergyman, and war hero General Pershing. President Hoover insisted that rugged individualism "requires" an open shop. Unlike the farmers, labor organizers would always be made to fight against the flag, which, in this case, was owned by the owners.

In October 1931, just as the weather was turning colder, the textile companies in Lawrence, Massachusetts, announced a pay cut of 10 percent. Some 23,000 workers went on strike. The AFL signed up 7,000 members, but its general ineffectiveness drove 5,000 other workers to create their own, unaffiliated unions. Communists enrolled 1,000 workers in their union, only to be bitterly criticized by their own members when party stalwarts attacked the government; the always patriotic workers wanted a living wage, not a revolution. Dissociating themselves from the Communists, they also formed their own union and cooperated with the police to deny the Communists the right to speak in public.[26]

Nineteen thirty-one was also the year that coal-mining operators warred against the miners in Harlan County, Kentucky. John Dos Passos, who covered the story, realized there was something different about the miners.

The fact that the exploited class in Harlan County is of old American pre-Revolutionary stock, that the miners still speak the language of Patrick Henry and Daniel Boone and Andrew Jackson and conserve the pioneer traditions of the Revolutionary War and of the conquest of the West, will perhaps win them more sympathy from the average American than he would waste on the wops and bohunks he is accustomed to see get the dirty end of the stick in labor troubles.

These miners fused the patriotic traditions of the Iowa farmers with the politics of the Lawrence workers, and the result was explosive: when they went on strike they were armed. These mountaineers turned miners had always considered a rifle a necessary feature of American liberty and an essential piece of domestic furniture. They fought and died to protect their families and to win industrial reforms that would improve their lives. They were defending the American way as they understood it.

The workers revived the old locals of the then-defunct United Mine Workers. Those who took the first steps were fired, blacklisted, and evicted from their company houses. Three unions, one of which was Communist, competed for the miners' allegiance. Dos Passos noted that the miners were so desperate they would join any organization that promised even a hint of help. He knew miners who joined all three unions.

Management's response was fierce. The owners' Coal Operators' Association blew up soup kitchens, kidnapped activists, and murdered organizers or ran them out of town. The publisher of a country newspaper sympathetic to the miners was shot from ambush, and a Federated Press reporter was taken for a ride and killed.

Union men were often arrested on the charge of criminal syndicalism. One miner so charged was asked what it meant. "The best I can give[,] it is going against your country, but that is something I never did do. I never thought about such a thing. . . . My family always fought for the country and I've always been for it." Another miner concluded that they were called Reds because they were so skinny that the sun shone right through them.[27]

Yet there was no revolution during the Great Depression because even suffering workers took pride in the fact that they were good and patriotic Americans who would not support an alternative political future; instead, they perceived Franklin Roosevelt as a friend and the federal government as a potential ally. They demanded relief from industrial oppression within the framework of the political system as it was, or as FDR might decide to change it. With time, the industrial workers of the depression and their children, some of whom were to ascend into the middle class, became the nation's most enthusiastic advocates of free enterprise.

Southern blacks had always endured hard times on their own. For them depression was not novel. Engulfed by systemic hatred, they were abused as tenant farmers, subjected to the paranoia and greed of the white man, and were the poorest, least-educated, and probably the most-deprived group in the nation. They survived as gardeners and small farmers, manufacturers of moonshine, and menial laborers. But even the economic threat paled in the face of the Ku Klux Klan's lynching orgies of the thirties. Two southern blacks were lynched each month of FDR's first term, and black railroad workers were routinely murdered so that whites could take their jobs.[28]

Like the city poor, these blacks were socially unorganized. Many of them realized that they had to fend for themselves. One woman remembered that when she was a young bride in Mississippi she "thought that the Depression would have pulled people together, but that sure didn't happen. Everybody went their separate ways. Nobody tried to help anybody else. I guess everybody was too busy trying to take care of themselves."

Walter Bennett survived by doing odd jobs, such as picking blackberries. His family lived on about $20 a month, and his wife found sporadic work as a maid for $2 a week. He remembered that "most folks was too proud to ask they neighbor for a helping hand. All the folks was out to help they self. Wasn't no neighborhood help. People didn't care 'bout nothing but they self. Times was hard."[29] These black Americans were surely too preoccupied with avoiding starvation and murder to worry about adopting middle-class values or overthrowing the government.

The people of Muncie, Indiana, were probably typical of the middle-class response to the depression and the New Deal. Because the town's basic industry was the manufacture of durable goods, mostly car parts, the depression hit hard. In 1929, Muncie had 106 factories; by 1933, there were only 81.

Muncie's citizens revealed some of their intimate values in the ways they adapted their consuming habits to their unexpected distress. The sharpest drop (85 percent) in retail sales was in jewelry, then building supplies, new cars, candy, furniture, and eating in restaurants. Grocery volume dropped by half, while sales from the local dime stores were more steady, declining by a mere third. Retail sales of men's clothing fell off by two-thirds, while women's clothing sales only decreased by half. Apparently women would not tolerate as much shabbiness as men; nor did men challenge this peculiar arrangement, perhaps because a wife's attire represented the husband's status.

No one voluntarily stopped driving his car. The purchase of gasoline was scarcely affected, dropping by only 4 percent, while the number of filling stations in Muncie actually doubled between 1929 and 1935.[30] More than any other product, perhaps even more than adequate food, the automobile was indispensable to Americans. It was used to go to work, shop, drive to the countryside on Sundays, have a date in privacy, and proclaim that its owner could afford to be an owner with his foot simultaneously on the gas pedal and *somewhere* on the road to success. The alternative to somewhere was nowhere, and the surest way to get there was on foot.

Like the initial response to a death in the family, Muncie's first response to the depression was denial. For decades, the optimistic psychology of small businessmen had dominated the town's press and infused its citizenry's deepest sentiments. Even in the depths of depression these Hoosiers were enormously proud of themselves and their town. Optimism was the key to the future: "The year 1936 will be a banner year because people believe it will be." They were certain that they could control events. Cheerfully religious and socially conformist, they disliked change and what they perceived to be eccentricity, backslapped each other, and held themselves aloof from strangers. They rejected "Non-Protestants, Jews, and Negroes—as 'not quite our sort.' "[31] Muncie celebrated the school of not-so-hard knocks, denied class divisions, asserted that small businessmen were the soul of the nation, and prided themselves as being a model of right living for others to emulate.

The sum of these attitudes produced the diagnosis that the depression was "largely mental" and "merely psychological," as FDR maintained. Thus, when General Motors closed a plant, the town fathers went to Detroit and persuaded the firm not to board up the windows for fear of rattling popular confidence, which itself would prolong the misery. To the small businessman, it was axiomatic that hard work, good judgment, and optimism would enable him to support his family and grow to be less small. It was all up to him: "You win if you're any good and your winnings are caused by you and belong to you. . . . If a man doesn't make good it's his own fault."[32]

Following the lead of the town's wealthy factory owners, Muncie's small businessmen detested the social engineering and centralized planning of the New Deal, which they felt infringed upon their freedom. For small merchants, even those who had no employees, there was local prestige to be won by adopting the anti-union, anti–New Deal attitudes of big businessmen. "We small businessmen resent the way we've been soaked in the New Deal."[33] They felt soaked because some legislation required that they occasionally, though not often, think beyond their immediate self-interest. They accepted aspects of the New Deal that were helpful to them, but for the most part they denounced FDR as an enemy, proving to themselves that they had the right attitudes for future social and economic progress, and that they formed a voluntary fraternity with the rich. The truly rich—civic exemplars—would thus approve of them.

Although the workers of Muncie, a majority in the town, lived across the tracks from the middle class, they, too, embraced middle-class values. In the first years of the depression the majority of workers were unmoved by the prospects of union organization. Many of them had recently come from the farm and, according to Muncie's chroniclers, they

> share the prevailing philosophy of individual competence. Working in an open-shop city with its public opinion set by the business class, and fascinated by a rising standard of living offered them on every hand on the installment plan, they do not readily segregate themselves from the rest of the city. They want what Middletown [Muncie] wants, so long as it gives them their great symbol of advancement—an automobile. Car ownership stands to them for a large share of the "American dream."

Life magazine came to the same conclusion: "These earnest midland folk still steer their customary middle course, still cling to their old American dream."[34]

Of some 13,000 industrial workers in Muncie before the crash, 900 were union members. With the encouragement of the New Deal, union membership reached a high of 2,800 in 1934, but by the end of the next year it had slipped back to 1,000.[35] After a strike at a General Motors plant in Toledo, an industrial city where labor conflict was intense, the company moved its operation to Muncie, thus confirming the belief among Muncie's owners and workers that their anti-union, open-shop traditions benefited the people and the town. The move reinforced the values of even defeated workers who had memorized their parents' hymns to the ethic of work, to the importance of standing on your own two feet, and to the good fortune of being Americans, citizens of a nation where in time God helps those who help themselves.

In 1934, an Ohio newspaper conducted a field survey on what "the forgotten man" most wanted out of life. The responses of the twenty subjects added up to a small profile of frightened middle-class Americans. When asked what they needed for future happiness, nineteen answered "money," and one, a bank teller, said "security." When asked if they believed the government owed them a living, eighteen said no, a fifty-four-year-old mother in one of the New Deal's work programs said yes, and a twenty-seven-year-old hotel clerk also said yes but only on condition that he failed to find a job on his own. Whom or what did they blame for the depression? Bankers, "capitalism's greed," irreligion, World War I, and, most important, themselves: "we are all responsible" because they "all spent too much," or "high living by everyone" from the "wild spending" in the 1920s was at fault. Their hardship was caused either by some distant malevolent power or by their own earlier lack of discipline. They trusted in leadership and change imposed from outside their lives. Meanwhile, they would wait, find ways to economize (such as spending less on life insurance and health care), and look back in sorrow at their own mistakes.[36]

Americans could be beaten by the impersonal arithmetic of their mortgage debt. Because of their growing inability to make the required payments, millions faced the possibility of losing their homes, having their share of the American dream foreclosed. In 1926, mortgages on 68,000 homes were foreclosed; in 1930, 150,000; in 1932, 250,000; and in 1933 half of all mortgages were technically in default, with foreclosures proceeding at the rate of a thousand a day. Many of the victims were middle-class, experiencing a striking reversal of fortune for the first time in their lives.[37]

By refinancing mortgages at low interest, New Deal legislation solved the mortgage problem for many farmers and city people who applied. Nationally, 40 percent of eligible debtors were assisted. By 1935, over one million new mortgages were supplied by the Home Owners Loan Corporation and the Emergency Farm Mortgage Act. The government also changed the conventions of mortgages, extending the repayment period to a maximum of twenty years, when the debt would be fully paid. Nonetheless, because payments were, of course, still required, 40 percent of the homes saved by the government were eventually foreclosed on in various parts of the country.[38] After the years of struggle to buy a house, after the investment of hope and pride as well as money, the great danger that all would be lost naturally produced fear and perhaps despair, but only passivity not action. The New Deal's responsiveness to the mortgage crisis deflected widespread middle-class anger. In any case, relief from the mortgage crunch endeared the President and his programs to home owners across the nation, as insuring bank deposits did to people with money on deposit, as the support of collective bargaining did to workers, and as Social Security did to almost everyone.

The largest group in depression America that rejected middle-class resignation were those industrial workers who chose union organization, their only available vehicle for self-defense. Early in the New Deal the right to organize had been encouraged and was made the law of the land in the Wagner Act of 1935. Opposition to such efforts arose partly from the owners, as expected, and also from middle-class orthodoxy within the American labor movement itself. The canonical purity of the mainstream American Federation of Labor had decreed that for unionism to be consistent with American life unions must be limited to skilled workers organized by what they did—their crafts—and not by where they worked. The Federation's core membership had been unwilling to digest either the economic or the human implications of mass production, especially the reality that millions of other workers, including immigrants, were essential to the gigantic effort to satisfy the demands of a mass market. As a result, the AFL's membership was overwhelmingly "Nordic" and Protestant—British, Irish, Scandinavian, and German—with a remarkable absence of Poles, Hungarians, Czechs, Italians, Greeks, and others. Blacks and poor whites recently off the farm were also systematically excluded. In short, as Dan Tobin, head of the Teamsters Union, put it, the "rubbish." William Collins of the New York Federation of Labor, occasionally obliged to meet with the wrong people, was somewhat more explicit: "My wife can always tell from the smell of my clothes what breed of foreigners I've been hanging out with."[39] Like most American institutions, the AFL was deeply Aryan in its dogmas.

John L. Lewis led a movement out of the AFL to organize workers according to their industries. In a radio speech he declared that "craft unions have failed in the crucial task of organizing the great mass-production industries and the only way workers in these industries can achieve industrial freedom is through organization by industries."[40] Thus was born the Congress of Industrial Organizations. The energy and anger of the CIO matched and released the energy and anger of about two million American workers who, with evangelical fervor, set about to rescue themselves and their brethren from the punishment of the depression, the myopia of the AFL, and the passivity of the American middle class. The CIO enabled powerless Americans to cooperate with and gain strength from each other, and then act.

The experience of a single Detroit local of the United Auto Workers reveals the composition and values of the CIO's following. Young, married, American-born children of Slavic immigrants spearheaded the drive to organize this factory. They had broken away from the traditions and extended families of their parents, and the heavy drinking and religiosity required by the solidarity of the Slavic community of Hamtramck, and realized that, more than their parents, they were on their own, a decisive symptom of Americanization.[41] Close to but not of the immigrant experience, they were neither inspired by the canons of the self-reliant American pioneer nor caught in the tentativeness of first-generation immigrants. These Slavs were new Americans, free of the past, but not yet digested by the middle class.

Most of the native-born Americans working in this factory came from Protestant German or Scandinavian backgrounds, were highly skilled, better off than the Slavs, and more conservative. They did not live in Hamtramck and in the plant stayed aloof from the Slavs. The American-born Appalachian migrants, "the most lonely and isolated people in the plant," were especially resistant to unionizing: they "had no sense of society as such but couched all their thinkings about social and political issues in individualistic and specific nonpolitical terms." The Scotsmen in the inspection department also refused to cooperate. Both groups had to be persuaded or pressured into participation.[42] Thus, in this local the most antiunion workers were all individualistic, non-Slavic Protestants, seeking to be self-reliant, whose assumptions were middle-class.

A comparison with the English working class clarifies the American experience. The values of English workers rested on the conviction that their labor differed from other modes of work and led to a different kind of life. They assumed this difference would be permanent, and it translated into a moral code emphasizing group solidarity, cooperation, and the necessity to fight unendingly for economic justice. Because capitalists would always try to thwart progress, the struggle against the deprivations of the present would never cease. Therefore, the culture of English workers, more than that of their American counterparts, rested on a sharp sense of class consciousness, an expectation that they would not rise into the middle class, so that, if their interests were to be represented, they required their own distinct political organization, the Labour party.[43]

In contrast, worker solidarity was far less common in America, and even when present it was usually temporary, a stage in life or in the progress of generations. Most American workers assumed they would ultimately achieve economic security and integrate into American society. The acquisition of a house, schooling of children, acceptance of the principles of free enterprise, and the near veneration of FDR further weakened both class consciousness and, for many, commitment to union militancy. The American worker, like his middle-class boss, was an optimist, believing less in the likelihood of personal gain than in familial security, if not today then tomorrow. Harold Laski, a British political economist writing during the thirties, exaggerated the mobility of the American worker, but was essentially correct when he said, "The average American was too certain that he would climb out of his class to be willing to build organic expression of its purposes."[44] If necessary, the American worker could just wait for better times, which he always assumed were coming. This worker, a patriot, was deeply opposed to labor radicals, who seemed more determined to overthrow the government than to secure jobs and improve working conditions.

The American union movement flourished for the first two decades of the century but faltered under the affluence of the twenties and the widespread fear in the early depression. In 1920, 5 million workers were organized; by 1929 this number fell to 3.5 million and declined again to 2.7 million in 1933. Four years later, after widespread organizing activities, much of which elicited violent resistance by owners, the CIO enlisted almost 2 million members while the AFL's membership dropped. Organized labor comprised about 5 percent of the total work force in 1933, 7.4 percent in 1936, and, because of the successful organizing effort of the new CIO, rose to 13 percent in 1937.[45]

The speed with which the CIO organized the heaviest mass-production industries was striking. A new era of industrial democracy seemed to be dawning in which ordinary people would have a stronger voice and better security. But the CIO was not able to build beyond its first successes, and the AFL began to grow faster. By 1940 the AFL was twice the size of the CIO, which had barely advanced beyond its 1937 successes.[46] CIO members who did not think of themselves as a separate American class, and could therefore draw on no tradition of solidarity, began to withhold their union dues while others actually went on strike against the dues required by their own unions.

More than anything else, the tactic of the sit-down strike lost middle-class support for the union movement. In 1936, for the first time, large numbers of workers attempted to prevail by sitting down (instead of organizing successfully) in the Goodyear rubber factory in Akron, a one-industry city of predominantly native-stock Americans, where the CIO had achieved its first major success.

Akron, a city polarized between wealthy owners and struggling workers, was an ideal location for sharpening the class struggle, but three-fourths of the population, in the face of the sit-down strikes, expressed attitudes characteristic of the American middle class across the nation. Preferring not to think of themselves as different from the American public at large, even militant strikers did not regard themselves as separate. Most of the Akron rubber workers "do not want to feel that they have isolated themselves from the general run of 'middle class opinion' "[47]—like the majority of Americans everywhere.

In 1937 almost half a million workers sat down. The tactic spread to the auto industry and later to shipbuilding, baking, mining, and steel, among others. The sit-down was an unexpected tactic that confounded owners and prevented them from controlling their plants and machines, their property. Unsure

about how to regain control, they resorted to tear gas and con-
doned police brutality. Violence spread throughout Detroit, especially at Henry Ford's River Rouge plant.

Most of Akron's small shopkeepers, whose attitudes consistently represented those of most of its residents, did not con-
done the thuggery of the owners and police. One observed that
"tear-gas is not good. Police action does not help, but makes
more trouble." The middle class always disapproves of "trouble." A few shopkeepers blamed the workers: "They [the strik-
ers] should have left when told to, and this wouldn't happen.
I don't like to see trouble but they had to be gotten out."[48]

In the year of the sit-down strikes a great majority of Americans (76 percent), including Republicans (65 percent), approved of labor unions, while 59 percent favored the AFL over
the CIO. But this broad support did not extend to sit-down
strikes. Asked to choose between General Motors and the strikers, 56 percent supported the company; 66 percent agreed that
GM was right in refusing to negotiate with the strikers; and 62
percent believed that John L. Lewis did not represent the majority of workers. By early 1937 over two-thirds of the people
(80 percent of the Republicans) thought their state should prohibit sit-down strikes. By the summer, 57 percent believed "the
militia [should] be called out whenever strike troubles
threaten." By the turn of the year two-thirds (73 percent of car
owners) supported Ford against the workers. By 1939 three-
fourths of the nation believed that sit-down strikes should be
outlawed, and over 70 percent of Americans opposed a union
shop. Almost everyone in the general population preferred the
AFL to the CIO.[49] Instead of forming a new society, the CIO
had isolated itself from those who embodied the nation's values, the salesmen and shopkeepers, and middle-class Americans everywhere.

Many of the immigrants' children came of age during the depression. By 1930, the second generation had grown to approx-

imately twenty-six million; with their parents, they totaled forty million, or one-third of the nation's white population. Although the parents had by now accommodated in some fashion to American life, for them family and neighborhood remained central facts of life, the psychological realities which were, especially during hard times, alone dependable. In his autobiography, Irving Howe recalled the East Bronx, where he grew up. "Our parents," he wrote of himself and his friends, "clung to family life as if that was their one certainty: everything else seemed frightening, alien, incomprehensible." Consumed by the demands of everyday life, the inhabitants of these communities rarely expressed their politics through action. The things that mattered most to the first generation, aside from the welfare of the children, were interconnected: steady jobs, their houses and families, and neighborhood services. In this decade of European fascism and militarism, the fate of the homeland, or of group members left behind, also shaped the thinking of many parents and those of their children who were maturing politically.[50]

As many of the parents hoped, some of the children began to enter a different world. Lacking the intensity of old-world cultural and religious ties, the second generation was composed of new Americans who were more familiar with the wider society, more adept at dealing with strangers, better educated, fluent in English, much more dedicated to individual progress, which usually meant abandoning the family and neighborhood nests, and sometimes ashamed of the incomplete Americanization of their parents.[51]

The children's embarrassment at their parents' accents and food preferences could lead immigrant-watchers astray. Officials, teachers, and commentators continued to analyze the immigrants' alleged sense of inferiority, even though this assumption was based on no more than the children's uneasiness, not contact with the parents, who, often enough, were proud of their own and their children's accomplishments in the new world. An arrogant if well-meaning principal of a New York high school enrolling mostly Italian youngsters concluded from what the students told him that it was essential "to eliminate the feeling of inferiority due to foreign origin." Like many others, he relied on what he heard from the children to form opinions about the parents.[52]

The children had been encouraged to stay in school, learn the language and ways of the new land, and make the attempt, however difficult during the depression, to find work different from and better than their fathers'. As the younger generation began to find its way in the wider world, the parents could take pride in their children's ingenuity and prospects. But now the children painfully realized that their parents were foreigners, who did not measure up to "real" Americans, those who held the keys to the children's success.

Generational quarrels usually began with children complaining that their parents continued to speak their mother tongue not only to each other and the children, but worse, in public, where strangers could overhear and identify the family as greenhorns. In 1933, five brothers wrote a letter to the *Jewish Daily Forward:*

> Imagine, even when we go with our father to buy something in a store on Fifth Avenue, New York, he insists on speaking Yiddish. We are not ashamed of our parents, God forbid, but they ought to know where it's proper and where it's not. If they talk Yiddish among themselves at home, or to us, it's bad enough, but among strangers and Christians? Is that nice?[53]

The home's security depended upon shutting out strangers, the people an ambitious youngster yearned to meet. For the children to have a new life of their own it was necessary to leave home. Perhaps they would not repudiate their parents' world in their hearts, but the decision to leave frightened and possibly insulted parents who knew that their children had to go. For the older generation the flight of their young implied that what was good enough for them was not good enough for the young, a conclusion with which perhaps most parents agreed. Much as the grandparents had felt about their children leaving for the new world, these parents felt wrenched to watch this latest generation become emigrants from home. More than emancipation was at issue, as Irving Howe acknowledged: "The thought of bringing my friends home was inconceivable, for I would have been as ashamed to show them to my parents as to show my parents to them."[54]

Alfred Kazin, however, growing up in Brownsville, a different New York neighborhood, testified that his parents actually were ashamed of themselves. They expected him to excel, he wrote, for them as well as for himself. His achievement would "redeem the constant anxiety of their existence." Of course, his parents were not the first to live vicariously through the achievements of their children. But he was special, their first child born in America, "their offering to a strange new God; I was to be the monument of their liberation from the shame of being—what they were." "Everyone" in Brownsville was ashamed, he asserted, because none of them spoke English as easily, precisely, and as "refined" as was required in school.[55] Perhaps.

In any case, the second generation's fascination with English drew some of its brightest members into careers as professional literary critics, such as Howe, Kazin, Lionel Trilling, Leslie Fiedler, and the editors of the influential *Partisan Review,* or as poets, such as Delmore Schwartz. Other native-born Jews, riveted by American society, became sociologists, such as Daniel Bell and Seymour Martin Lipset, or were drawn to art criticism and moral philosophy. But regardless of their specific careers, they all looked at the dominant language and culture from a somewhat greater distance and sometimes with greater skepticism and less sentimentality than most of their colleagues.

This second generation of Jews embellished the wider society's attitudes toward the middle class. Emancipated from what many considered the parochial world of their parents, passionately committed to the life of the mind, they were freer, more cosmopolitan than most others. As the parents' authority waned, some of these young men raised themselves. Saul Bellow, for example, "recognized at an early age that I was called upon to decide for myself to what extent my Jewish origins, my surroundings (the accidental circumstances of Chicago), my schooling, were to be allowed to determine the course of my life. I did not intend to be wholly dependent on history and culture."[56] Nonetheless, for many the repudiation of the father's faith was painful, what some later in life called treason. They were ashamed of being ashamed of their parents. But the lives they wished to lead—and the individualistic instinct nourishing the wish—beckoned, and so they chose personal progress over strict adherence to the family's expectations and fears.

While losing their religion, however, members of the younger generation retained their sense of Jewishness. During the depression many became socialist defenders of the rights of workers and blacks as part of their commitment to social justice. Their empathy for the oppressed came partly from memories of their own poverty, resentments over anti-Semitism, the humanism of dinner-table conversations at home, identification with victims of Nazism, and educations that increasingly focused on critical social theory and the play of the imagination. Their devotion to education was virtually religious. Obviously, some of these attributes were inhaled from the parents' culture, as they would all acknowledge sooner or later, but the fact that they had not yet achieved the security and eminence that each was to attain, that they still had their noses pressed to the glass, indicated that they had not yet entered America. They were suspended between worlds, leaving one before the other was willing to accept them, aspiring to the middle-class work of intellectuals, and they found a temporary footing in the coherent explanations of socialism.

Even their specific politics were carried over from the ambience of their parents' neighborhoods. Of course, the Jewish tradition of political opposition did not begin in America. Se-

curely packed in the bundles carried by many immigrants, socialism was one way for Jews to comprehend poverty and
political oppression. The children grew up in homogeneous
enclaves in which, as many reported, it was difficult to find
anyone who was not a socialist. When Daniel Bell declared
himself a socialist at thirteen, his family's concern was not the
young man's radicalism, but whether he was leaning toward
the correct sect. Alfred Kazin reported that he "was a 'Socialist,' like everyone else I knew." Irving Howe, a socialist at
fourteen, had the same recollection; his parents were more upset by his returning home late from political meetings than by
the meetings themselves.[57]

Of course, the young intellectuals' experiences and aspirations scarcely reflected those of other second-generation Jews.
When Victor Gotbaum, later to become a distinguished labor
leader, was asked by a Jewish intellectual why he never joined
any of the radical political movements, he responded: "Maybe
I was the only worker you ever knew."[58] He had to work too
hard and too long for that sort of politics.

Because everyone was now in the same leaky boat, the realities of depression life brought many immigrant families closer
to the national experience, even as their religion and ethnic
culture continued to keep them separate. Like almost everyone
else, they dreamt of the day when they would be more secure,
although they realized they would never make much money.
That was for the children. If the children did not get lost in
America, did not become too busy for parental love, they would
justify the parents' struggle. For these ethnic parents, that was
the American dream, their version of middle-class aspirations,
which they experienced vicariously, through the children.

Not surprisingly, as available cash declined and anxiety rose,
personal decisions changed. During the first years of hard times
Americans married, bore children, and divorced each other at
steadily slower rates until 1932, when the marriage rate dropped

precipitously. For every thousand unmarried women in 1920, ninety-two married, but only seventy-five did so in 1929. Divorce and birth rates followed the same pattern. In some cases, a wife who found a job discovered that the strains of working and managing the home were too much. A scholar understood the quandary: "To the educated middle classes this [the wife working] proved to be the most effective contraceptive yet discovered."[59]

Statistics scarcely convey the hurt and desperation of people in trouble. The clawing struggle to survive was not lubricated with the milk of human kindness. Some families were destroyed by the emotional pressures resulting from the loss of status, security, and self-esteem. Domestic violence soared, men and boys and occasionally girls ran away and became tramps, and children were hungry, cold, and abused.[60]

Prostitution, facilitated by the universal attachment to automobiles, became a way out for increasing numbers of women. Even in respectable middle-class Muncie, prostitution, always a thriving local industry, increased, sometimes by wives trying to supplement their husbands' inadequate wages. A local judge called the car "a house of prostitution on wheels."[61] The testimony of a Chicago whore, not an aspirant to the middle class, illuminates her bitterness, class awareness, and helplessness:

. . . the dame who went to work for eight or twelve bucks a week, all she's getting now is fifteen, if she's still got a job at all, and I'll bet she looks like a wreck besides, worried all the time and more than likely got a couple of kids and a drunken bum in a room somewhere to take care of. . . . When a girl got nobody who cares and she got to quit school like I done, it don't matter much what line she goes into, she ends up pretty much the same way every time. Whether she hires out to cook some college-dame's meals and scrub her toilet . . . or tap tacks in a shoe factory, she's bound to take a beating in the end. The smartest just take it lying down. You last longer that way.[62]

Most young women could not become streetwalkers, mostly out of scruples but also because the profession was overcrowded. As a result, the professional had cut her rates so deeply that she could not pay for life's necessities. It was difficult and humiliating to locate a renter, "and the girls say you're lucky if you get fifty cents."[63]

The greater availability and use of contraceptives made prostitution safer and sometimes challenged conventional sexual standards. Two-thirds of the general population supported birth control, and contraceptives were available from the Sears catalogue and in gas-station restrooms. The contraceptive business boomed throughout the thirties. Seventy percent of a group of Muncie's young middle class acknowledged that they had had sex before marriage. Bickering between parents and children about the nature of morality in the modern world inevitably resulted from somewhat looser sexual practices among the young, and the stability of the American family seemed threatened from every conceivable direction.[64]

But ironically, the depression also strengthened the family. To the outrage of an audience of social workers, a Secretary of the Interior announced that hard times would bring families back together: "With adversity the home takes its normal place." A Muncie newspaper agreed: "More families are now acquainted with their constituent members than at any time since the log-cabin days of America." Families whose emotional relations were strong and resilient not only withstood economic crisis but drew closer together, circled the wagons. Connected to this was the peculiarly American elevation of motherhood to a mawkish divinity. An Indiana senator, obviously in a terminal swoon, relieved himself in print: "Were I to assign all the world of accomplishments in peace and war, the preservation of all that is clean and dependable and worth while in human affairs, the integrity of nations and the supremacy of wholesome manhood and womanhood, I would lay it all at the shrine of mother love."[65]

Cheap sentimentality aside, some mothers did hold their

families together, economically and psychologically. Their heroic struggles redefined ideal womanhood as a particular kind of moral strength. Throughout the culture of the depression, this rediscovered symbol of strong woman, also a feature of earlier pioneers as well as immigrants, helped people to think about the depression, find an emotional anchor and grounds for hope. Her radiance would warm the cold, protect the weak, and guard the only sphere that now truly mattered—the home.

The story of an Illinois farm woman speaks for thousands of others. Her husband was an incurably ill veteran and her seventeen-year-old son was a conscientious high school student who dutifully helped out at home. The family rented a nearby farm to work as sharecroppers, but the husband's recurrent hospitalization forced them to hire help, which drained their resources. The specter of relief tormented them: the woman explained that she had been raised to pay her debts and to take pride in independence. To avoid what she considered to be charity she found a job as a waitress in a tavern for $6 or $8 a week, depending on tips. "And some old fool who should have been home rocking his grandchildren was always patting me on the back or trying to hold my hand, and saying, 'Let me buy you a drink, little girl.'" She did not tell her husband about this because, had he known, he would have been heartbroken. She wondered if she had been a fool to try so hard to stay off relief, but thought she would do the same again. When her son eventually left home for good, she wanted to be able to say: "Pay as you go; never take something for nothing. It's the only way to keep your self-respect." She did not want him to respond by thinking, "Oh, yeah."[66] The outcome of her struggle is not known.

Most women, however, did not face such severe crises and coped with the depression by "making do," becoming heroines of small victories—buying stale bread and cheaper meats, going to fewer movies—and worrying about accidents or illness that would destroy their average household budgets of $20 to $25 a week. The middle-class woman's life was rooted in her home and she was required to make it function by doing the work herself, sewing more and better than she had, and shopping with a sharper pencil.

Inevitably, magazine ads played on every anxiety that flowed from these family pressures. In many of the ads, the wife controlled her husband's emotional state simply by using the correct product or creating a marital crisis if she did not. In one ad an angry husband barks at his frightened wife: "Last night's roast for dinner—so I came home to *this!*" The beleaguered wife, trying to stretch the family budget, must somehow placate her handsome, well-dressed monster of a husband. Not to worry. He gets a whiff of the delicious mustard she plans to serve, and decides he might be able to choke down the old roast after all. In another ad, a young, anxiety-ridden husband leans over his somber wife to scold: "The boss's party and you *would* spring a *run.*" His outstretched hand is open either to emphasize his point or to slap her.[67] Had she washed her stockings in the correct soap, they would not have run and she would have maintained her neat, womanly appearance, and avoided destroying her husband's reputation in the eyes of his boss, of all people. Her ignorance and thoughtlessness could cause the boss to select Hubby's competitor, who probably displayed better judgment in his selection of a wife. Soap was no laughing matter.

The home was not the center of life for poorer women whose husbands' wages could not feed the family. In the late thirties, 38 percent of black women worked outside their homes, a familiar pattern for Americans hardest hit by the depression. Obviously this was not characteristic of poor city women who could not find work. Often invisible, they stayed away from breadlines and flophouses, and would not apply for relief, though it was commonly known that thousands of such women, "unattached," were drifting somewhere. To be poor and unattached—unattractive and unwanted in the mirror or in others' eyes—was to be in cultural limbo, to lack personhood and to fail as a woman and become an outcast. Although previous

generations of "unattached" American women had often
yielded to such destructive self-perceptions, the depression
raised the stakes even higher, to the question of whether life
itself was worth it. For middle-class aspirants, the need to mask
such humiliation could not be suppressed. Social workers described four former salesgirls sharing a kitchenette and twice a
day eating

> meals easily prepared, for they consisted almost invariably
> of coffee, bread and bananas, these latter measured out
> by the inch and divided scrupulously. They used candle
> instead of electric light. When at last they were forced to
> apply for relief . . . they held a council to decide which of
> them should go, settling at last on the girl who had the
> best clothes and could still make a good showing.

One hungry girl had lost a job because she was so well
dressed that she did not appear to need work.[68]

Relief workers would sometimes humiliate desperate city
women in ways unknown to men. If the women was "unattached," her morality and thus eligibility were questioned "by
the virgin women who dispense charity." Others were deeply
ashamed of their clothing and would not risk public scorn or
pity. When their lives were at stake, one woman reported,
women might turn to a man, even a stranger, for help, but
rarely to another woman. Most likely, however, was a retreat
into isolated anguish: "A woman will shut herself up in a room
until it is taken away from her, and eat a cracker a day and
be as quiet as a mouse so there are no social statistics concern-
ing her." The defeated women of the city learned to be wary,
and, although a man might finally be the last resort, to distrust
men: "I ain't going to have nothing to do with guys. I'll have
a time. I want what I want. I'll drink when I like it and have
a time but no guys for me." Her attitude probably would not
change even if her circumstances improved.[69]

While working women ran afoul of conventional sex roles,
increased domesticity among middle-class women reinforced

cultural stereotypes. Women who found work became active partners in the struggle, while middle-class women, even more than usual, hunkered down in the home and spent what their husbands earned by managing the household with greater caution. For these women, the majority, the depression was less threatening or disorienting than for any other sizable group.[70] They were now compelled to do more of what was expected, to satisfy their families' and their own emotional needs by wiping the noses and eyes of others, as servants, nurses, and waitresses had always done. This behavior supported the depression's flourishing mythology of the strong woman in whose competent hands the future of men, children, and the nation rested safely. She was to provide a center and structure to lives in chaos.

Another result of the emphasis on the woman as domestic manager of things and emotions, moral gyroscope, and defender of civilization was the housewife's increasing isolation. Separated from the world by the centripetal forces of the home under siege, by her endless housework and selfless tending of others, it was not unusual for this middle-class woman eventually to lose contact with reality beyond her domain. One unemployed man in Philadelphia pleaded with a social worker: "Have you anybody you can send around to tell my wife you have no job to give me? She thinks I don't want to work."[71] A life composed entirely of domestic emotions obscured the fact that jobs were not to be had, the reality of the outside world.

The major obligation of the domesticated male was to earn money to support his dependent loved ones, who would respond with respect and, if he had secondary virtues, love. The unemployed male could become purposeless. He could see this in his mirror and in others' eyes. Victims of class opinion, many tried to fool their neighbors and friends and sometimes themselves. One unemployed newspaperman sat in his bedroom and typed, "Now is the time for all good men to come to the aid of their party,'' day after day to make his neighbors think he still wrote for a living. He carried a few silver dollars in his pocket so that the jingle would lift his spirits and those of the people he met, who would not have to worry that he was going to ask for a loan. He hoped to discover ''at what stage of your poverty other people realize or sense it, and pass you by as one no longer interesting or useful to them.''[72]

If the jobless male helped his wife around the house, he ran the risk of losing the respect of his children, especially his teen-age sons. If he ran the house while his wife brought home a salary, he had to face the demons of his soul for his incompetent womanliness. If he stayed at home while his sons worked, the universe became inverted: he could no longer discipline his children because, having lost his manhood, he had lost the right to do so. Prolonged unemployment often meant that the man of the house lost authority as a husband, a father, and a man. He was rejected not only by the marketplace but by his loved ones, and not only by them but by himself.

Sexual impotence was one ''common'' result of the American male's inability to make money, or enough money. ''Physicians, whom I met in Home Relief work,'' wrote a contemporary observer, ''informed me that Depression-induced impotence was common in men under forty. This was true not only of jobless workers, but of business men whose fortunes had been affected by the slump.'' One woman complained that ''they're not men anymore, if you know what I mean.'' Sometimes it was the woman who first perceived the diminished sexuality of her jobless husband. One such woman lost interest in having sex with her husband, but of course he insisted that the reduced activity was his idea.[73]

Male dominance, however, was not so easily undermined, not even in a culture that defined men by their work. One study discovered that prolonged unemployment drastically altered men's personalities in 25 percent of the sample.[74] This huge number, even if only approximate, illustrated the crunch between cultural demands and economic realities. But it simultaneously revealed that in most cases men retained their familial status in the face of their economic failure. Most wives and families accepted Papa's continued authority even in the absence of his weekly paycheck. Unlike the middle-class woman, the male had his soul threatened by the depression, and some of them were destroyed, but most held on, held out, and lived to stand erect another day.

The most destructive male attitude was also a cultural axiom: he was personally responsible for his economic failure (or success). Thus, with all of his other problems, the unemployed or demoted American often blamed himself for his fall. Guilt was the final bitter pill. "I would like . . . to put it down in black and white that I am to blame for my present state. It isn't the system. It's me. . . . It was drink that ruined me." Others blamed their failure on their lack of education, their physical frailty, or their careless spending.[75] Whatever their reasons, as Americans they were culturally required to blame themselves for what they thought was their failure as men. Otherwise they would have relinquished the right to take credit for their past and future successes. In a perverse way they were defending the legitimacy of their status by this self-flagellation. They were proving that, no matter what, they continued to subscribe to middle-class values. And this apparently eased the psychological load.

Early in the depression a woman told of her husband's futile search for a job. She worried over newspaper stories about male suicides, especially when her husband came home late after looking for work all day. From their terrifying struggle she concluded that it was "middle-class haughtiness" to blame the unemployed for not finding work. One night he did not come home and she looked all over the neighborhood for him, finally finding him on a park bench at 10 P.M. He was "sobbing like a child. 'I'm just no good,' he said, as I pulled his head down into my lap. 'Why, here I am, almost forty, and a failure. I can't even pay the rent and buy the groceries for my wife and child next week. I can't sell myself.'"[76] Although his

wife could repudiate the middle-class contempt for the unemployed, he could not. As an individual he, not she, was at the
sinking center of the whirlpool. But as husband and wife they
dropped together.

When mass culture succeeds in finding its audience—the average of the greatest number of people—it is an obviously useful clue about what is on the people's mind. The production
of mass culture in the depression inevitably focused on middle-
class anxieties. Comic strips, fashions, advertising, radio programs, and movies were used not only to persuade hard-pressed
consumers to spend but also to convince the middle class neither to despair nor swallow dangerous ideas.

In the early depression, *Little Orphan Annie* was the most popular comic strip; aside from appearing in newspapers across
the nation, it was dramatized on radio and in two movies. A
blizzard of letters steadily descended on Harold Gray, Annie's
creator. He once had Annie lose Sandy, her dog. Among the
anguished letters was a telegram: "PLEASE DO ALL YOU
CAN TO HELP ANNIE FIND SANDY. STOP. WE ARE
ALL INTERESTED. HENRY FORD."[77]

In 1932 Annie was offended because Lug, the newspaper
boy, delivered her paper late. Lug, the paper's only employee,
went on strike to get his salary raised from $1 to $1.50 a week.
He threatened to beat up any scab kid who tried to take his
job. Annie spoke for the entire middle class when she mused:
"If he doesn't want to work for decent wages, o.k.—but he's
got no right to keep anyone else from takin' th' job." She
flattened Lug with a right to the jaw. The paper's owner told
her that she was "a most resourceful young lady," and hired
her at the higher salary Lug had wanted. Annie was thrilled:
"''Magine a guy like that strikin' for more money, with jobs
as scarce as they are now—he should have been glad he had a
good job." The last panel of this strip was a soliloquy: "I'll
bet a lot o' birds, who never get ahead, would have lots better

luck if they'd quit squawkin' 'bout their tight boss and really get to work and *do* something to *earn* more dough.'' Reflecting Annie's wisdom, the president of General Foods, sponsor of *The Kate Smith Hour,* announced on the air: ''Real Americans want to work.''[78] The implication was inescapable and obvious: the unemployed did not want to work and so were not good Americans.

Early in the 1930s, following the lead of President Hoover, the *Ladies' Home Journal* described spending as a patriotic duty, a way to create jobs and end the depression. More than a year before FDR impressed the nation with his declaration, this magazine had instructed its female readers: ''There is nothing to fear—except fear.'' It tried to explain that in the depression ''spending money is the surest way of saving it, and . . . saving money is the surest way of losing it.''[79] Still faithful to the gospel of the 1920s—thrift prevents the good life—the commercial sponsors were slow to align their pitch with the reality that people would no longer deliberately puncture their life raft by frivolous spending. The producers of mass culture then changed the ways by which they hoped to persuade the public. Where the commercial message of the twenties supported cultural change, the mass voice of the thirties extolled tradition, and clothing fashions during the depression revealed that a cultural retreat was now sponsored by America's advertisers.

The plumage worn by a people reflects how they wish to be perceived, what they think of themselves, and their perceptions of their place in the social order. The male's choices are severely restricted by his culture, by what the people who matter to him think is appropriate, and by how he wishes to communicate his social standing. The woman is even more restricted because for her the culture assigns greater significance to her feathers and therefore stricter rules. For her, fashion reveals not only her taste and allure but her husband's status, her children's prospects, and her culture's sense of stability.

At first blush, it may seem puzzling that the length of women's skirts rises and falls in relation to the stock market. But when Americans and others perceive their world as dangerous they do not want to make matters worse by challenging social conventions. Recognizing personal risk led everyone, but especially young people just starting out, to embrace cultural conservatism. When they were afraid they retreated to the safest behavior they knew, to the faith of the fathers, to received standards of decorum. When the external world seemed safe, as it did during the twenties (and not again until the prosperity and cultural security of the sixties, despite the Vietnam war), the urban young pushed for greater sexual freedom, independence from the interdictions of parents and society, less discipline as that had been defined, and greater playfulness. Like spring's first robin the appearance of the female knee signified the end of the cold.

In the 1920s, when the young concluded that their environment was safe enough to attack conventionality, their first reflex was to emphasize their youthfulness. Women's fashions became girlish, all legs but no breasts or hips, concealing prospective maternity. During the boom, marriage was not the only way out of the parental nest. Jobs were available and women claimed an increasing share. Young, middle-class, urban Americans were taught that marriage, and especially motherhood, was the irrevocable end of youth, fun, and romance. Consequently, the average age for marrying rose. They would hold off the dread day as long as possible.

In the sour depression, life was threatening enough without the added risks of questing for greater personal freedom. It was awkward to dance the Charleston with one's nose to the grindstone. This was a time for becoming an adult as quickly as possible. Although marriage and babies might be postponed because of the economic risks, the quest for security required that women abandon whatever flappery they had recently enjoyed.[80] The flapper's corselet that flattened breasts was sur-

rendered, as was the tight-fitting cloche hat fabricated to hide
her hair, traditionally woman's crowning glory.

In the thirties, for the first time, breasts were raised and
separated, requiring new engineering of bras because now that
each breast was to lie in solitary confinement it was discovered
that women with the same bra size required different-size cups.
Sales of bras doubled. In 1932 *Vogue* declared: "Spring styles
say CURVES!" The waistline rose from the flapper's hips to an
area approximating the woman's own. What the middle-class
women of the depression wanted was a slim outline, a high
bust, an apparent but not constricted waist, a skirt tight across
the hips and thighs that thereafter fell to a foot or less above
the pavement. Shoulders were widened by ruffles or puffed-up
sleeves, and later in the thirties padding was used, so that by
1940 the shoulders were square, something along the lines of a
football lineman.[81]

The need for an anchor in perilous times resulted in a ma-
tronly look: more feminine-looking, longer hair, emphasized
hips and breasts, a marked waistline—in short, the woman as
mother not eternal girl. Farewell the knee, bony talisman of
the owner's safety. Adults not kids might find work. The goal
was to appear responsible, not chic, not a knowing member of
the subculture of youth but an earnest adult on whom others—
parents, teachers, the boss—could safely rely.

One woman remembered her exciting years as a coed at
Southern Louisiana University. Because she broke the rules,
she was nicknamed "Rebel." Her rebellion, however, was a
trifle obscure:

> By the early thirties we had really rebelled against the
> "flapper" image. We let our hair grow long, parted it in
> the middle, and wore it in a bun. Delores del Rio fashion.
> And we didn't use a lot of makeup like our older sisters.
> We wore none, except for lipstick. . . . And another re-
> bellious thing we did . . . ha . . . and the girls today think

they invented this. We wore no bras. I was considered a devil because of this. You see, we were always trying to be different, but somehow we ended up in the same old thing. The normal fashion for dancing was a kind of Scarlett O'Hara dress—ruffles, crinoline, and all that.

She was invited to be the sweetheart of Sigma Chi at the University of Alabama. Her dress "was white chiffon—Southern virgins wore white." Although she thought her bralessness devilish, she bowed to the demands of the moment for this magical evening: "I was flat-chested or thought I was, and had Kotex stuffed in my brassiere that night."[82]

Given the single purpose of their cultural role, men's fashions underwent no significant variations for over a century. The male function was to provide, to make money, and the established "business suit" was designed to radiate middle-class solidity, sobriety, security, and success. There were moments when no one, however much out of the swim, could avoid the uniform. Huey Long, everyone's favorite fake redneck, was invited to a Mardi Gras ball: "I went down to a pawn shop and bought a silk shirt for six dollars with a collar so high I had to climb up on a stump to spit." During the 1930s some marginal types, brazen artists or intellectuals, actually appeared tieless in public. In a comprehensive survey, however, *Fortune* magazine learned that corporate recruiters on college campuses looked for a "sales personality and pleasant appearance; a good chemist whose necktie is sloppily tied may miss out, for the sloppy tie may look, rightly or wrongly, like a symbol of maladjustment."[83]

The composition of a collar or the style of a tie might change, but substantial variations in male fashion would communicate the wrong signal. The middle-class American male, along with his European counterpart, did not dress to exude flightiness or variability. Changes in men's fashions were subtle: suit jackets, apparently designed to emphasize a male's manliness and physical power at a time when he needed all the help he could get, had broader, padded shoulders and were cut loose across the chest and tight against the hips. Men wore hats (but not the straw boater they had bought in the 1920s), cut their hair short, often combed it straight back without a part, and locked it in place with various forms of heavy-duty grease.[84]

As Franklin Roosevelt (and Hitler) understood, the radio played a critical role in the thirties. Americans spent about 150 million hours a week looking at movies but almost 1 billion hours listening to the radio. Radio ownership grew from 12 million sets at the start of the thirties to 40 million by the end. Eight out of 10 Americans could listen, including 5 million while driving their cars.[85]

After several years of local broadcasting in Chicago, *Amos 'n' Andy* made its network debut, sponsored by Pepsodent toothpaste, in the summer of 1929. A national craze developed as two-thirds of the radio audience tuned in to the fifteen-minute program to hear the latest gags delivered by Amos (Freeman Gosden), the hard-working aspirant to the middle class, and Andy (Charles J. Correll), a lazy hustler and domineering clown. Listeners followed the characters' misadventures as they moved north from Georgia to find their fortune. Amos and Andy purchased a wreck of a car with no top, an office desk and chair, and formed the Fresh Air Taxi Company, "Incorpulated." This program swiftly became the most popular show of the early depression, and its black-faced white stars were radio's highest-paid performers.[86]

Even during its heyday, people tried to discover the reasons for the program's success. The two stars attributed its mass acceptance to its human quality. The audience surely liked it because it was funny. But a Washington newspaperman offered another explanation: "Amos 'n' Andy is built around the theme of money. And money, as almost everyone is ready to admit, is the one thing dearest to the American heart and mind."[87]

Amos 'n' Andy caught the public's fancy because it was a caricature of life in depression America. The exaggerated silliness and ignorance of blacks were apparently more acceptable to the enormous audience than such qualities in whites would have been. Had whites been featured on the program, their actions could have been perceived as criticism, not entertainment, by whites mired in hard times. Amos's avuncular sermons about the essential soundness of the American way took the bite out of the program. And its fixation on money ensured that it would be heard as timely and relevant, even though it was about well-meaning but quite stupid black folks. It was appropriate that white men played the characters, who were designed not to ruffle the white audience, indeed to soothe and assure it that all was well, especially since that other race was having such a good time.

The chronic need to get money and to prevent someone else from taking it away dominated many, if not most, of the broadcasts. While Andy was a semi-genius at developing elaborate and futile schemes to get rich without really trying, Amos was a middle-class moralist, devoutly attached to Poor Richard's maxims:

> Times like dese does a lot o' good 'cause when dis is over, which is bound to be, an' good times come back again, people's like us dat is livin' today is goin' learn a lesson an' dey goin' know whut a rainy day means . . . so maybe after all, dis was a good thing to bring people back to dey're senses an' sort a remind ev'ybody dat de sky AIN'T de limit.[88]

At its peak, the show attracted 40 million listeners, none so avid as Henry Ford. The telephone company lost business during the fifteen-minute programs, movies were interrupted to broadcast the show in the theaters out of fear that people would otherwise stay home to listen, and Pepsodent's sales soared, a juicy fact not overlooked by other mass-production industries. However, the program did not fare as well among some black listeners: almost 750,000 black Americans signed petitions to have the program canceled because of its unfavorable portrayal of blacks.[89]

Radio comedy was popular but the daytime soap opera—"woman's serial drama"—was the characteristic form of American radio in the depression. There were three soaps in 1931, ten in 1934, thirty-one in 1936, and sixty-one in 1939. According to one advertising agency, a successful soap followed four requirements: strong women, of course; simple characters; understandable situations; and "philosophical relevance." It was necessary that the central characters be ordinary, just plain folks, with whom the plain folks in the audience could identify. The character may have had a somewhat exotic background but some misfortune or other would have reduced her to keeping house, worrying over money, caring for the incompetent husband and beautiful children, and muddling through in good spirits.[90]

One such show, *Old Ma Perkins,* was, like virtually all of the soaps, about the depression's strong woman, this time a widow who managed a lumber yard. She was described in the first program in December 1933:

> A woman whose life is the same, whose surroundings are the same, whose problems are the same as those of thousands of other women in the world today. A woman who spent all her life taking care of her home, washing and cooking and cleaning and raising her family. And now, her husband's death pitched her head foremost into being the head of the family as well as the mother.[91]

Ma's "philosophy" was always at the tip of her tongue. One day as she was walking in her little village of Rushville Center, inhaling the scents of autumn, she remembered that when she was a young girl watching some geese flying overhead a feather dropped at her feet. Her father told her to keep the feather because then the goose would return to give her another in the spring. She asked her father:

"Year after year, will that same goose be flying right over our house?" He smiled sadly, and said, "If *you'll* be here to find the feather, the goose will drop it for you." *(A tiny pause)* . . . And ever since I've *liked* the idea of year after year . . . the regularity of the seasons . . . the mysterious way of God, moving those birds across a thousand miles of day and night and empty air, and me standing there, a part of it, because I . . . well, because I'm a part of it. And that's what I'd like my children to know . . . especially Fay [mourning her husband's death] . . . I'd like *her* to see that if we'll only be there to find it, the gray goose feather will always come. Telling us that the world goes on, that all's right with the world.[92]

The depression soaps sought to emphasize life's most traditional verities. It was woman's function as wife and mother to create domestic order out of the chaos of the world and the lethal ineptitude of men, with the exception of wise and presumably sexually safe grandfatherly types. The problems of the principals were emotional and private. If only these could be overcome, life would be wonderful. But of course the emotional turbulence of life in soapland could never be calmed. Conflict, the frustration of males with functioning glands, and the daily turmoil of the interior lives of these heroines were ceaseless. *Our Gal Sunday* featured an orphan raised by miners, perpetually but vainly seeking a moment of peace now that she was married to England's richest nobleman. But every time success seemed within her grasp, a new, private emotional storm swept her away. Peace was an always-receding goal. The external world did not exist. The recoil from the cultural experimentation of the twenties and the subsequent preoccupation with personal caution gained full voice in the soaps' sounds of strife.

As always in American folklore, the small town was the home of traditional morality and therefore superior people. The popularity of Will Rogers rested on this hayseed, as he explained: "Country folks are smarter than city folks. You never have to explain a joke to country folks." Because it was assumed that real people lived in the towns while denatured deal-makers and their victims lived in cities, it was essential that the soap's locale be small-town America. This did not amuse James Thurber: "Almost all the villains in the small-town daytime serials are emigres from the cities—gangsters, white-collar criminals, designing women, unnatural mothers, cold wives, and selfish, ruthless, and just plain cussed rich men." As these crooks and perverts intruded on the town's serenity or, less often, as a virtuous provincial woman mistakenly made her way to the city's bright lights, the soap's heartbeat accelerated dangerously. Although the ensuing conflict between good and evil would be tense, it was not cause for alarm. Thurber understood the predetermined fate of the city slickers. "They always come up against a shrewdness that outwits them or destroys them, or a kindness that wins them over to the good way of life." [93]

The soap's characteristic message was the necessity of a return. Return to the time-tested values of yesteryear, to dear papa's wise advice. Hold on to what you know to be true. The world is evil. Ignore it. Change is bad. Your emotional conflict is the nucleus of the world. Seek happiness within yourself. Men are dangerous and must be housebroken. Sex is a snare. Be strong. Rise above it. Virtue is its own reward. This ideal, strong woman, enshrined in a soap bubble, reigned in her mind and her parlor, where the action was.

The ideal American male played his role far away from the confines of Mrs. Soap's immaculate living room, in a different sort of return, distant from the emasculation of civilization itself. "Return with us now to those thrilling days when the West was young and adventure lay at the end of every trail. The Lone Ranger rides again!" He rode three times a week over 140 stations. The announcement at the start of the broadcast sucked the audience into the adventure: "A fiery horse with the speed of light, a cloud of dust, and a hearty Hi yo Silver, the Lone Ranger." [94]

The one-thousandth program was broadcast in June 1939, and it epitomizes all the others. The people of Smith's Corners, not suspecting impending tragedy, watch a cattle herd approach the town. The sheriff recognizes the brand and knows trouble is afoot because the cattle are stolen. As a cover, bad guys stampede the herd into town while they rob the bank and murder a dozen townspeople. Old Ma Healy tells the sheriff that she could identify the killers, but he says, " 'Tain't no use, Ma!'' The forces of evil have overpowered the law. Ma is outraged: "An' the law cain't do nothin' . . . but sit with its fingers crossed. Why, blast yer hide, Sheriff.''

But along comes the masked Ranger and Tonto, his trusted Indian comrade, to enlist the locals in a posse to capture the criminals. Only Ma and the sheriff volunteer. The Ranger is disgusted with the townsfolk: "Two people! One of them an old lady! Your town isn't fit to be saved! But there are other towns to consider!'' He rides to a prison camp for army deserters and arranges a pardon for them if they will ride with him against the outlaws. One prisoner shouts: "Give us a fightin' chance tuh be free men! That's all we ask!''

When the prisoners approach the outlaws' hide-out, murderous gunfire makes them falter. The Lone Ranger reaches into his shirt for a brilliant-colored piece of cloth. "He unfolded it, and the moonlight showed red . . . white . . . and stars in a field of blue.'' The fleeing prisoners stop dead in their tracks, roused by the flag, and with renewed courage resume their attack. Cowards at heart, the bad guys surrender, and the Lone Ranger heartily praises his comrades: *"You men, you've showed the people of Smith's Corners what men can do!''* He concludes with a message for the nation: "It's up to those of you who are left to make this the sort of country your friends would be willing to give their lives for! That is the foundation of America.'' Hi yo, Silver! Away![95]

When the institutions of American life stopped functioning properly, when law could no longer protect the innocent, when fear turned even American citizens into jellyfish, the anony-

mous masked man, an outlaw himself, and the classic American renegade, the Indian, could with skill and bravery set
matters right. As the middle class always assumed, the individual may overcome anything, even the collapse of institutional
authority. It was uplifting in the depression's gray days.

Yet how long would the Lone Ranger have survived had he
encountered strong Ma Perkins instead of strong Ma Healy?
Could even this classic American male have avoided paper-
training? He was lucky to be responsible only for enforcing
justice in seven western states, where, in his life, women did
not count. In the myth of the sexes propagated by radio culture, the freedom of each sex depended upon the eradication
of the other's.

The depression's myth of the strong woman was not like
Marianne leading the French revolution. Ma Perkins's battlefield was the kitchen and parlor, the enemy whatever threatened domestic order, especially the dark world of unregulated
sexuality. Strong Woman carried the shield of civilization
against attacks from outsiders—masculine bums and adventurers. The Lone Ranger could be strong, manly, and free, as
Huck Finn knew perfectly well, only at great distances from
the modulating and castrating civilization of good women.

Movies were the most exciting form of mass culture. Although
many more people listened to the radio, the experience of
watching a movie was more intense. Watching and listening
in the dark with strangers, all eyes focused on the bright
screen's compelling images, was simultaneously communal and
isolating. The viewer's reactions were reinforced by the laughter or grasps of others, while he could also thrill to the depiction
of private fantasies. Visually freer and more accessible than
what was called "legitimate" theater, the talking movies arrived just in time to lighten the lives of depressed Americans.

They went to the movies in astonishing numbers. The movie
industry reported that as the movies learned to talk the average

weekly attendance reached about 100 million in 1929, a level it maintained the next year. Then, like the birthrate, it fell until 1933 and leveled off afterward at around 75 million a week for the rest of the decade. By 1935 about half of the nation's approximately 13,500 theaters showed double features, and 5,000 used various prizes, especially bank nights, to increase attendance. The average admission price was 25 cents. By the mid-thirties almost 40 percent of the nation's adults went to the movies at least once a week. (In 1983, 20 percent of the adults went at least once a month.) The rich went somewhat more often than the poor.[96]

Some 5,000 feature films were produced during the thirties. City children saw about 1,000 of these for a 10-cent admission to a double feature every Saturday afternoon. Also, about twice a month, parents took their children to double features at night to see what they described as better movies. In these theaters, the young learned the etiquette appropriate for their courtiers, how to board a square-rigged treasure ship, duel with pistols or swords, rob the local bank, and sweep girls off their feet or boys into marriage. Most of these movies were diverting junk, except of course the serials, especially Flash Gordon, which captivated the nation's young people. For millions of them the movies of the thirties were a central part of life, providing not only entertainment, but education, guidance, and a retreat into a better world, more interesting, exciting, and significant than the entirely too grim real world.

In the early thirties, the film industry maintained its lucrative menu of romance, sex, and violence. Of the five hundred movies made in 1930, 30 percent (down from the 1920s) were about love, 27 percent (slightly higher than the 1920s) were crime movies, while sex comprised 15 percent (about the same as the 1920s). Together, comedies, mysteries, and war made up the rest. There was one children's movie.[97] Overall, the movie studios continued their search for mass attendance by creating uninhibited movies for adults, occasionally depicting alternatives to middle-class values, and masking that fact through exotic settings, or by making otherwise marginal people—criminals, the very wealthy and their butlers, and the gorgeous, in short, freaks—central characters. The early depression did not impress the studios as a reason to change their spectacularly profitable ways. But the advent of sound inevitably forced changes in content as well as technique. The response at the box office was better than any sane accountant could have dreamed possible.

The gangster movies upset public moralists and delighted the rest of the world. The gangsters, especially Edward G. Robinson in *Little Caesar* (1930) and James Cagney in *Public Enemy* (1931), were an antidote to the depression's grayness. At least the gangster tried to do something about his problems, even if he had to die at the end. He was a reversed image of the middle-class audience: sneering at the law, contemptuous of education, and virtually anarchic. His rise was thrilling, and his downfall sad, if just.

Perversely, the gangster movies reflected the public's demand for truth and realism in their lives. This was displayed more explicitly in the fine documentaries made in the thirties, but the same impulse lay behind the depiction of crooks. In their movies, the unsentimental grittiness of everyday life became a routine subject, displacing the exotic appeal of Valentino and Theda Bara. With the gangsters, millions of Americans saw bits of their own lives on the screen, not so much the hero but the dirty dishes, street accents, family quarrels, and poverty. The gangster was not real, but his screen environment was. Ordinary people in the audience, law-abiding to the last, saw part of their world on the screen, and loved every minute.

When Mae West swung her hips and overflowing bosom across the screen, the audience was shocked and delighted. Middle-class Americans did not admire prostitutes, but Mae West was so outrageously funny, so obviously enjoying herself, and so much in command of her life that she was almost impossible to resist. She became a sensational star in *She Done*

Him Wrong (1933) and devoured Cary Grant along the way. Grant is a federal agent parading as a minister, naturally, and when he enters her saloon she sizes him up: "You can be had." Later she issues her famous invitation: "Why don't you come up and see me sometime?" Grant asks whether she had ever met a man who could make her happy, and she responds: "Sure. Lots of times." No actress on screen had ever before been so explicit about her enjoyment of sex and her lusty domination of men—"suckers," she called them, mere slabs of sexual beef. She had a tongue of brass, not a heart of gold. The twinkle of her eye, the open smile, and the twitch of her hips left no one in doubt. When she sang approvingly of "A Guy What Takes His Time," she announced that she was displacing men as the aggressive sexual animal. Although she finally marries Cary Grant's character, she will never succumb to middle-class expectations. As he slips the ring on her finger he mistakenly exults in bringing her to heel: "Surely you don't mind my holding your hand." She responds, "It ain't heavy. I can hold it myself." She soon made the second-highest income in the nation, just below that of William Randolph Hearst.[98]

In line with the cultural conservatism of the depression it was inevitable that something would be done to bring the Hollywood gangsters and whores into step with strong women like Little Orphan Annie and Ma Perkins. In alliance with others, Catholic bishops organized the Legion of Decency to pressure the studios to clean up their acts. Established as a grassroots organization across the nation, most active in the Midwest, especially in Chicago, the Legion's members threatened theater owners with boycotts or worse. The studios got the message and in 1934 agreed to enforce their Production Code. Victory was easy because the studios had fallen too far out of step with the wider culture's need for conventionality, lengthened skirts, and renewed pleasure in the feather of an absent goose. Married couples on the movie screen now slept in twin beds, pref-

too liberal

erably clothed from the chin down, and embraced only if each had a foot on the floor, and so on. Hollywood adjusted quickly: in the six months before the enforcement of the code the Chicago Council of the Legion rated 30 of 125 movies "immoral and unfit"; in the half year after enforcement it found only 4 movies worthy of this blanket condemnation.

The fate of *Yes, My Darling Daughter* exemplified the Legion's state of mind. This movie was the first to be found objectionable by Legion reviewers in New York, but not because of any single scene or sexual explicitness. What was offensive was that the daughter does not accept parental authority. Out of fourteen reviewers, ten objected to darling daughter's stinging admonition to her mother: "Don't be a hypocrite. It's too late in the day for you to take a moral stand. It's none of your business." What was at issue was an unchaperoned weekend with darling's boyfriend. One Legion reviewer wrote that the movie conveys the "false idea to young people that it is easy for two people in love to spend the weekend together without sin." After ten minutes of playing time had been cut, the Legion gave this movie an intermediate rating.[99] The Code continued to shape the movies for the next thirty years.

The change in titles of some of Claudette Colbert's movies reveals the extent of the cultural retrenchment under the code's influence: before the code she played in *Secrets of a Secretary, Misleading Lady,* and *The Wiser Sex;* afterward she appeared in *She Married Her Boss, The Bride Comes Home,* and *It's a Wonderful World.*[100] Shirley Temple replaced Mae West as America's leading actress. The gangsters were transformed into G-men, and Frankenstein's monster was given a bride. Frank Capra's screwball comedies before the code, especially *It Happened One Night,* starring Clark Gable and Claudette Colbert, became his sentimental celebrations of the nation in *Mr. Deeds Goes to Town* (1936) and *Mr. Smith Goes to Washington* (1939). The heroes in these movies naturally come from small towns to fight the villainy of big-city tycoons. (Good nature versus bad city was also the theme of *King Kong,* 1933.) In his concluding filibuster to create boys' camps, somehow the most important issue facing the nation, Senator Smith, played by James Stewart, declaims:

> Now, you're not gonna have a country that makes these kinds of rules *work,* if you haven't got men who've learned to tell human rights from a punch in the nose. And funny thing about men—they start life being boys. That's why it seemed like a pretty good idea to take kids out of crowded cities and stuffy basements for a few months a year—and build their bodies and minds for a man-sized job.[101]

In *Stagecoach* (1939) the director John Ford included as passengers on the coach the characters of a drunk, a whore, a gambler, and a crook. But not to worry. They all turned out to subscribe to "Christian charity, one for the other," to have hearts of gold.[102] Ma Perkins and the nation's salesmen were riding high. Hollywood was finally safe and sanitary, American.

During the depression, Americans needed to find solid footing. To do so they tried to reinvent their culture, became more nationalistic in a world perceived as mad, and seized on conventionality as protection against chaos, a major victory for custodians of American culture, those who feared change and revered the older ways of getting along. The depression taught people to reduce risks.

For the next twenty years, demands to deepen such cultural conservatism became even sharper. In a world war and a cold war, even more than during hard times, Americans wanted as much security as culture could provide. In the forties and especially the fifties, members of the still-expanding middle class hoped that order, regularity, and conventionality in the relations between people would keep them safe, or safer, than they would otherwise be. The middle-class separation of life into distinct spheres—public and private—continued and deepened, with the man in charge of the public, if he had a job, and the woman reigning over the home, even if she had a job. Money in the bank meant that the private lives of the middle class might be more secure, except for World War II, the cold war, and nuclear weapons.

30's a victory for conservative style; hope for return to all security — conformity, a guide to follow

4

COSTS
OF THE DREAM

World War II hardened the cultural conservatism of the 1930s. It was taken for granted that national security required uniformity as well as uniforms and Americanism became middle-class respectability. Military regimentation forced millions of Americans to shelve for the duration whatever residual individualism they had salvaged from their immersion in mass culture, even to yield their personalities, get haircuts, follow orders, no questions asked. A massive industrial semi-mobilization taught additional millions to punch time clocks, regulate their behavior, even their clothing and speech: "Loose lips sink ships." "The forties," according to a literary critic, "was not a time for experimentation in prose."[1] Neither was it a time for experimentation in thought, except as it related to the production of soldiers and their equipment.

Naturally, Americans approached the war with their pre-judgments intact. When asked what America "should do with Japan" after the war, one-third of the people answered that it should be destroyed as a political unit, and 13 percent replied that all Japanese should be killed. Later, a GI who had been in combat remembered that "this hatred toward the Japanese was just a natural feeling that developed elementally." A woman looking back on her wartime experiences explained what was different about the Japanese and how she learned about them: "They sure as heck didn't look like us. They were yellow little creatures that smiled when they bombed our boys. . . . In all the movies we saw the Germans were always tall and handsome." For reasons of race and culture Americans' attitudes were more lenient toward Germans, despite the treatment of the Jews. Even after the Americans learned about the German death camps, eight out of ten believed the Japanese were more "cruel at heart" than the Germans.[2]

American political culture was stunningly innocent, although, by the late thirties, two out of three Americans believed that the nation's involvement in World War I had been a mistake. They remembered that the earlier carnage had been touted as the war to end war. But now, as they looked around, it was hard to avoid feeling somewhat detached from the periodic European butchery. If the crazed Europeans again engaged in their mass slaughter of one another, why should American boys have to die? Few Americans knew what the approaching war was about, except of course to beat the bad guys. A woman recalled her own mental condition: "You won't believe how incredibly ignorant I was. I knew vaguely that a war had started, but I had no idea what it meant." In 1942 one-third of the nation could not name a single war aim. As late as 1944, two out of three people believed they did not take the war "seriously enough."[3]

Americans' opinions were formed by their own backgrounds as well as by what was happening over there. Thus, during the Spanish Civil War most American Catholics supported the fascist Franco while an even larger percentage of American Protestants sided with the Spanish republicans. A substantial majority of Americans whose fathers were born in America thought the arms embargo should be lifted, as did those whose fathers were born in Britain or Russia. But less than half of those whose fathers were German advocated repeal. Some ethnic differences persisted into the war. For example, most Irish-Americans (82 percent) mistakenly believed (or said they believed) that Ireland had entered the war.[4]

Mussolini's antics posed a searing dilemma for many Italian-Americans who, while loyal to America, felt emotional ties to their homeland. Il Duce ignited pride in Italian neighborhoods. Paul Pisicano, fiercely attached to his Sicilian heritage, reminisced about his compatriots during the early war years: "It was very painful to live in America. . . . Prior to Pearl Harbor you tried not to talk about the Italian thing." Reared on what he called "this macho crap," he believed that American Italians were more Italian than native Italians. "Staying in America was something that you did to make money. . . . Nobody ever confused America with leading the good life. . . . You always alluded to the return some way or other." Nonetheless, the "macho crap" required them to fight. "You enlisted to go into the marines or go into the navy. You never enlisted to defend America. No, America was like your boss."[5]

The approach of war encouraged probings into the nation's character. The popular press issued warnings about the softness and femininity of American life. The indictment blamed women for the nation's predicament: women valued comfort over strength and had converted their men to this suicidal view; obsessive attempts to satisfy women's wants had shaped American culture around nothing more important than shopping; women determined all of the nation's now merely "dainty" ideals; and women had convinced men that opportunity was dead—therefore security, a matriarchal ideal, had replaced the vital patriarchal values of competition and struggle. The grand result was, according to *Harper's Magazine*, not edifying: "For the past twenty years American civilization as represented by its great middle class has appeared to pursue no ideal more world-shaking than the attempt to get harder and harder butter on softer and softer bread." It questioned whether democracy could survive the fears and desires of its middle-class women.[6]

Reflecting their deepening conventionality, American men at war sang grotesquely sentimental hymns to motherhood and the purity of their daughters. Inevitably the "holy right and duty" of mothers was affirmed. Supposedly they would not wear uniforms or earn paychecks in war work but would continue to wash string beans, sew buttons, and clean floors. *"And therein lies our power,"* declared *American Home* magazine. "For by the very regularity of our simple earthbound tasks we have the power to preserve . . . righteousness and order."[7]

The popular press defined the war's purpose as the protection of Mother. The American Gas Association, for example, ran an ad showing a GI hanging a picture of his aproned mother, holding a dish she has just taken from the (gas) oven. The caption crooned: "You're my pin-up girl, Mom!" Nor was this view of the world at war limited to profit-making enterprises. The air cadets at a training school in Oklahoma arranged their packed parachutes in huge letters spelling out "Hi Mom." Pilots at Langley Field lined up at attention in the shape of a heart and saluted a mom, their guest of honor, standing in the heart's center. On Mother's Day, 1942, the military brass in Washington ordered officers and men to write to their moms "as an expression of the love and reverence we owe to the mothers of our country." A civilian magazine explained the mother's wartime function: "to make the harmony and beauty of . . . home a symbol, the embodiment of a dream." J. Edgar Hoover was more direct: "Mothers . . . our only hope."[8]

Such soupiness drove the writer Philip Wylie into a frothing distemper: "I cannot think, offhand, of any civilization except ours in which an entire division of living men has been used, during wartime, or at any time, to spell out the word 'mom' on a drill field." He seemed not to understand that it was men, not mothers, who had ordered such a drill, but he was just warming up:

Disguised as good old mom, dear old mom, sweet old mom, your loving mom, and so on, she is the bride at every funeral and the corpse at every wedding. Men live for her and die for her, dote upon her and whisper her name as they pass away. . . . The one indubitably most-needed American verity [is]: "Gentlemen, mom is a jerk."[9]

The same halo shone over daughters, and their protection also became the war's goal. In one advertisement, American girls faced a salivating Nazi, with a warning aimed expressly at Dad:

You they may cast aside and put to some ignominious task, such as scrubbing the sidewalks or sweeping the streets. But your daughter . . . well, if she's young and healthy and strong, a Gauleiter with an eye for beauty may decide she is a perfect specimen for one of their experimental camps. A high honor for your daughter.[10]

Of course the American girl was described as embodying the nation's virtue and nobility. Beneath a photograph of one specimen, perhaps eight years old, sporting pigtails and an apron and seated in a rocker before a fireplace, knitting, presumably a sock for a GI in combat, the copy explained:

She could belong to no other country. In her are summed up all the efforts and strivings of the past—all our hopes for the future. If you have a daughter like this, how proud you must be of your share of her destiny—proud that she can face the world strong in body and mind, confident and smiling! Yes, *smiling!*[11]

To keep her smiling it was necessary to use Ipana toothpaste and win the war.

Men claimed that the inspirational purity of American women made life worth living and the war worth fighting. Girls and mothers rather than wives or lovers made the men choke up. The wife's sexuality barred her from the pantheon of purity; unlike a mother, she might someday withdraw her love. Lovers then were unacceptable and presumably irrelevant to inspiration. The nonsexual female—mother and daughter—rose again as the icon of cultural stability, as she had when Huck Finn fled to the freedom of the wilderness to escape a kind woman's mortal threat to feed, love, adopt, and break him.

This time, however, the men of America's middle class could not flee. Instead, they embraced their ideal of the maternal woman with a vengeance. They wanted their lives to be organized around the small details of domestic life, pleasures of earning a decent living, and a trained inability to identify with external, even historic, struggles. Unlike Huck they sought security and approval, not freedom, a caress, not fame, to escape from the anticipation of mortal combat. Singing "I don't want to set the world on fire," they redefined Huck's thrill of adventure into a need to conform, thus transforming Huck's need to test society's limits into a quest for love, mother love if possible, romantic love as second best. As another song said, they longed for the girl who would be "just like the girl who married dear old Dad." As the culture of motherhood gathered force in the fifties, the peculiar definition of Mother as wife became sharper. In the *Reader's Digest,* for instance, a woman argued that man's "most basic" need was the love he knew "from his earliest moments." Thus, "marriage is for mothering" because it would lead the husband to feel virile and attractive.[12] The strong woman of the depression was being transformed into the good woman of the war and its aftermath.

After everything else had become anonymous, impersonal, and bureaucratic, Mom was the last cushion. Middle-class men sought the one remaining source of warmth and love. With smaller families, weakened community bonds, and the lethal dangers of a world in depression and war, Mother was reinvented to provide the only reliable emotional refuge. Huck had become a young Willy Loman, desperately needing to be well liked.

The wartime movies reinforced the song of national innocence, the American placement of female purity at the center of national aspirations. A pure woman's love of a man proved his worth. The cultural power of Mother created the American boy-man. Pauline Kael, the movie critic, understood these movies:

> The Americans [in the movies] were stereotyped, too. They were always clean-cut, wonderful kids from the Midwest, who had funny ethnics, Italians or Jews, as buddies, who were from Brooklyn. The films were condescending to everybody. The Americans from the Midwest were always so innocent they didn't know a thing. They were virginal boys. There was a sickly undercurrent.[13]

This sickliness referred to the Protestant (Midwest) boys' virgin worship, their fear of and aggression toward actual women. They preferred angels to persons. In another popular tune they sang of preferring a paper doll to "a fickle-minded real live girl." Nonetheless, actual women sometimes had their (base) uses. One such was illustrated when these clean-cut GIs practiced what they learned in these movies—for example, when they tried to pick up Pauline Kael by telling her that, because "they were going out and dying to protect you," she should therefore sleep with them. Presumably the non-Protestant children of immigrants, living on America's margins and providing comic relief, would have found reasons other than the woman's supposed feelings of guilt.[14]

As defined by men, the asexual angel, like the Virgin Mary, always forgave and comforted; she embodied hearth, home, and manners, not passion or adventure. She led the way to the higher, finer things, to abstract, solemn, and uplifting ideals, not to flesh and blood or fire in the belly. She inspired continuity, not astonishments, small movements, not the *beau geste*.

This might seem to be the least effective training for soldiers, but the love of gentle and nurturing, that is, safe, women supposedly inspired and thus compensated America's green warriors for their disbelief in the possibility of their own heroism, or bravery, or adequacy. Some were right to distrust themselves. One psychiatrist concluded that more than one-third of the men rejected by the army were "emasculated males" who wanted to be protected.[15] Even so, for those who fought, the cultural dream identified the love of pure women as a purpose of war. Accordingly, World War II, the greatest adventure in the lives of millions of Americans, was to be fought in implicit opposition to adventure.

But the experience of combat changed everything. In this war, like every other, comrades, not mothers, became essential to survival, a vital bond, like that to mom, that was usually not sexual or threatening. "What was worse than death," according to a former rifleman, "was the indignation of your buddies. You couldn't let 'em down. It was stronger than flag and country." Some of the innocents experienced what some of them had hoped for: the liberating rape of their conventional values, the violation of their innocence. "I went there a skinny, gaunt mama's boy, full of wonderment. I came back much more circumspect in my judgment of people. And of governments."[16]

There were alternatives to fighting for Mom and apple pie. The sexless angel spoke most clearly to recruits from the American middle class. Therefore, she held no meaning for some immigrants or their sons who were not yet fully assimilated, or for other young men who were not middle-class. Even some recruits from the middle class could ignore her if they were young enough, if they had not yet learned the middle-class lesson about investing in the future. If they were too young to imagine their own death they could reject her whispered assurances. Wanting to prove themselves to Huck, not to her, some of these boys were eager for adventure, for the rite of passage into manhood: "I was a . . . mama's boy. I was going to gain my manhood then. I would forever be liberated from the sense of inferiority that I wasn't rugged."[17] For those who had not yet been fully converted to the prudential middle-class outlook, the angel was grounded. Immature enough to dream along with Huck, these young men may even have shared his resentment of apron strings and his love of the wild. Later they would hurriedly put these childish things behind them, either because combat taught horrifying lessons or because they were demobilized. Their adventure was limited to and by the war.

In combat some GIs repudiated the passivity and hesitancy of the middle class, as they had to. They may not have been heroes, but their bravery was indisputable. Perhaps for the first time, and probably for the last, they approved of themselves as men. "They felt they were more important, were better men who amounted to more than they do now," said a former soldier, now a professor. "It's a precious memory."[18] With peace they would return to the reasonable and good life, perhaps silently resentful that they now lived the small moral lessons they were teaching their children.

Many unassimilated GIs—the adventurers—thought that European women understood them better than the girls they left behind. Instead of being treated as boy-men by their American girlfriends, they were charmed by European women, who regarded them not only as genuine men but as conquerors. In this view European women were really women, not like the spoiled and ambitious American girls stuck in bobby-sox adolescence, who insisted that their men spend too much money on them and who were, as a mass magazine said, "breathless keepers-up with the Joneses." A writer for *Collier's* magazine admitted that such an indictment was just, but, he maintained, men should be grateful to their pushy, complaining women because such dissatisfaction and greed created the world's highest standard of living.[19]

To the great annoyance of waiting American women, soldiers married 50,000 English women, 10,000 Australians, and 30,000 others, and even fraternized with German women, "the final insult."[20] The grooms thought they knew what was different about their foreign brides: they had been *"brought up to please men."* An observer explained: "Foreign women know a good deal more about cooking, sewing, and housekeeping than the cocksure, somewhat willful, and much more self-promoting American women do. The overseas woman attaches at least as much importance to what she can do in her feminine sphere as she does to how she looks."[21] Sergeant Gene Fortuna predicted that American women would be forced to enjoy "the role of second fiddle" or lose the great contest for "the magnificent American male" to the women of Europe and Asia.[22]

The American adventurers protested that the bobby-soxers were too competitive and demanded "a loud and full share of the conversation," unlike French women, who believed their "sole purpose [was] being pleasant to the man" and who let the man monopolize the talk. European women presumably wanted to create the most perfect home possible and were described as more serious than the hometown girls. This perfect home would be warm and loving, because a "real woman" not only accepted but relished the superiority and supremacy of her man. Even more aggravating to those soldiers who felt liberated by the war, American women complained constantly, especially about the nylon crisis, more than European women did about the death of their families.[23]

However, other GIs, those who fought under the middle-class banner, were offended by unsanitary foreigners, by various forms of dirt: the European woman's lack of American hygiene and of American morality. Many of these soldiers, according to an army psychiatrist, failed in their attempts at sex with foreign women because "they had discovered that what they wanted after all was not sexual intercourse but merely to be held, caressed, and petted by a woman—just as a mother would fondle her baby." When Bing Crosby sang for the troops in the South Pacific, the song they most often requested was Brahms' "Lullaby," while their favorite beverage was milk.[24]

Both in war and peace, American men were struggling to define their masculinity, and consequently to recognize the kind of woman who could support their hopes and alleviate their fears. The choice was between a "pure girl," whose domination and love would prove a man's virtue, and a "real woman," whose subordination and love would prove a man's manhood. This conflict intensified throughout the 1950s, and, as will be seen, its resolution deformed the psychology of the middle-class American male.

World War II created two stunning domestic facts: 16,354,000 young Americans entered the military, while the remaining civilians had to produce their weapons. In both cases the nation started almost from scratch. And, during the war, marriage and birth rates rose dramatically, at least while the supply of eligible young men lasted. Several reasons account for this: the end of depression-era postponement, available money either through wages or military allotments, and the desire to create a bit of stability in a world gone berserk. War brides and "good-bye babies" planned as a living memorial, just in case, were increasingly familiar. Just before the war only 7 percent of young (18- and 19-year-old) married white women had absent husbands; in 1944 the percentage rose to 56. Comparable figures for the 20- to 24-year-old group were 5 and 34 percent, respectively.[25]

The separations were particularly hard on women, and some could not bear the fear that at any moment, day or night, a telegram might come. Anguished over her inability to locate her husband, a lieutenant who had not yet shipped out, one army wife wrote him letters filled with fear: "You wouldn't have disappeared into thin air like this unless you had to . . . I feel as if you'd stepped off the end of the pier into fog. . . . It's making me frantic! Always before you've been *somewhere*."[26] It was especially lonely for the new wife living near her husband's last base or embarkation port, particularly when she could not quite remember what he looked like. Although the divorce rate did rise, most marriages survived.

Servicemen were younger, healthier, and better educated than the total male population. Married men with dependents were the last drafted, but as the pool of single men was depleted, three million husbands and fathers were inducted. The domestic consequence of this massive call-up made the civilian population "overwhelmingly" female, older, less-educated, less healthy, and disproportionately black.[27]

Blacks were underrepresented in the military because they were often rejected as volunteers. If the same percentage of blacks in the total population as of whites had been allowed to enlist, 130,000 more of them would have served, though most likely in segregated support units, not in combat. Ordinary white Americans, if they took any notice of race hatreds, were not visibly moved by the increasing determination of blacks to obtain justice. For the majority of whites, wartime was the wrong time to experiment with social change; blacks were expected to understand and be patient, even as they seethed over the nation's hypocrisy. One result was race riots against blacks in Los Angeles, Beaumont, Mobile, Detroit, and Harlem. One Italian-American remembered the spirit of the time: His friends were going to Harlem to "beat up some niggers! . . . it was wonderful. It was new. The Italo-Americans stopped being Italo and started becoming Americans."[28]

Despite bureaucratic tangles, shortages of materials, and occasional black-marketing, wartime production was a miracle. In 1939 America manufactured 2,000 military planes; in 1944 it made about 100,000, including 16,000 heavy bombers. By 1944, the American work force turned out almost half of the total armament production of all other nations, allies and enemies combined. Productivity increased as well. The first standard freighter, the Liberty ship, took eight months to build; before the end of the war it was finished in seven weeks.

This magnificent increase in production was caused by more people working and for longer hours. Before the war ended the work force increased by more than a third. This was accomplished by hiring the unemployed—thereby ending the Great Depression—and by employing women, blacks, youngsters below the usual working age, convicts, the retired, and in time disabled servicemen. The work week rose from about 38 to 47 hours, plus overtime everywhere.[29]

Yet America's industrial production was not totally dedicated to war. Half of its capacity was used for civilian needs, and purchases of consumer goods actually doubled during the war. The economist in charge of controlling prices remembered that "never in the history of human conflict has there been so much talk of sacrifice and so little sacrifice." In 1943 about 70 percent of the people said they had not made one real sacrifice. Women found it hardest to cut down on sugar and butter while men were most reluctant to reduce their ration of meat and gasoline.[30]

To gear up the "arsenal of democracy" and make a personal contribution to the war effort, some 20 million Americans left home to find work elsewhere. So many people quit the farms (7 million went into the military or war work) that draft boards increased farm deferments. Indeed, so severe was the shortage of farm labor that 2.5 million people moved from cities to farms, presumably to profit from soaring farm prices. The great war plants rose just outside the cities and drew millions of Americans away from their homes, including 200,000 migrants to the Detroit area and almost half a million to Los Angeles. The populations of thirty-five states declined, while the West Coast, with its shipbuilding and airplane construction, gained the most migrants. Between 1940 and 1945 California's population increased by almost 2 million, and in a modern gold rush its per capita income rose to the nation's highest.[31]

Women workers now appeared everywhere, though they were not always welcomed. On average they earned 55 percent of male wages, a drop from 1939, when they had made 62 percent. The percentage of female union members soared. Without day care or nursery services (often opposed by the Catholic Church, which wanted women home), many mothers dumped their kids in movie theaters, locked parked cars, or the streets, though in the popular press they were continually advised to stay home and raise the kids, to be "stay-at-home patriots." Yet 19.5 million women worked in support of the war effort, almost 9 million more than were employed in 1940, with older married women making up a large part of the increase. Still, patriotic appeals regularly enticed even more women to take jobs, to help prevent Hitler from turning them into "sex slaves." "Rosie the Riveter," a popular tune incessantly played on the radio, told how Rosie was "protecting" her marine boyfriend. In 1943 the War Production Board called for another 1.5 million women workers within a year, a target that was not met, for not all women dashed to the nearest factory. Half the nation's housewives rejected the idea of working on a machine, because for many middle-class women any sort of blue-collar job, however vital to the war effort, would be seen as a personal loss of status.[32]

For a middle-class woman who had never worked before, a job during wartime filled the need to do something while waiting for her man to return home, and to contribute however best she could to the production effort. But a deeper urge also prevailed: how could a woman remain idle when her husband was preparing to face and deliver fire? One sensitive woman, accustomed to leisure, wrote to her distant military husband about her decision to work. "The job is pretty much a moral as well as a financial issue. Even the kids saw that. It's the only way I can keep moving in the same direction with you: toward the future." For her, structuring time through work—not sleeping late, not wasting time—was the point. But she did not feel it was necessary to make a direct contribution to war work. She found a job on a newspaper.[33]

A young woman who followed her man or sought work away from the security of the family discovered either a significant fringe benefit or danger. For better or worse and usually for the first time, she entered the world on her own and became part of an anonymous mass. She exchanged the daily comfort of knowing her neighbors and local shopkeepers to become a worker in an alien and impersonal place. She would be tested and perhaps grow in ways her parents had never intended. She could learn that life might revolve around issues other than how often the curtains were washed.[34]

These young women accepted the risks of becoming adults, an extraordinary opportunity or crisis for the small-town American girl. One of them, Virginia Rasmussen, remembered: "I think the war caused a definite rootlessness in our society. We would marry servicemen and follow them from one camp to another, and suddenly all of our roots were gone." Barbara Norek could not adjust to a freedom that required strength: "I feel that I was a casualty of the war. I lost stability at home." She needed a moral guide. "I lost my companionship with my father when I truly needed it." Other women became too independent to regress upon a returning husband's request. Frankie Cooper's husband "would have been happy if I had gone back to the kind of girl I was when he married me—a little homebody there on the farm, in the kitchen, straining the milk. But I wasn't that person anymore."[35]

Women "complicated" the workplace for men suffering from testosterone poisoning. Men complained that the distraction of tight sweaters could endanger their lives. If they were working on a drill press, there was no telling what they might puncture if they concentrated on curves elsewhere. The war's "sweater girl" was the beginning of the mass male's growing fixation on breasts, the bigger the better. In what may be a distinctly American confusion of maternity and sexuality this breast pathology, as will be seen, ballooned over the next fifteen years.

One male reaction to women workers was to insist that the women remain "feminine" no matter how greasy or important their jobs. At least one personnel manager boasted about the neat grooming of his women workers: "It helps their morale.

It helps our prestige too." An ad in a woman's magazine announced that women served their country best when they "are most charming, for beauty is ever an inspiration to those who see it." Buy Avon products. A cosmetics maker admitted that lipstick alone probably could not destroy the *Wehrmacht,* "but it symbolizes one of the reasons why we are fighting . . . the precious right of women to be feminine and lovely."[36] The men could not openly admit that some of them felt diminished by the fact that women could do their work, sometimes better.

It was the female soldiers in the Women's Army Auxiliary Corps and other services, more than the workers, who most disturbed the cultural gate-keepers, the guardians of male privilege. When the time came, would the female soldiers exchange their khakis for aprons and perhaps lace? "Will this woman who gave the most serious side of her life to active military service be content to take her orders from mere man?" asked the writer of a wartime marriage manual.[37]

Some men felt that these women differed radically from their predecessors, that they had become a new, tougher species, but one, it was fervently hoped, that would be temporary, for the duration only.[38] Mass culture depicted the boom-towner as young and beautiful, a glamour girl doing emergency work, a temporary derangement of the natural order, not a permanent alteration of American womanhood. Meanwhile, women in overalls or uniforms discomposed those men who longed for a "normal" postwar world as they understood it, a man's world. The definition of "normal" was clarified by a *Ladies' Home Journal* poll of servicemen. What was their "blueprint for a dream girl, 1942 model"? The men fantasized about a "girl" who was short, healthy, and a housewife thoroughly devoted to her children. Her cooking mattered much more than her "braininess," and her figure was more important than her face. Such attitudes inspired at least one woman to react:

. . . the majority of you [men] think of women as either sex machines or glorified domestic servants whose job it is to feed you, wash for you, and nurse you. I must be fair and acknowledge that it is not deliberately your fault that you think this. You have been subjected to the same movies, the same books, the same newspapers that we [women] have since childhood.[39]

But the response of Cornelia Otis Skinner in the fifties was more characteristic of the majority of middle-class women:

Ladies, we have won our case, but for heaven's sake let's stop trying to prove it over and over again. By setting ourselves up as a race apart and special we lose many of the delights and fulfillments of being a woman. In the long run, we cannot do without men and men cannot do without us, not unless we drive them to it with our shrill cheering for our own accomplishments. If ever the day approaches when men *can* do without us, I will take out citizenship papers in another and more agreeable planet.[40]

The war ended with a series of news reports portending a historic divide, the end of an era, the sudden and numbing beginning of God knows what. After twelve years of leadership through national hardship and war, President Roosevelt was dead. Winston Churchill was voted out of office. Less than two weeks later Harry Truman, the new President, spoke to the nation: "An American airplane dropped one bomb on Hiroshima. . . . It is an atomic bomb."

The announcement of peace was thrilling, of course, but the nation could not bring the near future into focus. The immediate postwar mood was tentative and confused. Did peace mean a return of depression? Worried about dismantling the enormous war industries and finding jobs for the veterans, Americans naturally were eager to reconstruct their lives in ways that would not require more extraordinary sacrifices or heroism. After being coerced by external and impersonal events for so long, they now demanded control of their private lives. They wanted to concentrate on the intimate details of living rather than on historic events of great consequence, and went in quest of the prosaic—small, domestic, personal daily events. They had had enough of the insecurity and excitement of shared, involuntary dramas on a worldwide stage, and were rushing now to be left alone, like their parents in the 1920s.

The wish to withdraw further from public life required a certain optimism, a conviction that external help was not needed. The transition to peace occurred without a general trauma and, after a year or two of anxiety, it became clear that another depression was not an immediate threat. Then the postwar middle class began its most startling ascent into what many thought was a serene domesticity. It began to exhibit limitless faith in the victorious nation, as well as in itself and its future. Moreover, the postwar economy came together in ways that confirmed middle-class interpretations of civic scripture: if the world would do him the small service of getting out of the way, the middle-class breadwinner could take care of his family and ride the vicissitudes of life to an even higher standard of living. If only others, outsiders and politicians, would leave him be.

Postwar America prospered as never before, and the middle class was euphoric. Not only were high-paying jobs plentiful but millions of people suddenly expected to rise in social status. It was thrilling to know, absolutely know, that the next move would be to a private house, from the city to the green suburbs, that the new job would not only pay the bills but bring respect, and that the growing number of children would get the sort of education that would propel them into even more affluence. Roger Montgomery, a factory worker, remembered how it was:

I think that one of the important things that came out of World War II was the arrival of the working class at a new status level in this society. I don't think the people I worked with in the plant at Elyria, Ohio, realized how much their lives were about to change. Most of the people that I worked with lived in rented houses and close to slum conditions. By the fifties almost everybody in that kind of social world expected that they would live in a suburban house—one that they owned themselves. The war integrated into the mainstream a whole chunk of society that had been living on the edge.[41]

Nationwide, the percentage of families earning under $3,000 fell from 46 in 1947 to 20 in 1959, while the percentage of families earning between $7,000 and $10,000, a high middle-class income, rose from 5 to 20 during the same period.[42] The family was not only safe but on its way up, and however far one looked at the ever rising curve into the future no barriers were visible. For the middle class the dream was coming true. America was delivering, at last.

The GI Bill of Rights was indispensable to this economic surge. Signed in 1944, this legislation released millions of Americans to make choices that would otherwise have been impossible. It solved the problem of not having enough money saved to make a down payment on a house, buy a business, or go to college. The GI Bill was the alternative to the nest egg that even middle-class Americans did not have. It provided discretionary money, those funds that alone have social potency.

In 1945, some 22,000 veterans used the GI Bill to pay for more education; within one year the number approached a million and in 1947 almost 2 million. Altogether, about half of the war's 16 million veterans participated in this aspect of the program. By 1948, 1.4 million veterans took out guaranteed loans to buy houses; 45,000 used them for farm-related purposes, and 94,000 more for businesses. Others used the aid to learn ballroom dancing, archery, or, in one case in Iowa, to buy a good set of burglar's tools.[43]

Veterans Administration records do not show how different ethnic groups used the GI Bill, but Mike Royko recalled of his mainly Slavic community in Chicago: "The majority of guys from my neighborhood did not use the GI Bill for school. They used it for a loan for a home."[44] The ways in which different Americans defined security shaped how they would use the bill. It is likely that the veteran of parents who had little faith in personal economic progress invested in a house rather than in education, that is, his economic future. Consequently, he ran the risk of getting stuck somewhere on America's economic and social ladder. The choice was between a debt and an investment, and those who distrusted the economy and perhaps themselves chose debt. The most thoroughly middle-class GIs used the bill for college tuition. For them the dream house would be postponed until personal income, higher now because of additional schooling, rather than government assistance, could pay for it. The transforming potential of the GI Bill was most fully realized by middle-class soldiers who had a feel for postponement and the future.

The GI Bill significantly helped to make tangible the postwar premonition of sweet times ahead. As usual, the most revealing symptoms of such spiraling confidence were the decisions of millions of people to marry and have more children than their parents. As the economy flourished, the marriage industry roared and the babies boomed.

The first item on the social agenda was to send Rosie home. This was thought necessary for two reasons: to make room for the employment of returning veterans and to restore the nation's domestic heart to something like order and normality. The rate at which women quit their jobs was double and sometimes triple that of men. When they neglected to leave voluntarily they were fired at twice the rate of men, especially in heavy industry. Replacing women with men essentially erased the economic progress women made during the war, although many continued to work. Perhaps because the reasons for getting rid of the women were always justified on patriotic and cultural grounds, millions of women willingly went home, where, the guardians of culture insisted, they belonged.[45] Demobilization produced a nationwide scramble to shed the cultural malformations required by war in favor of normality, the newly possible pleasures of domesticity.

Advice to women about how to help the returning soldier adjust to civilian life burgeoned into a postwar growth industry. The veterans were portrayed as bearing almost no responsibility for their adjustment to peace. Rather it was the woman's duty to understand him, appreciate his experiences, rebuild his confidence, and reintroduce him to manners, prettiness, delicacy, sensitivity, and civilization. Without her guiding hand, he might murder the in-laws and eat the furniture. But success required that this woman honor such a brute's instincts. *House Beautiful* explained: "You, to whom the veteran is returning, are entrusted with the biggest morale job in history. . . . Your part in the remaking of this man is to fit his home to *him,* understanding why he wants it this way, forgetting your own preferences. After all, it is the boss who has come home."[46]

Such advice might have driven a sane woman crazy. On the one hand, she was urged to "remake" her man, and on the other, to submit to him. She was urged to repress the independence she may have enjoyed during the war, ignore her capacity to support herself, stop wearing slacks, forget that she may have learned something about world politics, and, in short, practice the rites of "self-abnegation." A sociologist interested in such matters insisted: "Above all, she must give him lavish—and undemanding—affection," while expecting "no immediate return." How to domesticate a warrior? Herbert I. Kupper, staff psychiatrist at a marine hospital, thought he knew the answer: "mothering."[47]

Although a middle-class woman with a mind of her own might have ignored these mewlings she was more likely to yield to the dictates of the fashion industry. Not surprisingly the two enterprises were dedicated to the same profitable goal: the "refeminization'' of the American woman. In 1947, Christian Dior had designed a silhouette he called the ''New Look.'' Because he hated women who looked like ''Amazons'' he reconfigured them, as he said, to have ''rounded shoulders, full feminine busts, and willowy waists above enormous spreading skirts.'' He instructed his models to pad their brassières ''to give prominence to this most feminine attribute,'' while he built his own padding into the bust and hips to make doubly sure. Bras were reinforced with strong wire and girdles made sufficiently tight to decrease the waist, thereby emphasizing breasts and hips. As the woman's or her husband's income rose the size of her waist diminished. Dior's alternative to the Amazon was a style that emphasized potential maternity: protruding breasts, overspreading hips, and no legs. American women said they detested the longer skirts, but to be fashionable would buy them.[48] A newly engineered mammilary culture now emerged and swept over the resentfully pliant middle-class woman, who, while complaining, was susceptible to the opinion of fashion because of her need for the good opinion of friends and her unwillingness to appear as an exception to her class.

One of the great cultural anxieties of this period derived from the metaphysical question of how small a woman's breasts might be or seem for her to be or feel ''flat-chested,'' unwomanly, unattractive, unemployable, unmarriageable, a failure. Men and women resolved the tension by assuming that good is big and best is biggest. In the process the culture ignored the breasts' natural function and focused on real or apparent mammilary extravagance as the indication of the good life: a woman who could give sex and comfort to a man aglow with gratitude. The merely normal-sized woman was in trouble, and she knew it.

Distraught over nature's perceived parsimony, average-sized women begged their doctors to correct what seemed to be their ''insignificant'' breasts. One woman told her doctor: ''I've stood it as long as I can, being shut out of all the good things of life because of the way I'm shaped!'' Now women had

"shapes," not bodies or even figures. A spokesman for the
nation's plastic surgeons declared that "a great many U.S.
women" were agitated about the fear of small breasts "to the
point of severe neurosis." One surgeon, Dr. Gustave Aufricht,
was old enough to recall the good old 1920s, when fashionable
women wanted flat chests, but now he was operating to move
fatty tissues from the buttocks to the bosom. Most of these
surgeons concluded that "the current concern over micromas-
tia is really a mass micromania—a 'culturally induced' delu-
sion of smallness."⁴⁹

Goodrich Schauffler, a distinguished gynecologist, observed
that his younger patients, in particular teenagers and younger
married women, had symptoms of "a sort of hysteria" because
of "an exaggerated interest in the female bosom." Ten-year-
old girls wore miniature falsies, other girls became psychiatric
cases from depression over their small breasts, and one of his
patients attempted suicide out of profile despair. These women,
he claimed, had succumbed to "bosom-worship in our culture." The "bosom inferiority complex" was depriving the
middle-class woman of her equilibrium.⁵⁰

Women's fashions both dictated and played into this fetish
of colossal bosoms. There is no better source than *Good Housekeeping* magazine: "Right now you have in mind the current
ideal—firm, full, cone-shaped breasts, standing up and out
without visible means of support." The ads in women's magazines were ecstatic over the ways in which their intricately
engineered bras and girdles could reshape lives as well as bodies. Encased in her Maidenform bra, a woman could live out
her fantasies: "I'm the Circe of the circus . . . the gal in the
gallery with the gala Maidenform figure! Clowns [*sic!*] jump
for joy in the center ring—and the applause is all for my
curves." In fact, however, this bra created dangerously pointed
and rigid projectiles, not curves. Not to be outdone, the Jantzen
Curvallure girdle took "two inches off your age." Formfit's
Life bras were designed not merely to fit but "to *elevate, separate,*

rejuvenate perfectly.''[51] The number of such examples is just short of infinite.

The writer Marge Piercy recalled her adolescent struggle with the absurdity of the brassières of the fifties:

> Longline brassieres underneath staved in the ribs, shoved the stomach up into the esophagus, raised the rigid breasts till their padded peaks brushed the chin. . . . If you reached upward, if you moved suddenly, the bra would remain anchored like a granite ledge. The freed breasts would pop out. Suddenly you stood, Diana of Ephesus with four boobs.[52]

Because of the obligatory weight they carried on their chests, the physical proof of their talents, Hollywood's new sex queens clearly suffered from the constant peril of falling forward. In *The Outlaw,* a popular movie starring Jane Russell's bosom, Russell played a wooden but essential supporting role. To advertise this movie, Radio City Music Hall's marquee invited tittering:

THE MUSIC HALL GETS THE BIG ONES!

WHAT ARE THE TWO GREAT REASONS FOR
JANE RUSSELL'S RISE TO STARDOM?[53]

The first issue of *Playboy,* December 1953, displayed Marilyn Monroe's barely concealed breasts on the cover, and further revealed them in her famous nude calendar pose inside, where the text complained that ''her curves really aren't *that* spectacular,'' meaning that there were other bunnies not limited to a mere thirty-seven-inch bust. Nevertheless, her ''curves'' made *Playboy* a hit and Hugh Hefner, its publisher, a mass culture star. The new voyeuristic age had dawned and peeping toms could now avoid arrest. *Playboy*'s success—one million subscribers by 1959—proved that what the American male of the fifties most wanted to peep at were patulous bosoms. The first editorial promised that these would provide "a little diversion from the anxieties of the Atomic Age."[54]

Playboy attempted to reform attitudes about sex the same way that mass culture of the 1920s had approached money. Both were teachers of modernity: forget the unsatisfying, unhealthy conventions of the past, relish the present, don't save, don't postpone, and you can do it by following the new rules, which see life as an itch to be scratched now. *Playboy*'s nudes challenged the cultural conservatism of the fifties and shocked the newly complacent middle-class defenders of cleanliness and order, just as the rush into debt during the 1920s outraged that decade's ministers of thrift.

Playboy's world offered a single, simple message: women, like men, are in eternal and overpowering heat, live truly only through their genitals, and those who pretend otherwise merely play games designed to add fleeting and delicious preparatory tension to their inevitable surrender. The activating principle of life is female lust, promising Everyman relief from a groin in flames. Now American boy-men could fantasize about safe conquests by melting over *Playboy*'s paper dolls they could call their own. The large breasts of this safe doll were displayed as her only erogenous equipment. She could never witness the boy-man's failure.

Yet, despite its vulgarity and depiction of plastic women, *Playboy*'s message also contained a hint that women, because they were like men sexually, had human needs. This point, mightily obscured by everything else in the world of bunnies, was a bit helpful in the struggle to free women from conventionality's suffocating weight, especially the boy-man's adoration of the virgin and his aggression against non-virgins. *Playboy* attacked the masculine attribution of bloodlessness to the angels, mother and daughter, and at least implied that the virgin was a woman connected to universal biological realities. In seeking to reveal the sexual availability especially of virgins— the nudes were composed to evoke the "girl next door"— *Playboy* explicitly demeaned and implicitly humanized women.

While *Playboy* hoped to make lust respectable, Dr. Alfred Kinsey in his research on women's sexuality, also published in 1953, revealed that the white middle-class American woman was not the juiceless angel forever celebrated by the nation's moralists. Kinsey discovered that half the nation's brides were not virgins. Partly because of Kinsey's huckstering, the report sold in the hundreds of thousands. The popular response was entirely predictable: gratitude or outrage. The women's magazines seized on his work as providing essential information to improve their readers' sex lives and thus strengthen their marriages, while the Catholic press declared that the research was unscientific and, in any case, did not apply to Catholics.[55]

Beyond the debates about women's sexuality, the middle class was moving in a different though equally breast-centered direction. In 1949, Betty Friedan, a professional writer and editor, future leader of a revitalized feminism, recognized her growing acceptance of the middle-class package of values, the entire lot, and how easy, even pleasant it was to contemplate giving up her career for middle-class motherhood.[56]

Security, defined as money and marriage, came first, then came babies. "The end of the war," according to Winona Espinosa, interviewed years later, "was a real setback for women. We all sank back into our shells. The fellows came back home and everybody made babies." Postwar optimism, unaccustomed prosperity, and the desire to make up for lost time produced a nationwide invasion of infants. *Fortune* magazine estimated that 2.5 million postwar births had been postponed from the depression. But the widely accepted connection between a booming economy and increased fertility is not an adequate explanation. After all, birthrates fell during the booming 1920s and began to pick up in the depressed 1930s. Though the state of the economy was important, the kind of life that women envisioned for themselves was central. For the middle-class woman of the twenties careers often took precedence over romance. By the late thirties most women imagined this in reverse, but without children. The postwar middle-class woman decided that she was a nester after all.[57]

The young woman who married in the late 1940s was born in the late 1920s. The depression and the war had shaped her decisions and dreams until she became something of a free agent only on V-J Day. No longer would she have to worry about the shortage of money during the depression and the shortage of men during the war. Although millions of women (about 40 percent) continued to work after the war, most women chose domesticity, perhaps as a way to catch their breath, find out what motherhood felt like, and explore a different meaning of womanhood, one that everyone including themselves assumed was "normal," but that they had never known. It was as if millions of Americans decided to try to renew the world, at least their world, and women returned to the home with astonishing ease. However abrupt their individual decisions were to abandon their wartime independence for domestic femininity, their longing for what they considered normality was understandable.

The choice between working and domesticity was of course largely determined by the family's status. Middle-class women could find "women's" work, as secretaries or clerks, with relative ease, and they did so to help their family secure or expand its middle-class beachhead. Indeed, millions of families rose to a higher middle-class status only through the efforts of a second wage-earner. By 1956, 70 percent of middle-class families (in an income range between $7,000 and $10,000) included a second worker, usually the wife.[58] This working woman did not repudiate the culture of motherhood or the new domesticity. With her hands full of stenographic pads, shopping lists, and diapers, she embraced both worlds, often with amazing dexterity and energy.

The American house in the fifties contained seven times as much equipment as it had had in the twenties. The result was a slight increase in the amount of time the housewife spent doing her work: the fifty-two-hour week of the twenties house-wife became fifty-six hours thirty years later. New standards of cleanliness and the dispersion of stores created more work. For example, laundry took the same time in the fifties as it had in the twenties because the modern woman washed more often. The time spent on cooking and washing dishes declined by about thirty minutes a day, while that required for shopping increased by an additional thirty minutes. The fifties housewife spent about one day a week on shopping. In her nationally syndicated newspaper column, one of Heloise's hints to house-wives demonstrated how to squander the possibility of more freedom: "Silver polish does wonders for shining curtain rods."[59] The modern housewife's life was not simplified by all her "labor-saving" machines; on the contrary, she was as har-ried as her mother had been.

Yet the stereotype of the 1950s is wrong: middle-class Amer-ican wives were not wasting away in empty days of domestic boredom. Increasing numbers of them were experiencing empty days of doing "women's work" for low pay outside the home. Millions of women found new jobs, "ladylike jobs," precisely in order to advance their new domesticity. Working had now become essential to the protection of the home. In fact, the increasing prosperity and aspirations of the middle class required that more women work. By the end of the decade the number of working wives had doubled, the number of working mothers had increased by 400 percent, and the median age of working women was forty-one. In 1940, married women workers generally came from the working class; fifteen years later they were equally represented within the well-educated middle class.[60]

The marriage industry flourished and the mass production of babies would have gladdened the hearts of the nation's effi-ciency experts. In the first year of peace, 2.2 million couples married, more than double the number of any prewar year, and a record unmatched for a generation. Younger than be-fore, they had more years in which to deliver the goods. By the end of the fifties, 14 million seventeen-year-old girls were engaged. In the fifteen years after Pearl Harbor the percentage of men who married in their early twenties actually doubled, as did the fertility rate of women the same age. In the mid-1950s one-half the women in college dropped out to marry or to avoid acquiring so much knowledge that they would frighten men.[61]

Once motherhood began, its own logic took over. It became a middle-class axiom that a single child was deprived and that a full nest made for healthier chicks. By 1953 a national poll revealed that 30 percent of Americans considered three children the ideal number; an equal number chose four, and 12 percent wanted five or more kids. A Harvard senior tried to explain: "I'd like six kids. I don't know why I say that—it just seems like a minimum production goal." What actually happened fell short of these goals, but the national increase was huge, and among all the industrialized nations of the world, the postwar baby boom took place only in America, not devastated by the war, by a people awash in optimism.[62]

The significance of the 32 million babies born in the 1940s can be grasped if they are contrasted to the 20 million immigrants who came to America in the first two decades of the century. Then during the fifties 41 million more kids appeared. This eruption of babies was not caused by a return to the sprawling farm families of the past. It was a consequence of fewer unmarried women, childless marriages, and only children. There was a vast increase in the number of women who had two or three or sometimes four children.[63]

For decades, experts assumed that wealth and higher education caused sterility. The rich get richer and the poor get children. But after the war, educated, middle-class couples reversed the conventional wisdom by planning the number and spacing of their children. Indeed, the fertility gap between the college-educated and others narrowed. From 1940 to 1947 the birthrate among college graduates increased by over 80 percent; for grade-school graduates, the increase was 29 percent, even though non-college-educated women continued to produce an overall larger crop. Mass magazines were ecstatic about the economic implications of this nationwide epidemic of babies. *Life* gushed: "Kids: Built-In Recession Cure—How 4,000,000 a Year Make Billions in Business."[64]

With the mass fixation on bosoms it might have been expected that this nation of new mothers would breast-feed their babies, and some did. Though it was not fashionable, Betty Friedan recalled the "moral, political seriousness of breast-feeding. . . . It's so *natural,* we gloried, feeling only scorn for our superficial selfish sisters who thought breast-feeding was animal and would spoil their figures." Perhaps the inclination to breast-feed was thwarted by the fear that doing so would cause breasts to sag, thus altering the profile on which her own and her husband's self-esteem depended. Given the folklore of the time, women had to choose between using or protecting their breasts. The number of breast-fed babies released from hospitals fell from 65 percent in 1946 to 37 percent ten years later and to 27 percent ten years after that. A scholar came to the only possible conclusion: "The baby boomers wound up as the *least* breast-fed generation in our history."[65]

Because of a postwar housing shortage and the bursting national nursery many new parents were forced to find a different way to live. In 1947, six million families lived with relatives, while 500,000 others were housed in temporary shelter, such as Quonset huts, abandoned trolley cars, and grain bins.[66] Many could afford to move, almost always to the new suburbs, because of the employment boom and also because easy credit for veterans greatly increased the number of middle-class families.

The federal government put its resources behind the American Dream, the desire to own a house. The New Deal's Federal Housing Authority and the postwar VA both ensured lenders of mortgage money. The down payment required to buy a house dropped from 50 or 67 percent before the New

Deal to 10 percent after the war, and the repayment period was extended from ten to thirty years. Government guarantees reduced interest payments by two or three points, and tax breaks on interest and real-estate taxes further reduced the cost. The effect was often to make owning a suburban home less expensive than renting a city apartment. One couple paid $50 a month for an apartment in New York City before they bought a suburban house in New Jersey for a monthly payment of $29.[67] Such economics made possible the suburbanization of the blue-collar middle class, in its own suburbs.

The postwar improvement in the standard of living led to another swarming migration of the American people, like the vast dislocations of the war, only this time to the suburbs. It was not unusual for veterans to represent 90 percent of a suburb's population, while half the new village men and 25 percent of the women were college graduates. By 1955, four thousand families a day were leaving the cities for the suburbs, where 25 percent of the nation already lived. At the decade's end, one-third of the nation's population was suburban, many having moved into the 19 million houses, mostly colonial or ranch style, that had been built since the war.[68]

This was more than a change of location. It was a conscious attempt by the new migrants to distance themselves from the unpleasantness of the world, the crowded and expensive city, urban risks, blacks, and history. The goal was the comfort of being alone together with like-minded people. The new suburbanities viewed their new, clean, green communities as the best of all possible worlds in which to bring up the kids.[69]

The desire for a secure job and house was neither novel nor neurotic. What was new about the postwar Americans' longing was the frenzy surrounding their quest, sometimes revealed in support for the strident anti-Communist Senator Joseph McCarthy, atomic-bomb drills in the schools, or a massive withdrawal from politics. This was a time for small steps, carefully controlled personal change, order, and avoiding risk. The aim of the rearing and education of the fifties was safety. During the war the veterans had learned not to volunteer.

All of the postwar suburbs proclaimed the advantages of newness, an American tradition especially attractive to the young. Newness promised freedom from crust, dirt, prior owners, and vandals, and offered material objects and social relations that people could embrace as their own from the start. At first the emphasis was on objects: "Well, moving into a new house, you want everything new." But this desire for the new soon included people: "Nearly everybody is new. . . . I mean they are newly married and new to the community." Freed of the anchors of the past, the suburbanites created a claustral world in their own image. Levittown, with seventy thousand inhabitants, was the nation's largest community without blacks.[70] The wholesale flight from and deterioration of the nation's cities had begun.

To protect mortgage guarantees the FHA developed criteria for housing investments that promoted white flight from the cities, racially segregated housing, suburban home ownership, and inadequate funding for urban reconstruction. The two most important criteria stipulated that any house purchased must be located in a neighborhood of "relative economic stability" and that it have "protection from adverse influences." The government opposed racially diverse communities, densely populated neighborhoods, renovation of older houses, and lower-class occupancy. In short, the FHA recoiled from what it called "inharmonious racial or nationality groups," and it identified entire city neighborhoods whose diversity was considered a bad investment. Closely attuned to the spirit and fears of the white middle class, the government was in the business of ensuring white peace of mind.

The growth of the suburbs was enormous. About 100,000 new houses were built in 1944, almost one million two years later, and the all-time record to date of 1.7 million in 1950. Within the next twenty years the suburban population doubled from 36 to 74 million people, and for the first time more of a nation's citizens lived in suburbs than in cities or on farms.[71]

Having freed themselves from the past, from the restrictions and pleasures of the city's more traditional way of life, the most characteristically middle-class suburbanites had also freed themselves from attachment to place. The move away from family customs and from the sights and sounds of the city produced a thrilling feeling of liberation, of floating: if one suburb was a good place to live, any similar one would also do. Americans moved more than anyone else: the average suburban family moved every three years.[72] They could never "go home," back to the city, for that would be an admission of failure in the new and free American way. The first break from the city made the second move easier and the young middle class became chronically transient; the more education its members had, the more economically mobile they were and the more often they packed.

The commitment to the job was deeper than familial or personal roots. In the mid-fifties, 40 percent of Americans reported that they enjoyed working more than being at home. Moving companies reported that 40 percent of their business came from junior executives transferred by their firms. Because of corporate expansion and decentralization, America's attractive managerial jobs were increasingly accessible from the new suburbs, so life came to be lived on a checkerboard.[73] Consequently the stake in immediate family relationships intensified. In a world of friendly strangers, the floating husband and wife depended more on each other for emotional support. Commuting husbands might hope to be recharged on weekends; isolated wives might learn to postpone their needs to an indeterminate future, maybe when their husbands' salaries increased.

The lack of a past obviously created a dependence on the present for mastering the techniques and standards of daily life. A need for the community's approval inevitably made the young suburban families conformist, outgoing, friendly, and warmly cooperative, discouraging eccentricity and "snobbishness" in the process. Suburban homogeneity raised Americans' historical susceptibility to public opinion to a level approaching tyranny, but, because it confirmed the attitudes of its victims, it was apparently unobtrusive, even comforting. Such a tyranny enhanced individual security, but there were costs. One of the new villagers explained, "If you have any brains, you keep them in your back pocket around here." The rule for getting along was plain: "It's more fun to have a group. You all do things together." One typical reaction was presented apparently without irony: "In the city I knew a lot of intellectual, progressive-type people. I'll admit they are more stimulating, full of ideas, always wanting to talk about India or something. But I like the stodgy kind now. They're more comfortable."[74]

In focusing on the business implications of suburban middle-class psychology, *Fortune* magazine offered advice to advertisers: sell to the group, not the individual, because "suburbanites are growing more than ever concerned with the opinions of others in their group." Key to suburban living was the recognition that no one wanted to stand out, to emerge from the mass, so that it was understood everywhere that "the modern suburbanite tries to keep *down* with the Joneses," to spend no more conspicuously than his neighbor, though the average suburban family was 70 percent richer than the national average.[75]

Shared spending habits created the appearance of a united front composed of similar houses and cars, the new uniform of jeans and T-shirts for children, and women wearing slacks and shorts in public. Almost immediately suburbia's informality hardened into a rigid conventionality established by the need for like-minded neighbors to like each other. The compulsion to adjust to community norms filled family-room bookcases with self-help, junk psychology, and mindless educational literature, all focused on the joys of belonging and the fun of learning. Senator McCarthy exploited this desire to become indistinguishable from others. Indeed, the passion to adjust, especially in the suburbs, became an inquisitorial demon that could devour the odd unbeliever. David Riesman called it "other-directedness." Apparently, there were terrible pressures embedded in the comfortable safety achieved by middle-class Americans. Within three years of its appearance on the market, 1.2 million pounds of Miltown, the new middle-class tranquilizer, were consumed.[76]

Moving from the city and the past created special difficulties, even anguish, for the children of immigrants. Maintaining ethnic or religious traditions in the new villages required extraordinary determination and agility. Joining the group while guarding memory was not easy unless, of course, one moved to an ethnic suburb. Indeed, many of the suburbs were as distinctively Italian, Irish, or Jewish as the ghettos had been. Nonetheless, the move to suburbia, a badge of having arrived, of respectability and white bread, presented problems for people who once had prided themselves on standing a little apart from what they and especially their parents had considered the shallowness of American culture. In separating from the family's past, the new suburbanites faced the pleasures and pain of re-creating themselves, becoming more rootless, less ethnically identified, more American.

In the early fifties, Harry Gersh, an official with a Jewish family agency in New York, moved to Westchester County, where he expected to find a less Jewish environment. Deciding where to move was a simple matter of arithmetic:

> When we looked over the communities into which we might move, we checked around to find out whether there were other Jews living there. If there were none, or too few, we presumed that positive efforts had been made to keep them out. . . . So we looked further. And when we found that the community was 99 per cent Jewish, we also looked further.

In fact, the groupiness of the suburb strengthened this family's sense of Jewishness, but the Gershes worried that the heritage they cherished would still be diluted beyond recognition in their children. "Our earlier Jewishness was untroubled and untortured. Today it has a nagging quality. . . . There's a consciousness of loss that cannot be exactly pinned down." Yet, Mr. Gersh concluded, "we haven't really sold out."[77]

Paul Pisicano, an unreconstructed urbanite, was less equivocal. For him the suburbanization of the Italians destroyed their culture. After the war "we looked up, we owned property. Italians could buy. The GI Bill, the American Dream. Guys my age had really become Americanized." They moved to the suburbs to avoid blacks. Once rusticated, his friends let their minds go fallow. "The war bred the culture out of us." It used to be that opera for Italians was like cars for Americans. Not in the suburbs. "Oh, God, I see the war as that transition piece that pulled us out of the wine cellar. It obliterated our culture and made us Americans. That's no fun."[78]

Suburbs were not invented after World War II. They had long existed as havens from the city's unpleasantness for the wealthy. In the postwar years, however, the suburbs were consciously designed for the new middle class, both blue- and white-collar. The architectural and psychological conformity offended almost everyone except the people who were the first in their families to own their own houses and little plots of land. They did not move to starve the cities or segregate the blacks. Rather, they wanted to segregate themselves, and some regretted the larger social consequences of their actions. But tens of millions of Americans found a way to live that was better for them than what they left behind. Critics complained of the sterility and homogeneity of suburbia while more modest people realized their most cherished dream: they had some space, some cleanliness, some security, and were offended by accusations that they were transforming the nation into something others found ugly, racist, and dehumanizing.

The 1950s were reputedly the Golden Age of television, although a movie critic with less nostalgia and more accuracy

dubbed the decade "the Age of Golden Syrup." The growth
of the TV industry was sensational: 8,000 households had television sets in 1946, 5 million four years later, and 44 million in
1959. The significance of American TV was the viewing habit,
not the programs. As a historian of TV wrote: "Television
viewing is the evening's pastime, and it continues regardless
of content."[79]

Television swept away all competition in mass culture, and
reduced attendance at movies, baseball games, and restaurants. Because the viewers watched, they did not do other
things. They entertained, conversed, and worked around the
house less than they had before they bought TVs, and less than
others who did not own sets. They went to fewer parties and
dances while buying more liquor at package stores and less at
bars. TV dinners appeared in 1954 and some women cooked
less, buying the newly popular frozen foods in gigantic quan-
tities. Americans read fewer magazines. Because TV offered
its shorthand fifteen-minute version of the news—what politicians say and other disasters—increasing numbers relied on it,
and not newspapers, as their primary or only source of news.
But television, of course, also replaced language, ideas, and
analysis with pictures, required minimal attention, and thus
was only "half-observed." In 1952, 18 percent of the Americans
surveyed in a poll (compared to 55 percent in England) said
they were currently reading a book. In studies of metropolitan
New York and Bloomington, Indiana, half the population reported they no longer read books. At a time when 60 percent
of American men and three-quarters of the women could not
identify Karl Marx and 80 percent could not name the three
branches of government, the new television habit made masses
of Americans politically and culturally illiterate.[80]

A Roper poll found that "the new world of video is primarily a home-loving life."[81] This small screen seemed to be a
magnet for family "togetherness," a powerful bulwark to the
new, increasingly mute domesticity. Obviously viewers looked

at the set, not at each other. Conversation had become an intrusion, except for urgent matters: "The telephone's for you," or "Quiet, I can't hear."

No other mass-culture medium was as thoroughly commercialized from its inception as TV. Because the medium was the commercial, and because sales could be matched against advertising costs, the industry had a quantifiable index to prove its effectiveness. The electronic salesman first drew tens of millions of people into their living rooms and then sent them into the stores. Life now followed a somewhat different rhythm, orchestrated by Milton Berle, Lucille Ball, *Gunsmoke,* and the sponsors.

Seeking the largest possible number of shoppers as viewers, the TV producers intended to irritate no one and avoid controversy, while necessarily reflecting the shibboleths of the middle class, generally defined as represented by a twelve-year-old child with a below-average education. In 1949, for example, Faye Emerson became television's first female "personality" by interviewing talkative guests. More important, she wore low-cut gowns that held out the hope of a peek into paradise, thereby creating a "nationwide furore."[82]

Guns and bosoms, on the news as well as entertainment programs, were designed to trigger fantasies about social and individual potency, to depict solutions to the nagging deficiencies of real life. Family comedies, like the radio soaps of the thirties, reflected middle-class aspirations. In every case watching TV made the real home the center of private fantasy and semi-social laughter at a moment when American home life was not a laughing matter. In retreating from the complexities, frustrations, and satisfactions of the external world, Americans made more emotional demands on their immediate families and home life than could possibly be satisfied.

This increasingly absolute reliance of marriage partners on each other for all their emotional needs was, in its totalism, a relatively new challenge to increasingly brittle marriages. If I don't feel good it's your fault. This created a psychological dependency that led to a need for constant, unreasoning love, like idealized mother love, that would produce lifelong emotional security. Marriage was defined as chronic romance, not the best model for the psychologically dependent and needy children the adults were raising. (In the mid-eighties, six out of ten baby-boom daughters divorced when they reached their thirties.) Some psychiatrists found that unmarried women were happier than their married patients.[83] An enormous number of middle-class families had attained incomes that they had merely dreamed of only a few years before, and yet family difficulties not only remained but seemed to multiply. Everyone agreed that the problems of raising children, when they were not agglutinated to the tube, were becoming trickier. A decent and rising income, a private house and car seemed not to be sufficient ingredients, as they were supposed to be, for the good life. It was as if the solution, or near-solution, of the economic equation revealed an underlying psychological crisis. Glib critics called the fifties the age of anxiety, the aspirin age, or the age of passivity. Since many Americans had already accumulated an abundance of things, what went wrong?

By the 1950s, the rules for being a good parent had been rewritten and appropriated by a growing number of experts, including physicians, psychologists, counselors, teachers, social workers, juvenile courts, and newspaper columnists. Motherhood had become a profession requiring advanced study and credentials, along with never-ending vigilance not only over her child's behavior and development but over her own motives, feelings, and expert knowledge. She was obliged to conform to the "scientific" advice of others on whom she now depended. She assumed that on her own she would damage her child. *Newsweek*'s science editor commiserated with the modern mother, who, he said, was "untrained, vulnerable, insecure, young, inexperienced, and incompetent."[84] This was probably the world's first generation of mothers who were told—and believed—that they did not know what they were doing.

Dr. Spock's *Baby and Child Care,* published in 1946, became a textbook required by this new lack of self-confidence. His basic message was that mothers should work full-time at raising their babies and learn to trust their own instincts. But the modern mother could not follow either suggestion. Having endured the depression, war, and separation from the world of her parents, rising economically, this suburban mother was without tradition, without an organizing vision of life, and could raise but not educate her children. Her state was a consequence of her immediate family's mobility and freedom. Her need for authority and external validation led her to rely upon experts to lead her through parenthood. She wanted to be a rational mother. Because she equated her rootlessness with freedom, she prided herself on providing a better, more reasonable world for her children than what she remembered as her own closed and unenlightened childhood.

Every aspect of American culture seemingly conspired to convince the new parents that they could raise happier children than they themselves had been. The new credo was simple: old-fashioned parental authority would stunt the authenticity, creativity, and spontaneity of the child, who would positively bloom under the gentle care of democratic parents carefully tuned to the subtlest vibration from the newly imperial infant.

The professionalization of parenthood left some mothers with a kind of distanced, detached love to extend to their offspring, while the mother's own emotional dependency prevented her from disciplining the child. She depended on the infant's love as much as the child needed hers. Made up entirely of the present, her world and her role focused on the emotional needs of the children. Her best hope for their future was naturally defined in emotional terms, that they should be happy. In place of teaching and training—and restraining—the child, some parents, to retain their own youthful appearance and attitudes, tried to become their children by adopting the youngsters' clothing, slang, and music.

In a world of feelings, of disparate facts without knowledge, there was not much such a family could teach. Without knowledge of the past, of alternative ways of living, the parents could not evaluate or resist the present. Consumed by work, measuring itself against like-minded friends and neighbors, this family could not transmit to the young what it did not have: a coherent moral vision, a sense of what ought to be. It could not explain. It had no book of light in which it believed. Bombarded by incoherent facts, this family was necessarily reduced to the futile hope that someone else, teachers perhaps, would fill the void that only the family could occupy. But this family, of course including the children, did not know what to believe. It stayed afloat on information not knowledge, training not education, specialization not the humanizing quest for the answer to the question why.[85]

Rejecting conflict as an anachronism, such parents resorted to a thousand manipulative subterfuges, including bribery, to induce the child to change his demands. Christopher Lasch, the cultural historian, persuasively argued that this parental abdication of adulthood destroyed "the generational continuity on which every culture depends," as it also undermined the children's initiative and self-reliance. The adults' self-loathing was symptomatic of a grave social and individual pathology, obviously not universal but sufficiently widespread to be more than a clue to the culture at large.

The suburban home was designed as a sanctuary from a dangerous world, but it functioned as a nursery that tyrannized the willing mother. The denial of this reality led to the mawkish celebrations of "togetherness" (the name of a commercial campaign started by *McCall's* magazine in 1954) and to a massive desire to conform to external standards: those of the community, school, peers, neighbors, church, mass advertising, or any other socially approved external agency. Living according to the expectations of others reduced or distorted the mother's love as she marched mechanically through the day performing obligatory rather than felt duties, and refused to submit her breasts to the deformation she feared from her child.

Frenetic "activities"—Cub Scouts, Little League, ballet lessons, visits to the orthodonist—consumed the mother-as-chauffeur along with the children, and motion replaced the sort of healthy parental strength and affection that rests on self-confidence. Instead, these parents aspired to become their kids' best friend. By wanting something else, by finding best buddies elsewhere, such children could tyrannize their parents. A psychiatrist at the time called for "a father or mother who can say 'No' without going through an elaborate song and dance."[86] What was missing in this new child-centered world was not the arbitrary paternalistic authority of the past, but an enlightened adult authority necessary for children's development. But the emotional dependency of parents on their children made responsible authority impossible. The very idea of authority conjured up the past from which these free Americans had fled.

Except for her candor and understanding, Maxine Schnall seems to have been a typical fifties mother. In retrospect she believed that she became a mother when she was too young because she thought it was expected of her. Reflecting on her relationship with her daughters, she explained:

> I rationalized my inability to say "no" to their demands, even if it was clearly in their best interests to oppose them, on the grounds of enlightenment. I thought I was promoting the full flowering of their initiative and creativity. Yet I was aware that, in my older daughter's case, there were times when I was handing her a power over me that she neither wanted nor was ready to handle. . . . My own sense of self was so shaky that I couldn't stand *their* withdrawal of love.[87]

She fled not from the frustration of her children, but from her fear of the possible emotional penalty her children would exact for her authority.

In the absence of the father, the mother's behavior encouraged the child to exaggerate his importance, even omnipotence, as he fantasized about replacing the absent father. Such a child could do this through another fantasy about becoming famous or notorious by accomplishing some wildly dramatic and unattainable goal. This child was profoundly or pathologically confused about the lines between his own sense of self and the outer world, was transfixed by celebrity, could not sustain friendship, and detested competition. He longed for but avoided love.[88]

Obviously, the behavior of children born in the 1940s and growing in such a hothouse would change. Early in the century, in response to urbanization and mobility, the institution of dating replaced courtship. In the twenties and thirties dating was designed to display a wholesale popularity, a public competitive advantage, that was not intended to lead to marriage. "The modern girl," according to *Good Housekeeping* (1940), "cultivates not one single suitor, but dates lots of them. . . . Her aim is not a too obvious romance but general popularity."

After World War II, when for the first time women outnumbered men, adolescents began to "go steady," and their "steadies" became a haven from the competitiveness of American life, a way to satisfy young people's hunger for security. But having a "steady," especially for the precocious ten-year-old, obviously did not portend marriage. Going steady was an opportunity to play the roles of marriage without a long-term commitment. The characteristic form of going steady was a series of exclusive arrangements that permitted the partners to avoid the possibly tormenting competition of dating. With marvelously tangled logic, going steady proved one's popularity. About 70 percent of a national sample disapproved of going steady, but by 1959 a poll revealed that 57 percent of the nation's teenagers were doing so. Many parents complained that their teenage children were boring, "square," and "middle-aged."[89] Apparently parents could not see that some of their kids were following their own example by trying to avoid risk.

Nonetheless, one of the middle class's obsessions was with the new, incomprehensible, and ominous antics of young people. From the middle of the war until the mid-fifties, the nation was deluged with warnings and wailings about the rise of juvenile delinquency. The contemporary comprehensive high school, mixing social classes from different residential neighborhoods, was dimly viewed as the headquarters where the culture of barbarians—working-class, black—would defile the more delicate rituals of the middle class. Movies and comic books were blamed for the reported increase in violence. The Senate held ponderous inquiries, and the nation's sullen guardians lectured and scolded.

Toward the end of the decade, this shocking younger generation seemed a little less threatening, perhaps because of an intuition of what was behind the hula hoops, Davy Crockett caps, rock and roll, hot rods, and even alcohol. Although millions of teenagers worked during the war, the New Deal's child-labor legislation had signaled that Americans wanted their children in school. Postwar affluence created the first generation of adolescents who did not work, and high school attendance for every class and age group rose dramatically. The nation's producers and merchants began to understand that they were confronted with a potentially luscious new phenomenon—a distinct youth group, a separate culture, which, if approached properly, could create exciting new consumers. It is not surprising that this new world of teenagers was so closely identified with its toys, including Elvis Presley's recordings. Replicas of Crockett's coonskins added up to $100 million in sales. Obviously, the "delinquents" influenced purchases beyond the $9.5 billion spending money they carried in their own jeans pockets in 1959. A consultant to American business explained what was happening in terms the middle class would understand: "If you can buy as an adult, you are an adult."[90]

What frightened parents and others was that the advertisers, especially on television, interjected themselves between parents and their children. This was new, and the teenagers defended themselves by accusing their democratic parents of being old-fashioned and preventing their children from being popular or even being accepted by their friends. Baby-boom children could resist parental authority, yield to group pressure, and contribute to the nation's economic growth. The fact is that the mass culture of the young was a money-making enterprise.[91] When this was realized, however dimly, the children seemed less delinquent, even if increasingly bad-mannered.

The white-collar American male, like men during their transition away from manual work in other cultures, underwent a cultural transformation that was exceedingly difficult to absorb. He was losing the ancient mantle of masculine authority at home and at work, not because of the demands of women, but because of the nature of his family and his work. The clearest expression of the psychological and cultural costs of economic progress came when an individual moved from traditional "man's work" into the white-collar world of the office. Frank Rissarro, a pseudonym created by the researchers who told his story, was a third-generation, middle-aged bank clerk who lived in a Boston suburb. A high-school dropout, he had worked hard for two decades as a meat-cutter. The availability of work during the fifties convinced him to apply for a low-level job in a bank, processing, but not making decisions about, loan applications. He realized that by most standards he was a success: "I know I did a good job in my life," is the way he put it. He wore a suit to work and was able to buy many desirable objects. But he was ashamed of his work: "These jobs aren't real work where you make something—it's just pushing papers." To gain the respect of others, including his family, he had moved up in the world, at the cost of losing respect for himself.[92]

An increasingly democratic family and a bureaucratic job

gave others, including his children, unfamiliar control over him. By his own transitional values—admiring the stronger men of the past while striving to be a gentler, more sensitive, democratic man—he accepted the fact that he was in his own eyes becoming diminished.

The generation of upper-middle-class men who graduated from college in the early thirties knew that they wanted to make money but they were not wedded to the ways they would go about it. In fact, their charging ambition led them to change jobs often. They accepted risks, and some even sought adventure, believing that one good break would lead to another. Far wealthier and more secure than their fathers had been in the depression, the privileged graduates of the fifties were in a greater hurry, not to leave a mark on the world, but to occupy the precise economic niche that they had already defined for themselves while in school. They restricted their aspirations to the middle ground, to comfort and some sort of inner equilibrium that apparently would be disturbed by ambition. A Harvard senior explained why he had decided not to go to medical school: "I think contentment is the main thing." A Princeton senior went even further: "In fifteen years I look forward to a constant level of happiness." They were equally specific about the kind of wife necessary for their chronic happiness: "She shouldn't be submissive, she can be independent on little things, but the big decisions will have to go my way . . . the marriage must be the most important thing that ever happened to her."[93]

When the middle-class male arrived at his office, he found himself in an unfamiliar and threatening world. Like three-quarters of the American middle class, he was an employee. Most suburbanites were professionals, bureaucrats, small businessmen, salesmen, or skilled workers. If the suburban husband's dream came true he worked for a large corporation, the kind that he assumed would not go broke in hard times and offered the most generous insurance and pension plans. He was more or less aware of the fact that the road to his success was radically different from what he had been taught as a boy. He could not behave like the swashbuckling businessmen of the past. A senior at Princeton was explicit: "Let's face it, I'll be on salary, not making capital gains, even at 36. . . . Why struggle on my own when I can enjoy the big psychological income of being a member of a big outfit?" The child of an immigrant had to acknowledge that he did not have his father's nerve, required for going it alone as a farmer, pushcart peddler, independent craftsman, or speculator in stocks and bonds. For the son of the middle class, immigrant or not, success meant a promotion, not a killing in the market.[94]

The bureaucratic employee's fate depended on pleasing his supervisor, not on making a better mousetrap. Because his necessary aim was to please, he learned that the "personality" he displayed was his best and only weapon. In his relationship to his supervisor he was required to play the role of a fifties wife, subordinate, ingratiating, and devious. He had to "sell himself," and if he was liked, well liked, he and his family might be secure. Along with Arthur Miller, the sociologist C. Wright Mills spotted this trend at the beginning of the fifties: "The main chance now becomes a series of small calculations, stretched over the working lifetime of the individual: a bureaucracy is no testing field for heroes."[95] As personality replaced character, the struggle to survive was transformed into the struggle to be liked. William H. Whyte baptized the fifties bureaucrat as "the organization man." Corridor politics became essential to advancement, so powerlessness, fragility, and anxiety were likely consequences. Before the war no one had been brought up to think of the American breadwinner in such terms.

At least the father would be home on the weekends, in his own safe house in the green fields of suburbia, where he could escape from his impersonal office to the warm love of his family. He could cozy up to what F. Scott Fitzgerald called "a fresh green breast of the new world," a pastless world in which older ways of thinking would not interfere with his growing need for comfort and security. He could be healed from the week's humiliations, the wounds of modern bureaucratic work. His wife could nurse him back to functioning strength while the baby's bottle was propped on a pillow in the crib.

The emerging middle-class male adjusted to his family by surrendering, by retreating from guiding and disciplining his children, and by regressing to an infantile and ambiguous sexual relationship with his wife. Because the wife was responsible for home and family, she was also accountable for her husband's happiness. Some things belonged to her, but she belonged to him. In the early fifties, Erik Erikson observed that the modern male, "while exhibiting the necessary toughness in business, is shy in his intimate relationships and does not expect to be treated with much consideration at home."[96]

A case study, appropriately reported in *Woman's Home Companion* and appropriately entitled "I Thought I Married a Man," illustrates the domestic regression, the emotional malformation, of the modern American husband. Dr. David R. Mace, the chairman of the International Commission on Marriage Guidance, recounted the marital problems of Walter and Marion. Walter had just been passed over for the presidency of his company, and Marion tried to talk him out of his sulking. He became furious and found his way to Dr. Mace. Walter explained that "along with the strain of my work and responsibility, I'm finding my situation at home more than I can bear." He told Dr. Mace that Marion was cold and had never been sexually responsive. "He had dreamed of a wife who would be loving and tender." He said he was starving for love. Reared by his comforting, undemanding, and reassuring mother, he expected his wife to play the same role. But Walter now believed his wife had a "split personality" and needed therapy.

Marion agreed to see the doctor. She explained that her husband was professionally successful and had a "strong persuasive personality." He was clever, knew his job, was determined, and "incurably ambitious." But he "hasn't the first idea of how to live with a woman. He alternates between being a bully and a baby." He was ignorant about sex, about a woman's needs, and he refused to talk about it. In fact, he was "rather prudish." She elaborated: "He doesn't know how to give love. He does the routine things—but in an awkward perfunctory way, like a schoolboy. He seems to want to behave like a child. It's odd. When I think of his power and influence over men, I can't understand why he should want to be babied at home."

She had refused to coddle Walter, fearing he would become still more dependent and immature. She did not want a divorce, because she was afraid of loneliness, enjoyed her standard of living, and still felt a little affection for her husband. He refused to acknowledge that he had contributed in any way to his marital storms; instead, it was all Marion's fault. At Dr. Mace's suggestion she began to yield a little, to pet her husband, and to everyone's surprise he was so appreciative they did not divorce. She resigned herself to the fact that her husband could not be an independent adult.[97]

The modern man attributed his lack of active interest in sex to fatigue from work. At the office he still displayed competence, if not mastery, and he understood that it was his function to make money. If he had not risen from poverty himself, he was usually the child of impoverished immigrants or a depression family and, in either case, was familiar with his father's struggle, which he now idealized. The old man became a hero, whose funeral was a procession toward his son's future: commuting, accumulating, and lowering his own aspirations. Now that the man of the fifties had money, probably more than his father, his bank balance—not strength or courage—became his measure of manhood. He tried to convince himself that money meant strength, yet the old man had had something else, a presence to which others responded, moral clarity, and indisputable authority. Capable at work and regressive at home, the modern man was caught in a confusing tangle of cultural myths over a manhood that he could not personify or even approve of, but whose imperatives might continue to drive him, partly because he did not know what to put in their place.

For the men of postwar America the memory or myth of a strong father or grandfather shaped the son's perceptions. By braving the ocean and the new world, building American industry, and reconstructing the nation with their own strong hands, these older men loomed in their sons' memories as heroes, not as the wretched of the earth, and certainly not as schlemiels. "When my kids start complaining," a struggling steamfitter reported, "I tell them they should know what their grandfather went through." Far from embarrassing the sons, the poverty of the older generation was now a source of pride, the benchmark proving how much had been endured and how far the grandsons had come.[98]

The grandfathers and some of the aging fathers were America's last representatives of a simpler and more coherent moral code, whether opposing blacks in the South, defending religion and the old ways in the ghetto, or asserting Yankee certitude of the world's order and God's grateful approval. They were, in Erik Erikson's language, "masterly and cruel with good conscience, disciplined and pious without loss of self-esteem." For the men of the fifties, the grandfather—the father's masculinity might have been whipped by the depression—grew in stature to become the standard of maleness: active, powerful, confident, and masterful. Such "mastery persists in their grandsons as a stubborn, and angry sense of superiority. Overtly inhibited, they yet can accept others only on terms of prearranged privilege."[99] Although they had surrendered the house and the children to the wife, these husbands would not relinquish control of their wives, which might be exercised by appealing to the authority of the masculine tradition they were losing.

In the fifties, the American male lost the battle between cultural myths and personal reality. A white-collar employee relying on charm at the office, he could no longer lay claim to traditional manhood. He was not a hunter, farmer, or soldier,

and could not use his hands. He was neither self-sufficient nor
proud of his physical power. By himself, he could not protect
himself or his family. The new man often needed his wife's
help to bring home enough bacon. Playing the wife's role at
work and the child's role at home, the modern man was losing
masculinity and responsibility. The middle-class American man
was becoming androgynous without resentment. A potential
victim at work, in the streets, and perhaps even at home,
standing in line to see a John Wayne movie, he realized that
his father's funeral was a tragedy, not a liberation.

Arthur Miller understood the power of the strong ancestor's
ghost. Willy Loman's older, adventurous brother, the old
man's authentic heir, tells Willy about their father. "Father
was a very great and a very wild-hearted man. We start in
Boston, and he'd toss the whole family into the wagon, and
then he'd drive the team right across the country." Willy, slipping toward his inevitable destruction and sensing that his
salesman's life and occupational dreams were finished, always
knew that selling was unmanly. But this was knowledge he
could not live by. To locate his pride and manhood, he built
things in his house. "A man," the salesman boasted, "who
can't handle tools is not a man."[100]

In the opening pages of *Growing Up Absurd,* a book that became a guide to the perplexed youth of the sixties, Paul Goodman declared, "It's hard to grow up when there isn't enough
man's work." He defined "man's work" so simply that he
thought a clever boy would understand it more readily than
adults: "To produce necessary food and shelter is man's
work."[101] Regardless of how well it paid, the world of bureaucratic work was an assault on the meaning of masculine labor
that began when God condemned Adam to sweat. Antiperspi-
rants became popular when men no longer sweated.

On the other hand, lower-middle-class males, whose work
and family responsibilities were not as sexually ambiguous,
represented a different cultural reality. Their work was still
connected to a definition of honest labor retained from the past

even as their unions succeeded in improving pay packages and mechanization increasingly eased the physical demands made on them. Nonetheless, many remained faithful to aspects of the old ethnic values. They did not, indeed could not, permit their wives to work. The man close to the margin of class differentiation, fearful of slipping, believed that his manhood would be compromised if he had to "send his wife to work" because he could not "provide for the family" on his own. The nation's factory workers, small farmers, policemen, bus drivers, mailmen, and soldiers perceived the white-collar male as something of a traitor to his sex. From this perspective the white-collar man was soft, undependable, essentially useless if not a direct economic threat in the form of politicians, lawyers, accountants, government bureaucrats, and especially doctors.

The more traditional blue-collar men came to see their affluent brothers as mincing and weak in every way save one: they were capable of deflecting the nation from its tested traditions, its very soul. Made up of bleeding hearts, more concerned for blacks and foreigners than for decent white American workers, the white-collar men were coming to be viewed as traitors to the nation because they were traitors to their sex. The man of the threatened lower middle class assumed that it took a strong and independent American male to uphold the real nation. The increasingly affluent middle-class gentlemen could not deliver. From the blue-collar perspective the nation was being riven by the emergence of a rigged conflict between themselves, real but culturally marginal men, and fake but politically influential men.

For the white-collar middle class, blue-collar masculinity was primitive and linked to superannuated cultural and political values. Blue-collar males assumed that white-collar men did not really work for a living, were not bone-tired after a day of sitting in a chair, and so did not value honest labor. The blue-collar man struggled with economic precariousness, which led to a compensatory cultural rigidity. The white-collar man grappled with the loss of masculine self-esteem in the context of an unappreciative family and boss. As white-collar men became somewhat contemptuous, blue-collar men became increasingly resentful. This mutual rejection would eventually explode into political warfare, played out not strictly in economic terms, but as a cultural conflict whose goal was no less than the definition of what it meant to be a man, an American man.

Middle-class sons could learn to both love and despise their powerless, sedentary fathers. *Rebel Without a Cause,* an influential movie of 1955, focused on the comfortably middle-class Stark family and on the son's (James Dean's) rage at the father's social impotence, especially toward his wife. The son is lost, wanders in quest of an alternative to his father's weakness, and experiments with masculine strength. At the end his father offers the boy the best consolation he can imagine: "I'll try and be as strong as . . . as you want me to be."[102]

The assault on adult authority in the family spread to America's industries, and for the same reasons. The culture of motherhood understood itself as therapeutic and defined problems as little illnesses, usually psychological, that would yield to "cures," not conflict, logic, or politics. Psychology displaced politics, and a form of personal introspection substituted for institutional change. If this was true of human relations within the family, it was also true of human relations elsewhere, especially in America's business bureaucracies. In 1946 Henry Ford II announced: "If we can solve the problem of human relations in industrial production, we can make as much progress toward lower costs in the next 10 years as we made during the past quarter century through the development of the machinery of mass production."[103]

What America's senior management wanted was a "cure" for the familiar problems of absenteeism, turnover, low morale and productivity, and trouble with unions. It believed that psychology and sociology held the keys to the kingdom. Across the nation the most powerful corporations installed a variety of therapeutic schemes to increase employees' contentment. Personal counseling, noncash incentives, more sensitive communications, friendliness instead of hierarchical power, and dozens of other psychological strategies were seized upon to cure employees of their bad and expensive habits.

The fifties were preeminently the time for creating the appearance of a humanized bureaucracy. This was to be accomplished by convincing employees that management really cared about their psychological health. Thus power was given a prettier face, consensus became a universally desired goal, and therapy at work augmented therapy in the home. Manipulation was now powerfully established everywhere that mattered, and it always described the enemy as antiquated authoritarianism.[104] It appeared that the social and family fathers were being killed every day.

At home and at work aspirations centered on adjustment, not change. To grouse at a world that seemed fundamentally good was to risk appearing neurotic, not justifiably angry at injustice. When therapy (adjustment) displaced politics (struggle over resources), the status quo was invested with the authority that individuals were losing. In the therapeutic environment, no individual, and certainly not the non-directive psychiatrists, could resolve conflict. The sovereignty of the self required the displacement of external authority, as both mental health and middle-class democracy supposedly required. The collapse of authority, legitimate or oppressive, began with the search for therapy in the 1950s, not the protests of the 1960s. The struggle of men and women to redefine who and what they were would, in the following decade, be interrupted by the children, who had their own case to make.

These were the children in school in the fifties, a time when the nation faced a staggering shortage of teachers and facilities as the baby-boomers began to make their way into the schools. Americans were forced to admit they did not know how to educate the young. Some believed that progressive education, after its triumphs in the interwar period, had degenerated into a mere sect and was dying of hardening of the arteries.[105] But the "professional educationists" were still entrenched, especially in teachers' unions and schools of education. In 1957, they were blamed for the Soviet Union's victorious launching of *Sputnik*, the world's first artificial satellite. In a national torrent of self-abuse Americans suddenly awoke to the crisis of the schools because *Sputnik* evidently proved that Russians were smarter and more serious. This Cold War contest unified the nation, inspired the President to propose legislation, and imbued PTAs with a new purpose: reform the schools before it was too late, before the alarming mediocrity of the nation's young people permanently crippled the nation.

Many Americans agreed that their schools were too soft because of too much emphasis on therapy or "life adjustment," and not enough on physics and foreign languages. By the fifties the passion of progressivism had become domesticated into a focus on adjustment to the family, the community, the nation, the status quo. Teaching and learning had deteriorated into "a group process" in which the brilliant, cantankerous, or eccentric had no place. Courses in "Basic Living" or "Common Learnings" became the new educational chic. In some school districts all textbooks were eliminated as part of the search to make learning fun. But Admiral Hyman Rickover suggested that courses in love and marriage might not be essential: "You can learn how to make love outside of school in the good old-fashioned ways."[106] What the admiral failed to understand was that "happiness" was an acceptable substitute for competence and achievement.

As a special feature in *Life* magazine tried to show, Soviet children went to school to work hard, not to have fun. The article contrasted a day in the life of Stephen, an average anti-intellectual eleventh-grader in Chicago, with that of Alexei, a tenth-grader at Moscow's School 49. Alexei read Shakespeare and Shaw while Stephen had just finished *Kidnapped*. Alexei went to school six days a week to learn Russian literature, sixth-year English, fifth-year physics, fourth-year chemistry, mathematics, and astronomy. His homework took more than three hours a night, and his teachers were well trained and ran their classes with full authority. He had only recently made his first shy advances to a pretty girl in his class, but he seemed to prefer playing chess and going to concerts.

In contrast, Stephen met Penny, his steady girlfriend, every morning, just before his typing class. He also took English, history, geometry, and biology, but his studies were less advanced than Alexei's work. "In English," *Life* reported about Stephen's school, "students seldom bother to read assigned books and sometimes make book reports based on comic book condensations." But Stephen did throw himself into nonacademic activities with interest and verve. He was the school's star swimmer and a leader in student affairs. Because this took so much time, his teachers believed, he was behind in math and the rest of his grades were poor.[107]

Life's article provoked a national outcry. A man from Illinois wrote: "As long as Steve has a chick like Penny and Alexei has homework, I figure that Steve is the winner." A woman from New Jersey: "Count the smiles of the Russians and those of the Americans. Surely this must be worth something." An association of high school principals urged a boycott of *Life*. Spencer Brown, a teacher in a private school in New York City, had heard all of this before. Dismayed over the simple-minded criticisms, he wearily concluded: "What purports to be criticism of American education is merely [*sic*] criticism of America."[108]

Just so. More than those of any other nation, America's schools reflected what the community wanted. The schools could not afford to ignore the preferences of tax-paying parents, organized or not. Though 80 percent of the principals polled realized their schools demanded too little from the students, only half of the parents agreed, and some thought that too much work was already required.[109] The values of the American middle class dictated that children's happiness should not be disturbed by the imposition of discipline, a regimen explicitly rejected in the democratic family. Smiles must be worth something. The modern parent's aspiration for well-adjusted, fun-loving children conflicted with academic standards, and the schools could not overcome this even if they wanted to, which they did not. The absurd preparation of uneducated teachers in schools of education produced the "experts" who would, as many parents wished, pacify the youngsters.

As in education, so in religion. The nation congratulated itself over what many assumed was a religious revival in the 1950s. The apparent religiosity of President Eisenhower and John Foster Dulles, the Secretary of State, seemed to reflect a spiritual stirring in the people. But so acute an observer as Reinhold Niebuhr concluded at the time that "religious emotions," not religion, were what was catching fire.[110] Religion in America became faith in religion, any religion. The bumper sticker of the moment proclaimed: "The family that prays together stays together." Just as there were to be no failures in the schools, there were to be no losers in the domesticated religiosity of the fifties. In both instances, the acceptance of a standard against which to judge performance would have injected into polite discourse an unwanted authority of the past. The middle class would have none of it. If the price of mental health was that the winner's laurel was given to every participant, that evidently was good for democracy and the achievement of happiness.

More people said they attended church and believed in God. The American Legion led a movement "Back to God." The Pledge of Allegiance was placed "under God." For the first time dollar bills sang "In God We Trust." In twelve states agnostics could not become notary publics, and in most states they could not adopt children. This faith in faith was obviously a cold-war weapon against atheistic communism. But at its heart it too devolved into therapy, a compensatory cult of reassurance, a spiritualizing of the American need for the happy end. Faith's message was the need to adjust to other people, institutions, and the national credo.

The Reverend Norman Vincent Peale catapulted to fame by preaching *The Power of Positive Thinking*. Drive-in churches brought the American automotive icon directly into worship, suburban churches sprouted across the nation, and, in the spirit of suburban homogeneity, ecumenical intermarriages threatened the ethnic identities of the immigrants' children. Most of all, evangelical preachers on TV and in tented revival meetings appealed to southern and western Protestants, who "decided for Christ" in gratitude for healing, reassurance, and patriotism. The vulgarization of religion was not new, but its mass marketing was. As the religious soup was watered beyond recognition, Americans needed stability, yearned to belong to something, anything acceptable. The need was deep to find solace and pride by participating in the mass celebration of individual goodness and ultimate reward.[III] In this economy of salvation, like the family and schools, there was no shame.

There had always been crosswinds. The vacuity of television culture, the religion of reassurance, affluence itself, and the growing complacency of the middle class offended a few people. *Father Knows Best* and *Leave It to Beaver* represented perfect middle-class families, cozy at home and in thought. They dispensed comfort to their viewers at a level that could, and occasionally did, induce gagging. They could also inspire some children to decide *"not* to grow up to be Robert Young," once they recognized that there was a different world out there. The middle-class pursuit and achievement of comfort could seem suffocating, not only to well-known critics, but to some of the carefully nurtured children of the middle class itself. Even parental care could seem overripe, rancid. A few quietly thoughtful young Americans believed that shopping was not life's purpose, that privilege for some, even most, did not justify or explain injustice elsewhere. But it was difficult to resist what seemed like universal middle-class contentment. How to fight a fog? Writer Marge Piercy remembered what it was like: "To live in the fifties and think that the way this society distributes money, power, resources, prestige, and dirty work was wrong was to stand up in a stadium during a football game and attempt to read aloud a poem."[112]

That is precisely what the beatniks did. They organized their lives around sex and drugs and roaring up and back across the country. Because they were scruffy, obscene, and funny, they made riveting copy for the popular magazines. Partly a joke, although potentially dangerous, Jack Kerouac and his tiny band of wild men were recognized as a cultural shadow in this time of apparent middle-class harmony. Allen Ginsberg, however, was no joke. When he published *Howl* in the mid-fifties, he made it known that he was watching, keeping a cultural scorecard:

> I saw the best minds of my generation destroyed by madness, starving hysterical naked. . . .
> who were burned alive in their innocent flannel suits on Madison Avenue amid blasts of leaden verse & the tanked-up clatter of the iron regiments of fashion & the nitroglycerine shrieks of the fairies of advertising & the mustard gas of sinister intelligent editors, or were run down by the drunken taxicabs of Absolute Reality.[113]

Nevertheless, in January 1960, *Look* magazine published a poll that revealed all was right with the world. Most Americans were satisfied, expected their standard of living to improve every year, and believed that God was pleased with them. The opinions of adolescents reflected those of their parents. The curtain falls with the dream glowing: Americans "naturally expect to go on enjoying their peaceable, plentiful existence—right through the sixties and maybe forever."[114]

5

CULTURE
WAR

The 1960s appalled parents whose children were lost in sex and drugs, children whose middle-class parents were locked into a bureaucratic and uncomprehending world, blacks frustrated over the stalled civil rights movement, whites enraged by city riots, embattled young people protesting an escalating war, draftees' parents surrounded by antiwar protests, presidents afraid to leave the White House, and rioting police. The middle years of the decade were bad enough, but 1968 was inconceivable. For the first time a majority of Americans actively turned against a war in progress. In this exhausting year, Americans witnessed the Tet offensive, President Johnson's abandonment of power, the murders of two national leaders, the surrealistic Democratic convention, and misleading whispers about Richard Nixon's "secret plan" to end the war.

The middle-class compulsion to be reasonable, exercise control, and maintain order was of course exploded. The economy continued to boom, and parents might have hoped for some continuation of the surface calm of the fifties, perhaps finally somewhat aware of the strains and agonies of that deceptively quiet time. But now a curtain was raised, and the isolated, personal strains of that era erupted into a full-scale national convulsion. Suddenly, it seemed, everyone had become a passionate member of some psychosexual, racial, or political camp.

Parents were forced to choose. If they followed the lead of their rebellious children, they could slip into the unaccustomed role of advocating social change. If they disapproved of the demonstrations, riots, and new talk of freedoms, if they stuck to their last, they ran the risk of losing their children, defending the war, attacking the welfare system, resenting the progress and demands of blacks, detesting what they perceived to be the flaunting of female sexuality and male irresponsibility, especially in regard to the war, and usually feeling powerless in the process. But middle-class parents knew they could keep their sons out of Vietnam by exploiting student deferments, and perhaps some understood the implications of their privileges for poorer families and their sons.

The sheer number of young people made the sixties different, indeed even discontinuous. In the past, as more Americans lived longer, the proportion of the young had been decreasing. By the sixties the babies of the boom were growing up and swamping the nation. By way of comparison, in the 1920s the number of Americans between 18 and 24 years old increased by .19 percent; in the forties it fell by .03 percent. But the increase from 1960 to 1970 was an engulfing 53 percent, an addition of over 8.5 million people, more than the combined increases of the rest of the century. For the first time in two hundred years the proportion of young to old increased.[1]

The baby-boomers had lived with the boom throughout their young lives (and still do). They were jammed together in nursery schools, pediatricians' offices, schools, and at the movies, bowling alleys, dances, and drive-ins. For them life was a crush, and the fear of anonymity was pervasive.[2] The need to express individuality—to locate personal authenticity and be sincere and noticed—became irresistible. Anything was better than invisibility.

The inescapable crowds had two effects: first, quantity validated the young as important, and led them to make political or cultural statements based on the numbers they could amass. Businessmen continued to drool over the economic resources of the teenage market, and teenagers recognized the impact of their collective decisions on adults. It was inevitable that mass demonstrations, including mammoth rock concerts, became the collective signature of this generation. The second result was the need to stand out and be separate in ways that demonstrated solidarity with the culture of youth. Eager to exhibit the symbols of belonging, they all looked as if they came from the same cookie cutter of dress and behavior. The fears of anonymity dissolved before the exhilarating prospect of closing ranks against what was vaguely referred to as the enemy, the clean-cut, corseted, and starched middle class.

Whatever their other confusions, however, the children were certain that they knew better than their parents how to reorder human relations. They declared that their elders did not know how to love or live. At best, the older generation may have known better, but it did not live by what it knew. The parents were too often hypocritical, so the young would base their relationships on honesty, a central rallying cry. They could make a sport or a religion out of sex, but they insisted that, unlike older people, they would not sell out, betray their principles, or allow fear of public (the older public) approval to influence them. They called this freedom and integrity, attributes of which they said their elders were either ignorant or afraid.

Four different cultural wars, sometimes overlapping and mutually supportive, sometimes not, defined the decade: the redefinition of conventional morality, civil rights, radicalism, and alienation. Together and separately they were called "the movement." All were a direct repudiation of middle-class values and achievement. Each battle was an extension of earlier struggles, and a common state of mind connected them. They all demanded greater flexibility, revaluation of the past's usefulness, suspicion of established institutional and personal authority, trust only in peers, refusal to accept previous middle-class dictates of living, dressing, eating, and loving, and a commitment to greater democracy and equality, if not for outsiders from a different class, race, or age, then at least for one another, although movement women continued to be subordinate.

Most upsetting to the culture's custodians was the new morality and its fashions. Next in line was the stunted civil rights movement, and political radicalism had the least impact then and later. (This ranking would be reversed if the criterion were intellectual, not cultural, significance.) For the middle class, nothing was as disturbing as long hair, short skirts, reports of orgies, drug use, and other evidence that the younger generation was destroying itself. Parents became increasingly bewildered, then despairing or angry. For instance, one runaway daughter finally telephoned to say she was working in New York, but would not give her father an address or phone number. The mother took the phone and the daughter immediately said, "It's okay, Mother, I'm being a good girl." The father despaired that "she thinks we're more concerned about her chastity than we are about her as a person."[3]

It was not just that the young were not supporting the country's presidents, who, the elders continued to believe, knew best, or that they even disagreed with their own parents; this time the young's disaffection appeared different from usual youthful rebellion. This time, it seemed, some of the wayward young were becoming traitors, killing themselves with drugs, or turning into barbarians who could never recover from their ignorance, inarticulateness, and sloth. In the eyes of their elders, the young had become scornful and obscene and needed a bath; from the perspective of the young, the older generation had become a threat to freedom and, by supporting the war in Vietnam, to life itself.

Late in 1959, when life still seemed ordered and etiquette was not considered a disguise for power, *Newsweek* magazine declared it was rare for high school students to have sex because "most girls" refused. Furthermore, there would be no future sexual or social difficulties beneath the ferns in this repressed paradise. "Rebel?" asked one boy. "What have we got to rebel about?" A cabinet secretary somehow knew that "97 per cent of our youth by every standard are good."[4] An object small enough to hide in a purse would soon disturb this false sense of peace.

On May 11, 1960, the Food and Drug Administration approved the G. D. Searle pharmaceutical company's application to produce the world's first oral contraceptive. This was the first medicine designed for long-term, nonmedical use by people who were not ill. By its hormonal effect the pill ingeniously tricked the woman's body into thinking it was pregnant so it stopped ovulating.[5] For the first time a woman could feel reliably freed from the tyranny of anatomy in her intimate life. In decoupling sex and procreation, the pill gave women a wider range of choice and control. All the other contraceptive devices and schemes—diaphragms, foams and gels, condoms, withdrawal, rhythm—were apparent to the partner, but the pill could be the woman's secret, and she now was potentially less vulnerable and more autonomous. But, because she was now deprived of the major reason to say no to her mate, she faced greater pressure to be sexually active.

Even so, the pill freed women to accept and assert their sexuality, to demand recognition as human beings with sexual appetites no less pronounced than men's. This realization affirmed earlier acceptance of female sexuality, but it also moved beyond the adolescent postwar fixation on nourishing and comforting breasts. Now the complete woman was more human and also more dangerous than before. The pill represented an enormous advance in the emancipation of women, arguably the largest single step ever taken, not only because it afforded greater sexual freedom, but because it permitted women to regulate or forgo childbirth altogether in favor of pursuing jobs or careers.

The pill's primary beneficiaries were middle-class, as were most advocates of women's alleged asexuality. Responding to a *Good Housekeeping* survey, most women disapproved of giving the pill to unmarried women, not because they favored motherhood but because they disapproved of sex for single people. For them, the future of America was at stake. A comment from a woman in Washington State spoke for millions of Americans everywhere: "If this nation doesn't begin living the way God intended us to, we are lost."[6]

By 1965, 42 percent of married women aged fifteen to twenty-nine were on the pill. Before the scare in 1970 about side effects, including cancer, 8.5 million American women depended on it. Like others, Catholic women hurried to get prescriptions. They knew that the alternative to what their priest probably called sin was yet another baby, and their choice was clear if not easy. By the mid-sixties, about two-thirds as many Catholic women as Protestants used the pill.[7]

Preaching and posturing against the pill became not only pointless but damaging to the authority of church and state. A Catholic priest realized that "the moralizers got so out of touch . . . that after a while nobody listened."[8] The first blow against institutionalized authority in the sixties was struck by people who dismissed the strictures against freer sex as hypocritical, a defense of custom for the convenience of bureaucrats afraid of public opinion and parents afraid of everything. Given the nature of middle-class fears and obsessions, the generation gap of the sixties, such as it was, had more to do with sex than with politics or drugs.

Of course, the great question still concerned the bride's wedding-night gift of virginity. Every middle-class impulse supported the continuing demand for premarital chastity, useful for so long for regulating youthful curiosity and appetites. Roper polls taken in 1937 and again in 1966 showed that in both years slightly over half of the respondents said that both bride and groom should be virginal.[9] But one unmarried young woman in the Midwest who sought the pill from her doctor dismissed his worries about her endangered future:

> Have you ever stopped to think that you might someday want to marry a man who holds virginity in high regard?
>
> Yes . . . but I'm not at all sure I want to marry a man like that.[10]

A male student in Ohio, surely speaking for a vocal and growing number of college students in 1964, expressed himself in a way that might have but did not compel attention: "Premarital sex doesn't mean the downfall of society, at least not the kind of society we're going to build." However, a great deal of building would be required, as suggested by the more representative response of a senior at Columbia University when asked whether he favored sex before marriage: "For me—or my kid sister?"[11]

Whether there was, as the popular press loved to trumpet, a "sexual revolution" is a matter of definition. There is, however, no doubt that there was a revolution of the mouth, of public discussion, not so much by the young, although many of them delighted in provoking their elders with hints about passions unleashed in the dark of the moon, but by the press, which never tired of printing shadowy photographs of naked men and women under such provocative titles as "The Free-Sex Movement" or "The New Morality." Because as always it was particularly the colleges that seemed to be ersatz houses of ill-repute, noncollege youngsters were presumably safe, at least for a while. By the end of the decade a *Mademoiselle* survey disclosed that 42 percent of its young readers were still virgins, while 3 percent were promiscuous. The even younger audience for *Seventeen* not surprisingly revealed that conventionality diminished with each passing adolescent year, that teenage girls did not take the pill (out of ignorance or embarrassment, not carelessness), and that teenagers on the West Coast engaged in the most premarital sex, while those in the Northeast, presumably restrained by indigenous Puritan ghosts, experienced the least.[12]

The sexual right wing, the party of conventional morality, firmly decreed there was a revolution among the young, and that it was concentrated among middle-class young women, precisely the group about whose virtue the right was most worried. Obstetricians reported a rise in pregnancies among unmarried middle-class coeds. But researchers on the sexual left, the party advocating freedom, insisted that the change in actual behavior was slight, about the same as it had been during the 1920s.[13] While the conclusions of both were merely assumptions, those of the calmer, more skeptical left were probably closer to the truth.

It was not the miniskirted young woman or her long-haired boyfriend of the sixties who led the revolutionary sexual vanguard of the twentieth century but the rebellious young people of the 1920s who first faced the enemy, the middle-class Victorian custodian of tradition, with his watch chain across his paunch, vengeance in his eye, and conventionality in his soul. The flappers flamed and roared less than the fathers proclaimed, and tumbled in the rumble seat less often than they were accused of doing or might have wished, but they lifted the social lid, and repression in America was never the same. A scholar was succinct: "It was the flapper, not the hippie, who 'discovered sex.' "[14] Since the flapper's moment in the moonlight, the amount of premarital sexuality probably increased with each passing decade, until by the sixties it was declared a "revolution" largely because it had been taken out of the closet and used to twist the tail of the fretful middle class.

Regardless of the actual change in behavior, the young became freer to find the pace and nature of their own sexuality, and much freer to talk about it. Freedom, of course, had its pitfalls. If sex turned into therapy, it led people to seek satisfaction for themselves rather than for the mate, to engage in a soliloquy rather than a dialogue. Surely not for the first time, but probably more pervasively, sex as rebellion became theatrical. This made the reaction of the absent audience central to the experience, perhaps more gratifying than the act itself. For instance, "Julie," who lived in the Berkeley underground, had a lesbian encounter. Her description of this "mad affair" elevated the intended audience into central actors: "It was really a gas, some of the shocked expressions I'd get from people when I told them about it. My parents, of course, just about died."[15]

The young's choices were difficult, and some floundered in their most intimate conduct. For some, the new morality was confounding, especially for those who had not repudiated their middle-class origins, as a seventeen-year-old painfully tried to explain:

> Do I have sex because they [her peers] want me to, because I want to, because my parents are worried about it? You know, rebellion, the independence thing? Do I have it because you [an adult male sociologist] say I don't have to, or because I'm not attractive? And if I do, will I have to keep doing it? Will I want to keep doing it?. . . . Am I going to become a whore? Is that what I'm supposed to get out of my college education?[16]

Institutions could not adjust to the new sexual reality in time to save themselves and everyone else from immeasurable grief. As youth ghettos, colleges were especially vulnerable, and those that retained the old strictures against sexual experimentation appeared to their students as hypocritical and cowardly in the face of ignorant legislative, alumni, and parental pressures. They could continue to prohibit and punish or they could face the facts of real life. They could futilely attempt to retain the old order and risk student contempt, or they could permit students some privacy and risk the outrage of their public supporters.[17] The choice, especially for the large public universities, came down to suppressing student rebellion or facing reduced budgets.

Although the number is not known, by the late sixties more unmarried couples had begun living together. The reasons given for rejecting marriage were varied, but usually included some explicit repudiation of the middle-class way. A pattern emerged: as much as possible, the men rejected the ethic of work and commitment, the middle-class catechism of discipline in the name of future prosperity, while the women recoiled from the routine and boredom they associated not only with housewifery but with wifery in general. What resulted was consistent with some of the deepest strains of modern American life: a symbiotic pairing of men allergic to obligation and women reaching for independence and adult responsibility. The woman led the man and both were relieved.[18]

Sex had become a social weapon: given the traditional adult middle-class acceptance of repression, partly for themselves but mostly for their children, what else could more efficiently accelerate the social transformation advocated by the young? Because controls were breaking down, because an assortment of institutional leaders were obviously lying about sex, pot, and what presidents were doing, the young sought their own code to replace Mom's (Dad was busy and too shy) fears, social embarrassments, personal resentments, and such moral convictions as she may have had.

It is obvious that the pill affected men also, though this was not often discussed. Even without the social and personal complications created by the pill, it was not a good time to exult in conventional manhood. The war in Vietnam, with the customary wartime celebration of the most primitive machismo, provided a context that reinforced the American male's discomfiture with himself. For fathers and sons alike, sexual anxiety was only the starting point: the young had to grapple with peer pressure and worries about being drafted, while their fathers coped with the emotional enervation of bureaucratic work and the mounting frustration of watching their sons flounder.

And because some fathers, at least, realized they had been too distracted while the kids were growing up, they feared they would lose their children, not because of the revolt of the young, the culture war, but because they had failed to discharge an elemental responsibility, perhaps even failed in love.

The American male was different from men of other cultures because America was different. No other culture admired the strong, self-reliant male in quite the same way Americans did; only Americans celebrated the trailblazer, cowboy, and gangster (if not Al Capone, then Edward G. Robinson), none of whom was famous for adult relationships with women. As cultural myths go, it was only a small step from these heroes, always operating where social restraints were ignored, to the business entrepreneur struggling to be among the enduring fit who made the most lucrative use of those he deemed less fit. Like everyone else, middle-class American males thought this folklore was ancient history and fun, but presumably pointless. They were mistaken.

When the breadwinner blamed himself for his family's plight during the Great Depression, when the executive of the fifties sang the praises of his grandfather's manliness while disparaging his own paper-pushing comfort, those cultural echoes from a time long gone became nagging. John Wayne and what he represented did not create the middle-class man's growing discomfort, but Wayne was a memento of a self-reliance and virile competence that now could only be imagined.

As the prime arena for personal economic struggle, for wrestling over the prizes of the world's least-restrained individualism, America was a perfect laboratory to test whether the struggle to deliver in the daytime could be sustained at night. Could a worker, especially a psychologically drained bureaucrat, survive in his world of active manipulation of and by other people and still be sexually interested or interesting at home? The question was less one of fatigue than of the limits of active engagement with other people, sensory overload and the need for privacy, a moment to lick one's own wounds, to recoup energies for tomorrow's struggles. On the other hand, money was important and available, and naturally it led away from home and family.

In America, more than elsewhere, money determined worth, not only financial but moral and occasionally even intellectual. Because money was the way to measure who you were in comparison with everyone else, you packaged your wife to tell your story, regardless of mere economic debt. This was not only an economic contest. As the folk expression says, "Money is the way to keep score." What mattered was one's place in the economic hierarchy, so that relative standing counted more than the absolute net worth that determined it. The need to beat other men, called "the competition," was the psychological reality. It was a struggle to prove one's masculine prowess through the accumulation of approved objects on display in sufficient quantity. Playing by these rules meant that every single middle-class American male, as breadwinner, would fail. Somebody—too many somebodies—was always ahead.

For the middle class, the apparently eternal struggle must always be lost. The cliché said it all—grow or die. For some, this psychoeconomic requirement made sexual activity seem a distraction from life's tougher realities, and yet another challenge to an ego already challenged enough. In economic and sexual contests a comparison was essential to savor the apparently delicious fact that so many others were losers. Since the stock-market crash of 1929, nothing had changed. A psychiatrist reported that during a decline of the market in the sixties and early seventies the number of his "sexually impotent male patients increased about 300 per cent."[19]

Individually, none of the pressures on the middle-class American male was unique to America, but together they were. The sexual undertone of America's commercial culture, its seductiveness, succeeded for a reason. No natural law decreed that a display of varying expanses of female flesh would irresistibly draw people to purchase automobiles or take out bank loans. Such inescapable sexual suggestiveness must have been telling people what they wanted to hear. It was obvious that the moist lips and swaying hips on television could tantalize but not materialize. They were alluring but unattainable and therefore safe images that fed individual fantasies. Commercial sexuality's secondary message was *look, don't touch;* its subliminal primary message was *we know you'd rather look than touch.* It succeeded because it told a truth.

This was apparent in young people's new dances: they stopped touching and the male no longer led, something like the Charleston of the twenties. The young made the sexuality of dancing visual, and emphasized the expressiveness of the self rather than of the couple entwined. Look, don't touch.

The androgyny of young men was different from that of their fathers. The sons rejected their fathers' struggle to improve their status, a struggle that drained energy and love, and led to ineffectiveness and emotional impotence. Moreover, the young, middle-class male also repudiated the supercharged machismo of war culture, the kind of mentality that their fathers had admired in their own grandfathers. These young men, also moving toward androgyny, but with crucial differences, were trying to define masculinity in a way that would distinguish them from their passive, middle-class fathers. Because their dissatisfaction did not spring from psychic exhaustion, they wanted to reach out to others, to become more sensitive and responsive, as equality required. In the late sixties, the emergence of feminism caused many young women to insist that the new definitions of masculinity that their male friends were attempting to formulate should now be completed. And, imbued with a newly acquired feminist awareness, some of these younger women were moving toward their own androgyny.

Yet the American woman's increasing sexual confidence resulted in a corresponding rise in impotence among some men, not from overt conflict between the sexes but because women were maturing and the affluent older men and the sexists among the young were not. Sex counselors happily predicted that the pill would enhance women's lives by alleviating their fears of pregnancy, enabling them to be more spontaneous and expressive. They could take the initiative in bed, play the aggressor if they wished, and in other ways seek to arouse and satisfy their mates as traditional men had always done, or were supposed to. In short, women could now take on the sex roles traditionally reserved for men and some men were not delighted, while others, fearing yet more competition in their lives, collapsed. "Guilt," *Newsweek* reported, somewhat overstating the case, "used to be the leading cause of impotence; in the era of sexual freedom, it is anxiety over performance."[20]

Reporting in the *Ladies' Home Journal,* Dr. Robert W. Kistner of the Harvard Medical School explained that "the liberating effect of the Pill on the wife evokes all the latent emotional and sexual immaturity in the husband, once he is faced with real demands on his sexuality." Arguing that in sex the male ego is more vulnerable than the female, that male impotence is more devastating than female frigidity, Dr. Kistner asserted that American men were beginning to feel used, a little like sex objects or sexual service-station attendants, by their pill-popping women: "No longer the virile attacker, he becomes the docile partner rendering mere service."[21] The question of whether men or women suffered most is pointless, while it is true that the culture made greater demands on the male's capacity actually to perform in bed and everywhere.

For men and women, the pill was a great contribution to the middle-class demand for autonomy and prudential planning, its wish for order and predictability, and its hatred of surprise. For women, middle-class or not, unanticipated pregnancy rooted them in the rigors of biological logic to a degree that made the claim of equality and the dream of independence always conditional on the odds of avoiding childbirth. Now, for the first time, millions of middle-class women could rationally and safely plan careers, conceive of marriage as a true partnership, calculate the rational economic future of the family, and think differently about what it meant to be a woman of the middle class.

For men, athletic competition has always been a contest of manhood, a ritual designed to measure strength and speed relative to others. Since the 1920s at least, American men have been transfixed by sports, usually as spectators. Their athletic struggles have been fought by paid champions and their sense of prowess has risen or fallen with the fortunes of their surrogates. For actual participants, sandlot baseball and street-corner basketball were probably no different from schoolyard soccer in other cultures. The universal cruelties boys inflicted on one another, not only on the short, weak, and uncoordinated, but on everyone who could not excel, were not unique in America. But the implication that an uninterested or incompetent adolescent was a "sissy," strange, queer, potentially or actually gay, was in its terrors peculiar to America.

More than other cultures, America equated performance anywhere with masculinity everywhere; any failure in the approved masculine world—in the woods, locker room, marketplace, or bed—betrayed a disabled man. What should a real man be? One answer disclosed the lacerations endured by the American male in the sixties: "A man cannot stand a weak person." Another man thought his healthier response was nevertheless "a hell of a way for us to live. . . . I do what I suppose most men do: take a little pride in 'masculinity' where I can manage it, and scorn the idea where it's out of my reach."[22]

As a result of such expectations, the male's failure to perform on view, at home plate, inevitably raised questions about his delivery in private, at home. An eighteen-year-old male blurted out: "I can't make it. I can't perform and that's what America's all about, isn't it?" Because human relations were a contest for superiority in skill and size—for one's place in the hierarchy—there had to be winners and losers everywhere, on the sandlot and in bed. Such competition turned the American male into a hothouse specimen of anxiety. As one man complained, men "are supposed to be a cross between John Wayne, the Chase Manhattan Bank, and Hugh Hefner. We are only human, for christsake."[23]

Because sex was a contest requiring prowess, the pressures on the boy to hit a home run, or at least not to strike out, when he could not do the first or avoid the second, could torment him when he was still swinging at air as an adult. For this masculine culture, often applauded by women, the degree of violence and the degree of bravery required to face it measured the degree to which a sport reflected this conception of manliness—thus the national delirium over football. Dropping the ball did not mean the American male should find another activity. All other activities were suspect. In fact, there were no other activities. In American culture, sport defined masculinity in ways that only a few superboys could achieve. And when superboys defined manhood for adults, men (and women) were in trouble.

Among themselves, boys could relax, assert their masculinity, drink too much, and spit on the floor, if they wished. The fear of seeming gay usually was not raised by participation in the conventionally approved male associations, always organized on a class basis: beer at the bowling alley, scotch at the golf course, or white wine at the marina. Or at male colleges. When monosex colleges became coed in the sixties, women did not lose status by attending a formerly male institution. But a young man who deliberately sought the daily company of women by attending a formerly female institution inevitably ran the risk of seeming a eunuch. A male sophomore at masculine Yale wondered about the men who were breaking the sex barrier at Sarah Lawrence:

I know a Sarah Lawrence boy—he's really typical. He's about 5'3". Not real long hair, but it sort of comes out to here and stops! He sort of looks like a pig with hair.

He's a nice guy. He's not a snob or anything, but sort of a pseudo-intellectual. Last year Sarah Lawrence had sixteen boys. They were all shorter than 5′6″ and fat. The little piggies.[24]

These pressures on the middle-class male, young and old alike, predated the rebirth of feminism. But now that neither partner could use fear of pregnancy as a way to regulate sex, the absence of the old excuse compelled different dodges or else led to the truth. Ralph Greenson, a UCLA psychoanalyst, was not surprised by the apathy of husbands whose wives used the pill: "American men are becoming more and more lethargic in their sex lives anyway." His prediction might have been put to music: "American men are beginning to show a preference for demure, passive women. Perhaps the golden day of the shy Southern belle is due for revival." Meanwhile, decidedly unshy women also complained about the deformation of the too nice, too acquiescent, and too sensitive American male. "You don't excite us," one of them complained. "We feel more like your mothers than your wives."[25]

The culture of the pill emerged at the same time as the civil rights movement. Connections were rarely made between these two affronts to American habits, but a Chicago psychiatrist, writing in *Ebony* magazine, was astute. Dr. Kermit Mehlinger observed that for his typical woman patient "20 tiny pills have given her 20 days each month to celebrate her newly acquired emancipation. It's as if she received an added dividend from the civil rights movement—sexual rights." For him, civil rights was a black battle, while sexual rights was more white. But there were reciprocal benefits from both. In the politically charged atmosphere of the sixties the attempt to take control over one's sexuality became a political statement just as the struggle to obtain long-denied basic rights was deeply personal. The Victorian black woman was described as more repressed, more anxious to conform, more perfectly attuned to the middle class than her "puritanical" white sister. Dr. Mehlinger recognized that, although the pill could liberate black middle-class women, this was the group in black America that most resisted change, just like, he did not point out, its counterpart in white America, even if both groups also contained rebels.[26] Coming from unlikely places—a chemical laboratory and somewhere called Greensboro, North Carolina—sexual liberation and civil rights held out the promise of greater freedom.

Change was inevitable when the Supreme Court, which had earlier sanctioned state-sponsored racism, fired its opening volley against racial injustice in America. In 1954 the Court decided that separate school facilities were not equal and therefore that public school segregation was illegal. The southerner's instinct was to thwart desegregation with the shield of states' rights. But this overlooked a major cultural transformation of the postwar world: the Americans had already become almost entirely nationalized. World War II made the nation more of a community than ever before—or since. Even though the military had been segregated, millions of GIs lived and fought with others they ordinarily would never have met. The war introduced uniformed Americans to each other.[27]

The vast wartime relocations of the work force and, later, the mobility of the suburban middle class also weakened attachment to regional culture and place. The almost universal experience of national television contributed to diminishing localism. The wartime migration of blacks took them out of the South and off the land. By 1950 half lived in the North and West. Some southerners' fears of blood pollution and their obsession with the mythical sexuality of the black male were perhaps somewhat alleviated by this great reduction in the numbers of their black neighbors. Although the lives of the majority of black southerners had not yet been affected, each step away from the customs of the American grandfathers helped advance the black campaign for justice.

Postwar attitudes toward integration bore this out. Because

of their weakened attachment to regional and parental customs, whites' attitudes toward blacks greatly improved after the war. In 1942, only 40 percent of the white population thought that blacks were as intelligent as whites; by 1956 the percentage had actually doubled. The number of southern whites who acknowledged equality rose from 20 to 60 percent. Support for school integration increased with education, and more Americans were going to college. Outside of the South, 75 percent of white college graduates, and half the grammar school graduates, endorsed integration; the figures in the white South were 28 and 5 percent respectively. Everywhere young people were more decent than their elders.[28] Given the historical intransigence of American racism, these postwar attitude swings were remarkable, and they set the stage for the court's great reversal of itself.

During the 1950s, as the white middle class was enjoying its delivery from the historic traumas of depression and war, some southern blacks began to challenge the daily routines of the nation. Civil rights became the first postwar claim on the public's conscience, the first inescapable intrusion into peacetime privacy. This movement involved individual Americans in the prosaic facts of life; it was domestic and close to home.

The movement initially coalesced around the small, degrading details of blacks' daily lives. In 1955, on a bus in Montgomery, Alabama, Rosa Parks refused to give up her seat to a white because she was tired after working all day and her feet hurt. She was arrested and was bailed out by a railroad porter, who telephoned the news to the city's young new pastor, Martin Luther King, Jr. The two men called on Montgomery's blacks to boycott city buses until blacks could choose where to sit. To everyone's surprise, despite arrests, intimidation, and terrorism, the boycott was carried out with dedication and efficiency for over a year until the blacks won through a Supreme Court decision.

King became the undisputed leader—the voice and conscience—of the first phase of the movement. For him, Christ furnished the spirit and Mahatma Gandhi the technique: non-violent resistance was the way to convert hate to love, integrate blacks into middle-class America, and finally offer the nation the chance to redeem itself from centuries of bad faith.[29] Because of King, the movement became indistinguishable from black religion in the South, and it rested on his conception of Christian love and duty, and on his faith that the nation's bigots would ultimately be converted to rationality. He was certain that sooner or later the thugs would become sated with the blood of the meek, and the spectacle of beasts again devouring Christians, even black Christians, would finally stir the nation's conscience. Such optimism revealed how much he was a part of the American middle class.

His profound religious faith and diction indicated that he knew that the alternative to mainstream America for blacks was the culture of the rural South. His cadences, the songs of his followers, the appeal to the Christian virtues of his people, and his utter faith that the conscience of the enemy would eventually overwhelm its bigotry obviously spoke to the hearts of millions. It may be that the failure to appreciate the rural South as a cultural foundation for blacks explains why none of King's successors—distracted by Africa, Arabism, individualism, and ideology, their too obvious scorn for middle-class values—could unify, even if for only a relatively brief time, American blacks as he did.

Spontaneously, the children led the next stage. In their late-night bull sessions at a black college in Greensboro, North Carolina, four seventeen-year-old students argued, as freshmen used to do, about the meaning of justice and the obligations of a moral man. One of them insisted that they had to act as well as talk, that Gandhi, not King, had showed the way. They were dedicated to nonviolence and described what they were planning to do simply as "Christian." Their target was a segregated lunch counter at the local Woolworth's. The plan was politely to ask for service and then sit there until they got it or were arrested. During the first day—February 1, 1960—

some white shoppers congratulated them: "Ah, you should have done it ten years ago," while a black dishwasher called them "troublemakers." Despite the presence of an increasingly angry policeman, they stayed until closing time.

On the second day, twenty other black students joined them; on the fourth day, the first white student participated. In the second week, sit-ins spread throughout North Carolina. At the peak of enthusiasm in Greensboro, about ten thousand people wanted to sit in. After ten days the sizzling energy of the students erupted in Virginia. After ten weeks protests had occurred in every southern state, and by then some fifty thousand students had found a way to face down a small but powerful part of the segregationist South. They had exposed the vulnerability of southern racism.[30]

The four Greensboro students ignited a social reaction that instantly passed them by. They had no desire to pursue a sustained protest and no intention of bidding for leadership. What is rare actually happened: ordinary people took over a symbolic act and transformed it into a popular movement. The students showed how young blacks could act in their own behalf. After the success of the sit-ins it was no longer as necessary for blacks to wait passively through the delays and mysteries of court cases fought for them by white lawyers.

Something new had been created, especially for the students themselves, most of whom came from a tradition that trained them to be more buffed and polished, more correct in public behavior, and more deferential than the most tenderly reared child of the white middle class. The conservative behavior of black students in the South of 1960 must be understood to appreciate the accomplishment of the new rebels. Life at the black colleges was a full-dress rehearsal for middle-class conformity:

Absolutely no forms of rebellion exist: no bohemianism, no orgies, no riots, no radical discussion groups—not even walking on the grass! Everyone dresses like the pictures in Sunday magazines—pressed pants, shined shoes, ivy shirts and flouncy dresses. Girls, as a rule, must be safe in their dormitories by 10:30 P.M.—even on weekends—and to be caught drinking is cause for expulsion.[31]

This explains the students' discipline. They displayed their middle-class aspirations along with tactical good sense by dressing neatly, as was customary for them, and protesting courteously. Their goal was to join America. They hoped their moderation, in contrast to the bug-eyed hatred of screaming white racists, would persuade the nation that they posed no threat, not even to decorum. Even so, the majority of people polled nationally and in the South believed that the demonstrators were damaging the prospects for integration in the South.[32]

Nonetheless, the early sit-ins successfully attacked Jim Crow in the name of middle-class fair play, closely targeting the enemy so as to frighten no one else, if possible. Yet, however careful they were, the young protesters could not avoid frightening older blacks for whom the status quo offered some sort of equilibrium. A middle-aged black porter watching the protesting students shook his head: "I jes' don't understand what's getting into people these days." Of course, the racist city attorney of Montgomery believed that "the mature, substantial Negro . . . is not taking part in this uprising."[33]

The chaotic spontaneity of the sit-ins led to the creation of an organization to channel and sustain the students' energy. Students established the Student Nonviolent Coordinating Committee. SNCC, as it was called, served several purposes: it was a vehicle to disseminate information about local struggles, to provide an arena for young blacks to test and sharpen their political skills, and later to serve as a laboratory in which to experiment with alternatives to middle-class movement strategies. Still, one observer's characterization was correct: "SNCC began as a religious band of middle class, rather square reformers, seeking only 'our rights.' "[34] The young SNCC activists were buoyant, and their goal was not the consumption of greasy hamburgers but the reformation of the republic, for which they assumed all good and decent Americans would proffer thanks. When this bubble burst, it collapsed in bitterness and hate.

SNCC realized that the federal government would have to intervene against the South if segregation was to be uprooted, but the massive struggles of the early sixties had not moved the government to such unambiguous action. It had always been clear that left on their own blacks could be slaughtered. Assuming that the government and the television networks would react with dispatch to the death of white civil rights workers, SNCC invited hundreds of white, northern college students to work for black voter registration in Mississippi, the vortex of southern racism. It was not clear whether the movement would be helped more by the safety or the deaths of the visiting white babes in the piny woods. Among the SNCC staffers, however, there was great fear that the introduction of so many whites into a SNCC project might endanger black leadership.

After white students were screened to eliminate the more unlikely prospects, about seven hundred summer volunteers collected in Ohio for training. Most had already worked for civil rights in the North, and because they could afford not to work during the summer and could pay their own transportation (and bail money, if necessary), it was assumed that they were relatively affluent children of the middle class. Robert Moses, the black leader of the summer project, described what he liked about them: "They're from good schools and their parents are influential."[35]

The resulting class difference between the local SNCC workers and the white volunteers strained relationships within the summer project. The whites deferred to the blacks, never the reverse, and the air remained electric throughout the summer. However, white guilt made things easier. Shortly after arriving in Mississippi, a white volunteer recognized that the local blacks were "very much an in-group, because of what they have gone through together. They tend to be suspicious of us, because we are white, northern, urban, rich, inexperienced. We are somewhat in awe of them, and conscious of our own inferiority."[36]

Congress finally passed civil rights legislation in 1964 and 1965 that secured basic legal rights. The essential combination of the economic boom plus the anti-segregation legislation caused the size of the black middle class suddenly to double, a gain that surpassed black progress of the previous half century. The boom of the fifties did not lift black Americans because of Jim Crow; the civil rights of the seventies failed to help as much because of unemployment and inflation. The necessary conditions came together only in the sixties. In 1960, about 13 percent of black workers were in middle-class jobs; by the end of the decade the percentage was 27. And the social rewards of the integrationist laws most directly benefited middle-class blacks, those who could afford to patronize previously segregated restaurants and hotels, and afford the tuition while giving up the potential earnings of their college-bound children.[37]

While blacks considered the civil rights legislation a good beginning, white America viewed them as a triumph. Distracted by the escalating war in Vietnam, frightened by anti-war demonstrations and urban riots, tired of being challenged by civil rights moralists, the white middle class heralded the civil rights legislation as the culmination of a struggle. Consequently, the genuine legislative achievement derailed the civil rights movement so that it never again recaptured its former enthusiasm and support, driving into militancy some young blacks who knew that justice had not yet been secured.

As a result, a connection developed between increasingly radical SNCC workers and the emerging white student protesters across the nation. In their short history, SNCC activists had already taken on the aura of veterans in the war for justice against the hypocrisy of the complacent middle class. Some morally disquieted white college youth regarded the SNCC workers as social commandos who had secured the moral

beachheads of the 1960s, the vanguard in the struggle for political conscience. For these potentially influential white students,
SNCC people were a rebuke to the passivity of other young
men and women, the too comfortable and too talkative.

The early civil rights movement aimed to open middle-class
opportunities to black people. Many white college students participated to show their increasingly explicit rejection of the
middle class by siding with justice for blacks, identifying with
black music, slang, sometimes food, and, displaying their own
residual racism, with what they thought was black sexuality.
Turning from their own domestic comforts, many white workers in the cause idealized poverty as proof of virtue. Adorning
themselves with the clothes of poverty, nicely shocking to their
parents and the middle class in general, the white dissidents
consistently disclosed self-repudiation. As the black students in
the sit-ins dressed up, white students dressed down. By assist-
ing in the movement, whites seemed determined to transcend
who they had been in the fifties, and they needed black allies.

During the forties and fifties the left had become politically
pointless in America, but it had not actually died. It continued
to sputter along in the memories of aging veterans of the sectarian wars of the thirties, and in the zeal of some young men
and women who had just discovered Marx for themselves. By
following the Rosenberg trial, McCarthyism, and the Cold War
of Eisenhower and Dulles, they witnessed what their leftish
parents had been saying all along. The young found intellectual excitement in sharing insights into the reasons behind the
nation's shortcomings, but the society was sufficiently impervious so that the left shrank into a network of friendships, not
in Communist cells or as agents of the Soviet Union, but
among students or assistant professors who, as they understood
it, were keeping the flame of justice burning. They did their
part by learning and talking.

The isolation of the left lent a touch of bohemianism to their encounters. They welcomed the beats as grungy allies, but not as like-minded spirits. Jack Kerouac and his excited band of bikers and poets were too literary and crazy—uneducated, emotional, rootless, and irresponsible. But the imagined Left Bank bistros, with red-and-white-checkered tablecloths lit by candles dripping over Chianti bottles, with close friends huddled together, mulling over the failure of the working class, nourished the vision of the young American left wing as President Eisenhower was preparing to leave office.

The political atmosphere was filled with indecipherable premonitions of what was to come. Some on the left conceded that postwar America was reducing economic scarcity. Of course poverty and black oppression were ever present, but both were easing somewhat. Of course workers were still exploited, but this seemed not to be the major issue on which the world would turn. The booming economy itself, however, raised questions about human costs. What were the psychological costs of living a life devoted to things? Was the nation's morality overwhelmed by its inventory? Like many others, a young college instructor was grappling with the choice between radicalism and a comfortable middle-class life: "Somewhere inside I knew what attitudes and feelings were required for entry into this good life: despair, boredom, the relentless drive to keep moving, being 'realistic' by putting society's demands first and my own second, giving up on happiness, lying about pain."[38]

Who became President was not the issue. The culture of the middle class, not conventional politics, was the target. Rebels without a cause, as well as those who had a reasonably clear political agenda, were nauseated by success. They viewed the achievement of the American dream as a barrier to political progress because that very success seemed to make the nation less just at home and more dangerous abroad. Increasingly, its citizens seemed not so much evil as coarse, unfeeling, and bloated.

These students were raised in the comfort of two decades of prosperity. They had never faced the dangers their parents overcame in depression and war. As a result, the students seemed to assume that, whenever necessary, they could earn a living. But, more important, because they had not struggled to acquire the wealth or things valued by the middle class, they were indifferent to or scornful of such comfort and such possessions.[39] As they understood it, their idealism was the antidote to the poisonous materialism of the middle class. For the young, the middle class was blindered, if not blind, and a cultural revolution was of the essence if ever men and women were to be free. The fight between morality and immorality was the strategy of both armies in what had to be a war between cultures.

The early leaders of the new student left made their values the centerpiece of the Port Huron Statement, the 1962 manifesto of the Students for a Democratic Society. The statement opened with a reference to the fact that they had been raised "in at least modest comfort . . . and many of us began maturing in complacency." The American middle class, it said, was not so much contented as glazed. Thus, they felt obliged to make their own values explicit as the way to counteract somnambulistic middle-class Americans.[40] This was to be a struggle between energy and entropy, morality and greed, sensitivity and callousness. Who could doubt the outcome, even if organized power was all on the wrong side?

The students were thinking their way to the conclusion that their rebellion would be for themselves, not the proletariat. They understood that universities had become the gateway into the good life of the middle class. But, unlike the middle class, the young left believed that the function of higher education was to free people's intelligence, not serve as the nation's employment bureau. They challenged the university to assist in the revolution of intelligence and imagination by teaching the truth. If it failed to do the former, it would fail to do the latter. "Sadly," said Tom Hayden, an early leader and spokesman, "the university in America has become part of . . . [the] hierarchy of power, rather than an instrument to make men free."[41] Though this was hardly an original thought, it was an important discovery for young people whose lives were rooted in the very institution they now recognized as corrupt. Perhaps only the young, with more energy than the skin could contain, and blessed ignorance of the power of state legislatures, could have solemnly decided to change all this.

The technique for change was "participatory democracy." When leadership arose from below, the manipulation of people by élites would obviously cease. If people contributed to decisions affecting their own lives, they would become active democratic agents instead of objects deployed for the profit or convenience of others. Of course SDS tried to apply participatory democracy to itself and thereby created an uncoordinated, free-flowing, unmanageable spasm, not an organization. Following the lead of SNCC, with its own hatred of bureaucracy and ambivalence toward structure and leadership, SDS was practicing improvisational radicalism.

SDS was a genuinely native left, and the first organized and run by young people. They came from middle-class America, from affluent parents who were professionals. The colleges that drew them were the most selective and distinguished private liberal-arts colleges, some state universities, including those at Berkeley, Madison, and Ann Arbor, and the most prestigious private universities. More than other students, they majored in the liberal arts rather than in professional programs, and they were the best students.

Many had been raised by parents who themselves had been on the left when they were younger, before working their way into postwar success. These "red-diaper babies" were not rebelling against their parents, nor did they accuse them of hypocrisy; rather, they were maintaining family traditions of intellectual independence and critical thinking. One young college radical discovered that his family's values were really his, too. The difference was that "they were no longer my family's, because I had to defend them now on my own." Not surprisingly, a disproportionate number of Freedom Riders and early new leftists were Jewish, often because of a radical link somewhere in the Jewish family background, especially for those who had come from Tsarist Russia. Moreover, the parents' struggle to escape the dominion of others by working for themselves, and their commitment to higher education for their children, contributed to a heightened sensitivity to social injustice among young Jews and placed them in the universities where the action was.[42]

Because of its fluid structure, it was impossible to tell how many "members" SDS actually had. And however many there were at any given campus, a much larger group of supporters could be recruited if the issues were right. The ineptitude of administrators and police usually made the issues seem right, and thus both became unintentional but reliable allies. In 1969, a poll attempted to determine how the political pie was sliced among the young. Allowing for the expected ambiguities about definitions, the poll disclosed that 1 percent of the young were revolutionaries, 10 percent radical dissidents, 23 percent reformers, 48 percent moderates, and 19 percent conservative. In the same year the Gallup organization learned that 28 percent of college students nationally had participated in a demonstration, with the highest percentage in the East and the lowest in the South. Graduate students protested most (41 percent), and seniors least (24 percent). But these percentages conflated too many categories. An actual protest was more illuminating. In 1968, when SDS and some black students temporarily joined forces to seize buildings at Columbia, 58 percent of the Columbia students agreed with the protesters' goals but 68 percent opposed their tactics.[43]

Collectively, the young people in the emerging left were searching for ways to reshape the nation into a more moral order, into a culture that encouraged rather than stifled what they considered to be desirable individual and communal aspirations. Almost none of them approached the new left with a personal commitment to the ideological and sectarian struggles of the past. They were not conspirators. They believed that America could actually become more humane. At first, many saw themselves as the best kind of patriots, who wanted to reclaim their country's most decent ideals. Taken together, these highly privileged and idealistic shock troops were determined to force America to reexamine itself, an exercise deeply resented by the war managers, racists, and much of the complacent middle class at large.

In many ways the culture of youth in the sixties was no different from the immemorial rebellion of young people against the arbitrary rules of the older generation. This was the nation's best-educated generation, an achievement that created trouble between children and their less educated parents, but such had been the case for most of the century. This generation was not more alienated than the drunks of the twenties, nor was it more political than the debaters of the thirties. It probably did not fight with its parents any more than previous generations had with theirs. At the start of the decade, most of the nation's young people shared their parents' politics. The exception, of course, was to be expected: about 30 percent of the men and 20 percent of the women in college disagreed with their parents' politics. Toward the mid-sixties, parents and their children continued to agree on many issues, while the sharpest disagreements were found between young people in college and those who were not, between youngsters from the middle class and those from the lower middle class. By the end of the period, three out of four young people still supported their parents' values and ideals, and even more acknowledged that their parents lived up to their own values. But by then a slight majority revealed that their parents disapproved of the way the younger generation expressed itself. The difference between this generation and its predecessors was education, which also explained the rift within the younger generation itself.[44]

From 1963 to 1973 college enrollments actually doubled (a $100 billion explosion) to almost 10 million students. Five times as many students now went to college as in 1940. For every professor who left the faculty, five replacements had to be hired. To manage the invasion some large state universities flunked more than a third of each freshman class. Whether they wanted to or not, the draft forced the men to stay in school. It was not surprising that this student generation developed an aversion to competition that for many became a principle of life,[45] or that students perceived the university as a machine designed to manipulate or destroy young people. Universities became the battleground in the war for personal and political identity, and epitomized for students the inhumanity of oppressive bureaucratic society and schooling. The campus became both youth's front line against a failed society and a sanctuary for attacking adulthood's calcified institutions. Classes with over a thousand students seemed remarkably like an assembly line, proof that the university was as soulless as the Pentagon, and increasing numbers of students hated it all.

At the University of California at Berkeley in 1964—the year the first wave of baby-boomers entered college—these tensions erupted into the Free Speech Movement. This had almost nothing to do with some students' wish to shout obscenities, but concerned rather the students' demand to be free to act politically. By interfering with free speech the university administration elevated a dispute into a crisis. The student leaders, many of whom had participated in the Mississippi Summer just past, felt oppressed by the facelessness of their opponents, the emptiness of their education, and the power of distant political pressures. With splendid redundancy, they avowed not to trust anyone over thirty. When they carried signs proclaiming, "I'm a U.C. student. Don't Fold, Spindle, or Mutilate," they were obviously protesting the academic assembly line. The FSM's leader, Mario Savio, a veteran of Mississippi, voiced their repudiation, phrased in terms familiar throughout the industrial world:

There's a time when the operation of the machine becomes so odious, makes you so sick at heart, that you
can't take part, you can't even tacitly take part. And
you've got to put your bodies upon the gears, and upon
the wheels . . . and you've got to make it stop. And you've
got to indicate to the people that run it, the people who
own it, that unless you're free, the machine will be prevented from working at all.[46]

The FSM demonstrated to the nation's students that the
universities were not sanctuaries from a mad society. This was
the first organized protest in the name of the students themselves rather than on behalf of segregated blacks or exploited
workers. Now the privileged young of the middle class fought
for what they called student power. This latest crusade particularly provoked parents who could not afford to send their
children to college, and whose sons consequently were slogging
through rice fields in a distant and dangerous place.

The oppressive regimentation and political agnosticism of
the "multiversity" were symptomatic of a larger enemy—the
mush of American culture. It was not merely suburban or familial affluence that disturbed the young, but the uncertain
direction of life, the vapidness of political morality, middle-
class complacency, and a maddening nationwide numbness,
usually translated into indifference over the fate of the weak.
Apart from the acquisition of money, life seemed frightfully
pointless. Early in the decade, a New England college senior
described this mood: "What I worry about most is the most
terrible of all curses, found in the Book of Isaiah: 'Make the
heart of this people fat, make their ears heavy and shut their
eyes.' I would like to see the opposite of this." The culture of
his peers, however, was as banal as that of his elders: in a list
of people the young admired most, rock stars—Elvis Presley
and the Beatles—ranked higher than an amateur violinist, Albert Einstein.[47]

Yet racial discrimination did focus the political conscience of some American youth, especially because their elders were at best vague about the issue. The example of young blacks demonstrating in the South galvanized some middle-class white young people who had not thought much about the possibility of social change, especially change induced by the young.[48]

The cause of the street politics of the sixties did not lie in the psychological relationship of the dissidents and their parents, or in "permissiveness," but in massive official misconduct, whose consequences eventually drove two presidents from office. The behavior of their elders in authority—in the universities, the White House, the Pentagon, courthouses across the South, police precincts in northern ghettos—further fed their growing hostility to what seemed like the destructive nature of American life. They struggled for justice for blacks, peace in Vietnam, and the restoration of integrity to American institutions. Many of the dissident students were authentic patriots; they envisoned an America more decent than the actual country oftimes crudely defended by their adult opponents. When the young demanded to know how their elders could live with the disparity between the ideal and the actual America, and were given political lullabies for a mindless answer, they became outraged, burned their draft cards, marched on Washington, educated themselves about American power, and smoked pot. These were the political members of the generation, the new left, and they were on the attack.

Like a charging bull and a red flag, youth culture and the Vietnam war were made for each other. Along with the size of the younger generation, it was the war that made this decade unique. From their moral high ground, the young watched Lyndon Johnson dissemble about the war. With his childlike sensitivity to criticism and dislike of other people's disorder, the President concluded that the nation's crazed children were giving comfort to an enemy at arms. But in 1966, a year after the teach-ins began and the first 3,500 marines splashed ashore at Danang, 72 percent of the students polled at the University of Wisconsin approved of the war.[49] Many of the nation's young people supported the presidents to the end. The radical students and their middle-class supporters, however, concluded that LBJ was a liar and a murderer. *"Hey, hey, LBJ, how many kids did you kill today?"* The protesters assumed that only the concerted power of their numbers could force his hand, not in the name of Ho Chi Minh, and not even in the name of America, but in the name of what was more important, the young people of the nation and the world. They spoke of love and truth. He spoke of honor and freedom.

It is not possible to disentangle the antiwar and antidraft movements. Opposition to the war was based on principle or on a desire not to fight, or perhaps both.[50] In either case, the surging population of male adolescents was a recruiter's dream, the largest pool of potential soldiers in the nation's history. The male half of the Vietnam generation was composed of some 27 million young men, sooner or later all the right age to be drafted. About 2.2 million men were drafted; 8.7 million enlisted (many to escape the consequences faced by the draftees, including dangerous infantry assignments); and some 500,000 chose criminal resistance or draft evasion. About 16 million were deferred, exempted, or disqualified.

Students, primarily the children of the middle class, were deferred. This policy made every male student vulnerable for years, long enough to ponder the future and sharpen antiwar skills. So long as the privileged college students retained their exemptions, their parents, potentially the most vocal and political segment of the American middle class, would remain relatively quiescent. It would not be their war. But the grunts in Vietnam—working-class, blacks, and Puerto Ricans—knew exactly what the draft signified. Steve Harper, a poor kid who was drafted in Ohio, reasoned, "The critics are pickin' on us, just 'cause we had to fight in this war. Where were their sons? In fancy colleges?" Even General William Westmoreland, the commander in Vietnam, recognized that the draft was "discriminatory, undemocratic and resulted in the war being fought by the poor man's son."[51]

Students frequently claimed they had a right to evade the draft because of the immorality of the war. They did not often question who was being sent in their place, or whether the substitutes thought the war was just. When graduate-school deferments ended in 1967, a Harvard *Crimson* editorial complained that the new regulation was "careless expediency" and "unfair." Graduating seniors could no longer rely on admission to graduate school for continued immunity from the draft. Graduation now meant they were abruptly eligible. The immediate result was that some 40,000 students joined 220 major demonstrations against the war on over 100 campuses in the first few months of 1968. The nation's politically oriented students were now truly mobilized, and the Secret Service could no longer guarantee the President's safety on the nation's campuses.[52]

In July 1967, one-third of Americans in their twenties and half of those over fifty thought the war a mistake; by October 1969 the percentages had risen to 58 and 63, respectively. Thus, the older middle class was more skeptical of the war than the young. While the middle class continued to prosper in the economic boom, most were unhappy with the war, because America had intervened in the first place and because they were frustrated by limited war and wanted dramatic, decisive action to force a quick victory. The Americans' faith in their nation's moral superiority and their naïve confidence in technology persuaded them that the nation was right and could win. The endless and frustrating talk about controlled bombing and limited war contradicted their deepest intuitions. The country was torn between doves who wanted to get out and hawks who wanted to win. Neither side supported the prolonged agonies of "rational" warfare, carefully calibrated to just the right level of death. It was becoming obvious that a president who refused or was unable to find a way out or a way to win would be in trouble.[53]

Middle-class fathers, gentler and more sensitive than their lower-middle-class counterparts, as well as their own fathers and grandfathers, generally opposed the Vietnam war. Their sons who found ways to avoid the draft were equally at variance with conventional masculine imperatives and, like their fathers, were doves. He-men hard-hats, whose sons did much of the fighting in Southeast Asia, supported the presidents' war, accused middle-class, long-haired opponents of being emasculated, and eventually mourned the lost war as a betrayal of the nation's manhood. Middle-class responses were more convoluted, blaming defeat on errors of judgment, musclebound bureaucracy, or inept generals. A few thought of scrutinizing American culture itself to understand how so powerful a nation could be defeated, as the bigotry during war expressed it, by short Asians in black pajamas. The squeamishness of the middle class and the pugnacity of the lower middle class contributed to the war's basic confusions, while misguided national policy first created and then lost the war.

Much of this came to a head in 1968, partly because SDS had now defined itself in Marxist terms as a revolutionary vanguard. If revolution was the goal, SDS's frustrating but authentic participatory style of making decisions would be threatened, the qualifications of members would become relevant for the first time, and the relationship of specific actions to the larger goal would have to be rethought. A strategy of revolution probably meant that tactics would replace morality, while it surely meant that some earnest young people were now capable of deceiving themselves about the fundamentally middle-class nature of American society. Improvisational politics was also becoming delusional.

SDS learned from all of this that it should ride the wave, abandon fears of a backlash, and mobilize around the call for revolution. Its leaders exulted in the press coverage of each fresh outrage, especially the police riot during the 1968 Democratic convention in Chicago. SDS was sharpening its analysis, attempting in vain to exert some vague control over itself, and was becoming increasingly clever at provoking the reactions it wanted. But it was simultaneously losing its sense and purpose.

It came to a dreary and self-righteous collapse at its 1969 convention, where the organization disintegrated into warring sects,[54] lost what little contact it had with the rest of America, and became hopelessly anti-American, battling not only the huge and complex institutions of American life, but Americans themselves. A fireman's wife who had lost a son in Vietnam resented what she saw as the middle-class privileges of the students and their rejection of her:

> Those kids, they are in college. Those are the people who want us to surrender. They say they don't want more killing. They say they're worried about that place in Africa where they were starving, and Vietnam and the colored in the South. Do they ever stop and think what *we* think? They don't come out here and try to talk with us. They march over to the colored slums, or they demonstrate downtown or in the colleges. Are *they* America? I don't believe it. I'm against this war, too—the way a mother is, whose sons are in the army, who has lost a son fighting in it.[55]

By 1971, Rennie Davis, a veteran of many SDS confrontations, was lamenting: "We see that a movement unable to relate to tens of millions of Americans who are angry and frustrated is a movement that is out of touch with its own country and time."[56]

The movement was over.

Martin Luther King understood that black power grew out of the failure of white America to respond to legitimate cries for justice. Liberals pressured him because he was going too fast, while the black left, especially SNCC, criticized him for proceeding too slowly. He resisted both factions, but particularly the dithering of the liberals. Finally he concluded that the call for moderation, superficially reasonable, endangered the Lord's justice, that shallowness was more threatening than hatred. He feared drowning in the middle-class devotion to manners and, above all, order.[57]

Black power was as much a separatist movement from King and the established black civil rights organizations as from white America. Its advocates told white allies to go back where they came from, to organize white racists into a more just community, and then the two sides could meet again to negotiate remaining differences. Young black radicals remembered the Black Muslim Malcolm X's earlier incendiary sermons about white devils, recalled the humiliations and fears they had suffered themselves, the harsh discipline and suppressed rage that nonviolence required, and they discovered that they hated the white race in its entirety.

Stokely Carmichael, originally a Trinidadian and a veteran of countless civil rights battles, became SNCC's president in 1966. Though he had only the vaguest idea of what it meant, he built his reputation by preaching black power. He announced that integration into middle-class life was no longer the goal, that blacks would no longer work with white allies, and that henceforth blacks would find ways to develop and express their collective pride and power. The Christian commitment to nonviolence was no more: "Those of us who advocate Black Power are quite clear in our own minds that a 'non-violent' approach to civil rights is an approach black people cannot afford and a luxury white people do not deserve."[58] He was becoming a black nationalist, and he called for a black nation that would reflect either a new cultural or a new political reality, he was not sure which; this nation would emerge from within the context of American pluralism or through revolution, and he advocated both.

Either way, the slogan of black power galvanized young blacks who were dissatisfied with the victories of nonviolence, and alarmed white America and the NAACP, who feared that the hot-headed youngsters had gone too far. King repudiated this separatism, knowing that a minority's rejection of allies, along with a commitment to violence, was ultimately suicidal, but he no longer wielded his former influence. Most white civil rights activists were hurt by their sudden exclusion and, some thought, the ingratitude of their former comrades. Some SNCC workers exulted at their new militancy even as the organization was beginning to flounder. Was SNCC's mission to organize black communities or to lead a crusade for ideological purity? When it embraced separatism, SNCC fell into the trap of attempting to impose its ideology on ordinary blacks, who insisted on thinking for themselves. When SNCC embraced black nationalism it sacrificed its energizing connection to the rural South and began its decline. Dogmatism had now replaced its earlier fluidity and commitment to change.[59]

Advocates of black power rejected southern culture because they were committed to modernity—the world of cities, factories, and rising expectations. The militants wanted a different past for American blacks, one more coherent and aggressive. They thus invented an African and a Muslim, and occasionally an Arab, history. Black, not Negro; wearing the dashiki, not a suit; learning Swahili; demanding that Black Studies be taught in colleges; and adopting names common to Islam—all reflected this need for an alternative to white America. This fictitious African bond spoke not to the ordinary blacks of the nation, but to the ideological needs of the young blacks within SNCC. It represented their growing anti-Americanism, their solidarity with worldwide struggles of peoples of color, and their hunger for a different world. But it came at a cost: by emphasizing the African connection, young militants deflected attention from the reality that the black movement for justice began and succeeded where cultural ties to the rural South were strongest, in the segregated churches and schools, led by churchmen, not intellectuals, and aimed at the end of segregation, not common cause with Islam.

"We must stop being ashamed of being black," exhorted Carmichael. "We are black and beautiful."[60] This version of black power probably affected more blacks, even if they did not adopt the external symbols, than did the politics. It was a cry from the heart for a past, for an identity separate from whites, and for pride in blackness. This reformation of black psychology was intended to end racism, to alter white behavior by strengthening black confidence and esteem, and by sloughing off white attitudes forced on them for centuries.

Black nationalism reemerged at about the same time the nation's ghettos burned. The official report of a national commission calculated that 16 urban riots or clashes took place in 1964, 23 in 1965, 53 in 1966, 82 in 1967, and 65 in 1968. The riots in the Watts district of Los Angeles (34 killed, 1,000 injured, and 4,000 arrested) and Detroit (43 dead, 324 hurt, and 7,200 arrested) were the most devastating. Despite the confusion that still surrounds the riots, three white assumptions proved to be wrong. The rioters did not represent a tiny fraction of the ghetto residents; they rioted as a political protest, not merely for free-for-all looting; and they did not dwell on the consequences of future backlash. Most rioters, in fact, thought the flames and blood would do more good than harm, and onlookers took pride in the extent of the damage. Nonetheless, looting was still the motivation for some. As Efelka Brown of Watts expressed it: "We don't want to overthrow the country—we just want what we ain't got." King recognized that the violence was aimed more often at property than at people, and especially at shops that took advantage of the residents. At least, he noted, the opportunity to kill whites was "sublimated into arson, or turned into a kind of stormy carnival of free-merchandise distribution."[61]

The national response to the city riots was sharp: law and order must be restored at once, the guilty punished, and no more coddling. The Rochester, New York, riot of 1964 elicited a vehement rejection of ghetto conduct and goals. According to the polls, the percentage of those who disapproved of rioting rose to 88 during the summer of 1967. The rioters frightened the middle class, which feared for the safety of its neighborhoods. Whites deeply resented the noisily articulate black spokesmen who either defended or explained away the riots, and abhorred the great, fun-filled looting spree. The long, hot summers promised continued heat, for the political initiative in the ghettos now lay in the hands of angry young men who could not be soothed by Christian hymns or whispered assurances of better times in the by and by.

At the beginning of the sixties, many young Americans had felt overwhelmed or confused rather than angry. A young man in New Orleans was thinking about generational differences. With regret that he was born too late to participate in momentous events, he tried to speak for his generation: "Look, we have neither the naïveté nor the urgency of our parents. They felt that they mattered; that they could do something about conditions. We feel that nothing we do will make any difference." Somewhat reminiscent of his predescessors in the 1920s, he was weary. For him and others like him, the time for effective action was past, despite JFK's exhortations to the contrary. "You know, there are no individuals any more. There are no more Lindberghs flying the ocean alone, or real men with real names and real identities exploring the frozen north. It's all done by teamwork and helicopters and submarines backstopped by a thousand scientists and technicians. Even the astronauts are not people; they're a team."[63]

One young man in Florida attributed the malaise to the pacifying years of the Eisenhower administration, in which the nation had been soothed instead of led. During those eight years, almost half of this youth's life, "we've been told that everything is peachy fine. Now we know it's not. Americans have been treated like children, and denied the harsh truths. Now we're told to act, but we don't know what to do. I'm confused."[64]

The fathers of the 1950s had looked back in pride on the achievements of their grandfathers, while their children, the students of the sixties, often idealized the seemingly heroic struggles earlier fought by their own parents. A young man in

Seattle understood the rueful pleasure of paying homage to forebears whose triumphs diminished their children's lives: "Our parents led a tougher life—they fought a depression and a war. And they've protected us." A goodly number of young people began the sixties with attitudes toward their parents—and not just the fathers—that echoed the hero worship their fathers practiced toward their fathers. "Goals?" asked a high school student in California. "We've got no goals. Our parents have achieved them all for us."[65] There was nothing to do.

If only life were not so complicated, some of the more fragile young people would not be sinking into alienation and passivity. If only rationality and freedom did not overwhelm emotional and intellectual resources. If only someone could lead the young to believe—anything. Even fascism would be a relief. One college sophomore poured out his guts:

> If I had been brought up in Nazi Germany—supposing I wasn't Jewish—I think I would have had an absolute set of values, that is to say, Nazism, to believe in. In modern American society, particularly in the uppper middle class, a very liberal group, where I'm given no religious background, where my parents always said to me, 'If you want to go to Sunday School, you can,' or 'If you want to take music lessons, you can,' but 'It's up to you,' where they never did force any arbitrary system of values on me—what I find is that with so much freedom, I'm left with no value system, and in certain ways I wish I had had a value system forced on me, so that I could have something to believe in.[66]

A father was missing. One West Coast psychology student recognized the growing deprivation in American culture: "We need fathers. . . . This is not the America I dreamt about."[67] Nostalgia for strong fathers could be transformed into a longing for fascism, but, despite the overheated metaphors of man-haters, strong fathers and fascism were not identical.

The achievements of the past, the triumphs of the older generation, had drained the present of meaning. Admiration for the elders' accomplishments was usually tinged with resentment for inheriting a middle-class life chokingly pleasant, safer than what the old folks had, less testing, and less proving. These young people felt useless and torn. They argued that the domesticated present was oppressive, yet insisted that only the present mattered. They saw the past as irrelevant to their lives but were terrified by the future. When young people could not reconcile this tension, paralyzing alienation became a generational epidemic.

Although young people in the sixties might idealize their parents, the anxious middle-class American male student probably admired his mother a little too much. For these young men the focus on Mother emphasized what marriage had compelled her to give up. The strong woman of the thirties, and the good woman of the postwar decades, now was seen as the martyr, society's victim, who had sacrificed herself to the needs of her husband and children. In his study of alienated students at Harvard, Kenneth Keniston preserved the language of some of the sons: "She showed early talent as a pianist. . . . Nothing ever came of it." "When she was young, she had ambitions to be a writer, and she told me she hated to settle down to the dreary task of becoming a housewife, and she would have preferred to write." "My mother thinks she could have been a good actress, but doesn't really regret having married my father." These young men also described their mothers as domineering, possessive, and neurotic, but blamed their fathers for their mothers' frustrations. They resented their fathers' weaknesses, their willingness to be dominated, and the consequent "selling out" of their youthful ideals to become trivial, unworthy successes. According to the sons the fathers were uncommunicative, reserved, and lonely. In therapy these young men would only mention their fathers if pressed, and then condemned them for choosing to become broken men, for trading the dreams of youth for nothing more than middle-class comfort.

These students also reported that they preferred never to initiate any contact or action on their own behalf, hoping, especially in their sexual relationships, that they would succeed without effort. Such passivity guarded them against rejection and assured them a life without responsibility. In short, they did not want to become adults, at least not the men their fathers had become, because they hated the cultural and psychological roles assigned to men. Because there seemed to be no way out, they were choosing not to make choices, to become distanced not only from the surface textures of American life, but from life itself.[68]

Less troubled young people also rejected the dictates of traditional masculinity. In retrospect, it seems inevitable that the boys' early defiance would center on the length of their hair. Inspired by the Beatles to wear what later seemed like dainty "Prince Valiant" hairstyles, American teenagers and college students dared parents and teachers to find a way to compel them to submit to a barber. At first the parents tried. "Moptops," as they were too cutely called in 1965, were expelled from school, convicted in a jury trial of disturbing the peace, made to wear dog tags, and, most serious, forced by a gym teacher to wear pink hair nets.[69]

The reason adults panicked was obvious. One student told his teacher that "the trouble is my father can't believe that anyone but a sissy would wear his hair the way I do." His teacher's cousin was even more indignant: "Long hair had one connotation and one only—it meant that a male wasn't really a male. At best he was some kind of an arty phony; at worst a homosexual, a beatnik." But for blacks, longer hair, the natural or Afro, conveyed the opposite message: pride in blackness, an open rejection of white standards of grooming and beauty, and greater strength.[70]

For most of the twentieth century, the convention for male hair fashion dictated looking "clean-cut," tidy, unthreatening, safe, acquiescent, respectful—middle-class. Until the mid-sixties, short hair was a symbol of adjustment, acceptance of authority, even patriotism. Long hair—women's "crowning glory"—was consigned to male misfits—"phony" poets, painters, and other social freaks. The hair frenzy of the mid-sixties, however, signified that the culture of youth was less malleable than it had been, and that it had found a way to bewilder or, even better, anger adults. And those who were angry understood the message. A man in Lawrence, Kansas, admitted that he hated long hair: "To me I guess it's a symbol they're against me."[71] Girlfriends of long-haired males frequently encouraged the rebellion, occasionally for purposes of protest, but more often because they thought long hair symbolized greater gentleness, sensitivity, and thoughtfulness than the crew-cuts of marines.

Young men found other ways to communicate their rejection of the American he-man. Perhaps influenced by a convention in black music, the prevalence of soprano voices or falsettos over bass voices in musical groups reinforced not only the youth of the castrato impersonators, but their sensitivity and vulnerability. Not surprisingly, country music, then the music of those least swayed by the winds of fashion, the music of rugged Americanism, continued to feature men with deep voices.

The truly alienated were engaged in a search for perception and deep, clear, intense feelings. Keniston explained that for them, "Experience is defined as subtlety, sensitivity, and awareness: the purpose of existence is not to alter the world so as to create new experiences, but to alter the self so as to receive new perceptions from what is already there."[72] Much of what was to unfold within American youth culture by the mid-sixties was consistent with the reactions of these wounded, bright, articulate, clinically alienated students. From their private agonies, their quiet search for dignity among the wounds, a lunatic tribe of acolytes was let loose.

The counterculture in America was a worshipful celebration.[73] As the hippies decorated themselves with daffodils, beads, feathers, fringes, bells, and painted faces, these young souls were replaying aspects of the sixteenth-century Protestant Reformation. They did not know this, of course, for their spirituality depended on an encyclopedic ignorance. What they thought they knew, or rather sensed, was that the modern world was deranged and dangerous.

For them, the devil's mutiny had finally succeeded and he was now in charge. His names were many, but "materialism" and "rationality" were the most common. He lived everywhere, but seemed most at ease on Wall Street and in the Pentagon. His form was infinitely changeable, but he usually paraded in the world as either General Motors, Columbia University, or the President of the United States. Most of all he enjoyed mass murder, so he invented napalm and loved Vietnam. Masses of moderately sane young people enjoyed the entire cornucopia of the occult, especially astrology and witchcraft. They were drawn to everything science had disposed of and reason had refuted, partly to display their freedom from fact and logic, but, more important, to replace truth with a substitute that helped them pretend they could control their lives, perhaps with a macrobiotic diet or by embracing the cosmos.

Like the Anabaptists of Martin Luther's era, these new reformers were separatists. Both reacted to similar perceptions: a spoiled world gone rancid, fatal to the soul. Optimists might try to improve such a world, but they had to believe it was still possible to locate some pathetic but redeeming little flame of goodness flickering somewhere. This was what the English Puritans attempted. They thought their terrible state church could be purified, while the separatist Pilgrims fled to Holland and the New World to escape its limitless and contagious corruption.

Because the Anabaptists were not sanguine about the world, they wanted to get away from it, in the process becoming sixteenth-century hippies. They created communes separate from the world's stench, shared their worldly goods with each other, became pacifists, practiced polygamy, and met persecution passively. Some, in paroxysms of piety, ran about naked, babbling incoherently. It was said that some seduced simple women with the argument that the Lord decreed that only the sinner willing to part with what was most precious would enter paradise. They preferred to make love, not war. They scandalized the burghers by their outrageous dress, and went about their business with palpable piety, for they were citizens of heaven with duties owed to no earthly state.[74]

To be a devout counterculturalist in the sixties was a full-time commitment. There were masses of plastic hippies, sometimes called "yo-yos," who fled their parents to cavort on the weekends, but the true believers, the vanguard of the international revival of the young, were obliged to live their beliefs daily. Joyce Francisco, a twenty-three-year-old worker on a hippie newspaper, displayed the quivering piety of the newly converted: "I pray in the morning sun. It nourishes me with its energy so I can spread my love and beauty and nourish others. I never pray *for* anything; I don't need anything. Whatever turns me on is a sacrament: LSD, sex, my bells, my colors . . . that is the holy communion, you dig?"[75]

The counterculture's first commandment was, Thou shalt not commit gainful employment. Its members staked their claim on love as the replacement for every form of competition, every sort of battlefield, and they wanted no tests or struggle. Absolutely committed to the union of what the modern world violently shattered—men and women, person and nature—they could not honor the rules of the middle-class world, for they were on the exclusive track of feelings. This new imperium of the emotions required the overthrow by the power of flowers of that other world, which reeked of reason, restraint, progress, order, and other related misfortunes.

They had both larger and more focused goals: the achievement of ecstasy was a celebration of nature or God, if there was a difference. The elements of the counterculture's liturgy were inseparable. Their quest for humanness, which, by its mere existence, was the equivalent of truth and beauty, took them through higher, more intense layers of sensation to sex, drugs as the new eucharist, especially LSD, and occasionally, when all the vibrations were harmonious, to communion with their peers. The massive rock concerts, where the music played so loud it flapped the pants legs of those who were dressed, signified that youth existed and was different. What always lifted the celebrants to a feeling of oceanic oneness with each other was the revelation that young people could be nice, nicer than anyone else.

This church was not universal and tried to enforce its rules for admission (although some others, too old for automatic inclusion, insisted on sneaking in). It was for the young, longhaired, sandaled, gentle souls, devoted to love and each other, who hated the middle-class straight society, old and dried-out people who prevented the angelic young from loving each other, sent them to war, to factories, to schools, and in countless other ways broke the spirit, tormented the flesh, and poisoned the earth.

The new fingering of sensation repudiated the entire universe the middle class had constructed for itself, the buttoned-up loving and living and working of the past. It celebrated what could be if people would only breathe freer, love easier, and follow the lead of spontaneity and joy. The counterculture was clearest about what it rejected: wealth prevented a full and happy life; the struggle of ordinary people to achieve economic independence was pathetic and suicidal; and education destroyed freedom and happiness. These refugees from the middle class sought release from crippling adherence to conventional values, including the value of work, competition, marriage, the family, patriotism, democracy, and equality. They sought freedom from oppressive social institutions and conventional authority, including the law, police, universities, politicians, and corporations. They hated alcohol, preferring other, more liberating agents of transient psychosis, and, out

of their need for community, detested the middle-class obsession with privacy.[76]

The genealogy of hippies traced back through the beats of
the fifties to the lost generation of the twenties, and beyond to
the bohemians of the world. In the Summer of Love in 1967,
they coalesced in the Haight-Ashbury section of San Francisco
and the Lower East Side, now called the East Village, in New
York. Buses from straight society brought middle-class tourists
to gawk at the hairy bipeds. In Hashbury a hippie occasionally
would run alongside the bus holding up a mirror to the riders.
In retribution for the tourist buses jamming up St. Mark's
Place, sixty East Village hippies rented a bus to tour Queens
and inspect the natives. At departure the bus driver asked, "Is
everybody on?" "On what?" came the reply.[77]

There were limits to the hippies' capacity for love. The males
were confused about, if they did not actually hate, women, and
they were as racist as the mainline society they were escaping.
A street bulletin disclosed part of the truth:

> Pretty little 16-year-old middle-class chick comes to the
> Haight to see what it's all about & gets picked up by a 17-
> year-old street dealer who spends all day shooting her full
> of speed again & again, then feeds her 3,000 mikes [LSD]
> & raffles off her temporarily unemployed body for the big-
> gest Haight Street gangbang since the night before last.
> The politics and ethics of ecstacy. Rape is as common as
> bullshit on Haight Street.[78]

The hippie woman's role was to serve men. Performing the
usual housewifely functions of cooking and cleaning for her
man and his friends, she was free to be as pretentious as she
wished. A woman named only Martine explained herself: "I
spend all day cooking, sewing, straightening the house. I used
to think I wanted to be an artist. But now, I am." The sex
roles of hippie women drove some of them to levels of degradation hard to imagine. Being passed from one crotch to an-

other, unable to protest for fear of violating the hippie covenant, the women proved their right to exist by becoming groovy communal spittoons. A woman described the hip man as a predator. She realized that the hippie woman's straight mother at least got a home and security out of her relationship, and that prostitutes got cash. "But," she said, "the hippie woman is bereft of all that. . . . The sons have really outdone the fathers."[79]

Attracted to cheap ghettos, the middle-class runaways practiced their gentleness, displayed their love for all living things, and became easy targets for robbery, rape, and murder. Out of fear for their physical safety they relearned to hate blacks, called "spades." This was a departure from the earlier world of the beatniks, who often thought of black culture as superior to that of whites. Hippies in Hashbury used the Hell's Angels to protect them from marauding blacks. The street wisdom of 1967 was "SPADES ARE PROGRAMMED FOR HATE."[80]

Poor people in the neighborhoods resented the hippies for playing at poverty for only as long as it amused them, and for mocking what Hispanic and black families were striving to achieve, a toehold in the middle class. A black East Villager complained that "the hippies really bug us, because we know they can come down here and play their games for a while and then escape. And we can't, man." A Chicano school principal in Taos, New Mexico, accused the local hippies of "making fun of our poverty and our fight for survival."[81]

Hippies soon grew sick of the danger and death of the ghettos and resolved to "go to the country," to form tribes and live in communes. About ten thousand of them settled on more than five hundred communes across the nation.[82] By 1968 youth thought it was replacing economic class, social rank, and racial identity as a new, independent social category. Many of the young thought of themselves as a distinct social reality, a separate nation, or, in moments of high enthusiasm, a separate race. Their religiosity was intensifying.

Whatever they were and from wherever they came, 400,000

of them assembled in late summer, 1969, on Max Yasgur's Bethel, New York, farm. Known formally as the Woodstock Music and Art Fair, and informally as "An Aquarian Exposition," it was, according to *Time,* the largest happening in history, one that "may well rank as one of the significant political and sociological events of the age." This overheated conclusion was itself proof of the transforming spirit, some said magic, of what happened in Yasgur's sodden fields. Leading rock groups played, of course, but the crowd was the real attraction. It was estimated that over a million would have come if the logistics could have been arranged. Hippiedom's style had apparently seized the imagination of an entire generation of American youth. There were so many young people who wanted to huddle with each other that any place could be filled. A Hollywood promoter sighed with frustration. "I wish I could rent Utah."[83]

In their strange and wondrous garb, the young displayed the potential power of their numbers. To middle-class, middle-aged television viewers it seemed more like the reinvention of Sodom, complete with disgusting nudity and rampant sex, a drug-maddened release of the dark forces civilized society was supposed to subdue. For the participants in the festival, the mystic sense of community transcended every other feeling, with the possible exception of the self-celebration of innocence. The main point, according to a nineteen-year-old student from the University of Chicago, was that

> there were no fights, no hassles, no pushing, no stealing. Everybody shared everything he had, and I've never seen such consideration for others. . . . It was the extraordinary demonstration of how good people can be—really *want* to be, if they are left alone. . . . We were exhilarated. We were in a mass of *us*. . . . [At the end of an antiwar song an army helicopter flew over.] The whole crowd— all those hundreds of thousands of people—looked up and waved their forefingers in the peace sign, and then gave a cheer for themselves.[84]

With their worship of love, these young people could become
an irresistible force if, the straight world said, they could get
themselves organized and accept leadership. Janis Joplin responded for them all: "We don't need a leader. We have each
other. All we need is to keep our heads straight and in ten
years this country may be a decent place to live in."[85]

The adherents assumed that the generational pressures unleashed at Woodstock would finally free America. They believed that the amplified sounds of their weekend would
continue to reverberate until the walls of mainstream America
actually did come tumbling down. Middle-class values—
competition, commercialism, individualism, and élitism—were
falling from their own decadence. And the young would inherit
the earth. But an observer worried about the middle-class environment in which youth was struggling:

> The new culture has yet to produce its own institutions
> on a mass scale; it controls none of the resources to do so.
> For the moment, it must be content—or discontent—to
> feed the swinging sectors of the old system with new ideas,
> with rock and dope and love and openness. Then it all
> comes back, from Columbia Records or Hollywood or
> Bloomingdale's in perverted and degraded forms. But
> something will survive, because there's no drug on earth
> to dispel the nausea. . . . But the urges are roaming, and
> when the dope freaks and nude swimmers and loveniks
> and ecological cultists and music groovers find out that
> they have to fight for love, all fucking hell will break
> loose.[86]

In the early seventies part of hippiedom found its way back
from drugs as "Jesus freaks." This melding of fundamentalist
Christianity with the flower child's ecstatic innocence, and even
the exaltation akin to the acid head's psychedelic trips into
space, was easy. Young people's craving for simplicity, for a
faith that explained everything, could apparently be satisfied
by reading tarot cards, watching in drugged delight as the side-

walk turned into the world's grooviest chick, or venerating Christ, greatest guru of them all. Straight Christians, a bit offended by the style, were generally pleased with young people's proclamation of their Christianity. Norman Vincent Peale was put off by the bumper sticker "HONK IF YOU LOVE JESUS," but he recognized "that's exactly what I have been doing in my pulpit for almost 40 years." In *Godspell* and *Jesus Christ Superstar* the religion was toned down, the glamour turned up, as Broadway required, but the message was inescapable: Jesus is coming. Praise be to Him. Oh, wow. The Pentecostal climax of the counterculture revealed the emotional strands, the force of irrationality, that had held it together from the start.[87]

This cultural foray based on unreason was intended to liberate the human spirit, introduce the world to peace and love, and drive the computers out of the temple. Unreason, however, had other uses, which the hippie vision and style also venerated. It was later made explicit in the ritual murders by the psychopathic Manson "family," and again at a place called Jonestown.

Not coincidentally, this was a moment of overweening confidence in the power of rationality to manage a distant war and, through Lyndon Johnson's Great Society programs, to improve the lives of the poor and despised at home. A hypertrophy of rationalism was driving some powerful men a little mad. No war had ever been as carefully managed as Vietnam. The systems analysts in the Secretary of Defense's office calculated with marvelous cleverness what the troops needed. It was becoming increasingly hard to recognize that technology had limits. Secretary Robert McNamara himself explained that it was vital to keep Vietnam a cool war, emotionless if possible, lest the people become excited and demand, in their irresponsible way, a wider and deadlier conflict. McNamara, displaying an advanced case of American technophilia, once declared: "The greatest contribution Vietnam is making—right or wrong is beside the point—is that it is developing an ability in the United States to fight a limited war, to go to war without the necessity of arousing the public ire.'' In this one sentence are combined the typical New Frontier's offhanded dismissal of morality, its failure to understand that it is right for a people to get fighting mad before they go to war, and the peculiar assumption that life is a puzzle that can be solved. When it suited him, Admiral Hyman G. Rickover, a lord of technology himself, revealed more insight into the mad rationality of the Pentagon: ''At one time the Pagan Gods ruled the world. Later the Kings. Then the Warriors, followed by the Lawyers. Now it is the Cost Accountants.''[88] The times were ripe for a cultural mutiny, a recoil from demented rationalism, a movement toward drug-supported exploration of feelings and mindlessness, performed to a deafening and obliterating beat, over which the middle class was panic-stricken because it all seemed so irrational.

Beyond the blacks, radicals, and hippies was the largest group of young people, the enormous middle-class contingent that was neither separatist nor political, but participated in the generation through the consumption of goods. Purchases were sometimes intended to reveal solidarity with whatever it was others were trying to accomplish. More often the new objects were meant to signify the owners' newfound freedoms, acceptance of the symbols of their tribe. They bought Beatles' records, motorcycles, amplifiers, granny dresses, and other chic revolutionary products. Their revolution raised the national expenditures for clothing and fashion between 1963 and 1967 by 40 percent, a figure that before 1963 represented an entire decade of consumption. The president of a New York City advertising agency recognized that for them ''the consumption of goods and services appears to be life's goal.''[89] Some of the new goods riled the parents and churchmen, but the manufacturers were poised at the ready.

Their problem was to design merchandise that could satisfy

the desire of young men and women from the middle class to mark themselves off from the middle class in ways that might be perceived as naughty but not really offensive to the middle class. The choices were limited: increased sexuality for women, decreased sexuality for men, and a little touch of apparent poverty for everyone. For the young this naturally resulted in short skirts, long hair, and jeans.

The most significant research on the cultural changes in the late sixties and early seventies was conducted by Daniel Yankelovich. He discovered an amazing transformation in the culture of the young, one that people of the time sensed. The leftward movement of college students was abating, while nonstudents—workers, housewives, high school children—had now adopted the earlier, more radical, attitudes of the college students.

The perceptible change in college students' attitudes was by far the more dramatic. In the late sixties the campus rebellion was at its peak, and by the early seventies it was dying, a process to which Richard Nixon's substitution of a voluntary army for the draft contributed significantly. In the late sixties the cultural and political rebellions seemed synchronized; after, they diverged. Earlier, feminism seemed insignificant; later, it became central. In the sixties the value of education and the work ethic were repudiated, and racism was a major target; in the early seventies the idea of work was less repulsive and racial justice seemed less pressing. What was limited to the campuses in the sixties spread outward in the early seventies, so that the earlier intragenerational division over social and moral values between students and nonstudents virtually disappeared.[90] Once the movement was freed from politics and justice for others, from concerns external to the individual self, once it was brought exclusively to bear on the lives of young people themselves, it caught fire among the nation's young as a whole and lost salience for the left.

For adults who pined for their spent adolescence, who perhaps envied the students' freedom, and who could afford the

fullest package offered by the department stores, consumption
meant joining or copying the jet set, beautiful people, and what
Madison Avenue referred to as the "peacock revolution." Bill
Blass, the American designer, thought he understood why
American men were initially reluctant to accept ruffled shirts
and golden necklaces, but then rushed to buy: "At first most
men found it impossible to identify with the new fashions because many of the innovations were pioneered by the Negro
and the homosexuals. Then along came the young. That made
the difference."[91]

Profitably desexing the middle-class male required new
plumage, bright colors, hair stylists, perfumes, and other
equally significant changes in the cues you gave the world about
your social and sexual status, and your incapacity to do useful
work in the new public costumes. The respectable middle-class
male had always criticized men who challenged the conventions of clothing. But now the American male was, as *Newsweek*
gushed, "wrapping himself in form-fitting suits of every shade
and fabric; hanging pendants and beads from his neck; adorning his feet with bright buckled shoes, and generally carrying
on like a dandy."[92] The solidity and reliability conveyed by
the business suit were replaced with fashion, that is, flightiness,
sometimes whimsy, but always an expenditure of time and
money on objects that earlier would have caused shame. The
middle-class male of the fifties and early sixties would not have
wanted the world to know he had the time or inclination
to think about such matters as the curl of his hair. The new
middle-class male, however, paraded his skill with cosmetics
and fashion coordination. Androgynous man would not blush.
He did not want the fashion setters, those younger than he, to
perceive him as a bore, repressed, a square, too poor or timid
to emulate their apparently exciting behavior.

On Carnaby Street in London and in most other cities of
the western world, the miniskirt, like the flapper's hemline,
emblemized the owner's sense of security. The miniskirt had
securely arrived by 1966 and displaying ten inches of thigh was

proof beyond reasonable doubt that the new leggy girl was unconcerned about the reaction of parents, teachers, or employers. She required certain guarantees, however, before she ran such risks. In short, the girl's miniskirt proclaimed that she perceived the world to be safe. She had enough money and did not believe that Vietnam threatened her or her boyfriends. This war did not elicit the cultural retrocession characteristic of every other war of the century. This war did not count. The miniskirt revealed that Vietnam, bigotry, and poverty were someone else's problems.

Beyond a barometer of social confidence, the miniskirt, like the flapper's more revolutionary display of the knee, indicated youthfulness, usually prepubescence. When the breasts of the fifties were replaced by the legs of the sixties as the new zone of excitation, it was freedom, not maternity, that was being heralded—joyfulness, not responsibility; innocence, not sensuality; girlishness, not womanhood. At first bralessness was suggested for women whose breasts were small enough not to require support. An executive of a chain of boutiques described the ideal customer as "a little hollow-chested." The fifties were dead, and the standard for mass culture's new stylish female was seventeen and starved. She was personified by an English waif named Twiggy, described thus by a news magazine: "Four straight limbs in search of a woman's body, a mini-bosom trapped in perpetual puberty, the frail torso of the teen-age choirboy."[93]

To the degree that very short skirts evoked extreme youth they were also desexualizing, like the brief skirts of cheerleaders acceptable to all of middle America, innocently pleasing to the clerics and other sharp-eyed cultural watchdogs. The short skirt conveyed and required happiness. A twenty-seven-year-old businessman noticed a beautiful miniskirted girl who was frowning, so the effect was "a total, absolute loss." He diagnosed the problem: "The mini-skirt demands that you smile. Maybe it demands that you sort of skip every third step."[94]

The cultural devolution toward the age of skipping was inevitably exploited by advertising. One inspiration was the television show *Batman*—"the hottest property in Hollywood." The creative admen, as usual, fell into a lockstep, putting the comic book at the center of their persuasive arts. Captain Carbide sold Union Carbide and Superman hawked Continental Insurance. Airline stewardesses were required to wear "fun" things, such as plastic helmets, while Montgomery Ward's catalogue devoted a page to vinyl clothes. While the adolescents of the middle class were covering parts of themselves in plastic, the counterculture celebrated nature. For both groups the highest compliment in the new slang was "unreal."[95]

The paper doll of the 1940s had now been rebuilt in plastic, both nice only to play with. *Mademoiselle* magazine informed its middle-class audience what the American male took seriously: "All those little dolls you can take home and screw are still motivating the jerks who cruise the singles bars." The view from mass culture displayed relationships between brainwashed females and retarded males, yearning to be free through sexuality, attractive by correct consumption, and protectively colored through "unisex," what *Newsweek* in 1966 called "a peculiar new class of teen-age androgyny."[96]

The androgynous inclination of the adolescent males was, through example and advertising, becoming contagious. Revealing the female leg was not about sexuality, as the cheerleader's father understood. The vinyl packaging, and the short skirts over tights, celebrated affluence and profits, the masks of middle-class fashion, playfulness and youth, even innocence and virginity, almost everything but sex. But obviously the young were not becoming celibate. Their fashions conveyed what they believed was an appropriate message for the times: the men's long hair and the women's short skirts both proclaimed that the bearer rejected the middle-class adult world of demarcated sexes—barbarian males who destroyed each other in wars and conventionally fashionable women who bound their man's wounds, cheered his excess, and wept at his burial.

• • •

Participants in the middle-class youth brigades of the culture war felt safe enough to postpone decisions about their economic futures, or to assume that somehow everything eventually would turn out to be fine. These young people had been raised in amazing affluence. From 1960 to 1968, the total personal income of Americans rose more than 70 percent, and the gross national product almost doubled, while unemployment averaged 4.8 percent. Daniel Yankelovich discovered that while the historic events of the sixties unfolded, including the assassinations, civil rights and antiwar demonstrations, "the vast majority of Americans" went on with their lives "unruffled, their outlook on life hardly touched." But the state of the economy was more intrusive than blood and fire in the streets. Even a slight economic perturbation was likely to strike Americans as unfamiliar and ominous. In 1965, about one-quarter of the respondents in a poll said their chief concern was Vietnam, and an equal number worried most about the economy. Within a year, 60 percent of those polled answered that the economy was their most urgent problem, while only 5 percent replied that the war worried them most.[97]

In 1967, inflation began to undermine the nation's prospects. Then the average cost of living index was 100; by 1973, it was 133. The purchasing power of the dollar went from 100 cents in 1967 to 75 cents in 1973. In the middle of this spiral, after almost a decade of what inevitably was called the superboom, a relatively mild recession descended in 1970, against which there was a disproportionately severe reaction. Taxes also began to rise. Good times had rolled along for so long that the nation seemed less prepared than usual for what apologists were beginning to call "a pause." A news magazine made the obvious point: "Sidewalks are too narrow for protest marchers and food stamp lines."[98]

Of course the usual cultural retrenchment began at once; parental authority was reasserted, and increasing numbers of young people began looking for work, even though hair styles did not return to the pre-Beatles era. Because of the state of the economy as well as the diminution in the number of college-bound students, job prospects for graduate students—the group most active in the earlier political demonstrations—began a long decline. When the children's own futures were threatened it was predictable that they would adopt what they had to of the middle-class ethic against which they had been struggling, even while the middle class was embracing many of youth culture's innovations in personal appearance. The nation's retailers, recording companies, clothing manufacturers, drug smugglers, and advertisers, among others, found profit in this reciprocity of culture.

When rising inflation was accompanied by increasing unemployment—the new, ugly word was "stagflation"—optimism was bound to crash, expectations to lower, and concern for the plight of others to diminish. The great culture war finally gave way to its centrifugal separatism, its eventual devolution to the church of one. Then, as a matter of course, attention focused on the apparent impossibility of sustaining marriage and led to a reinvigorated national obsession with money. Nothing, neither civil rights nor political resistance, could withstand the unprecedented hypertrophy of the acquisitive urges. Economic pressure released the middle class from its fleeting concern for the republic's political health to regroup its energies for worrying about the economy, and for more shopping as a distraction from the worrying.

The weakened economy delivered an unambiguous message to the American people: there had been too little discipline, too much iconoclasm, too much passion, and, most of all, too much change. It was time now for anything but change. A judge in Milford, New Hampshire, resented young people for disdaining his values, but that was superficial. He really believed that "it's change, that's what's got Milford edgy."[99] The Watergate scandal, that series of events that drove Nixon out of the White House, was the most dramatic example of the corrosive consequences of an absence of controls. Once such chaos ended, the nation would demand renewed stability, and civil rights and other forms of social change would have to wait.

The famous American unconcern with history turned out to be a myth. The fear of change, of the future, characterized Americans as much as anyone else. They did not want the rules changed from those with which they had grown up. They were as conservatively rooted, treasuring memory, as anyone. Barbara Baisley, a thirty-four-year-old mother of four and wife of a lawyer in Glencoe, a Chicago suburb, was succinct: "I want my children to live and grow up in an America as I knew it."[100] Even the churches were unsettling worshippers. A former Minneapolis churchgoer attributed the decline of the churches to disorienting change: "I used to go to church and the preacher would talk about God, Jesus and the Bible. Now he tells me why I shouldn't buy grapes."[101] A government official worried along with the rest of the middle class: "The values that we held so dear are being shot to hell. Everything is being attacked—what you believed in, what you learned in school, in church, from your parents. So the middle class is sort of losing heart. They had their eye on where they were going and suddenly it's all shifting sands."[102]

Losing what had been previously accumulated, perhaps over generations, was the overwhelming fear, intensified by the fact of inflation and anxiety over unemployment. The fear of slipping to an earlier personal and family economic level focused the thinking of millions, especially those living close to the margin of the lower class. Many ethnic Americans belonged to the lower middle class, where the fears of black progress were most keenly felt, and where the children had not fought on the campuses as much as they had in Vietnam. It was widely understood, but not often said out loud, "that black militance can push some WASPS and some liberals around, but it will *not* push ethnics around."[103]

The middle class paid most of the taxes, but the lower middle class felt it was forced to pay most of the cultural and psychological costs. These ethnically conscious Americans believed they paid the real price for school integration, "while assorted social planners and liberal moralists retreat at night to their suburban fastnesses." For Americans near the class boundaries, "the smoked Irishmen—the colored . . . represent change and instability, kids who cause trouble in school, who get treatment your kids never got, that you never got. . . . The black kids mean a change in the rules." A West Coast carpenter did not report his moonlighting income to the IRS: "Screw the government," he said. "They just give it to some black bastard anyway for doing nothing."[104] These increasingly bitter people were the "forgotten Americans" and the "Silent Majority," to whom Richard Nixon appealed when he insinuated himself into the role of chief advocate for all true Americans.

What the lower middle class wanted most was respectability, value in the eyes of others. This was its version of the hierarchy of wealth that motivated the higher middle class. The badges that earned the respect of the family and community were known everywhere: "well-behaved children, neatly kept home and yard, and a *nice* neighborhood." All of this was now "threatened by a long-haired 'hippie' in the house, weeds in the neighbor's yard, and a Negro in the next block."[105] Manhood, self-esteem, and status were at risk. Especially for the members of this cultural stratum, still composed largely of the children of immigrants, respectability in an exaggerated way stood for wealth. It was the only shield the lower middle class had against the encroachment of the barbarians—the sexually ambiguous, the blacks, and the untidy.

On balance, it was not the sagging economy, the perceived unfairness of forced school integration, or even welfare and Vietnam that were the most unsettling. The underlying problem was not so concrete. The middle class had "a nagging sense that life is going sour—that . . . the whole society somehow has lost its way."[106] For all its need to maintain at least the appearance of control, the middle class now recognized that no one was minding the store they cared most about; that, while the body politic was crumbling out of reckless neglect, the nation's leaders seemed determined to fight the wrong battles, like busing, or were forced to fight destructive and distracting ones, like Watergate, and could not win in Vietnam.

Small-town, Protestant America allied itself with the urban, Catholic ethnics in demanding either a return to the good old days or, at least, some semblance of stability. These tensions replayed some of the social struggles of the 1920s, of the provincial mentality against more cosmopolitan Americans. The publisher of the El Dorado (Kansas) newspaper commented that he would like to build a fence around his town to protect it from the "Mickey Mouse" problems of—what? "They . . . want to withdraw from New York; Lindsayland and the other big U.S. cities are more alarming now than the jungles of Indochina or the wiles of Europe."[107] The great difference was that the forces of the city and its suburbs had grown much stronger since the twenties. Now the city represented black ghettos, not those of immigrants, and the arguments were over marijuana, not alcohol, votes for eighteen-year-olds, not women, and about a meaningless war in progress, not one just past. The old exhaustions receded as new angers took over.

The culture war attacked the self-esteem of the middle class. The thirties had threatened its wealth and the sixties challenged its worth. This was particularly hurtful because it was the children of the good life who rejected their parents' struggle to provide for the children. They not only dismissed the hard-won material progress of the middle class, but its very personality. The parents thought they had liberated themselves from the narrow and unenlightened world of their own childhoods. But now their children shouted that they had not gone far enough, that their success had made them unfeeling, too rational, guilty of every sin of omission, and unable to love. If the children, always designated as the major beneficiaries of middle-class success, did not value who the parents were or what they had, what was the point? The painful reconfiguration of the middle-class male, especially in his role as an unsure father—working endlessly, ambivalent about lost traditions, and paying the bills to raise and educate the young—was now described by dissident young people as a crime that, by silence, supported racism, the Vietnam war, and a culture satisfied with mere consumption, the goal this culture had always sought as its due—right, pleasant, and inoffensive.

Parents could hope that young people would recover from their spasms, would eventually come to their senses and finally get in line for a job so that they could join the generations in the serious business of living well. But, even so, it was obvious that both sides were scarred by the sixties, that things might never again be as pleasant as almost everyone thought they had been.

After the sixties there were no more courteous victims. Throughout American culture the level of civility crashed. Political noise, economic shoving, and cultural hatreds were everywhere. The etiquette of suffering was rewritten by the great and rancorous culture war. Other victims now demanded central positions on the stage. Having learned to elbow their way into the spotlight, they now sought to control the "social agenda," to dictate the way other people should live. The coming years were devoted to new struggles to redefine women, ethnicity, and the nation itself.

6

FREEDOM
FROM LOVE

A sense of belonging and psychological health require a plausible story of creation (now called "roots" in America), memories and myths of parental love and protection, and successful rites of passage into adult competence. By connecting the generations, these foundation memories emphasize the continuity of human experience. This was shattered by World War II and the transforming nature of postwar affluence, more than by the exercises of the 1960s. The Holocaust exploded the trust peoples of the earth thought they could safely invest in each other's inherent goodness, and the atomic bomb stripped science of whatever pretensions it may have had about being the only path to human progress.

After the war, recessive fathers and a rising standard of living provided young people with the motive and the means needed to break away, abandon tested and failed ways, and explore individual freedom. This quest culminated in a great escape, a transition from wanting to having freedom from one's own past.

As is well known, the cultural travails of middle-class America in the twentieth century produced the separate, sovereign self, the final logical extension of the Protestant Reformation's psychological torque that spun toward more and smaller sects until the irreducible sect of one was eventually reached. The new souls were free at last, craving expressiveness, sensitive to inner vibrations, radically alone, sometimes mourning the dissipation of tradition, by which was invariably meant a way of life that was not so cold.

Obviously, the transition to such freedom depended on rejecting the values and deceptions absorbed as a child, on becoming more truly uprooted than the immigrants ever were. Such a deconversion secularized the creation myths and facilitated a declaration of psychic independence. Such separatism created distance from the cult, the culture of fathers, the old ways, which were seen as comforting, unambiguous, and oppressive. There had been a time when such separation was called exile, never to be suffered save by threat of force. But it became a heartfelt prayer in the church of the single believer.

The velocity of change during the war and its aftershocks threw up a new psychological type, called "protean man" by Robert Jay Lifton, the Yale psychiatrist. This new man was detached from his own history and felt unloved and abandoned during a childhood remembered as empty, and subsequently was tormented by feelings of unworthiness and vulnerability. But protean man was extraordinarily adaptive, fitting in to the moment, able to change whenever desirable, and to do it again and again, not troubled by the abandonment of beliefs or the experience of wild contradictions, attracted to change as if he had no prior qualities to impede his next transformation. He was fascinated by innovation, experiment, improvisation, and action (as disclosed in the postwar fine arts—especially in aleatory music and action painting). He was flooded by bits of unconnected and superficial information, but because he had no enduring beliefs by which to organize this inescapable datachatter, his cherished sense of impermanence became at the same time a source of deepening anxiety. The ground seemed to move under his every step. He was a radically free man.

As such, in Lifton's words, "he requires a symbolic father-lessness."[1]

Throughout the century the conventional masculinity of the American father was progressively weakened. The immigrant's child, comfortable in the language of the streets and schools, familiar with the exotic customs of the Americans, often enough became ashamed of his father's accent, attitudes, and incompetence in negotiating the new culture. He thought that to become an American he had to leave papa behind, as papa may also have wished, but in sadness. Similarly, the generation that was lost in the 1920s experimented with ways to escape the clutches of vulgar and provincial fathers too occupied with making money and seeking middle-class approval. The fathers who could not support their families during the Great Depression, those who were debilitated by their well-paid bureaucratic jobs after the war, and those who repudiated young people in the sixties all risked losing their children.

Since mid-century, American poets had been obsessed with the absent father, a wholesale passion, according to Stanley Kunitz, that had not existed in other times or places. Kunitz observed that "The father-and-son poem, as written from the perspective of the son, carries a 'Made in America' label." He quoted Howard Moss's elegy which compressed the quest and the pain:

> Father, whom I murdered every night but one,
> That one, when your death murdered me.[2]

Finally, in the name of equality, feminism required adjustments in the daily lives of some men and women, educated, middle-class city people, often relatively well-paid professionals, those who were close enough to the protean personality to respond to the appeal of no horizons. Whether it was intentional or not, and it usually was not, the mere existence of the debate about women's independence further challenged male authority, not merely the oppressive, privileged authority as men, but the legitimate authority of adults, including men. Some feminists acclaimed the androgynous male as evidence of evolutionary progress away from the hairy, chest-thumping biped who for the sake of domestic tranquillity should be relegated to his cave.

As women sought jobs beyond the conventional definition of "women's work" and encountered stiff opposition from men in power, their political education became more intense and personal. Adopting the complaints of all excluded Americans, they struggled against discrimination in employment. The National Organization for Women (NOW), organized in 1966 by women who came of age during the war, in effect became the "women's rights" division of a still nascent feminism. Its primary goal was equality in public, beyond the home, while most women who felt oppressed assigned blame to their primary assignment as housewives, vaguer than discrimination in the workplace, but culturally approved and widely taken for granted by both men and women. So, NOW was also compelled to challenge the culture's ascription of sex roles if it was to succeed as a reformist organization dedicated to improving the working conditions of the professional middle class.

NOW struggled against intimidation, as blacks had also, and won important regulatory and legislative victories on the model of the civil rights movement. The connection between feminism and the black struggle was firm because feminism emerged just as the civil rights movement sagged. A woman scholar observed that "now it appeared that the predominantly White women's movement was going to reap the benefits that the Black movement had sown." More than blacks, women benefited from affirmative-action programs, especially in higher education, where white women were usually preferred to blacks. When some white feminists referred to themselves as "niggers," they disclosed the centripetal quality of their politics and the separatism of their vision. NOW did not and was

not intended to speak to a wider constituency. That was someone else's job.[3]

The roots of the new organized feminism lay in student radicalism of the sixties, especially the civil rights movement in
the South and SDS in the North. It was inevitable that the
students' struggle to liberate the oppressed would eventually
convince women that freedom begins at home. When women
radicals were assigned the tasks of taking notes and fetching
coffee the contradictions could not be suppressed, nor could a
distinct women's movement, the next phase of separatism. The
heart of their early struggle was a search for a politics of intimacy, focused on unequal relationships, in contrast to NOW's
more conventional view of politics and the law, analogous to
that of the NAACP. Younger feminists disdained struggle
within the terms set by conventional culture; they were determined to reconstruct culture itself. A key to success was "raising consciousness," teasing out the subtle oppressions of daily
life by sharing examples of coercion in loving, language, sex,
and the kitchen, as well as the workplace. The catalogue of the
male's spurious claims to inherent superiority and unearned
privilege began to expand.

The incremental growth of sexual freedom in the sixties also
forced some women to think carefully about the contrast between their role and that of their partners. Some men assumed
that greater sexual freedom had already liberated women to
the extent necessary, so that for them a women's movement
was pointless. The sexism of black radicals was the most blatant. In 1966, Stokely Carmichael announced that "the only
position for women in SNCC is prone," and a Black Panther
offered a slogan: "Pussy power!" When they attacked sexual
liberation, the early feminists struck home: "We have come to
see that the so-called Sexual Revolution is merely a link in the
chain of abuse laid on women throughout patriarchal history."
Feminism taught them to speak plainly: "What's in it for us?
And the answer is simple. We've been sold out."[4] The ex-

tremes of the sixties' sexuality served men who did not object
to consuming women, and women who were not yet able to
stand on their own feet.

As a separatist movement away from patriarchy, as a potential majority force, feminism outlasted the other passions of the
culture war, and although it did not convince the majority of
women or men, it changed the cultural ecology of the nation.
Even its opponents were now obliged at least to oppose what
they had earlier not even recognized. Its tactics evolved from
awareness to domestic politics to demanding equal rights under
the law and in the market to, finally, a determination to change
the patriarchal assumptions and habits of the culture.

The widespread view in the sixties of woman as martyr was
precisely what the new feminists determined to change, along
with the myths of strong woman and good woman, in favor of
woman as equal person. The hypertrophy of personhood in
every one of the sixties' movements inspired middle-class feminists, as it had blacks and white dissidents, and also the millions of somewhat rebellious children of the larger middle class.
For all, the question was always whether personhood and organized political behavior were reconcilable.

In the seventies and early eighties, feminism led to direct
action and self-help groups, including anti-rape and anti-
assault hot lines, shelters, health collectives, Women Studies
departments in colleges, bookstores, "networks" of supportive
women, and, occasionally, covens of witches. Inevitably, the
separatist mentality drove to destroy itself, on the model of
black power. Feminism led to the splintering off of radical les-
bians, who felt their ideological purity was endangered by the
compromises of the center.

By 1969 more men than women said they would vote for a
woman as president, while the percentage of women who would
do so had steadily dropped since the peak two decades earlier,
when the icon of the good woman organized middle-class assumptions. Polls in the early seventies disclosed that a majority
of women supported feminism in only half of the relevant is-

sues. In fact, most women were "apathetic" about their role in "this man's world." But a 1973 poll concluded that two-thirds of college women believed that discrimination against women was pervasive. As always, education was the key to conflicting politics. Noncollege women rejected ideas about sisterhood and the exploitation of women. But they supported equal pay for equal work, thought it very important for a "real man" to be concerned with the sexual satisfaction of his partner, and wanted equality in family decisions. College and non-college women strongly disagreed about the family: less than half of the students believed the family was most important, while 70 percent of the nonstudents thought so.[5]

By its adherence to conventionality and its inability or unwillingness to send children to college, Protestant, small-town America sheltered itself from feminism. In 1972, the residents of Hope, Indiana, a town where no one had gone to college and where cheerleading was still the most prestigious activity for girls, thought of feminism as "either a joke or a bore," if they thought about it at all. The women of this town opposed feminist radicals, "just like the radicals of the colored race," rejected women who demanded more equality because women were not "held down as much as they pretend to be," and laughed at the feminists' political ambitions because women are "so weak, they'd have headaches and wouldn't be able to run the country."[6]

The growing independence of the middle-class woman was caused more by education and work than by organized feminism. It cannot be argued that feminism created the extraordinary movement of women into the work force, because they were now returning to patterns typical of the first half of the century. They resembled their strong grandmothers more than their good mothers. The true demographic aberration occurred in the semi-domesticated fifties. Nonetheless, as a careful study showed, the sheer magnitude of women working—most often to solidify their families' middle-class status or as single parents to pay the bills—was unprecedented. By contrast, however, the number of women who expected to marry in 1980 was the same as it had been in 1960, and only 1 percent wanted no children. But the younger women were better educated, expected to work outside of typical "women's work," and did so. In 1984 more than 75 percent of women college graduates were employed.[7]

Feminism scored countless victories when women stood their ground. But they could not find ways to exercise political power or to develop a politics that extended beyond themselves, make their way to the top of the market's institutions, change the language as much as some demanded, pass the Equal Rights Amendment, solve day-care problems, prevent wife battering, or resolve female poverty and other problems that required a nonseparatist vision. They did force profound changes in their relationships with men, not the he-men, who continued to snicker, but the men whose work had for decades led them to undergo their own traumatic transformation into androgyny. The gentle men of freedom responded positively if not immediately to feminism.

In the early seventies, when the new feminism showed that it was durable, the psychologist Kenneth Keniston surveyed the shifting terrain:

> Many men at this point are trying to throw off the old images—the images that men cannot be sensitive and they can't be gentle and they can't cry and they can't like flowers and so forth. There's a whole kind of ethos of tenderness and sensitivity and the formerly feminine qualities, at the same time that women are moving in to more of the things that men had. But men are moving out of these positions; they don't want them anymore.[8]

Yet other men opposed feminism because of its new challenges, not only to the male's traditional sexual domination, but to his need to feel superior everywhere. A Yale student acknowledged that his opposition to feminism stemmed from his fear of sexual competition: "If I get shown up by a guy, well, I've had a fighting chance and he's smarter than I am.

If I get shown up by a girl, it's a blow to my ego—I'm not supposed to be shown up by girls."9

Some men accepted feminism because they imagined that it would lighten the load men, as conventionally defined, were supposed to carry, but no longer wanted to:

Women's lib is great. A man has enough of a burden.

It's good. . . . I would be glad to have the pressure off my shoulders.

[I]t frees me from being forced into the role of rough and tough, provider, insensitive male.10

For men, in ways not yet sufficiently studied or understood, androgyny led to a free-floating deference. A thirty-two-year-old woman, never married, described such men as "emotionally immature, self-indulgent, and unable to make commitments . . . they are little more than boys."11 This was difficult for her because she wanted children before it was too late, but she could not find an authentic man.

Should feminism assist, even as an unintended consequence, in the emergence of less-mature men, no one would benefit. Of course, maturity implies the exercise of legitimate authority—the sort that strengthens the dependent's own growing and independent authority. Parental authority, including that of the father, implies the strongest obligation to shape the moral universe for children. To abdicate this function is to create kinetic and uneasy children who, when they are able, will turn against and then away from their parents: protean children who may succeed in the market as they fail in love.

In 1982, the poet Robert Bly came to believe that the desirable cultural evolution of the American male had a price, that along the way to greater understanding and sensitivity something of value had been lost. In the process of becoming rounder and gentler and even more thoughtful, the American middle-class male had not become more free. "He's a nice boy who not only pleases his mother but also the young woman he is living with." Bly liked the "soft males" in his audiences for having lost the aggressiveness that led to war and to harming the earth. But they did not have much energy, knew more about preserving than giving life, and seemed to attach themselves to "strong women who positively radiate energy." Some women, according to Bly, exuded the message that they wanted softer males and some had, for sound political reasons, rewarded male passivity during the Vietnam war. He discovered that the modern middle-class male had learned to say to his wife or lover: " 'I can feel your pain, and I consider your life as important as mine, and I will take care of you and comfort you.' But he could not say what *he* wanted."

These men had lost the ability to be fierce, or even angry, when necessary. They needed the inspiration not only of the "Virgin Mary and the blissful Jesus, but . . . [of] the wildman covered with hair." The wildman was not the atavistic he-man of life before feminism, but the man who could roar when insulted or harmed, who would not shrivel in a corner imagining what might have been. The "soft males" took their cues from their fathers, who, as Bly understood, were "a little ashamed" of office work and found it hard to explain to their children, who then tried to uncover what was hidden, to probe for hypocrisy, to unmask Father. Father's remoteness, not his evil, drove the son. But the need both to escape from and to find the absent father remained: "the longing for the father, the confusion about why I'm so separate from my father, where is my father, doesn't he love me, what is going on?"[12]

As everywhere else in the postwar, bureaucratized world, but especially in America, it was becoming difficult to escape fatherlessness. This was most characteristic of the Americans because many of their prior inclinations—toward mobility and innovation—edged them closer to what they perceived to be intolerable frustration with restraints, away from the weak father who could not perform, and from the strong father who could, but thereby thwarted action and dreams. This was intensified by the American veneration of youth, the new beginning, the fresh start. Thus, some of the nation's central ideas about its own freedom coincided with the individual escape, the merging with the flux and the explosiveness of contemporary history. It is illustrative that psychoanalysts began to lose interest in oedipal relationships, concentrating instead on narcissistic disorders.[13]

Because the mechanism by which freedom was wrested from prior authority was the replacement—melodramatic psychoanalysts called this "murder"—of parents, freedom's price should have been guilt, which, however, presupposed acknowledgment of transgression. But the repudiation of androgynous fathers who did not constitute authority was, for protean Americans, a recognition of the fathers' psychic abdication—suicide!—and against them no action need be taken and no guilt felt. Males seemed to be failing at every important conventional task. Male suicides outnumbered female in every age group: the male rate steadily increased until, by age eighty-five, fifteen men killed themselves for every woman who did so.[14]

A result of fatherlessness was a weakened or malformed conscience.[15] Describing what he had learned in the Harvard Business School, a former student personified freedom from prior constraint: "You learn in school not to give a shit if the people you climb over are weak or sick or small or blind. You understand that everybody is your enemy, and you learn to fear and hate people."[16] Such freedom required redefining the self, work, wife, if any, and children, if any. It required cutting those threads of belief that for previous generations helped to make life seem coherent. Freedom now embodied incoherence, with attendant anxieties and drugs, but it was also assumed that incoherence and amorality switched on the green light that F. Scott Fitzgerald described as necessary to Americans. The question was no longer whether, but where, to go, and the new answer had to be: everywhere, no speed limits or other arbitrary interdictions, lest the sense of well-being be disturbed.

In postwar America, unprecedented numbers of ambitious

youngsters fled to college from what they felt was their parents' closed world. This institutionalized and camouflaged the escape, and did not always facilitate education. The energies of such young people were occupied by enormously strong inner pressures, which excluded less personally relevant information, such as the structure of the sonata, dispassionate science, or the history of other people. Many were most "comfortable" in psychology programs. Yet, because of their needs, such refugees were often the best students, ravenous for information and symbols to reinforce their break, delighting in their new anticommunity of isolated and iconoclastic readers. If they could read they had come to the right place to make their sense of unworthiness and fragility more intense. The voice of postwar American freedom was that of the most, perhaps best-educated generation in the nation's history.

Now an entire culture called for what it knew not, an elimination of the prohibitions that its members assumed crippled personality. For them, freedom meant a release of "creativity" and personality from the repressive ordinances of a prior culture. Because this older culture led its members to limit wants and fear novelty, what was required for greater freedom was to renounce repression, to search for and destroy the stop signs in the mind. Because culture is, in a sense, a shared agreement about what ought not to be enjoyed, the expansion of permissible pleasure threatened culture, the prior culture, the culture of the elders, the traditions of time and known civilization. The question then is whether love would be viewed as an unacceptable restriction of freedom. In popular parlance divorce is called "gaining my freedom."

Philip Rieff, the University of Pennsylvania sociologist, showed how the western world had slowly liberated itself from religious culture—the organization of thought by faith, acceptance of mystery, invention of music and architecture to glorify God, and the rationalization of social institutions, such as the patriarchal family, to reflect its God-centeredness. This ascetic culture, rich in symbols and nuance, based on conscience and guilt, thou-shalt-nots, was overthrown in favor of a psychological culture, symbolically impoverished and vulgar, based on intelligence, leading to a desire to feel good, and composed of members who believed they had passed into a world that seemed not to have evolved from their own childhoods: new people in a new world, free to worship each in his own closet, liberated from emotional bonds, emancipated from love.

In this new, irreducible church of solitary worship, impulse replaced prayer: "Religious man was born to be saved; psychological man is born to be pleased," as Rieff wrote. Stifling a want was the correlative of what used to be sin. Psychological man, unimpeded by belief, controlled by information, luxuriated in his power to consume. Neither the bread nor the wine would be taken, for fear of spoiling the larger appetite. He accepted whatever constituted therapy, although besieged psychiatrists could not help because of their own confusion about whether they approved of any renunciations. Psychological men dismissed heroes and guides, admired and envied each other, scorned the drones in the lower middle class, occasionally were cognizant of black Americans, about whom somebody, but not themselves, should do something, and were insensitive to the world.[17]

Still, the question remained: if prohibitions could be demolished, would happiness result? For all his illuminating crankiness, Freud thought not. Even Nietzsche, our great, thundering prophet of expressiveness, occasionally peered over the brink and recoiled. But the free Americans demanded everything. They insisted on the release of the isolated self, which, in the sixties, was called "doing your own thing," and which existentialists described as "authenticity," and by post-ascetic Americans, characteristically in a command: "Get out of the way." A twenty-five-year-old bicyclist ran over and killed an eighty-six-year-old woman because, he said in justification, "she got in my way."[18]

Hence, this transformation was no longer passive, as middle-class Americans with good prospects took the offensive, stalk-

ing previously settled convictions and assumptions, determined
to leave nothing standing of repressive and protective communal culture. For them, the past threatened the emerging synthesis of a personality resembling protean man, but
rounder, more detailed, and more dangerous. In postwar
America, obviously, the new man did not have the field to
himself. The older culture, which he despised and transcended,
was all around him, in the stubborn, sometimes quaint, but
always depressingly irrational customs and faith of the lower
middle class and its always present spokesmen: Father Coughlin in the 1930s, Charles Lindbergh in the 1940s, Senator
McCarthy in the 1950s, George Wallace in the 1960s, and fundamentalist Christians in the 1970s and 1980s.

The new freedom, experienced in the past by scattered individuals, was now a cultural fact. Where the American stood
was, as usual, determined by money and education. The well-
and the least-educated, the middle class and the poor, opposed
tradition. By contrast, the lower middle class, the Americans
who were stuck between the stronger and the weaker, buffeted
from both sides like the second of three children, asserted pride
in work and ethnic identity, clung to what they knew and had,
and constituted the nucleus of traditional America. They had
replaced the very rich, who used to guard what was thought to
be the nation's deepest values, while dabbling in a trivial gentlemanly education.

The Americans divided themselves between those who
wanted more and those who would not tolerate less. The poor
and those who were comfortable or affluent wanted more; the
lower middle class, afraid it would lose what it had laboriously
scraped together, was determined to hang on. Lower-middle-
class Americans did not expect to earn more discretionary
money each year, and usually did not, so they learned to seek
security, not progress. They sought the peace that came from
acceptance, from birth and death in the natural order of things,

from children's growth, and long association with close and known people who through practice understood forgiveness and shame. They were defensive and feared moral chaos. They strove for a shared happiness deriving from the ritual of family gatherings, where seating arrangements and conversation were identical from one occasion to another. This culture rested on intimate human associations that radiated warmth and sentimentality, with relatives as best friends who did not object to silence. Because mass culture no longer reflected their values, they stopped going to the movies, unless it was one of Disney's, were cautious about what they viewed on television, and read almost nothing. They feared and resented strangers who—they knew from watching Archie Bunker and suffering through ethnic humor aimed at them—thought they were laughable, primitives, and a drag on the enlightenment of the nation.

The free people of the middle class, by contrast, learned to be comfortable with strangers—they were strangers themselves, occasionally to themselves. They were driven by ambition, feared boredom, and believed that orderly change would be beneficial. They had isolated themselves, yet feared loneliness. After distancing themselves from their own communal and ethnic roots, for example, many academics contended that other Americans should find ways to live more communally. The cultural appetite of these strangers was voracious, and they enjoyed seeing and doing everything, while occasionally complaining about declining quality and standards. Irony seemed their natural vocabulary.

America had become two hostile cultures: shared and private; static and fluid; acquiescent and critical; local and cosmopolitan; ascetic and therapeutic; faithful and agnostic. During the sixties, each grew warier of the other. When lower-middle-class Americans—urban Catholics and rural Protestants—came to power, they demanded a restoration of (their) values, families, pride, and retribution against the arrogant strangers who had insulted and ignored them, sometimes smirked, and imposed taxes to help the blacks, who threatened the order and predictability on which the lower middle class depended to avert panic.

The Vietnam war, with its rancorous political divisions, taught both cultures, hawks and doves, that the war's leaders were either incompetent or vicious, maybe both. Doves, mostly middle-class, and hawks, mostly lower-middle-class, were maddeningly frustrated: doves because they could not stop the killing, and hawks because they could not have a victory. As 500,000 young men evaded the draft, as a majority of the people despaired of influencing the government, the war confounded what it meant to be a citizen. In fact, one of the major casualties of that war was the very idea of citizenship. If nothing could influence the government, if all the protests and all the death had neither effect nor purpose, then it was preferable to look out for oneself, to repudiate the government as a potentially lethal threat to domestic order.

Unless it was based on the maxim that love of country is blind, patriotism became confused. So much was thrown into question so quickly: Vietnam undermined confidence in the nation's political wisdom and military strength; Watergate, in its democratic processes; OPEC, its technological and industrial capability; and the inability to rescue hostages in Iran and Lebanon undermined the self-esteem of the people. Because of the nation's impotence, Americans could no longer confidently inhale its strength and glory.

People naturally concluded that life used to be simpler, not blighted by so many ambiguous, interminable, and inconclusive arguments, that (it was remembered through the usual haze of nostalgia) hard work had paid off and people were happier. Americans still showed their dazzling smiles in ads, but human relationships seemed increasingly mechanistic and empty: "Have a nice day." In a major poll in 1975, four out of five families responded that the nation was "doing badly," and over half believed that a depression was on the way. According to another poll, by the mid-seventies almost three-quarters of Americans assumed that the nation's leaders had, over the preceding decade, "consistently lied" to the public. A life-insurance study reported that half of the public did not believe that their vote mattered, or that important decisions should be trusted to the nation's leaders. The nation's happiness quotient was dropping—national and personal prospects were not encouraging—and life in America was turning sour.[19]

As always, more dangerous, unspoken fears lurked behind the politics. Many of the successful members of the middle class, those who were wealthy enough to want more, were looking for something difficult to define, some intangible element missing from American life. Some felt that the American air had become a little thin. For others, the responsibilities and conflicts associated with authority at work seemed burdened with gloomy consequences of loneliness, nostalgia for someone else's life. Some attempted to bury this dark side under wealth. For them, education could proceed and money could be made, despite inflation and other people's unemployment. Other people, other attitudes—music, ritual, and childhood—seemed not so much dangerous as pointless, not a threat as much as a mystery about why so many others found them satisfying, or said they did.

The world noticed that these Americans worked harder than others. If one of life's goals was consumption, they were the world's champions, the most comfortable diners and warmest players. Responding to financial incentives, not bureaucratic regulations or sentimental sermons, affluent middle-class Americans seemed not only to pursue but apparently to find happiness, and they did so by reimagining a world in which continuity was uninteresting and everything was possible.

Success required that the affluent learn to concentrate on themselves, which was apparently easy, and adhere to a crippling rationalism, also easy, even though its ineffectiveness had been brilliantly exposed in Vietnam. The costs of the emerging psychology of the middle class included divorce, an unwillingness to have children, and thriving industries in various therapies, drugs, and assorted escapisms, including television, spectator sports, theatrical sex, and compulsive consumption. Many people felt the need to reinvent themselves, especially women, who arduously attempted to reconceive not only their roles but their very nature, including the facts and implications of female biology. Recognizing that their pastlessness obscured their identity in the present, blacks celebrated their *Roots* on television, while half of the nation watched. Americans recalculated who they were and where they belonged in a culture that was losing its joy and coherence.[20]

Since 1968, a domestic battle had been waged between people committed to freedom—feminists and blacks—and those committed to virtue—ethnics and religious fundamentalists. The battle's earthly prize was the middle class, the onlookers whose sympathy or votes might aid one side or the other, and whose active participation, if this could be imagined, would determine the outcome. The troops for freedom summoned the state to act in their behalf; troops for virtue opposed state programs for other people, but wanted lower prices, job security, respect for themselves and their nation, and so supported huge expenditures for defense to feel strong and proud themselves, what they called "#1."

Communal, lower-middle-class Americans had confidence in their own ethnic cultures, which continued to rest on family and church. They dismissed such warnings as "You can't be Italian and be a good American." Retorted an Italian priest: "Who says?"[21] Their strength, as they understood perfectly well, depended on not assimilating into mainstream America, from which they were excluded anyway by lack of education. Their overriding demand was that freedom, as others defined it, not interfere with what they thought was their pursuit of a moral life and of ways to protect their supposedly vulnerable children. It was a time for ethnic pride, for the slow accretion of organic adaptation, not the brilliant schemes of crazed bureaucrats who did not understand real Americans. They were becoming a potent political force, not as workers or union members, not as a class, but as Poles, Russians, Irish, Italians, blacks, Vietnamese, Koreans, Chicanos, and Haitians, among others. It would be difficult to write rules by which this "team" would play.

The pursuit of personal and national salvation led millions of lower-middle-class people to reaffirm Christianity and fear the cities, especially if they lived in them. Religious revivalists and proud ethnics detested blacks who seemed never satisfied, courts that forced busing on unwilling parents, and the pampering of misfits and lunatics on the margins—criminals, homosexuals, welfare cheats, abortionists, and shrill women. Traditionalists in America had always connected religion to public virtue, and thus to patriotism. "One nation, under God" was understood literally. Piety, as they defined it, was integral to being an American. Thus, for them, pornography and abortion were seditious.

Having seceded from the moral culture, the free middle class abandoned all hierarchies except those based on personal wealth, the only ones that mattered. Of course, this was also true for middle-class blacks, estimated to comprise about 40 percent of the black population.[22] Egalitarian among themselves, the fatherless Americans demanded that money talk, with no distinctions between old and new, earned and unearned. Feminists, struggling with patriarchy, and middle-class blacks, resisting the residual social stigmata of color, represented their own interests in an environment that insisted that only legal tender be accepted, no questions asked, no quarter given, and no other language spoken.

Profoundly at odds with communal culture, psychological man sought better living, so he was completely at home in America. He had learned Freud's lesson to be satisfied with second-best, to accept the discontent inherent in his culture. Living was focused not around grand abstractions or glory, but around gaining freedom by withholding commitment. Living on the surface permitted only superficial wounds. For example, Bruce, the lover of a writer, believed that "there's nothing in life that's worth being unhappy about. You choose to feel pain. You can choose, just as easily, not to feel it." His lover asked, what about death? "I wouldn't mind dying," he responded, "and I wouldn't be sad if you died."[23]

There was now less to hide than there used to be. Communal culture still made its believers cringe, requiring skulking in the shadows to relieve this or that pressure. This older culture funneled illicit behavior toward the safety valves. But in psychological culture everything was licit, so there was no risk; everyone was a stranger and everyone knew the meaning of comfort. Every stranger was the same and thus familiar so that the old, stuffy formalities were consigned to history. Because none of us mattered, we were all friendly on the surface, comfortable only with first names.

We were all tolerant because we sought not to persuade, as zealots and missionaries do. Instead, like tourists traveling near other people's lives we wished to be left alone, avoid scenes, and smile indulgently on the way to somewhere else. Everyone's opinion was solicited, all criticism welcomed, because in therapeutic culture it did not matter. This culture was essential for the further social experimentation demanded by feminists, blacks, and others excluded from the center, while moral culture, squeezed between the affluent and the poor, fought to prevent further encroachment on its turf. Communal men protested because the men of freedom, inauthentic Americans, were destroying the strength and purpose of the nation.

Without knowing or intending it, the affluent middle class replaced culture with wealth. The first intuition of the turn-of-the-century immigrants turned out to be accurate: America was a place to make money. A bargain had to be struck between the greenhorn and mainstream culture: my culture for your money. America's song to the newest outsiders was invariable: abandon who you are in exchange for wealth, become one of us, share our education and values, learn to invest your aspirations and savings, and encourage your children to repudiate you so that they may become free to make more money than you have, be better than you, and, best of all, be free, especially from you.

The three million people who immigrated in the first half of the 1980s were unlike the earlier arrivals. Almost half of the recent newcomers were Asian, while 37 percent were from Latin America and only 11 percent from Europe. Almost half of the Asians spoke English well, were college graduates, affluent, and settled in prosperous suburbs, intermixed with white Americans, who generally did not object (unless the new neighbors were uneducated refugees, a relatively small number).[24] A middle-aged American in Westchester County, New York, spoke for many: "Thank God for the Asians. They're bringing back standards to our schools. And they're so successful in small business." The Asians' median income was $23,600 while American families earned $20,800.

Asians accomplished in one generation what earlier Europeans took two or three to achieve, but Asians, like the Europeans, understood that success depended on retaining their native customs while adapting to the ways of the middle class. Everything hinged on whether what they brought was consistent with what they found. Native Asian culture, said an Indian bank officer, meant "family, education, discipline, and hard work."[25] Time will tell whether the emphasis on family can withstand the pressures of the other values. In any case, the Asians in particular brought a variety of values consistent with the requirements of the middle class. They were ready to begin as soon as they stepped off the airplane.

The course of freedom in America, as embodied in the progress of ordinary people in the middle class, moved toward an acceptance of alienation and the fragility that adheres to isolation. Of course, there can be no return to an earlier status, and no safety. For the middle class, personal wealth is the only shield, although it is useless against nonfinancial anxiety. Wealth can, however, keep the dangerous external world from intruding, unless it explodes in general war or economic crisis. But the shield is effective against other people. It is a barrier that isolates while it protects.

For the members of the middle class as employees, ownership, such as that of the earlier family farm or small business, is no longer the origin of wealth or the means to make a living. The salaries of some élite employees are high enough to create disposable income for investment in a variety of wealth-producing instruments, including real estate that generates equity and sometimes income, stocks and bonds, limited partnerships, income-producing insurance, money-market packages, and pension funds. For a few, such investment produces wealth beyond a mortal's ability to consume, as well as water wings for any but a cataclysmic future. They continue to work because they enjoy it or to heap more on their pile, not because they must. Of course, this élite wishes to retain and expand what it has, and, on the model of the old, classic capitalists who personally owned the means of production, to ward off challenges to its privileges. This most advantaged stratum of the middle class, like the earlier owners of America's enterprise, is conservative in its very reflexes.

But for the great majority of middle-class Americans, current salaries are essentially all there is. Although they no longer seek property as the means of their livelihood, they are less vulnerable to economic vicissitudes than the earlier owners of small family farms and businesses. The fortunes of these small entrepreneurs were almost always determined by the condition of the general economy as it applied to them, except that they were usually in a more fragile state than current employees. The great size of contemporary firms is a buffer against economic perturbations that would have been fatal to owners of small enterprises. In fact, size alone can now be used successfully as a persuasive argument for the public, through government, to bail out an incompetently managed automobile company or bank, if it is large enough. That the size or financial strength of a firm is a bureaucratic security blanket has been lost on no one. This makes government employment especially attractive for some. The security of bureaucratic employees, as dependents, in the public or private sector, rests on the continuing favor of the supervisor who authorizes the paycheck. Earlier owners of the means of production were vulnerable to economic forces; current middle-class employees are susceptible to the psychology of the boss.

The first concern of bureaucratic employers is their reputation at work, a more immediate concern than the firm's general prosperity. The conservative implications of such dependency prove to be irresistible. Such employees have no suggestions to make, wish only to work hard at whatever the boss initiates or seems to want. They seek the security that comes from a reputation as "a good corporate citizen," the protection of masks, the safety of unidentifiable agents. Much like the student who wills himself to become invisible when the teacher asks a difficult question, such dependents spend part of their working lives trying not to be noticed, attempting to deflect trouble by avoiding personal responsibility, which implies risk. They have no political existence at work or in their private lives, and shun active participation in public affairs.

What the middle-class employee owns is his skill—what working people have always offered employers—but now with a computer, legal brief, or ledger, not with a lathe. Because corporate fortunes are seen to be more dependent on the judgment of such employees than on the individual worker on the factory floor, the bureaucrats command commensurately higher salaries. Throughout the twentieth century, and even earlier, the skills that create the financial strength of corporations have been changing, and such evolution has created the opportunities for larger numbers of people to work their way upward. Job descriptions in middle management require specific forms of specialized "education," increasingly accessible to middle-class students. Training has replaced the capital once required to start a business. Those with such vocational training—professionals they are called—are paid accordingly, and the nature and quality of their private lives depends on the degree of their perceived value to their supervisor.

The private lives of dependent employees are not, of course, shaped exclusively by the nature of their work or the size of their paychecks. Nonetheless, it is arguable that dependency, coupled with the emphasis on what are often the intangibles of reputation at work, cannot reinforce strength and independence in the family or community. Some might compensate for bureaucratic humiliation and office frustration by exhibiting traits of independence away from the job. But because American men especially have been adjusting to dependency for decades, it is likely that significant numbers of them seek to avoid trouble—a basic middle-class imperative—wherever they find themselves. Such dependency reinforces the heightened tendency of men, as well as of the rising number of women bureaucrats, to seek equality with each other, with the men relinquishing prior privilege, and adjusting to equality with their children, with parents rejecting the antiquated authority of less enlightened eras. Psychological equality obviously obliterates authority. Fearful of conflict at work and elsewhere, the middle of the middle class seeks to give everyone what he or she wants. They can do so when such largess has no impact on the reputation at work which determines wealth and worth.

Dependency at work is reflected everywhere, because it is necessary to security in professional, personal, and even intimate relationships. It sets the limits of consumption and therefore prestige. It affects personality in ways that radiate everywhere, from demanding that political leaders be glamorous, courageous, and decisive but they take no actions that will intrude on domestic rhythms, to the celebration of others who seem to have managed their lives differently, who stand out from the cautions of middle-class lives: a straight-talking business executive, a tough-talking military officer, or a sweet-talking movie star.

Because personality is perceived to be the very heart of the middle-class regimen, its members are riveted by the personalities of others, especially when great wealth or power seems to have flowed from the consumption and display of a special self. In no other time or place has the cult of personality been so pervasive. Venerating personality as life's nucleus, the middle class demands to consume the details of personality of everyone who seeks its favor. Candidates for high, and not so high, office know that they ignore this at risk of exposure as misfits, and certain failure.

Personality has become the decisive private property of the American middle class. It is nurtured and fondled as avidly as Midas caressed his gold. It is the psychological bullion of the middle class on which its actual wealth depends. Economic man has become psychological man, and competition has been replaced by manipulation, struggle by therapy.

The therapeutic tropism of the middle class inevitably has led it to seek the help of professionals, and not only for domestic reasons. On the model of the Catholic Church's sale of indulgences to forgive sin, the new psychological confessors cannot absolve a sinner but can redefine sin as disease, which they then can attempt to cure. Greed, formerly a deadly sin, was described as an addiction by a psychiatrist with a consulting firm on Wall Street. He understood that this redefinition "puts the problem into a clinical rather than a moral framework," and thus made "money addiction" susceptible to his ministrations.[26]

The history of middle-class Americans shows that economic pressure may produce anxiety, even fright, but that they will tenaciously retain their belief that they are where they want to be, that next week will be better, and that the nation will not let them down. Some observers believed that the future of the middle class was threatened because of the economic restraints of the 1980s—deeper poverty for the poor, homelessness, more and poorer single mothers, a continuing squeeze on small farmers, low wages in service jobs, reductions in industrial jobs, the frustrations of minorities and women who are not moving upward, and the inability of many young people to buy a house. Such injustice and pain led to a conclusion that the middle class is shrinking, that America is becoming a two-tiered nation, which it always was. Defined in strictly economic terms, the middle class may for a season not be able to recruit an ever-expanding crop of replacements. Defined culturally, however, middle-class assumptions and values, hence behavior, are characteristic of both comfortable and deprived Americans. It seems reasonable to speculate that the tested ability of Americans to dissociate themselves from the material facts of their economic lives will not soon dissipate. The middle class weathered the Great Depression intact. The cultural barometer is steady, indicating no significant change in the way the American wind blows. It is not reasonable to predict the foreseeable transformation or diminution of the American middle class as an overwhelming cultural and political force.

With the evolution of more freedom for psychological man, the field of action for the vanguard of the middle class increasingly shifted to financial markets. It is therefore an error to think that wealth, because it destroyed what was familiar and revered in the lives of people in the western world, obliterated all culture. It did destroy the high culture precious to intellectuals and esthetes, as well as the folk culture of the now pointless communal life among the lower middle class. But it created a new culture required by the market, and a new psychology essential to do work there.

When psychological man entered the market he found his home, at last. Now his skill matched the work to be done, and he discovered that his freedom created a nimbleness that, if properly nurtured, assisted him in landing on his feet. For in the market he was betting his personal welfare against vast, impersonal, often worldwide economic forces impossible to foresee or manage. He was now enmeshed in a world that was himself writ large. His prospects depended on reading the tea leaves of transient and apparently motiveless forces in the international economy. Citizens of the international republic of money, psychological men freed themselves from more parochial loyalties, so that the liquidity of a distant bank was more personally interesting and important than the mobilization of deadly military forces along archaic political borders. The market men, the new pathfinders of the middle class, had come home to where political life generally was purposeless, conventional values distracting, and loyalty a restriction on freedom.

The market is a tight and disciplined world whose psychology suits the new men and women. They have discovered that they do not have to train themselves, as they have been warned and taught, to become secretive and inexpressive; they have been so as far back as they can remember. Revering information and intelligence as the only bulwark, however leaky, against the irrationality of market forces, they must squelch those qualities that impede clear thought. They recoil from sentiment and nurture their inclination to be pitiless.

If you had the right sort of technical or professional education and learned to live by your own rules without the rituals that had punctuated life over millennia, life in contemporary America could seem sweet. These middle-class Americans never tired of repeating that they were satisfied with lives they acknowledged to be full but not intimate. A psychologist reported that "more and more of my patients are coming in and saying, 'I have it all, or I'm getting it all, and it's not making any difference.' " She learned that "there really is less sex out there now."[27] The uncertainties centered on a personal identity that seemed to be dissipating, and the absence of guideposts, particularly since the important milestones in their new lives measured wealth, not place. Their bumper stickers proclaimed (not, perhaps, without a certain irony): "WHOEVER DIES WITH THE MOST TOYS WINS." The new man had the toys everyone wanted, but having turned from freedom in the sixties to being pleased in the seventies, he was obliged to measure others by the degree of pleasing they offered. If he was not pleased, not happy, it was someone else's fault. In a peculiarly American way, the new people explored the technologies of happiness, as in adherence to assorted gurus, primal screaming, fake Zen, singles bars, and group therapy for various addictions. In the atmosphere of progress, logic, the rigors of the computer's algorithms, pleasures of personal acquisition, and attenuation of a sense of connectedness, many of the highest-flying Americans concluded they were not in good health. The market men showed that there were compensations.

Success, of course had a single definition, as did excellence, purpose, and life itself. This required a profound ignorance and usually a distrust of those aspects of the world that seemed not to relate to the ownership of wealth. As a senior partner of a major New York brokerage house commented when he lost a talented junior executive who wanted to spend more time with his family: "Regrettably, if you're going to be a world class player, along with the money and the glamour and the pizazz goes a lack of personal time." As usual, the choice was between power and love, wealth and belonging. Friends of the departing executive could not believe what he was throwing away. And it was hard to explain: "You're giving up the American dream. And what you're getting is so intangible. . . . It's so gooey compared to what your bonus was."[28]

The new, free men of the market occupied what surely was a logical terminus for the American journey. In this as in so much else, America sets the example for the rest of the world. This is revolutionary, and the march of the market men in time will probably sweep everything before them, as no mere ideological barriers will long withstand the power of mass culture and the force of market psychology, or the charms of incorporating the self as its very own cult.

Attainment of personal wealth had always been the middleclass definition of the good life. As this class expanded throughout the twentieth century, the pecuniary values of the grandchildren of peddlers, iron workers, and miners swamped the nation. As Rieff observed, quantity really did become quality: "Our cultural revolution has been made from the top, rather than from the bottom. It is anti-political, a revolution of the rich."[29] This cultural revolution was fought and won for the great purpose of living more pleasantly, for money in hand and the balance wisely invested. In the new world, freedom's green goal could be achieved.

Rieff doubted that "Western men can be persuaded again to the Greek opinion that the secret of happiness is to have as few needs as possible."[30] This is not quite accurate, because the American middle class had actually eliminated many of the needs that motivated and therefore restricted the ancient Greeks: intellectual curiosity, the ability to understand each other, the necessity of beauty, and a deep sense of proportion. The middle class had simply substituted its pecuniary standards for the culture of what it considered an irrelevant civilization. What happened was clear to a writer in *Vogue* magazine: God rested on the seventh day, but "we watch [the television program] *Lifestyles of the Rich and Famous.*"[31] Sophocles's ghost cannot be serene.

Above all, wishing to be undisturbed in the pursuit of additional wealth, the market men and their envious and admiring epigoni have learned to despise politics. It is not clear under what circumstances, if any, they could be moved by what used to be called the claims of citizenship. They fear the irrationality of the world because it introduces additional uncertainty into the market. They became the model to be emulated by the cream of the new student generation.[32] The market men became the future—free, masterless, fatherless.

• • •

Just before World War II, Stanley Kunitz, in a poem he called "Father and Son," cried out for the attention and help of his dead father:

> At the water's edge, where the smothering ferns lifted
> Their arms, "Father!" I cried, "Return! You know
> The way. I'll wipe the mudstains from your clothes;
> No trace, I promise, will remain. Instruct
> Your son, whirling between two wars,
> In the Gemara of your gentleness. . . ." [33]

These sad tales of the death of fathers, of the passing of their quaint but inefficient world, also recount the children's release from the past's dead hand. Freed from civilization's shalt-nots, and from poverty's constraints, the new Americans, especially those born in the late forties and fifties, may now enjoy the perquisites of status, and liberation from the obligations and limitations imposed by love. While a rose, an infant, or a sonata does not produce advantageous cost-benefit ratios, this cold new world evidently does. Although extreme individualism necessarily shades into isolation, although a hypertrophied rationalism must become callous, although commodity fetishism can never be satisfied, all nevertheless apparently justify the abandonment of place and intimacy. The cost of success, then, is a redefinition of pleasure, and thus also of pain. The fathers knew there was risk and pain in love and life. Fleeing this human adventure, the children calculated their progress toward a better life—the contemplation of all that success may produce, life as work, the happiness produced by objects, the envy of strangers, and the freedom to float above the struggles of others, in warmth and comfort, alone.

Notes

INTRODUCTION

1. See, for example, Lawrence Stone, *The Family, Sex, and Marriage in England,* 1500–1800 (New York, 1977); Leonore Davidoff and Catherine Hall, *Family Fortunes: Men and Women of the English Middle Class,* 1780–1850 (London, 1987); and Simon Schama, *The Embarrassment of Riches: An Interpretation of Dutch Culture in the Golden Age* (New York, 1987).

I. ASSAYING THE GOLDEN LAND

1. John Adams to John Taylor, JA, C. F. Adams, ed., *Works* (Boston, 1850–56), VI, pp. 461–62.
2. Marcus Lee Hansen, *The Immigrant in American History* (Cambridge, Mass., 1940), p. 85.
3. Robert H. Billigmeier, *Americans from Germany* (Belmont, Cal., 1974), p. 29.
4. Quoted in S. E. Weber, *The Charity School Movement in Colonial Pennsylvania* (Philadelphia, 1905), p. 11; Billigmeier, *Americans from Germany,* pp. 29–35.
5. Henry Nash Smith, *Virgin Land* (New York, 1957), p. 138.

6. Adam Clymer, "Poll Finds Most Americans Cling to Ideals of Farm Life," *New York Times,* Feb. 25, 1986, p. A 22; "Looking Backward," *ibid.,* March 1, 1986, p. 26.

7. Carl Wittke, *We Who Built America* (New York, 1939), pp. 122, 186, 204; Hansen, *The Immigrant in American History,* pp. 61-68.

8. Quoted in Billigmeier, *Americans from Germany,* p. 71.

9. Carl Wittke, *Refugees of Revolution* (Philadelphia, 1952), pp. 280-87.

10. Wittke, *We Who Built America,* pp. 134-35, 147.

11. Kerby A. Miller, *Emigrants and Exiles* (New York, 1985), p. 327.

12. Oscar Handlin, *Boston's Immigrants* (New York, 1970), pp. 62-63, 71-77, 131, 176-77, 192-93, 239.

13. Edward Alsworth Ross, "Immigrants in Politics," *The Century Magazine,* LXXXVII, 3 (Jan., 1914), pp. 392-93, 395.

14. Miller, *Emigrants and Exiles,* pp. 142-43, 167-68, 280, 327-29, 349-52, 492-97, 569, 582.

15. Computed from U.S. Bureau of the Census, *Historical Statistics of the United States* (Bicentennial Ed., Part 2; Washington, D.C., 1977), p. 105; "Shall We Restrict Immigration?" *The Outlook,* XCVI (Dec. 31, 1910), p. 1003.

16. John Bodnar, *The Transplanted* (Bloomington, Ind., 1985), pp. 54-56.

17. Computations based on Bureau of the Census, *Historical Statistics,* pp. 105-106; computations based on Moses Rischin, *The Promised City* (Cambridge, Mass., 1962), p. 270; Marshall Sklare, *America's Jews* (New York, 1971), p. 38; Lucy Dawidowicz, *On Equal Terms* (New York, 1982), p. 167.

18. Abraham Cahan, *The Education of Abraham Cahan,* tr. by L. Stein *et al.* (Philadelphia, Pa., 1969), p. 354; Dan Vogel, *Emma Lazarus* (Boston, Mass., 1980), pp. 14-24.

19. Daniel Patrick Moynihan, "What Wretched Refuse?" *New York,* XIX, 9 (May 12, 1986), p. 59.

20. Henry Cabot Lodge, "A Million Immigrants a Year," *The Century Magazine,* LXVII, 3 (Jan., 1904), pp. 466-69.

21. Richard Hofstadter, *The Age of Reform* (New York, 1960), pp. 91-93.

22. John R. Commons, "Amalgamation and Assimilation," *The Chautauquan,* XXXIX, 3 (May, 1904), pp. 218-21; and " 'Americanization' by Labor Unions," *ibid.,* p. 225.

23. Edward A. Ross, *The Old World in the New* (New York, 1914), p. 286.

24. Frank P. Sargent, "The Need of Closer Inspection and Greater Restriction of Immigrants," *The Century Magazine,* LXVII, 3 (Jan. 1904), p. 470; Clarence H. Matson, "The Immigration Problem," *The Outlook,* LXXVII (June 25, 1904), pp. 462-64.

25. Thomas Kessner, *The Golden Door* (New York, 1977), p. 42.

26. Immigration Commission, "Distribution of Immigrants, 1850–1900," *Statistical Review of Immigration, 1820–1910* (Washington, D.C.: Government Printing Office, 1911), pp. 288–92; U.S. Bureau of the Census, *1970 Census of Population* (Washington, D.C., 1972), I, Part A, Section 1, pp. 1–116; U.S. Bureau of the Census, *County and City Data Book* (Washington, D.C., 1983), Table C, pp. lxiv, 649–809.

27. Caroline Golab, *Immigrant Destinations* (Philadelphia, 1977), pp. 171–72.

28. Constance McLaughlin Green, *The Rise of Urban America* (New York, 1965), p. 105.

29. Salvatore J. LaGumina, *The Immigrants Speak* (New York, 1979), pp. 34–35; John Higham, *Strangers in the Land* (New York, 1978), pp. 90–91.

30. Stefano Miele, "America as a Place to Make Money," *The World's Work*, XLI, 2 (Dec., 1920), p. 204.

31. *Ibid.*, pp. 205–206.

32. Kessner, *The Golden Door*, pp. 28–32.

33. Hutchins Hapgood, "The Foreign Stage in New York," *The Bookman*, XI (Aug., 1900), pp. 546, 553.

34. Giuseppe Cautela, "The Italian Theatre in New York," *The American Mercury*, XII, 45 (Sept., 1927), p. 109.

35. "An Italian's Advice to Italian Immigrants," *The American Review of Reviews*, LXI, 1 (July, 1917), p. 100.

36. Laurence Franklin, "The Italian in America," *Catholic World*, LXXI, 421 (April, 1900), pp. 75–76.

37. Ernest Crosby, "The Immigration Bugbear," *The Arena*, XXXII, 181 (Dec., 1904), pp. 596, 601. Also see Kate Holladay Claghorn, "Our Immigrants and Ourselves," *Atlantic Monthly*, LXXXVI, 516 (Oct., 1900), pp. 535–48.

38. Yoshio Markino, "My Experiences in California," *McClure's Magazine*, XXXVI, 1 (Nov., 1910), p. 109; "The Confession of a Japanese Servant," *The Independent*, LIX, 2963 (Sept. 14, 1905), pp. 661–68; Yone Noguchi, "Some Stories of My Western Life," *Fortnightly Review*, CI, 566 (Feb. 2, 1914), pp. 263–76; Maxine Schwartz Seller, ed., *Immigrant Women* (Philadelphia, 1981), p. 56.

39. Fred W. Riggs, *Pressures on Congress* (New York, 1950), p. 8.

40. Marie Prisland, *From Slovenia to America* (Chicago, 1968), p. 55.

41. Emory S. Bogardus, *Essentials of Americanization* (Los Angeles, Cal., 1919), p. 89; M. E. Ravage, "My Plunge into the Slums," *Harper's Monthly*, CXXXIV, 803 (April, 1917), p. 659; Robert E. Park and Herbert A. Miller, *Old World Traits Transplanted* (New York, 1969), p. 275.

42. Miele, "America as a Place to Make Money," *World's Work,* p. 204; Michael Pupin, *From Immigrant to Inventor* (New York, 1922), p. 53; Manuel Gamio, *The Mexican Immigrant* (New York, 1930, 1969), pp. 13, 46, 49, 53, 60, 67, 96, 126, 131, 148, 159, 173, 181.

43. Abraham Mitrie Rihbany, *A Far Journey* (Boston and New York, 1914), p. 215.

44. Oscar Handlin, *The Uprooted* (Boston, 1951), p. 6.

45. Isaac Don Levine, "Letters of an Immigrant," *American Jewish Archives,* XXXIII, 1 (April, 1981), pp. 53-83.

46. Park and Miller, *Old World Traits,* p. 277.

47. E. V. Eskesen, "A Dane Who Came—and Stayed," *The World's Work,* XLI, 4 (Feb., 1921), p. 381.

48. Anzia Yezierska, "The Miracle," in Alice Kessler-Harris, ed., *The Open Cage* (New York, 1979), pp. 16-17.

49. Robert E. Stauffer, *The American Spirit in the Writings of Americans of Foreign Birth* (Boston, 1922), p. 141; Elizabeth Ewen, *Immigrant Women in the Land of Dollars* (New York, 1985), p. 73; Emily Greene Balch, *Our Slavic Fellow Citizens* (New York, 1910), p. 421.

50. Park and Miller, *Old World Traits,* p. 23.

51. Alan Conway, ed., *The Welsh in America* (Minneapolis, Minn., 1961), p. 209.

52. Isaac Metzker, ed., *A Bintel Brief* (New York, 1971), p. 58; Mary Van Kleeck, *Working Girls in Evening Schools* (New York, 1914), p. 24.

53. Bodnar, *The Transplanted,* pp. 83-84.

54. William I. Thomas and Florian Znaniecki, *The Polish Peasant in Europe and America* (Urbana, Ill., 1984), pp. 153-54; Erik H. Erikson, *Childhood and Society* (New York, 1963), p. 294.

55. Jane Addams, *Twenty Years at Hull House* (New York, 1910, 1981), p. 179.

56. Park and Miller, *Old World Traits,* pp. 102-103.

57. Peretz Hirshbein, "Green Fields," in Joseph C. Landis, ed., *The Dybbuk and Other Great Yiddish Plays* (New York, 1966), p. 140.

58. Irving Howe, *World of Our Fathers* (New York, 1976), p. 25; for one example, see Rose Pesotta, *Bread Upon the Waters* (New York, 1944), p. 9.

59. Abraham Cahan, *The Rise of David Levinsky* (New York, 1917), p. 459.

60. Arthur Liebman, *Jews and the Left* (New York, 1979), pp. 141, 142; Gerald Sorin, *The Prophetic Minority* (Bloomington, Ind., 1985), pp. 4-7, 68-71.

61. Quoted in Howe, *World of Our Fathers,* p. 75.

62. "More Are Leaving America's Shores," *New York Times,* March 13, 1985, p. A15.

63. Anzia Yezierska, *Children of Loneliness* (New York, 1923), p. 15; Carl W. Ackerman, "The Book-worms of New York," *The Independent,* LXXIV, 3347 (Jan. 23, 1913), pp. 199-201; Maxine Seller, "The Education of the Immigrant Woman," *Journal of Urban History,* IV, 3 (May 1978), pp. 313, 326.

64. Metzker, *A Bintel Brief,* p. 42.

65. Howe, *World of Our Fathers,* p. 82; Sorin, *Prophetic Minority,* p. 55.

66. Howe, *World of Our Fathers,* pp. 80-83.

67. Ravage, "My Plunge into the Slums," *Harper's Monthly,* p. 664.

68. Cahan, *The Education,* p. 287.

69. Thomas Sowell, *Race and Economics* (New York, 1975), p. 69.

70. Bodnar, *The Transplanted,* pp. 138-43.

71. Billigmeier, *Americans from Germany,* pp. 142-46.

72. Higham, *Strangers in the Land,* pp. 194-222.

73. Franklin K. Lane, "The New Americans," *Ladies' Home Journal,* XXXVI, 10 (Oct., 1919), p. 37; Gregory Mason, "Americans First," *The Outlook,* CXIV (Sept. 27, 1916), pp. 193-201.

74. John Kulamer, "Americanization," *Atlantic Monthly,* CXXV, 3 (March, 1920), pp. 419, 421; Oscar Leonard, "An Immigrant's View," *The Nation,* CXIII, 2928 (Aug. 17, 1921), p. 175; Sarka B. Hrbkova, " 'Bunk' in Americanization," *The Forum,* LXIII (April-May, 1920), p. 438; Edward Corsi, "The Voice of the Immigrant," *The Outlook,* CXLVII, 3 (Sept. 21, 1927), p. 89.

75. Walter E. Weyl, "New Americans," *Harper's Monthly,* CXXIX, 772 (Sept., 1914), pp. 615-22.

2. THE WONDERFUL WORLD OF DISSATISFACTION

1. Henry F. May, *The End of American Innocence* (New York, 1959), p. 350. Also see Christopher Lasch, *The New Radicalism in America, 1889-1963* (New York, 1965), pp. 253-54. The surge of poetry in the twenties similarly began with the prewar generation; see Conrad Aiken, "Poetry," *Civilization in the United States,* ed. Harold E. Stearns (New York, 1922), p. 217.

2. F. Scott Fitzgerald, *The Crack-Up,* ed. Edmund Wilson (New York, 1945), p. 70; F. Scott Fitzgerald to M. Perkins, May 21, 1931, Andrew Turn-

bull, ed., *The Letters of F. Scott Fitzgerald* (New York, 1965), p. 225; Ernest Hemingway, *A Moveable Feast* (New York, 1964), p. 29.

3. John F. Carter, Jr., "These Wild Young People," *Atlantic Monthly,* CXXVI, 3 (Sept., 1920), p. 302.

4. *Ibid.,* pp. 302–304.

5. Quoted in Warren Susman, *Culture as History* (New York, 1984), p. 136.

6. *Ford Ideals* (Dearborn, Mich., 1922), pp. 154, 156–57, 293.

7. *Ibid.,* pp. 401–404.

8. Henry Ford, *The International Jew,* ed. Gerald L. K. Smith (Los Angeles, [1948]), p. 30; "What About the Jewish Question?" *Dearborn Independent,* XXVI, 212 (March 6, 1926), p. 6; Henry Ford, *My Life and Work* (New York, 1973), p. 251.

9. "Ford Now Retracts Attacks on Jews," *New York Times,* July 8, 1927, pp. 1, 10; "Henry Ford's Apology to the Jews," *The Outlook,* CXLVI, 12 (July 20, 1927), pp. 372–74; "Mr. Ford Retracts," *The American Review of Reviews,* LXXVI, 2 (Aug., 1927), pp. 197–98; Alfred D. Chandler, Jr., ed., *Giant Enterprise* (New York, 1964), pp. xi, 17, 145, 166.

10. "Why They Love Henry," *The New Republic,* XXXV, 447 (June 27, 1923), p. 112.

11. H. L. Mencken, *Notes on Democracy* (New York, 1926), p. 129; Louis R. Reid, "The Small Town," in Stearns, *Civilization,* p. 286.

12. "What America Thinks of Votes for Women," *The Literary Digest,* LI, 15 (Oct. 9, 1915), p. 753.

13. Bart Landry, *The New Black Middle Class* (Berkeley, Cal., 1987). pp. 1–2; Irving Bernstein, *The Lean Years* (Boston, 1966), pp. 47–50.

14. Andrew Sinclair, *Prohibition* (Boston, 1962), p. 163.

15. Hiram Wesley Evans, "The Klan's Fight for Americanism," *The North American Review,* CCXXIII (March–May, 1926), pp. 35, 40, 49.

16. Quoted in Stanley Coben, *A. Mitchell Palmer* (New York, 1963), p. 198.

17. *Ibid.,* p. 227.

18. Sinclair, *Prohibition,* p. 290; Norman F. Furniss, *The Fundamentalist Controversy* (New Haven, 1954), pp. 39–41.

19. Quoted in Lawrence W. Levine, *Defender of the Faith: William Jennings Bryan* (New York, 1965), p. 279.

20. *Ibid.,* p. 289.

21. Preston William Slosson, *The Great Crusade and After* (New York, 1935), pp. 163–72.

22. David John Hogan, *Class and Reform* (Philadelphia, Pa., 1985), pp. 115–17.

23. *Ibid.,* p. 182; Kenneth T. Jackson, *Crabgrass Frontier* (New York, 1985), p. 196.

24. John Bodnar, *The Transplanted* (Bloomington, Ind., 1985), p. 180.

25. Hogan, *Class and Reform,* pp. 117-20.

26. Jane Addams, *Twenty Years at Hull House* (New York, 1981), p. 181.

27. Hogan, *Class and Reform,* pp. 126-33.

28. Deborah Dash Moore, *At Home in America* (New York, 1981), pp. 43, 51-53.

29. John Dewey, *The Public and Its Problems* (New York, 1927), pp. 122-23, 134-35, 139.

30. Clayton R. Koppes, "The Social Destiny of the Radio," *South Atlantic Quarterly,* LXVIII, 3 (Summer, 1969), pp. 363-76.

31. Quoted in Stuart Ewen, *Captains of Consciousness* (New York, 1976), p. 161.

32. *Ibid.,* p. 46.

33. Roland Marchand, *Advertising the American Dream* (Berkeley, Cal., 1985), pp. 66-69.

34. Otis Pease, *The Responsibilities of American Advertising* (New Haven, 1983), pp. 41-42. Cf. T. J. Jackson Lears, "From Salvation to Self-Realization," in Richard W. Fox and T. J. Jackson Lears, *The Culture of Consumption* (New York, 1983), pp. 3-38.

35. Pease, *The Responsibilities of American Advertising,* p. 23.

36. *Ibid.,* p. 42.

37. Slosson, *The Great Crusade and After,* p. 181; Marchand, *Advertising the American Dream,* p. 158.

38. Pease, *Responsibilities of American Advertising,* pp. 38-40.

39. Marchand, *Advertising the American Dream,* pp. 238-41.

40. Frank Presby, *The History and Development of Advertising* (Garden City, N.Y., 1929), pp. 560, 564; George Mowry, *The Urban Nation* (New York, 1965), p. 13.

41. Marchand, *Advertising the American Dream,* pp. 6-7, 157-58.

42. Siegfried Giedion, *Mechanization Takes Command* (New York, 1948), p. 520.

43. Ruth Schwartz Cowan, "Two Washes in the Morning and a Bridge Party at Night," in Lois Scharf and Joan M. Jensen, eds., *Decades of Discontent* (Westport, Ct., 1983), pp. 177-93.

44. Slosson, *The Great Crusade and After,* pp. 142-47; Frederick Lewis Allen, *Only Yesterday* (New York, 1931), pp. 115-16; G. V. Hamilton and Kenneth Macgowan, "Marriage and Love Affairs," *Harper's Magazine,* CLVII (Aug., 1928), p. 281.

45. Regina Malone, "The Fabulous Monster," *The Forum,* LXXVI, 1 (July, 1926), p. 26.

46. Ben B. Lindsey, *The Revolt of Modern Youth* (Seattle, Wash., 1925), p. 54.

47. Eleanor Rowland Wembridge, "Petting and the Campus," *The Survey,* LIV, 7 (July 1, 1925), p. 395.

48. Anne Temple, "Reaping the Whirlwind," *The Forum,* LXXVI, 1 (July, 1926), pp. 22, 25.

49. Mary Agnes Hamilton, "Where Are You Going, My Pretty Maid?" *Atlantic Monthly,* CXXXVIII, 3 (Sept., 1926), p. 302.

50. Chicago *Tribune* excerpted in "Courting Danger in the Automobile," *The Literary Digest,* LXXXII, 1 (July 5, 1924), p. 35.

51. May, *End of American Innocence,* p. 339; Valerie Steele, *Fashion and Eroticism* (New York, 1985), pp. 237-38.

52. Paula S. Fass, *The Damned and the Beautiful* (New York, 1977), p. 280.

53. F. Scott Fitzgerald to E. Wilson, Spring, 1925, and to his daughter, Oct. 5, 1940, in *Letters,* pp. 96, 342.

54. Fass, *The Damned and the Beautiful,* pp. 262-68, 276, 278, 307.

55. "Is the Younger Generation in Peril?" *The Literary Digest,* LXIX, 7 (May 14, 1921), pp. 9-12 ff; "The Case Against the Younger Generation," *ibid.,* LXXIII, 12 (June 17, 1922), p. 42.

56. "Today's Morals and Manners," *ibid.,* LXX, 2 (July 9, 1921), pp. 36, 39.

57. Allen, *Only Yesterday,* p. 109.

58. Quoted in Fass, *The Damned and the Beautiful,* p. 291.

59. Eleanor Rowland Wembridge, "The Girl Tribe," *The Survey,* LX, (May 1, 1928), p. 158.

60. Fass, *The Damned and the Beautiful,* p. 326.

61. Richard Schickel, *Intimate Strangers* (Garden City, N.Y., 1985), pp. 39-60, 91.

62. Foster Rhea Dulles, *A History of Recreation* (2d ed.; New York, 1940, 1965), pp. 299, 303.

63. This and the preceding paragraphs draw on Mary P. Ryan's informative essay "The Projection of a New Womanhood: The Movie Moderns in the 1920's," in Jean E. Friedman and William G. Shade, *Our American Sisters* (2d ed.; Boston, Mass. 1973, 1976), pp. 366-83.

64. Quoted in Ernest W. Mandeville, "Gutter Literature," *The New Republic,* XLV (Feb. 17, 1926), p. 350.

65. Ludwig Lewisohn, *Up Stream* (New York, 1922), p. 186.

66. Harold E. Stearns, "The Intellectual Life," in Stearns, *Civilization,*

p. 149. See, however, Lewis Mumford, "The Emergence of a Past," *The New Republic*, XLV (Nov. 25, 1925), pp. 18-19.

67. Walter Lippmann, *A Preface to Morals* (New York, 1929), p. 6.

68. *Ibid.*, p. 18.

69. Sherwood Anderson, *Dark Laughter* (New York, 1925), p. 230.

70. Lyman P. Powell, "Coué," *American Review of Reviews*, LXVI (July-Dec., 1922), pp. 622-24; Allen, *Only Yesterday*, p. 102; John Dewey, *Individualism Old and New* (London, 1931), p. 91.

71. Joseph Wood Krutch, *The Modern Temper: A Study and a Confession* (New York, 1929), pp. 22-23.

72. *Ibid.*, p. 237.

3. THE TRIUMPH OF THE MIDDLE CLASS

1. Interview of March 4-9, 1939, George H. Gallup, *The Gallup Poll* (New York, 1972), I, p. 148.

2. Lewis Corey, *The Crisis of the Middle Class* (New York, 1935), p. 276.

3. Alfred Winslow Jones, *Life, Liberty, and Property* (New York, 1964), pp. 346-47.

4. Richard Hofstadter, *The Age of Reform* (New York, 1955, 1960), pp. 131-48.

5. Robert S. Lynd, "Democracy's Third Estate: The Consumer," *Political Science Quarterly*, LI, 4 (Dec., 1936), pp. 513-14.

6. George E. Sokolsky, "The Temper of the People," *New Outlook*, CLXI, 7 (April, 1933), p. 13. Cf. Lawrence W. Levine, "American Culture and the Great Depression," *Yale Review*, LXXIV, 2 (Winter, 1985), pp. 196-97; Earl Browder, "The American Communist Party in the Thirties," in Rita James Simon, ed., *As We Saw the Thirties* (Urbana, Ill., 1967), p. 236.

7. Samuel Rosenman, ed., *The Public Papers and Addressses of Franklin D. Roosevelt* (New York, 1938-50), II, 12-16.

8. Frances Perkins, *The Roosevelt I Knew* (New York, 1946), p. 330.

9. *Ibid.*, p. 328.

10. John Kenneth Galbraith, *The Great Crash, 1929* (2d ed.; Boston, 1961), pp. 22, 71, 146; George E. Mowry, *The Urban Nation* (New York, 1965), p. 66.

11. Galbraith, *The Great Crash*, p. 146.

12. National Industrial Conference Board, *Major Forces in World Business* (New York, 1931), p. 11; Lionel Robbins, *The Great Depression* (New York, 1936), pp. 210-14; League of Nations, *World Economic Survey, 1939-1941* (Ge-

neva, 1942), pp. 18–22, 108–10, 198, 206; Edward Robb Ellis, *A Nation in Torment* (New York, 1970), p. 231; Edmund Wilson, *The American Jitters* (Freeport, N.Y., 1932, 1982), p. 132; *Business Week* (Oct. 7, 1931), pp. 32–33.

13. Quoted in Ellis, *A Nation in Torment,* p. 250; Edmund Wilson, "The Literary Consequences of the Crash," March 23, 1932, *The Shores of Light* (New York, 1952), pp. 498–99.

14. Irving Bernstein, *The Lean Years* (Baltimore, 1960, 1966), pp. 316–17; National Industrial Conference Board, *Economic Almanac,* ed. G. Deutsch (New York, 1962), p. 36; Broadus Mitchell, *Depression Decade* (New York, 1947, 1969), pp. 97–99.

15. American Institute of Public Opinion and *Fortune* polls of October, 1936, June 20, 1937, and July 26, 1939, in Hadley Cantril, ed., *Public Opinion, 1935-1946* (Princeton, N.J., 1951), pp. 1044–45.

16. Bernstein, *The Lean Years,* pp. 319–20; U.S. Bureau of the Census, *Historical Statistics of the United States, Colonial Times to 1970* (Washington, D.C., 1975), Part 1, Series D, pp. 167–68.

17. Bureau of Labor Statistics, "Costs and Standards of Living," *Monthly Labor Review,* LI, 2 (Aug., 1940), p. 393; "Food Expenditures of Wage Earners and Clerical Workers," *ibid.,* p. 251; U.S. Bureau of the Census, *Historical Statistics of the United States, Colonial Times to 1957* (Washington, D.C., 1960), pp. 186–87; Bureau of Labor Statistics, "Food Expenditures," *Monthly Labor Review,* XXXVII, 5 (Nov., 1933), pp. 250, 259.

18. Quoted in Ellis, *A Nation in Torment,* p. 254.

19. Gerald W. Johnson, "The Average American and the Depression," *Current History,* XXXV (Feb., 1932), p. 671.

20. *Ibid.,* pp. 672–73, 675.

21. Arthur M. Schlesinger, Jr., *The Crisis of the Old Order* (Boston, 1957), pp. 459–60.

22. *Fortune* poll of Jan., 1938, in Cantril, *Public Opinion,* p. 896; Samuel Lubell and Walter Everett, "The Breakdown of Relief," *The Nation,* CXLVII, 8 (Aug. 20, 1938), pp. 171, 173.

23. Ellis, *A Nation in Torment,* pp. 231–34; Census Bureau, *Historical Statistics . . . to 1970,* series C, pp. 93–95.

24. Mary Heaton Vorse, "School for Bums," *The New Republic,* LXVI, 856 (April 29, 1931), pp. 292–94.

25. Bernard Sternsher, ed., *Hitting Home* (Chicago, Ill., 1970), pp. 106, 114–19.

26. Edmund Wilson, "Lawrence, Mass.," *The New Republic,* LXIX, 886 (Nov. 25, 1931), pp. 36–39.

27. John Dos Passos, "Harlan: Working under the Gun," *The New Republic*, LXIX, 887 (Dec. 2, 1931), pp. 62–67.

28. "No Checks on Mobs," *The Crisis*, XLIII, 5 (May, 1936), p. 145; Milton Meltzer, *Brother, Can You Spare a Dime?* (New York, 1969), pp. 60–61.

29. Lawrence Gordon, "A Brief Look at Blacks in Depression Mississippi," *Journal of Negro History*, LXIV, 4 (Fall, 1979), pp. 382, 385.

30. Robert S. Lynd and Helen M. Lynd, *Middletown in Transition* (New York, 1937), pp. 9–11.

31. *Ibid.*, pp. 406, 418.

32. *Ibid.*, pp. 17, 19, 24.

33. *Ibid.*, p. 24.

34. "Muncie, Ind. Is the Great U.S. 'Middletown,' " *Life*, II, 19 (May 10, 1937), p. 24.

35. Lynd and Lynd, *Middletown in Transition*, p. 27.

36. Reprinted in "Off the Record," *Fortune*, X, 4 (Oct., 1934), p. 20; Institute of Life Insurance, *Life Insurance Fact Book* (New York, 1950), p. 16; Census Bureau, *Historical Statistics . . . to 1970*, Part 1, Series no. 440, pp. 318–19.

37. Kenneth T. Jackson, *Crabgrass Frontier* (New York, 1985), p. 193.

38. *Ibid.*, pp. 196–97.

39. Quoted in Arthur M. Schlesinger, Jr., *The Coming of the New Deal* (Boston, 1959), p. 411.

40. "Lewis Pushes War on Form of Union," *New York Times*, Nov. 29, 1935, p. 5.

41. Peter Friedlander, *The Emergence of a UAW Local* (Pittsburgh, Pa., 1975), pp. 26–29.

42. *Ibid.*, pp. 45–46, 66–67, 98, 100–103.

43. Eric Hobsbawm, "The Formation of British Working-Class Culture," *Workers* (New York, 1984), pp. 176–93.

44. Harold J. Laski, *Democracy in Crisis* (Chapel Hill, 1933), p. 46.

45. Census Bureau, *Historical Statistics . . . to 1970*, pp. 177–78.

46. *Ibid.*, p. 177.

47. Jones, *Life, Liberty, and Property*, pp. 287, 331–32, 345.

48. *Ibid.*, p. 233.

49. Gallup, *The Gallup Poll*, I, pp. 31, 48–49, 52, 62–63, 85, 143, 158–59.

50. Richard Weiss, "Ethnicity and Reform," *Journal of American History*, LXVI, 3 (Dec., 1979), p. 567; Irving Howe, *A Margin of Hope* (New York, 1982), pp. 4–5; John Bodnar, *The Transplanted* (Bloomington, Ind., 1985), pp. 213–15.

51. Alexander Bloom, *Prodigal Sons* (New York, 1986), pp. 20-21.

52. Weiss, "Ethnicity and Reform," p. 583.

53. Isaac Metzker, ed., *A Bintel Brief* (New York, 1971), p. 157.

54. Howe, *A Margin of Hope*, p. 5.

55. Alfred Kazin, *A Walker in the City* (New York, 1951), pp. 21-22.

56. Saul Bellow, "Foreword," in Allan Bloom, *The Closing of the American Mind* (New York, 1987), p. 13.

57. Bloom, *Prodigal Sons*, pp. 49-50; Howe, *A Margin of Hope*, pp. 4, 9.

58. Victor Gotbaum, "The Spirit of the New York Labor Movement," in Bernard Rosenberg and Ernest Goldstein, eds., *Creators and Disturbers* (New York, 1982), p. 247.

59. Census Bureau, *Historical Statistics . . . to 1970*, Part 2, pp. 49, 64; Richard Malkin, *Marriage, Morals and War* (New York, 1943), pp. 33-34.

60. Cf. Thomas Minehan, *Boy and Girl Tramps of America* (Seattle, Wash., 1934, 1976), *passim;* Bernstein, *The Lean Years*, pp. 327-29.

61. *Ibid.;* Lynd and Lynd, *Middletown in Transition*, pp. 162-64.

62. Nelson Algren, "Ellen O'Connor," in Ann Banks, ed., *First-Person America* (New York, 1980), p. 179.

63. Meridel Le Sueur, *Ripening*, ed. Elaine Hedges (Old Westbury, N.Y., 1982), p. 140.

64. Susan Ware, *Holding Their Own* (Boston, 1982), p. 7; Lynd and Lynd, *Middletown in Transition*, p. 169.

65. Bernstein, *The Lean Years*, p. 329; Lynd and Lynd, *Middletown in Transition*, pp. 146, 174-75.

66. Anonymous, "A Letter from Illinois," *Saturday Evening Post*, CCIX, 42 (April 17, 1937), pp. 27, 49.

67. *Ladies' Home Journal* (May, 1938), p. 97; *ibid.* (April, 1938), p. 82.

68. Ware, *Holding Their Own*, pp. 2-13; Emily Hahn, "Women without Work," *The New Republic*, LXXV, 965 (May 31, 1933), p. 64.

69. Le Sueur, *Ripening*, pp. 141, 151.

70. Ware, *Holding Their Own*, pp. 13-14.

71. Ellis, *A Nation in Torment*, p. 234.

72. Frank G. Moorhead, "Broke at Fifty-five," *The Nation*, CXXXII, 3436 (May 13, 1931), pp. 528-30.

73. Louis Adamic, *My America* (New York, 1938), p. 293; Ware, *Holding Their Own*, p. 8; Mirra Komarovsky, *The Unemployed Man and His Family* (New York, 1940), p. 77.

74. Komarovsky, *The Unemployed Man*, p. 23.

75. *Ibid.*, p. 118. Cf. Studs Terkel, *Hard Times* (New York, 1970), pp. 421-27.

76. Anonymous, "Man Out of Work," *Harper's,* CLXI (July, 1930), pp. 195-201.

77. Bruce Smith, *The History of Little Orphan Annie* (New York, 1982), p. 35.

78. Harold Gray, *Little Orphan Annie and Little Orphan Annie in Cosmic City* (New York, 1926, 1932, 1933), pp. 128-33; Max Wylie, *Best Broadcasts of 1938-39* (New York, 1939), pp. 113-14.

79. "It's Up to the Women," *Ladies' Home Journal,* XLIX, 1 (Jan., 1932), p. 3.

80. Caroline Bird, *The Invisible Scar* (New York, 1966), p. 285.

81. Joan Nunn, *Fashion in Costume* (New York, 1984), pp. 184, 192; Frederick Lewis Allen, *Since Yesterday* (New York, 1939), p. 137.

82. Jeane Westin, *Making Do* (Chicago, 1976), pp. 105-108.

83. Quoted in Allen, *Since Yesterday,* p. 189; "Youth in College," *Fortune,* XIII, 6 (June, 1936), p. 162.

84. Nunn, *Fashion in Costume,* pp. 176-77, 181.

85. Hadley Cantril and Gordon W. Allport, *The Psychology of Radio* (2d ed.; New York, 1935), p. 14; Foster Rhea Dulles, *A History of Recreation* (New York, 1965), pp. 333-34.

86. Arnold Shankman, "Black Pride and Protest," *Journal of Popular Culture,* XII, 2 (Fall, 1979), pp. 237-38.

87. "Amos 'n' Andy: The Air's First Comic Strip," *Literary Digest* (April 19, 1930), reprinted in Daniel Aaron and Robert Bendiner, eds., *The Strenuous Decade* (Garden City, N.Y., 1970), p. 375.

88. Arthur Frank Wertheim, *Radio Comedy* (New York, 1979), p. 44.

89. *Ibid.,* pp. 48-49; Shankman, "Black Pride," *Journal of Popular Culture,* pp. 236-49.

90. J. Fred MacDonald, *Don't Touch That Dial!* (Chicago, 1979), pp. 240-41.

91. *Ibid.,* p. 243.

92. Max Wylie, ed., *Best Broadcasts of 1940-41* (New York, 1942), p. 326.

93. Wertheim, *Radio Comedy,* p. 73; James Thurber, *The Beast in Me and Other Animals* (New York, 1928-61), pp. 209-10. Cf. Dale Kramer, "Main Street in 1940," *Forum and Century,* CIII, 4 (April, 1940), pp. 166-73.

94. Vincent Terrace, *Radio's Golden Years* (San Diego and New York, 1981), p. 161.

95. Max Wylie, ed., *Best Broadcasts of 1939-40* (New York, 1940), pp. 279-99.

96. *The 1936 Film Daily Year Book of Motion Pictures* (N.P., 1936), p. 39;

Richard Gertner, ed., *1985 International Motion Picture Almanac* (New York, 1985), p. 30A; *Fortune*, XIII (April, 1936), p. 4.

97. W. W. Charters, *Motion Pictures and Youth* (New York, 1933), p. 49.

98. Ware, *Holding Their Own*, pp. 182–83.

99. Paul W. Facey, *The Legion of Decency* (New York, 1974), pp. 106–109. Cf. Catherine Covert and John Stevens, *Mass Media Between the Wars* (Syracuse, N.Y., 1984), pp. 184–87.

100. Ralph A. Brauer, "When the Lights Went Out," in M. T. Marsden *et al.*, eds., *Movies as Artifacts* (Chicago, Ill., 1982), p. 34.

101. *Mr. Smith Goes to Washington*, in John Gassner and Dudley Nichols, eds., *Twenty Best Film Plays* (New York, 1943), p. 643.

102. Robert S. McElvaine, *The Great Depression* (New York, 1984), p. 219.

4. COSTS OF THE DREAM

1. Chester E. Eisinger, *Fiction of the Forties* (Chicago, 1963), p. 17.

2. Studs Terkel, *The Good War* (New York, 1984), pp. 61, 110–11; interviews of Nov., 1944, March, 1945, and May, 1945 in George H. Gallup, *The Gallup Poll* (New York, 1972), I, 477, 499, and 509.

3. Terkel, *The Good War*, p. 108; interviews of Oct., 1939, Dec., 1942, and April, 1944, in Gallup, *The Gallup Poll*, I, 189, 359, 444.

4. *Ibid.*, pp. 123, 125, 128–29, 132, 137, 145, 149, 150, 153, 154–55, 175, 178, 180–81, 184–85, 323.

5. Terkel, *The Good War*, pp. 139–41.

6. Roy Helton, "The Inner Threat," *Harper's Magazine*, CLXXXI (Sept. 1940), pp. 337–43.

7. Rachel Rubin, "We Build Morale," *American Home*, XXVII, 6 (May 1942), p. 4.

8. *Better Homes and Gardens*, XXI, 10 (June 1943), p. 11; *Life*, XII, 21 (May 25, 1942), p. 28; Rachel D. Cox, "Home Front Communiqué," *Hygeia*, XXII, 8 (Aug. 1944), p. 575; J. Edgar Hoover, "Mothers . . . Our Only Hope," *Woman's Home Companion*, LXI, 1 (Jan. 1944), p. 20.

9. Philip Wylie, *Generation of Vipers* (New York, 1942), pp. 184–86.

10. Quoted in Richard R. Lingeman, *Don't You Know There's a War On?* (New York, 1970), p. 295.

11. *Collier's*, CIX, 25 (June 20, 1942), p. 3.

12. David Riesman *et al.*, *The Lonely Crowd* (New Haven, Conn., 1950, 1961), especially pp. 234–35; Hannah Lees, "What Every Husband Needs," *Reader's Digest*, LXXI, 426 (Oct. 1957), pp. 137–40.

13. Terkel, *The Good War,* p. 124.

14. "Paper Doll," recorded in 1942 by the Mills Brothers, reprinted in Reader's Digest, *Treasury of Best Loved Songs* (Pleasantville, N.Y., 1972), p. 265; Terkel, *The Good War,* p. 124.

15. Robert Coughlan, "Modern Marriage," *Life,* XLI, 26 (Dec. 24, 1956), p. 113.

16. Terkel, *The Good War,* pp. 7, 60.

17. *Ibid.,* p. 39.

18. *Ibid.,* p. 68.

19. *Collier's,* CXIV, 1 (July 1, 1944), p. 70.

20. Beth L. Bailey, "Conventions of Desire: Courtship in 20th Century America," unpublished Ph.D. dissertation, Northwestern University, 1985, p. 25. This study led me to the debate about the comparative qualities of European and American women.

21. Leland Stowe, "What's Wrong with Our Women?" *Esquire,* XXX, 3 (Sept. 1948), p. 96.

22. Gene P. Fortuna, "The Magnificent American Male," *ibid.,* XXIV, 1 (July, 1945), pp. 54, 147-49.

23. Victor Dallaire, "The American Woman? Not for This GI," *New York Times Magazine,* March 10, 1946, p. 15.

24. Edward A. Strecker, *Their Mothers' Sons* (Philadelphia, 1946), p. 32.

25. D'Ann Campbell, *Women at War with America* (Cambridge, Mass., 1984), p. 244.

26. Margaret Buell Wilder, *Since You Went Away* (New York, 1943), p. 171.

27. Mapheus Smith, "Population Characteristics of American Servicemen in World War II," *Scientific Monthly,* LXV, 3 (Sept. 1947), pp. 246-52.

28. Paul Pisicano interview in Terkel, *The Good War,* pp. 141-42.

29. A. Russell Buchanan, *The United States and World War II* (New York, 1964), I, pp. 138, 140.

30. John Kenneth Galbraith interview in Terkel, *The Good War,* p. 323; interviews of Aug. 1943 and Jan. 1945 in Gallup, *The Gallup Poll,* I, pp. 406, 488.

31. Lingeman, *Don't You Know There's a War On?,* pp. 66-69.

32. Alice Kessler-Harris, *Out to Work* (New York, 1982), pp. 275-78, 289-91; Ethel McCall Head, "It's Harder to Stay Home," *American Home,* XXX, 4 (Sept. 1943), p. 4; interview of Feb.-March, 1942 in Gallup, *The Gallup Poll,* I, p. 326.

33. Wilder, *Since You Went Away,* pp. 12, 16.

34. Margaret Mead, "The Women in the War," in Jack Goodman, ed., *While You Were Gone* (New York, 1946), pp. 284-85.

35. Mark J. Harris, Franklin D. Mitchell, and Steven J. Schechter, *The Homefront* (New York, 1984), pp. 247-49.

36. *Ibid.,* p. 288; Lingeman, *Don't You Know There's a War On?,* pp. 85-87; A. A. Hoehling, *Home Front, U.S.A.* (New York, 1966), pp. 56-61; *Woman's Home Companion,* LXXI, 5 (May, 1943), p. 49; Susan M Hartmann, *The Home Front and Beyond* (Boston, 1982), p. 199.

37. Richard Malkin, *Marriage, Morals, and War* (New York, 1943), p. 125.

38. Elizabeth Field quoted in Leila J. Rupp, *Mobilizing Women for War* (Princeton, 1978), p. 146.

39. The *Ladies' Home Journal* and Susan Anthony II are quoted in *ibid.,* pp. 151, 153.

40. Cornelia Otis Skinner, "Women Are Misguided," *Life,* XLI, 26 (Dec. 24, 1956), p. 75.

41. Interviewed in Harris *et al., The Homefront,* p. 241.

42. U.S. Bureau of Census, *Historical Statistics of the United States* (Bicentennial Ed., Part 2; Washington, D.C., 1975), p. 289.

43. Administrator of Veterans Affairs, *Annual Report, 1948* (Washington, D.C., 1949), p. 229; *ibid., 1955* (1956), p. 241; Sar A. Levitan and Karen A. Cleary, *Old Wars Remain Unfinished* (Baltimore, Md., 1973), p. 145; Alicia H. Munnell, "Wars Are Expensive," *New England Economic Review* (March-April, 1983), pp. 61-63; Eric F. Goldman, *The Crucial Decade* (New York, 1956, 1960, 1961), p. 49.

44. Terkel, *The Good War,* p. 137.

45. Kessler-Harris, *Out to Work,* pp. 286-87, 292, 295-99.

46. Marion Gough, "Home Should Be Even More Wonderful," *House Beautiful,* LXXXVII, 1 (Jan., 1945), p. 29.

47. Herbert I. Kupper, *Back to Life* (N.P., 1945), p. 184.

48. "Some Basic Statistical Data on Our Most Numerous Sex," *Life,* XLI, 26 (Dec. 24, 1956), p. 27; Hartmann, *The Home Front,* p. 203.

49. Henry Safford, "Tell Me Doctor," *Ladies' Home Journal,* LXX, 10 (Oct., 1953), p. 188; Goodrich C. Schauffler, *ibid.,* LXXVI, 12 (Dec., 1959), p. 38; "Building Up Bosoms," *Time,* LXX, 21 (Nov. 18, 1957), p. 59.

50. Goodrich C. Schauffler, "This Bosom Business," *Reader's Digest,* LXVII, 400 (Aug. 1955), pp. 22-23; "Dangerous Curves," *Newsweek,* XLIV, 26 (Dec. 27, 1954), p. 49; "Bosom Foe," *Time,* LXIV, 26 (Dec. 27, 1954), p. 52.

51. Ruth Murrin, "What You Can Do to Have a Beautiful Bosom," *Good Housekeeping,* CXXXVIII, 5 (May, 1954), p. 153; *Ladies' Home Journal,* LXX, 3 (March 1953), pp. 16, 83, 210.

52. Marge Piercy, "Through the Cracks," *Partisan Review*, XLI, 2 (1974), pp. 209-10.

53. Joseph C. Goulden, *The Best Years* (New York, 1976), p. 197.

54. *Playboy*, I, 1 (Dec. 1953), p. 3.

55. Alfred C. Kinsey *et al.*, *Sexual Behavior in the Human Female* (Philadelphia, 1953), p. 287; "Sex vs. America," *Newsweek*, XLII, 10 (Sept. 7, 1953), p. 20; "Report on Kinsey," *ibid.*, 11 (Sept. 14, 1953), p. 115; "Letters," *Life*, XXXV, 11 (Sept. 14, 1953), pp. 17-18; "Letters," *Look*, XVII, 21 (Oct. 20, 1953), p. 12; Barbara Benson, "What Women Want to Know," *Ladies' Home Journal*, LXX, 9 (Sept., 1953), pp. 52-53; Lena Levine, "A Woman Doctor Interprets . . . Kinsey's Report," *Woman's Home Companion*, LXXX (Sept., 1953), p. 30; Charles G. Wilber, "But Is It Science?" *America*, XC, 1 (Oct. 3, 1953), pp. 19-20.

56. Betty Friedan, *It Changed My Life* (New York, 1963-1976), p. 8.

57. Harris *et al.*, *The Homefront*, p. 249; "Sixty-six Million More Americans," *Fortune*, XLIX, 1 (Jan. 1954), p. 166; Peter F. Drucker, "Are We Having Too Many Babies?" *Saturday Evening Post*, CCXXII, 45 (May 6, 1950), p. 40.

58. Sara Evans, *Personal Politics* (New York, 1979), p. 9.

59. Maxine L. Margolis, *Mothers and Such* (Berkeley, Cal., 1984), pp. 166-69.

60. *Ibid.*, pp. 218-19.

61. Landon Y. Jones, *Great Expectations* (New York, 1980), pp. 24-25; Betty Friedan, *The Feminine Mystique* (New York, 1963), p. 16; Mirra Komarovsky, *Women in the Modern World* (Boston, 1953), p. 70.

62. William Peterson, "The New American Family," *Commentary*, XXI, 1 (Jan. 1956), p. 4; interviews of May 1953 and Feb. 1957, Gallup, *The Gallup Poll*, II, pp. 1156, 1474; David Riesman, *Abundance for What?* (Garden City, N.Y., 1964), p. 321; other nations experiencing a baby boom were Canada, Australia, and New Zealand, Jones, *Great Expectations*, p. 21.

63. Frank W. Notestein, "As the Nation Grows Younger," *Atlantic Monthly*, CC, 4 (Oct., 1957), p. 13; Jones, *Great Expectations*, pp. 28-29, 336.

64. "Sixty-six Million," *Fortune*, p. 165; Friedan, *It Changed My Life*, p. 12; *Life*, XLIV, 24 (June 16, 1958), cover and pp. 83-89; "The Population Boom," *Time*, LXII, 11 (Sept. 14, 1953), p. 96; "37 Million Babies," *U.S. News & World Report*, XXXIX, 5 (July 29, 1955), pp. 30-32; and "What 4 Million Babies Mean to Business," *ibid.*, XLII, 13 (March 29, 1957), pp. 38-39.

65. Friedan, *It Changed My Life*, p. 14; Jones, *Great Expectations*, p. 49.

66. Kenneth T. Jackson, *Crabgrass Frontier* (New York, 1985), p. 232.

67. *Ibid.*, pp. 204–206.

68. Frederick Gutheim, "What Makes a Good Suburb?" *House & Garden,* CVII, 1 (Jan. 1955), p. 31; "The Roots of Home," *Time,* LXXV, 25 (June 20, 1960), p. 14.

69. Gutheim, "What Makes a Good Suburb?," p. 31.

70. Harry Henderson, "The Mass-Produced Suburbs," *Harper's Magazine,* CCVIII, 1242 (Nov. 1953), pp. 25–27; and "Rugged American Collectivism," *ibid.*, 1243 (Dec. 1953), p. 85.

71. Jackson, *Crabgrass Frontier,* pp. 207–209, 233, 283–84.

72. Douglas Miller and Marion Nowak, *The Fifties* (Garden City, N.Y., 1977), p. 136.

73. Interview of June, 1955, Gallup, *Gallup Poll,* II, p. 1350; William H. Whyte, Jr., "The Transients," *Fortune,* XLVII, 5 (May 1953), pp. 112–17, 221–22, 224, 226.

74. Henderson, "Rugged American Collectivism," *Harper's,* p. 81.

75. "The Lush New Suburban Market," *Fortune,* pp. 128–29, 131.

76. Miller and Nowak, *The Fifties,* p. 138.

77. Harry Gersh, "The New Suburbanites of the 50's," *Commentary,* XVII, 3 (March 1954), pp. 218–21.

78. Interviewed in Terkel, *The Good War,* pp. 142–43.

79. Stanley Kauffmann, "A Carpenter, An Architect," *The New Republic* (March 31, 1986), p. 24; Bureau of the Census, *Historical Statistics,* pp. 93, 796.

80. Quoted in Miller and Nowak, *The Fifties,* p. 368; Gallup, *The Gallup Poll,* II, pp. 1109, 1217, 1378; Leo Bogart, *The Age of Television* (New York, 1972), p. 133.

81. Bogart, *The Age of Television,* pp. 103–105.

82. Irving Settel and William Laas, *A Pictorial History of Television* (New York, 1969), p. 57.

83. Friedan, *The Feminine Mystique,* p. 25.

84. Edwin Diamond, "Young Wives," *Newsweek,* LV, 10 (March 7, 1960), p. 59.

85. Cf. Allan Bloom, *The Closing of the American Mind* (New York, 1987), pp. 57–60.

86. Quoted in Christopher Lasch, *The Culture of Narcissism* (New York, 1978), p. 165. I am in debt to Lasch's scholarship and wisdom in these paragraphs on the family in the 50s.

87. Maxine Schnall, *Limits* (New York, 1981), pp. 86–87.

88. Lasch, *The Culture of Narcissism,* pp. 162-80.

89. Bailey, "Conventions of Desire," Ch. 2, pp. 1-69; interview of Feb., 1955, Gallup, *The Gallup Poll,* II, p. 1325.

90. James Gilbert, *A Cycle of Outrage* (New York, 1986), p. 204.

91. *Ibid.,* pp. 13-19, 209, 215.

92. Primo Levi, *The Periodic Table,* tr. R. Rosenthal (New York, 1984), p. 24; Richard Sennett and Jonathan Cobb, *The Hidden Injuries of Class* (New York, 1973), pp. 18-30.

93. Riesman, *Abundance for What?,* pp. 318-20.

94. Henderson, "Mass-Produced Suburbs," *Harper's,* p. 27; Riesman, *Abundance for What?,* p. 315.

95. C. Wright Mills, *White Collar* (New York, 1951), p. 263.

96. Erik H. Erikson, *Childhood and Society* (2d ed., New York, 1950, 1963), pp. 308-309.

97. David R. Mace, "I Thought I Married a Man," *Woman's Home Companion,* LXXXI (Jan., 1954), pp. 17, 47.

98. Robert Coles, *The Middle Americans* (Boston, Mass., 1971), p. 4; William Jovanovich, "My Illusions and Yours," *Harper's,* CCXXXV, 1409 (Oct. 1967), p. 57.

99. Erikson, *Childhood and Society,* pp. 314-15.

100. Arthur Miller, *Death of a Salesman,* in *Collected Plays* (New York, 1957), pp. 154, 157, 222.

101. Paul Goodman, *Growing Up Absurd* (New York, 1956-60), p. 17.

102. Leonard J. Leff, *Film Plots* (Ann Arbor, Mich., 1983), pp. 295-300.

103. Henry Ford II, "Human Engineering Necessary for Further Mass Production Progress," *Automotive and Aviation Industries,* XCIV, 2 (Jan. 15, 1946), p. 39.

104. Loren Baritz, *The Servants of Power* (Middletown, Conn., 1960), pp. 186-87.

105. Diane Ravitch, *The Troubled Crusade* (New York, 1983), p. 78.

106. Quoted in Sloan Wilson, "It's Time to Close Our Carnival," *Life,* XLIV, 12 (March 24, 1958), p. 36.

107. "Schoolboys Point Up a U.S. Weakness," *ibid.,* pp. 25-35.

108. "Letters to the Editor," *Life,* XLIV, 15 (April 14, 1958), p. 10; "Reaction to a Letter," *ibid.,* 17 (April 28, 1958), p. 16; Spencer Brown, "Have Our Schools Failed?," *Commentary,* XXV, 6 (June 1958), p. 462.

109. "Painful Crisis," *Life,* XLIV, 16 (April 21, 1958), p. 34.

110. Reinhold Niebuhr, "Is There a Revival of Religion," in William L. O'Neill, *American Society Since 1945* (Chicago, Ill., 1969), pp. 30-36.

111. Geoffrey Perrett, *A Dream of Greatness* (New York, 1979), pp. 390–405.

112. Sam Merrill, "The Hollywood Laugh Track," *New Times*, X, 1 (Jan. 9, 1978), p. 29; Piercy, "Through the Cracks," *Partisan Review*, p. 216.

113. Allen Ginsberg, *Howl*, Barry Miles, ed. (New York, 1956, 1986), pp. 3, 5.

114. William Atwood, "How America Feels," *Look*, XXIV, 1 (Jan. 5, 1960), pp. 11–15.

5. CULTURE WAR

1. Landon Y. Jones, *Great Expectations* (New York, 1980), pp. 80–81.

2. "The Face of the Future," *Look*, XXIX, 1 (Jan. 12, 1965), p. 73.

3. Quoted in Bill Moyers, *Listening to America* (New York, 1971), p. 193.

4. "Our *Good* Teen-Agers," *Newsweek*, LIV, 21 (Nov. 23, 1959), pp. 69–70.

5. Loretta McLaughlin, *The Pill, John Rock, and the Church* (Boston, Mass., 1982), pp. 108–45.

6. "Should Birth Control Be Available to Unmarried Women?" *Good Housekeeping*, CLXIV, 2 (Feb. 1967), p. 14; Tom Flaherty, "In Defense of Traditional Marriage," *Life*, LXXIII, 20 (Nov. 17, 1972), p. 59.

7. Steven Spencer, "The Birth Control Revolution," *Saturday Evening Post*, CCXXXIX, 2 (Jan. 16, 1966), p. 22; "The Pill," *U.S. News & World Report*, LXI, 2 (July 11, 1966), p. 65.

8. Quoted in "Anything Goes," *Newsweek*, LXX, 20 (Nov. 13, 1967), p. 75.

9. Sandford Brown, "May I Ask You a Few Questions About Love?" *Saturday Evening Post*, CCXXXIX, 27 (Dec. 31, 1966), p. 26.

10. Spencer, "Birth Control Revolution," *Saturday Evening Post*, p. 66.

11. "The Morals Revolution on the U.S. Campus," *Newsweek*, LXIII, 14 (April 16, 1964), pp. 52, 59.

12. "Students," *Time*, LXXXVII, 10 (March 11, 1966), p. 66; "Mlle's Modest Little Sex Survey," *Mademoiselle*, LXX, 4 (Feb. 1970), pp. 220–21; "Teen-Agers and Sex," *Seventeen*, XXVI, 7 (July 1967), pp. 88, 130.

13. Andrew Hacker, "The Pill and Morality," *New York Times Magazine*, Nov. 21, 1965, pp. 32, 140; Spencer, "Birth Control Revolution," *Saturday Evening Post*, p. 66; Muriel and William Peters, "Love, Sex and Marriage," *Good Housekeeping*, CLXX (June 1970), p. 162; Ira L. Reiss, "How & Why America's Sex Standards Are Changing," in J. R. and J. S. DeLora, eds., *Intimate Life Styles* (Pacific Palisades, Cal., 1972, 1975), pp. 72–79.

14. John Cuber, "How New Ideas about Sex Are Changing Our Lives," in DeLora, *Intimate Life Styles,* p. 80.

15. Michael Miller, "Letter from the Berkeley Underground," *Esquire,* LXIV, 3 (Sept., 1965), p. 85.

16. Thomas J. Cottle, "The Sexual Revolution and the Young," *New York Times Magazine,* Nov. 26, 1972, p. 37.

17. John T. Rule, "Must the Colleges Police Sex?," *Atlantic Monthly,* CCXIII, 4 (April, 1964), p. 57.

18. Arno Karlen, "The Unmarrieds on Campus," *New York Times Magazine,* Jan. 26, 1969, pp. 29, 77–80.

19. Bettie Wysor, "Sex . . . Up With the Stock Market," *Vogue,* CLVII, 4 (Feb. 15, 1971), p. 87.

20. "All About the New Sex Therapy," *Newsweek,* LXXX, 22 (Nov. 27, 1972), p. 66.

21. Robert W. Kistner, "What 'The Pill' Does to Husbands," *Ladies' Home Journal,* LXXXVI, 1 (Jan. 1969), pp. 66, 68.

22. Shere Hite, *The Hite Report on Male Sexuality* (New York, 1981), pp. 61, 67.

23. Cottle, "The Sexual Revolution," *New York Times,* p. 108; Hite, *Male Sexuality,* p. 66.

24. Janet Lever and Pepper Schwartz, *Women at Yale* (Indianapolis, Ind., 1971), p. 193.

25. Quoted in Kistner, "What 'The Pill' Does," *Ladies' Home Journal,* p. 68; Patricia Coffin, "A Message To: The American Man," *Look,* XXXI, 1 (Jan. 10, 1967), p. 14.

26. Kermit Mehlinger, "The Sexual Revolution," *Ebony,* XXI, 10 (Aug. 1966), pp. 57–62.

27. Studs Terkel, *The Good War* (New York, 1984), p. 39.

28. Herbert H. Hyman and Paul B. Sheatsley, "Attitudes Towards Desegregation," *Scientific American,* CXCV, 6 (Dec., 1956), pp. 35–39.

29. *Playboy* interview in Martin Luther King, Jr., *A Testament of Hope,* ed. James M. Washington (New York, 1986), pp. 343–44; Martin Luther King, Jr., *Stride Toward Freedom* (New York, 1958), p. 212; Martin Luther King, Jr., *Strength to Love* (New York, 1963), pp. 138–39.

30. Franklin McCain, "The Student Sit-Ins," *ibid.,* pp. 75–82; Clayborne Carson, *In Struggle* (Cambridge, Mass., 1981), pp. 10–11.

31. Jeremy Larner, "The Negro in the South," *New Leader,* XLIII, 35 (Sept. 12, 1960), p. 11.

32. Hazel G. Erskine, "The Polls: Race Relations," *Public Opinion Quarterly,* XXVI, 1 (Spring, 1962), p. 145.

33. Quoted in Hodding Carter, "The Young Negro Is a New Negro," *New York Times Magazine,* May 1, 1960, Sect. 6, p. 11; "Everywhere: Tension," *U.S. News & World Report,* XLVIII, 12 (March 21, 1960), p. 75.

34. Jack Newfield, *A Prophetic Minority* (New York, 1966), p. 100.

35. Harvard Sitkoff, *The Struggle for Black Equality* (New York, 1981), p. 172; quoted in Carson, *In Struggle,* p. 112.

36. *Ibid.*

37. Bart Landry, *The New Black Middle Class* (Berkeley, Cal., 1987), pp. 3, 68, 72, 83.

38. Ronald Aronson, "Dear Herbert," in George Fischer, ed., *The Revival of American Socialism* (New York, 1971), p. 268.

39. Allan Bloom, *The Closing of the American Mind* (New York, 1987), p. 49.

40. Quoted in Kirkpatrick Sale, *SDS* (New York, 1973), p. 53.

41. *Ibid.,* p. 43.

42. Quoted in Kenneth Keniston, *Young Radicals* (New York, 1968), p. 113 and pp. 16–36, 111–32, 305–20; Allen J. Matusow, *The Unraveling of America* (New York, 1984), pp. 308–10; Lewis S. Feuer, *The Conflict of Generations* (New York, 1969), p. 423; Irwin Unger, *The Movement* (New York, 1974), pp. 128–31; Nathan Glazer, "The Jewish Role in Student Activism," in Fortune eds., *Youth in Turmoil* (New York, 1969), pp. 94–107.

43. CBS News and Daniel Yankelovich, Inc., *Generations Apart* (New York, 1969), p. 39; Gallup International, Inc., *Gallup Opinion Index: Results of Survey of College Students* (Princeton, N.J., 1969), p. 13; Allen H. Barton, "The Columbia Crisis," *Public Opinion Quarterly,* XXXII, 3 (Fall, 1968), p. 336.

44. George Gallup and Evan Hill, "Youth," *Saturday Evening Post,* CCXXXIV, 51 (Dec. 23–30, 1961), p. 78; Yankelovich, *Generations Apart,* pp. 5, 12; Louis Harris and Associates poll, "Change, Yes—Upheaval, No," *Life,* LXX, 1 (Jan. 8, 1971), p. 22.

45. *Ibid.,* pp. 82–84.

46. Quoted in Unger, *The Movement,* pp. 71–72.

47. Quoted in George B. Leonard, Jr., "The Explosive Generation," *Look,* XXV, 1 (Jan. 3, 1961), p. 20; Louis Harris survey, in "The Teen-Agers," *Newsweek,* LXVII, 12 (March 21, 1966), p. 60.

48. Harold Taylor, "The New Young Are Now Heard," *New York Times Magazine,* Sect. 6, Jan. 29, 1961, p. 66; Leonard, "The Explosive Generation," *Look,* pp. 17, 36b–d; Gallup and Evans, "Youth," *Saturday Evening Post,* p. 78; "The Face of the Future," *Look,* pp. 74, 76.

49. "Poll Contradicts Students' Image," *New York Times,* Jan. 16, 1966, p. 66.

50. The best discussion is James Fallows, "What Did You Do in the Class War, Daddy?," *The Washington Monthly* (Oct. 1975), *passim.*

51. Quoted in Murray Polner, *No Victory Parades* (New York, 1971), p. 27; William Westmoreland, "Vietnam in Perspective," *Military Review* (Jan. 1979), p. 37.

52. Lawrence M. Baskir and William A. Strauss, *Chance and Circumstance* (New York, 1978), p. 7; Jones, *Great Expectations,* p. 96.

53. Hazel Erskine, "Is War a Mistake?" *Public Opinion Quarterly,* XXXIV, 1 (Spring 1970), p. 134; Loren Baritz, *Backfire* (New York, 1985), *passim.*

54. Todd Gitlin, "The Dynamics of the New Left, Part 2," *Motive,* XXXI, 2 (Nov. 1970), pp. 43–67.

55. Robert Coles, *The Middle Americans* (Boston, Mass., 1971), p. 134.

56. Joseph Lelyveld, "Status of the Movement," *New York Times Magazine,* Nov. 7, 1971, Sect. 6, p. 105.

57. Martin Luther King, Jr., "Letter from Birmingham City Jail," April 16, 1963, *A Testament of Hope,* pp. 293–95.

58. Stokely Carmichael and Charles V. Hamilton, *Black Power* (New York, 1967), p. 53.

59. Martin Luther King, Jr., *Where Do We Go From Here?* (New York, 1967), pp. 23–66; Carson, *In Struggle,* pp. 287, 300.

60. Quoted in *ibid.,* p. 217.

61. Hugh D. Graham and Ted R. Gurr, *Violence in America* (A Report Submitted to the National Commission on the Causes and Prevention of Violence; New York, 1969), p. 555; Joe R. Feagin and Harlan Hahn, *Ghetto Revolts* (New York, 1973), *passim;* Bayard Rustin, "The Watts Manifesto," in Joseph Boskin, *Urban Racial Violence in the Twentieth Century* (Beverly Hills, Cal., 1969), p. 109; David O. Sears and T. M. Tomlinson, "Riot Ideology in Los Angeles," in James A. Geschwender, ed., *The Black Revolt* (Englewood Cliffs, N.J., 1971), pp. 377–78; Rodney Allen and Charles Adair, eds., *Violence and Riots in Urban America* (Worthington, Ohio, 1969), p. 70; King, *A Testament of Hope,* p. 649.

62. Hazel Erskine, "Demonstrations and Race Riots," *Public Opinion Quarterly,* XXXI, 4 (Winter, 1967–68), pp. 655–77.

63. Gallup and Hill, "Youth," *Saturday Evening Post,* p. 66.

64. *Ibid.*

65. *Ibid.,* p. 80.

66. Quoted in Steven Kelman, "These Are Three of the Alienated," *New York Times Magazine,* Sect. 6, Oct. 22, 1967, p. 39.

67. Louis W. Cartwright, "The New Hero," in Otto Butz, ed., *To Make a Difference* (New York, 1967), pp. 28–29.

68. Kenneth Keniston, *The Uncommitted* (New York, 1960, 1962, 1965), pp. 108–18, 124–25, 176.

69. "Big Sprout-Out of Male Mop-Top," *Life,* LIX, 5 (July 30, 1965), p. 58.

70. Mary Groves, "An Open Letter to the Father of the Boy Who Won't Get His Hair Cut," *Good Housekeeping,* CLXV, 5 (Nov. 1967), pp. 62, 64; David Llorens, "Natural Hair," *Ebony,* XXIII, 2 (Dec. 1967), pp. 139–44.

71. Moyers, *Listening to America,* p. 99.

72. Keniston, *The Uncommitted,* p. 181.

73. Cf. Tom Wolfe, "The 'Me' Decade and the Third Great Awakening," *New York,* IX, 34 (Aug. 23, 1976), pp. 34–36.

74. Eugene F. Rice, *The Foundations of Modern Europe* (New York, 1970), pp. 136–39; cf. Paul Goodman, "The New Reformation," *New York Times Magazine,* Sept. 15, 1969, pp. 145–46.

75. Hunter S. Thompson, "The 'Hashbury' Is the Capital of the Hippies," *New York Times Magazine,* May 14, 1967, p. 123.

76. Daniel Yankelovich, *The New Morality* (New York, 1974), p. 10.

77. Thompson, "The 'Hashbury,' " *New York Times Magazine,* p. 123; "60 Hippies in a Bus," *New York Times,* Sept. 23, 1968, p. 24L.

78. Quoted in Joan Didion, *Slouching towards Bethlehem* (New York, 1961, 1968), p. 101.

79. "Dropouts with a Mission," *Newsweek,* LXIX, 6 (Feb. 6, 1967), p. 92; Vivian Estellachild, "Hippie Communes," *Women,* II, 2 (Winter, 1971), pp. 40–43.

80. Ralph J. Gleason, "The Power of Non-Politics," in Jesse Kornbluth, ed., *Notes from the New Underground* (New York, 1968), p. 220; Nicholas Von Hoffman, *We Are the People Our Parents Warned Us Against* (Chicago, 1968), p. 112.

81. Richard Goldstein, "Love: A Groovy Idea While He Lasted," in Kornbluth, *Notes from the New Underground,* p. 257; "Hippies," *Time,* XCIII, 25 (June 20, 1969), p. 55.

82. "Year of the Commune," *Newsweek,* LXXIV, 7 (Aug. 18, 1969), p. 89.

83. "The Message of History's Biggest Happening," *Time,* XCIV, 9 (Aug. 29, 1969), p. 32; "A Whole New Minority Group," *Newsweek,* LXXIV, 9 (Sept. 1, 1969), p. 22A.

84. "The Talk of the Town," *The New Yorker,* XLV, 28 (Aug. 30, 1969), pp. 19–21.

85. "The Message," *Time,* p. 33.

86. Andrew Kopkind, "Coming of Age in Aquarius," in editors of *Ramparts, Conversations with the New Reality* (New York, 1971), p. 44.

87. Norman Vincent Peale, "We *Need* Their Faith," *Reader's Digest,* XCIX, 596 (Dec., 1971), p. 140; "The Jesus Movement Is Upon Us," *Look,* XXXV, 3 (Feb. 9, 1971), pp. 15-21; "The New Rebel Cry: Jesus Is Coming!," *Time,* XCVII, 25 (June 21, 1971), pp. 56, 59-63; James Nolan, "Jesus Now," *Ramparts,* X, 2 (Aug., 1971), pp. 20-26; Robert Lynn Adams and Robert Jon Fox, "Mainlining Jesus," *Society,* IX, 4 (Feb., 1972), pp. 50-56.

88. Quoted in Harry G. Summers, *On Strategy* (Novato, Cal., 1982), p. 18; U.S. Congress, House of Representatives, Committee on Appropriations, Subcommittee *Hearings* (90th Cong., 1st sess.; Washington, D.C., 1967), p. 43.

89. For an earlier view, see "A New $10 Billion Power," *Life,* XLVII, 9 (Aug. 31, 1959), pp. 78-85; Eleanore Carruth, "The Great Fashion Explosion," *Fortune,* LXXVI, 5 (Oct. 1967), p. 162; quoted in Vance Packard, *The Sexual Wilderness* (New York, 1968), p. 25.

90. Yankelovich, *New Morality,* pp. 3-6, 23, 93.

91. "Male Plumage '68," *Newsweek,* LXXII, 22 (Nov. 25, 1968), pp. 75, 76.

92. *Ibid.,* p. 70.

93. "Fashion," *Time,* XCIII, 20 (May 16, 1969), p. 62; "Twiggy," *Newsweek,* LXIX, 15 (April 10, 1967), p. 62.

94. "Charming a Man," *Mademoiselle,* LXV, 3 (July 1967), p. 51. Cf. Charlotte Cook and Joel Butler, "Short Skirts and Symbolism," *Corrective Psychiatry and Journal of Social Therapy,* XIV, 2 (1968), pp. 103-105.

95. "The Story of Pop," *Newsweek,* LXVII, 17 (April 25, 1966), pp. 56-58; Joyce Maynard, "An 18-Year-Old Looks Back on Life," *New York Times Magazine,* April 23, 1972, Sect. 6, p. 80.

96. "From Hot Panting to Hotpants," *Mademoiselle,* LXXIII, 3 (July, 1971), 140; "Uni-Sex," *Newsweek,* LXVII, 7 (Feb. 14, 1966), p. 59.

97. Daniel Yankelovich, *New Rules* (New York, 1981), p. xiii; "The Mood of the Country," *U.S. News & World Report,* LXIII, 24 (Dec. 11, 1967), pp. 91-92; Hazel Erskine, "Hopes, Fears, and Regrets," *Public Opinion Quarterly,* XXXVII, 1 (Spring, 1973), pp. 139, 141. Cf. Peter Clecak, *America's Quest for the Ideal Self* (New York, 1983), pp. 188-200.

98. Standard & Poor, *Basic Statistics* (New York, 1984), p. 76; U.S. Bureau of the Census, *Statistical Abstract of the United States: 1981* (102d ed.; Washington, D.C., 1981), p. 458; Peter Vanderwicken, "The Uses of Economic Adversity," *Time,* XCVII, 8 (Feb. 22, 1971), p. 17.

99. Ira Mothner, "If New Hampshire Makes It," *Look,* XXXV, 1 (Jan. 12, 1971), p. 36.

100. "Man and Woman of the Year," *Time,* XCV, 1 (Jan. 5, 1970), p. 13.

101. "The Troubled American," *Newsweek,* LXXIV, 14 (Oct. 6, 1969), p. 49.

102. *Ibid.,* p. 31.

103. Michael Novak, *The Rise of the Unmeltable Ethnics* (New York, 1971, 1972), p. 168.

104. "Time to Remember 'Forgotten America,' " *Time,* XCIV, 6 (Aug. 8, 1969), p. 42; Peter Schrag, "The Forgotten Americans," *Harper's,* CCXXXIX, 1431 (Aug., 1969), p. 29.

105. "Revolt of the Middle Class," *U.S. News & World Report,* LXVII, 21 (Nov. 24, 1969), p. 55.

106. "The Troubled American," *Newsweek,* p. 34.

107. Henry Grunwald, "Thoughts on Troubled El Dorado," *Time,* XCV, 25 (June 22, 1970), p. 18.

6. FREEDOM FROM LOVE

1. Robert J. Lifton, "Protean Man," *Partisan Review,* XXXV, 1 (Winter, 1968), pp. 13–27.

2. Stanley Kunitz, "The Poet's Quest for the Father," *New York Times Book Review,* Feb. 22, 1987, Sect. 7, p. 36; Howard Moss, "Elegy for My Father," *Selected Poems* (New York, 1971), p. 21.

3. Paula Giddings, *When and Where I Enter* (New York, 1984), p. 308; Sara Evans, *Personal Politics* (New York, 1979), p. 19–21, 189.

4. Abe Peck, *Uncovering the Sixties* (New York, 1985), p. 208; Anselma Dell'Olio, "The Sexual Revolution Wasn't Our War," in Francine Klagsbrun, ed., *The First Ms. Reader* (New York, 1973), p. 125.

5. Hazel Erskine, "Women's Role," *Public Opinion Quarterly,* XXXV, 2 (Summer, 1971), pp. 275–76; Daniel Yankelovich, *The New Morality* (New York, 1974), pp. 41, 95–102.

6. Judy Klemesrud, "In Small Town, U.S.A.," in Gene Roberts and David R. Jones, eds., *Assignment America* (New York, 1974), pp. 242–46.

7. Battelle Memorial Institute study quoted in Nadine Brozan, " 'New Woman' Is Not So New," *New York Times,* Aug. 18, 1986, p. A18; U.S. Department of Labor, Bureau of Labor Statistics, *Facts on Women Workers* (Washington, D.C., 1984), p. 2.

8. Quoted in Janet Lever and Pepper Schwartz, *Women at Yale* (Indianapolis, Ind., 1971), p. 220.

9. *Ibid.,* p. 189.

10. Shere Hite, *The Hite Report on Male Sexuality* (New York, 1981), pp. 313, 314, 316.

11. Cary McMuhllen, Letter to the Editor, *New York Times,* Sept. 4, 1986, p. A26.

12. Robert Bly interviewed by Keith Thompson, "What Men Really Want," *New Age* (May 1982), pp. 31–37, 50–51.

13. Hans Loewald, *Papers on Psychoanalysis* (New Haven, Conn., 1980), p. 386.

14. National Council on Aging, *Fact Book on Aging* (Washington, D.C., 1978), p. 159.

15. Christopher Lasch, *Culture of Narcissism* (New York, 1978), pp. 177–80.

16. Peter Cohen, *The Gospel According to the Harvard Business School* (Garden City, N.Y., 1973), p. 169.

17. Philip Rieff, *The Triumph of the Therapeutic* (New York, 1966), pp. 1–27.

18. *Ibid.,* pp. 55–65; Sara Davidson, "Rolling into the 80s," *Esquire,* XCIX, 6 (June, 1983), pp. 406–407.

19. Yankelovich *et al., The General Mills American Family Report* (Minneapolis, Minn., 1975), p. 35; Peter N. Carroll, *It Seemed Like Nothing Happened* (New York, 1982), p. 235; Connecticut Mutual Life Insurance Co., *Report on American Values in the '80s* (Hartford, Conn., 1981), p. 19.

20. Robert N. Bellah *et al., Habits of the Heart* (Berkeley, Cal., 1985), pp. 23–24.

21. Bill Moyers, *Listening to America* (New York, 1971), p. 71.

22. Bart Landry, *The New Black Middle Class* (Berkeley, Cal., 1987), pp. 222–23; C. Vann Woodward, "The Dreams of Martin Luther King," *New York Review of Books,* XXXIII, 21 and 22 (Jan. 15, 1987), p. 9.

23. Davidson, "Rolling into the 80s," *Esquire,* p. 396.

24. John Herbers, "Suburbs Absorb More Immigrants," *New York Times,* Dec. 14, 1986, pp. 1, 44.

25. Robert B. Oxnam, "Why Asians Succeed Here," *New York Times Magazine,* Nov. 30, 1986, Sect. 6, pp. 70, 72, 75, 88, 89, 92.

26. Jay B. Rohrlich, "Wall Street's Money Junkies," *New York Times,* May 7, 1987, p. A35.

27. Stephen Drucker, "Psyching It Out," *Vogue,* CLXXVII, 1 (Jan. 1987), p. 258.

28. Gail Gregg, "Putting Kids First," *New York Times Magazine,* April 13, 1986, pp. 47, 104.

29. Rieff, *Triumph of the Therapeutic,* p. 240.

30. *Ibid.,* p. 60.

31. Drucker, "Psyching It Out," *Vogue,* p. 209.

32. Felix Rohatyn, "The Blight on Wall Street," *New York Review of Books,* XXXIV, 4 (March 12, 1987), p. 21.

33. Stanley Kunitz, "Father and Son," in *Selected Poems, 1928–1958* (Boston, 1929, 1958), p. 45.

Index

Adams, Henry, 24, 55
Adams, John, 8
Adams, Samuel, 8
Addams, Jane, 41, 73
advertising, 77–83, 143
  creation of consumers by, 78
  items to increase leisure time, 79
  Man at Work and, 81
  "new gospel" of consumption
    and, 79–83
  of 1920s, 79
  pressures on family during Great
    Depression, 143
  Printers' Ink on, 78
  romantic love and, 80–1
  women and, 83–5
American Federation of Labor
    (AFL), 129–30, 132–4
  ethnic makeup of membership,
    130
American Gas Association, 169
American Home, 169

"Americanization" campaigns,
    52–3
American Jews, 200–1, 253
  see also Jewish immigrants
American Revolution, 8
Amos 'n' Andy (radio show), 153–5
Anderson, Sherwood, 101
androgyny, 237, 282
Arbuckle, Fatty, 95
Aufricht, Dr. Gustave, 188

baby-boomers, 226–7
"Back to God" movement, 222
Baisley, Barbara, 285
Bara, Theda, 161
Batman (TV show), 282
Beatles, 256
beatniks, 224
Bell, Daniel, 137, 139
Bellow, Saul, 138
Bennett, Walter, 125

birth control, *see* contraceptives;
   "pill," the
Black Power movement, 262–5
   black nationalism, 262–5
   southern culture rejected by, 263
   urban riots and, 264
blacks, 69, 121, 124–5, 177, 241–9,
      245–6
   middle-class aspirations of black
      students, 245–6
   in military (World War II), 177
   postwar statistics on education,
      243
   procession in Harlem (1935), 121
   southern blacks in Great
      Depression, 124–5
   see also civil rights movement
Black Thursday, 113
Blass, Bill, 280
blue-collar workers, 217–18
Bly, Robert, 297–8
bohemianism, before World War I,
      58
   see also Jazz Age
Boone, Daniel, 25, 26
Boston, Irish immigrants in, 16–20
   collision with nativists, 17–18
   exploitation of, 17
   political power and, 18–20
Boston Brahmins, 18, 19
Bourne, Randolph, 99
Bow, Clara, 96
breast fixation, in postwar era, 187–
      91, 195
   breast-feeding and, 195
   fashion and, 188
   Hollywood stars and, 189–90
   importance of breast size, 187–8
   Playboy and, 189–91
Bride Comes Home, The (film), 163

Bronstein, Leon (Trotsky), 69
Browder, Earl, 110
Brown, Efelka, 264
Bryan, William Jennings, 70–1
buying on credit, 64, 80

Cagney, James, 161
Cahan, Abraham, 23, 49–50
Capone, Al, 76, 235
Capra, Frank, 163
Carmichael, Stokely, 262, 263, 293
Catholic Church, 18, 25
   see also Irish immigrants
celebrity, 76–7, 94–8
   conformity and, 94
   consumerism and, 76–7
   power over fans of, 95
   rise of idea of, 94–8
   silent movies and, 96–8
   tabloid press and, 95
Chaplin, Charles, 94
Chicago *Tribune,* 87
children
   comparisons with Soviet
      children, 220–1
   home ownership and child labor,
      73
   of immigrants, education of, 40–1
   parenting in postwar era, 204–10
   see also education
Chinese immigrants, 33–4
Churchill, Winston, 182
civil rights movement, 241–9
   anti-segregation legislation (1964–
      65), 248
   diminishing localism and, 242
   Greensboro lunch counter sit-ins
      and, 244–5
   Martin Luther King and, 243–4

Montgomery bus boycott, 243
the "pill" and, 241
postwar attitudes toward
integration, 242–3
sixties' achievements viewed by
whites as "total success," 248
SNCC and, 246–9
Supreme Court school decision
(1954), 242
Colbert, Claudette, 163
Collins, William, 130
Colonial America, 5–9
American Revolution, 8
birth of middle-class values in,
6–7
economic improvement and
immigration, 9–10
German immigrants in, 9–10
ideal of farmer in, 11–12
inherited wealth in, 6–7
Commons, John R., 25
Congress of Industrial
Organizations (CIO), 130,
132–4
"consciousness raising," 293
consumerism, 76–83, 114, 278–82,
305–6
advertising and, 76–7
celebrity and, 76–7
electrified kitchens, 83
Great Depression and, 114
installment plans and, 80
items to increase leisure time, 79
mass culture and, 77
"new gospel" of consumption,
79–83
romantic love and, 80–1
technology, fascination with,
76–7
women and, 83–5

see also consumerism (1960s)
consumerism (1960s), 278–82
"peacock revolution" and, 280–1
contraceptives, 141, 229–30
see also "pill," the
Coolidge, Calvin, 71, 114
Cooper, Frankie, 180
Cooper, James Fenimore, 11
Correll, Charles J., 153
Coué, Émile, 101
Coughlin, Father, 302
Crawford, Joan, 87, 95, 96
credit, buying on, 64, 80
Crosby, Bing, 175
cultural revolution (1960s), 225–88
alienation and passivity behind,
265–7
androgyny of young men and,
237, 282
baby-boomers and, 226–7
colleges and universities and,
233, 240, 254–5
consumerism and, 278–82
"cultural wars" of, 227–8
education and, 254–5
Free Speech Movement and,
255–6
generation gap and, 254
hippie counterculture, 269–77
idealism of students during,
249–51
inflation of 1967 and, 283–8
long hair on males and, 268–9
masculinity and, 234–7, 268–9
"massive official misconduct"
and, 256
national reaction to "too much
change," 284
new left, aims of, 253–4
1968 and, 225

cultural revolution (1960s) (*cont'd*)
 parents' choices forced by, 226
 the "pill" and, 229–30
 repudiation of middle-class
  values, 227–8
 SDS and, 251–4
 sexual revolution and, 229–34
 strong fathers, nostalgia for, 266–7
 transfer of leftward movement
  in, 279–80
 Vietnam war and, 256–61
Custis, Daniel Parke, 8

Dabrowskis, Helena, 40
Darrow, Clarence, 70–1
Davis, Rennie, 261
Dean, James, 218
Dearborn Independent, 63
DeMille, Cecil B., 96
Democratic convention in Chicago
  (1968), 260
Dewey, John, 102
Dior, Christian, 187
divorce, 84
Dos Passos, John, 122–3
Dulles, John Foster, 222

education, 40–1, 219–22
 "happiness" vs. "discipline,"
  221–2
 of immigrant children, 40–1
 parochial schools, 74
 in postwar era, 219–22
 rise in school attendance by 1930,
  74
 Soviets and, 220–1
Einstein, Albert, 256
Eisenhower, Dwight D., 222, 250

Ellis Island, 26–7
Emergency Farm Mortgage Act,
  129
Emerson, Faye, 203
employees, middle-class,
  310–12
Equal Rights Amendment, 296
Erikson, Erik, 40, 213, 215
Espinosa, Winona, 191
Etiquette (Post), 86

"famine emigrants," 15–16
farmers, 11–12, 67–8, 178
 Great Depression and, 119–20
 in 1920s, 67–8
fashion
 in Great Depression, 149–53
 in 1960s, 282–3
"Father and Son" (Kunitz), 318
Father Knows Best (TV show), 223
"fatherlessness," 266–7, 291, 298–9
Federal Housing Authority, 195, 197
feminism, 237, 291–9
 beginnings of, 294–5
 independence of middle-class
  women and, 295–6
 males opposed to, 296–7
 NOW and, 292–3
 political power and, 296
 sexual freedom of sixties and,
  293–4
 "woman as martyr" and, 294
 see also women
Fiedler, Leslie, 137
films, *see* movies; silent movies
Fitzgerald, F. Scott, 59, 89, 99, 212,
  299
 on flappers, 89
flappers, 87–93, 150–2, 232

college papers on dances done by, 91-2

disdain for parents as role models, 93

end of era in Great Depression, 150-2

fashion and style of, 88

as precedent for sexual revolution of sixties, 232

religious protests against, 90-1

seriousness behind antics of, 92-3

sexual mores and, 89-90

short hair of, 88

Flash Gordon (movie serial), 160

Ford, Henry, 61-5, 77, 82, 106, 114, 148, 154

    anti-Semitism of, 63-4

    conservatism of, 61-5

    hatred of the city, 62-3

    on motor car for multitudes, 62

Ford, Henry, II, 218

Ford, John, 164

Ford, Patrick, 20

"forgotten man," 128

Fortuna, Sgt. Gene, 175

Fortune, 199

forty-eighters, 13-14

Forward, Jewish Daily, 49-50, 136

Francisco, Joyce, 271

Franco, Francisco, 167

Franklin, Benjamin, 10

freedom, *see* new freedom

Freedom Riders, 253

Free Speech Movement (FSM), 255-6

Freud, Sigmund, 101, 301, 307

Friedan, Betty, 191, 195

Gable, Clark, 163

Gandhi, Mohandas K., 244

gangster movies, 161

General Motors Corporation, 63-4, 82, 126, 134

    innovations by, 64

generation gap, 85-7, 87-93, 99-102, 135-6, 254

    flappers and, 87-93

    in Great Depression, 135-6

    in 1920s, 85-7, 99-102

    in 1960s, 254

German-Americans, 51-2

German immigrants, 9-10, 12-14

    in Colonial America, 9-10

    forty-eighters, 13-14

    as ideal citizens, 9-10

    in nineteenth century, 12-14

    in Pennsylvania, 10

Gersh, Harry, 200-1

ghettos, 28, 43, 44-5

GI Bill of Rights, 184-5

Gibson girl, 88

Ginsberg, Allen, 224

Gish, Lillian, 96

Godspell, 277

Goldwyn, Samuel, 106

Good Housekeeping, 208

Goodman, Paul, 216

Goodyear rubber factory, 133-4

Gosden, Freeman, 153

Gotbaum, Victor, 139

Grant, Cary, 162

Gray, Harold, 148

Great Depression, 102, 105, 109-65

    advertising industry pressure on families in, 143

    Amos 'n' Andy as success during, 153-5

    blame for, 128

Great Depression (*cont'd*)
  clothing fashions during, 149–53
  consumer society and, 114
  cultural conservatism and, 164–5
  domestic life during, 139–45
  farmers and, 119–20
  flappers and, 150–2
  "forgotten man" and, 128
  generation gap during, 134–9
  Harlan County coal miners'
    strike, 122–4
  housewife's isolation during, 145
  labor union movement, 122–4,
    129–34
  mass culture in, 148–9
  men's fashions in, 152–3
  migrations from farms to cities,
    120
  momentum of stock market crash
    and, 113–14
  mortgage debt, 128–9
  movies during, 159–65
  in Muncie, Ind., 125–8
  New Deal and, 126–7
  optimism of middle class during,
    117–18
  prostitution during, 140–1
  radical social change, 110
  radio broadcasts during, 153–5
  sexual impotence and, 146
  as survival crisis, 116
  tenacious character of, 113
  urban poverty during, 120–2
  violence in cities during, 121
  wage cuts and cost of living, 115–16
  women as job holders during, 115
  women's strength and fortitude
    during, 141–4
Greenson, Ralph, 241
Growing Up Absurd (Goodman), 216

"Guy What Takes His Time, A,"
  162

Harding, Warren G., 67
Harlan County coal-miners' strike,
  122–4
Harper, Steve, 258
Harper's Magazine, 168
Hawthorne, Nathaniel, 7
Hayden, Tom, 251–2
Hays, Will, 95
Hearst, William Randolph, 162
Hefner, Hugh, 189, 240
Hell's Angels, 274
Heloise, 193
Hemingway, Ernest, 59
hippie counterculture, 269–77
  communes, 274–6
  criticism of, 277
  "devils" in society, 270
  geographical centers of, 273
  life-style and philosophy,
    271–3
  "love" and, 271–2
  in poor neighborhoods, 274
  as separatists, 270–1
  women and, 273–4
  Woodstock and, 274–6
Hitler, Adolf, 153
Ho Chi Minh, 258
Holmes, Oliver Wendell, 18
home ownership, 72–6, 128–9
  building and loan associations,
    72–3
  child labor and, 73
  foreclosures during Great
    Depression, 128–9
  as fulfillment of dream, 74–5
  Jews and, 75–6

in postwar era, 195-6
see also suburbs
Home Owners Loan Corporation,
129
Hoover, Herbert, 66, 110, 116, 122,
149
Hoover, J. Edgar, 169
Hoover vacuum advertisement, 78
Horner, Gov. Henry, 120
House Beautiful, 186
Howe, Irving, 44, 48, 135, 137, 139
on generation gap, 137
on Jewish immigrants, 44, 48
Howl (Ginsberg), 224
Hutchinson, Anne, 5

immigration and immigrants, 6-55,
68, 309
"acceptance," myth of, 23-4
"Americanization" campaigns
and, 52-3
Asian immigrants of 1980s, 309
assimilation and heritage, 32-3,
36-7
children's break from family
values, 41-2
Chinese immigrants, 33-4
in Colonial America, 6
condescension from nativists,
38-9
cultural cost of economic
opportunity, 36-7, 38-9
cultural transition and, 32-3
disorientation and
"uprootedness" of
immigrants, 35-6
economic improvement as goal
of, 9-10
education of children, 40-1

Ellis Island and, 26-7
family integrity and, 39-42
fear and resistance to, after
1880s, 22-6, 38
German immigrants, 9-10, 12-14
ghettos, 28
"heartless money machines,"
America viewed as, 37-8
increases in all ethnic groups
before 1900, 22-3
industrial boom of 1880s and,
21-2
Irish immigrants, 14-20
Italian immigrants, 29-32
Japanese immigrants, 33-4
Jewish immigrants, 30-1, 42-51
misperceptions of America by
immigrants, 34
New York City and, 27
Northeasterner and Populist
resistance to, 24-5
quotas imposed by 1924 law, 68
racism and, 33-4
"real men" and, 25-6
religious intolerance and, 25
settlement in cities (1900-20),
26-7
slums and, 28
from South and East Europe
(1880s), 21
unwillingness to become
"Americans," 32-5
urbanization and, 26-7, 54-5
Walter Weyl on urbanization,
53-5
World War I and, 51-2
see also German immigrants;
Irish immigrants;
Italian immigrants;
Jewish immigrants

installment buying, 64, 80

Irish Emigrant Society of New York, 15

Irish immigrants, 14–20
  in Boston, 16–20
  clannishness and conservatism of, 18
  economic need as motivation for, 14–15
  exploitation in Boston, 17
  "famine emigrants," character of, 15–16
  in New York, 18–20
  political activity in Boston, 18–20

Italian-Americans, 168–201

Italian immigrants, 29–32
  adjustments to American culture, 31–2
  contrasted with Jewish immigrants, 30–1
  prejudice against, 29
  as "temporary" citizens, 29–30

It Happened One Night (film), 163

It's a Wonderful World (film), 163

Japanese immigrants, 33–4

Jazz Age, 60–104
  advertising and, 77–83
  consumerism, rise of, 76–83
  economic boom of, 71–2
  emancipation of women in, 85–7
  flappers, 87–93
  Freud and, 101
  generation gap in, 85–7
  Henry Ford and, 61–5
  "ill-mannered" revolt of, 86
  obsession with young, 86–7
  Prohibition, 68
  Red Scare of 1919 and, 69

religious fundamentalism and, 69–71
  rural America and, 65–7
  Scopes Trial and, 70–1
  sexual ideal in, 84–5
  small-town America and, 60–1
  spiritual crisis and, 102–4
  youth's disillusionment with own rebellion, 100–1

Jefferson, Thomas, 8, 11

Jesus Christ Superstar, 277

"Jesus freaks," 276–7

Jewish Daily Forward, 49–50, 136

Jewish immigrants, 30–1, 42–51, 63–4, 75–6
  contrasted with Italian immigrants, 30–1
  development of own middle class, 50–1
  eastern European Jews, 45–6
  garment industry and, 48–9
  German Jews, 45–6
  ghetto experience of, 43, 44–5
  Henry Ford and, 63–4
  home ownership and, 75–6
  "Jewishness," sense of, in second generation, 138
  learning English, 47
  literary critics among second generation, 137
  Lower East Side (of New York) and, 44, 50
  materialistic America and, 46–7
  as more highly skilled than other immigrant groups, 44
  as peddlers, 47–8
  politics of, 49–50, 138–9
  second generation and middle-class attitudes, 137–9
  traditional values in new setting, 45

Jews, 200–1, 253
 see also Jewish immigrants
Johnson, Gerald, 117–18
Johnson, Lyndon B., 225, 256–7,
 277
Jonestown, 277
Joplin, Janis, 276
juvenile delinquency, 209

Kael, Pauline, 172
Kate Smith Hour, The (radio show),
 149
Kazin, Alfred, 137, 139
Keniston, Kenneth, 267, 269, 296
 on shifting sex roles, 296
Kennedy, John F., 265
Kerouac, Jack, 224, 250
King, Martin Luther, Jr., 243–4,
 261–2, 264
King Kong (film), 164
Kinsey, Dr. Alfred, 191
Kistner, Dr. Robert, 238
Krutch, Joseph Wood, 102–4
Ku Klux Klan, 68–9, 124
Kunitz, Stanley, 291, 318
Kupper, Herbert I., 186

labor unions, 122–4, 129–34
 AFL, 129–30
 CIO, 130
 English working class compared,
  131–2
 Harlan County coal-miners'
  strike, 122–4
 organization in Great
  Depression, 122
 sit-down strike tactic, 133–4
 statistics on (1936), 132–3

UAW, 130–1
 worker solidarity, 131–2
Ladies' Home Journal, The, 83, 149, 238
Lasch, Christopher, 206
Laski, Harold, 132
Lazarus, Emma, 23
League of Nations, 59, 67
Leave It to Beaver (TV show), 223
Legion of Decency, 162–3
Levine, Isaac Don, 35–6
Levittown, 197
Lewis, John L., 130, 134
Lewis, Sinclair, 66
Life, 127, 220–2
Lifestyles of the Rich and Famous (TV
 show), 317
Lifton, Robert J., 290–1
Lincoln, Abraham, 25
Lindbergh, Charles A., 76, 302
Lindsey, Judge Ben, 85–6
Lippmann, Walter, 100, 101
Lipset, Seymour Martin, 137
Literary Digest, 89
Little Caesar (film), 161
Little Orphan Annie, 148
"living together," 234
Lodge, Henry Cabot, 24
Lone Ranger, The (radio show), 157–9
Look, 224
lower middle class, 302–4
"Lullaby" (Brahms), 175

Mace, Dr. David R., 213–14
Mademoiselle, 231
Malcolm X, 262
Man at Work, The (advertising
 image), 81
Manson "family," 277
market men, 314–18

marriage, 97, 139–40, 176, 193–4,
    198–9, 213–14
  fifties couples, 213–14
  in Great Depression, 139–40
  in postwar era, 193–4
  in silent movies, 97
  suburban life and, 198–9, 203–4
  World War II statistics on, 176
masculinity, 145–8, 173–6, 234–7,
    291, 296–8
  absent father and, 291, 298–9
  competition and, 236
  corporate workers and, 211–12
  cultural myths about, 214–16
  defining, in World War II, 173–6
  feminism and, 296–7
  heroes, 235
  lower-middle-class males, 216–17
  money and issues, 235–6
  performance anxiety, 239–40
  sexual anxiety of the sixties, 234,
    235–6
  "soft males" and, 297–8
  sports and, 239, 240
  unemployment in Great
    Depression and, 145–8
  value of being "well liked," 212
  white-collar workers and, 210–11
mass culture, 77, 148–9
McCarthy, Sen. Joseph, 196, 199,
    302
McNamara, Robert, 277
Mehlinger, Dr. Kermit, 241, 242
Mencken, H. L., 55, 66, 70, 87
  on political power of "boobs,"
    66
Miele, Stefano, 29–30
Miller, Arthur, 212, 216
Mills, C. Wright, 212
Miltown, 200

miniskirts, 280–1
Misleading Lady (film), 163
Mr. Deeds Goes to Town (film), 163
Mr. Smith Goes to Washington (film), 163
Modern Temper, The (Krutch), 102
Molly Maguires, 19
Monroe, Marilyn, 189
Montgomery, Roger, 183–4
Moses, Robert, 247
Moss, Howard, 291
mothers and motherhood, 169–70,
    194, 204–6, 267
  as cultural icon of forties and
    fifties, 171–4
  Dr. Spock and, 205
  as martyrs and society's victims,
    267
  protection of, in World War II,
    169–70
movies, 159–65, 172
  gangster, 161
  in Great Depression, 159–65
  Legion of Decency and, 162–3
  Mae West and, 161–2, 163
  Production Code and, 162–4
  romance, sex, and violence, 160–4
  statistics on, 159–60
  World War II movies, 172
  see also silent movies
Moynihan, Sen. Daniel Patrick,
    23–4
"multiversity," 256
Muncie, Ind. (in Great
    Depression), 125–8
Mussolini, Benito, 168

National Association for the
    Advancement of Colored
    People (NAACP), 262, 293

National Organization for Women
(NOW), 292–3
Native Sons of the Golden West, 52
New Deal, 126–7, 129
new freedom, 289–318
  consumption and affluence,
    305–6
  dependency and, 312
  employee class and, 310–12
  "fatherlessness" and, 298–9, 318
  feminism and, 291–9
  freedom from past, 289–91
  fundamentalism and, 306–7
  incoherence and amorality and,
    299–300
  lower-middle-class Americans
    and, 302–4, 306
  market men and, 314–18
  masculinity and, 291
  new immigrants, 309
  personality and, 313
  personal wealth replacing
    cultural values, 307–9
  political system, lack of faith in,
    304–5
  postwar affluence and, 289
  "protean man" and, 290–1
  psychological culture replacing
    religious culture, 300–2, 307–8
  release of "creativity" and, 300
"New Look," 187
Newsweek, 228
New York Federation of Labor, 130
Niebuhr, Reinhold, 222
Nietzsche, Friedrich, 56, 301
1920s, *see* Jazz Age
1960s, *see* cultural revolution (1960s)
Nixon, Richard M., 225, 279, 284,
  286
Norek, Barbara, 180

Okies, 120
Old Ma Perkins (radio show), 155–6
"organization man," 212
"other-directedness," 200
Our Dancing Daughters (film), 87
Our Gal Sunday (radio show), 156
Outlaw, The (film), 189

Packard Motor Car Company, 52–3
Paine, Thomas, 8
Palmer, A. Mitchell, 69
parenting, 204–10
  lack of moral vision and, 206
Parks, Rosa, 243
parochial education, 74
"peacock revolution," 280–2
Peale, Norman Vincent, 223, 277
Perkins, Frances, 112
Pershing, Gen. John Joseph, 122
Pickford, Mary, 96
Piercy, Marge, 189, 224
"pill," the, 229–30, 238–9, 241
  civil rights movement and, 241
  effects on sexuality, 238–9, 241
  statistics on use of, 230
Pisicano, Paul, 168, 201
Playboy magazine, 189–91
Port Huron Statement, 251
Post, Emily, 86
postwar era (1945–59), 182–224
  births during, 191, 194–5
  breast fixation in, 187–91
  "chronic happiness," search for,
    202–3
  conflict and search for therapy,
    219
  dependency of parents on
    children, 205–10
  dissent in fifties, 223–4

postwar era (1945–59) (*cont'd*)
  education in, 219–22
  GI Bill of Rights and, 184–5
  housework in fifties, 192–3
  housing problems in, 195–6
  industry in, 218–19
  juvenile delinquency in, 209
  marital problems, 213–14
  masculinity myths and, 214–16
  the "organization man," 212
  parenting in, 204–10
  prosperity in, 182–5
  "refeminization" of women in,
    186–91
  religious revival, 222
  safety and security, importance
    of, 196–7
  second generation as corporate
    workers, 211–12
  sexuality in, 186–91
  Soviet education, comparisons
    with, 220–1
  suburban living, 196–201
  teen-age dating and "going
    steady," 208–9
  television and, 201–3
  "togetherness," 206
  white-collar work and
    masculinity issue, 210–11
  women replaced by men in work
    force, 185–6
Power of Positive Thinking, The
  (Peale), 223
Presley, Elvis, 209, 256
Printers' Ink, 78, 79
privacy, demand for, 57–8
Prohibition, 68
prostitution, 140–1
"protean man," 290–1
"psychological man," 300–2, 307–8

psychology of self, focus on, 57–8
Public Enemy (film), 161
Puritans, 3–5

racism
  Asian-Americans and, 33–4
  Ku Klux Klan and, 68–9
  in suburbs, 197
  see also blacks; civil rights
    movement
radio, 77, 153–9
  Amos 'n' Andy, 153–5
  growth in Great Depression,
    153–5
  soap operas, 155–7
Rasmussen, Virginia, 180
Ravage, M. E., 34
real estate, *see* home ownership;
    suburbs
Rebel Without a Cause (film), 218
Red Scare of 1919, 69
Reformation, 3–5
religion, 25, 222
  "Back to God" movement in
    fifties, 222
  fundamentalism in small towns,
    69–71
  intolerance toward immigrants,
    25
  Scopes Trial and, 70–1
Rickover, Adm. Hyman, 220,
    278
Rieff, Philip, 300–1, 317
Riesman, David, 200
Rissarro, Frank, 210
Robinson, Edward G., 161, 235
Rogers, Will, 156
Roman Catholic Church, 18, 25
  see also Irish immigrants

Roosevelt, Franklin D., 110–13, 124,
127, 132, 149, 153, 182
"ideology" of, 112
leadership qualities of, 110–12
middle class and, 112–13
Roosevelt, Theodore, 51, 84
Roots (TV miniseries), 306
"Rosie the Riveter," 179
Ross, E. A., 20
Royko, Mike, 184–5
Russell, Jane, 189

Sacco and Vanzetti case, 69
Sargent, Frank, 26
Savio, Mario, 255–6
Schauffler, Goodrich, 188
Schiller, Johann Christian
Friedrich von, 14
Schnall, Maxine, 207
Schurz, Carl, 13
Schwartz, Delmore, 137
Scopes Trial, 70–1
Secrets of a Secretary (film), 163
Seventeen, 231
sexuality, 84–5, 89–90, 98, 146,
229–34
flappers and, 89–90
ideal sexuality in 1920s, 84
the "pill" and, 229–30
sex-magazine editor's letter
(1926), 98
sex roles in 1920s, 84–5
sexual revolution (1960s), 229–34
in silent movies, 97–8
unemployment and sexual
impotence, 146
virginity in sixties, 230–1
see also feminism; masculinity;
sexual revolution (1960s)

sexual revolution (1960s), 229–34,
237–9
androgyny in young males, 237
colleges and, 233
confusion about sexual freedom,
232–3
flapper as precedent for, 232
"living together," 234
the "pill" and, 229–30, 238–9, 241
premarital sex and, 230–1
sex as social weapon, 234
virginity, 230–1
women's sexual maturation in,
237–9
She Done Him Wrong (film), 161–2
She Married Her Boss (film), 163
"Silent Majority," 286
silent movies, 96–8
consumerism and, 97
exploitation of sex in, 97–8
marriage and, 97
"new women" in, 96–7
sit-down strikes, 133–4
Skinner, Cornelia Otis, 182
slums, 28
Smith, Harry Nash, 12
soap operas (radio), 155–7
"soft males," 297–8
Spanish Civil War, 167
Spock, Dr. Benjamin, 205
Sputnik, 220
Stagecoach (film), 164
"stagflation," 284
Stein, Gertrude, 59
Stewart, James, 164
Student Nonviolent Coordinating
Committee (SNCC), 246–9,
261, 262, 263, 293
black nationalism and, 263
voter registration and, 247

Student Nonviolent Coordinating
    Committee (SNCC) (*cont'd*)
  white students in, 247–8, 249
Students for a Democratic Society
    (SDS), 251–4, 260–1, 293
  challenges university, 251–2
  collapse of, 260–1
  composition of membership in,
    252–3
  Jewish students in, 253
  "participatory democracy" of,
    252
suburbs, 196–201
  conformity and, 198–200
  ethnicity and, 200–1
  family difficulties increasing in,
    204
  freedom from attachment to
    place, 198
  growth statistics, 197–8
  racism in, 197
  see also home ownership
suicides, 299
Sunday, Billy, 70
Swanson, Gloria, 96

tabloid press, 95
Talmadge, Gov. Eugene, 116
technology and mass culture, 77
television, 201–3, 223
Temple, Shirley, 163
Tet offensive, 225
Thurber, James, 157
Tobin, Dan, 130
"togetherness," 206
Trilling, Lionel, 137
Trotsky, Leon, 69
Truman, Harry S., 182
Twiggy, 281

United Auto Workers (UAW), 130–1
United Mine Workers, 123
urban riots (1960s), 264–5

Valentino, Rudolph, 76, 161
Vietnam war, 228, 234, 256–61,
    277–8, 283, 304
  antidraft movements, 258–9
  confidence in government
    undermined by, 304
  draft deferments and, 258–9
  fireman's wife on student
    protests, 261
  national division caused by,
    259–60

Wagner Act of 1935, 129
Wales, John, 8
Wallace, George, 302
Washington, George, 8, 11
Watergate scandal, 284
Wayne, John, 235, 240
Wehl, Walter, 53–4
West, Mae, 161–2, 163
Westmoreland, Gen. William, 258
white-collar workers, 210–11, 217–18
Whitman, Walt, 12
Whyte, William H., 212
Williams, Roger, 5
Wilson, Edmund, 114
Wilson, Woodrow, 51–2, 59
Winthrop, John, 7
Wiser Sex, The (film), 163
women
  advertising and consumerism
    and, 83–5
  breast fixation in postwar era,
    187–91

domesticity as postwar choice, 191–2

emancipation in 1920s, 85–7

European women and American soldiers, 174–5

flappers, 87–93

in Great Depression, 115, 141–4

hippie counterculture, role in, 273–4

housewife's increasing isolation, 145

housework in fifties, 192–3

miniskirts and, 280–1

"new women" in silent movies, 96–7

nonsexual woman as icon of forties and fifties, 171–4

the "pill" and, 229–30

postwar sexuality and, 186–91

prostitution, 140–1

"refeminization" in postwar era, 186–91

right to vote, 66–7

sexual maturation in sixties, 237–9

single and poor women in Great Depression, 143–4

"softness" in World War II, blamed on, 168–76

veterans returning to civilian life and, 186–7

as work force in World War II, 178–82

see also feminism; mothers and motherhood; sexual revolution (1960s)

Women's Army Auxiliary Corps, 181

women's liberation, *see* feminism

women's suffrage, 66–7

Woodstock music festival (1969), 274–6

World War I, 51–2, 60

World War II, 166–82

attitudes toward enemy, 166–7

blacks in military, 177

combat experience and changing attitudes, 173–4

cultural conservatism of thirties and, 166

European women and American soldiers, 174–5

farm population and, 178

male reaction to women workers, 180–2

marriage statistics, 176

masculinity defined during, 173–6

political naiveté of Americans and, 167–8

population shifts during, 178

production during, 177–82

protection of mothers as aim of, 168–70

sacrifices during, 178

"softness" of Americans blamed on women, 168–76

women in work force, 178–82

see also postwar era (1945–59)

Wylie, Philip, 169–70

Yankelovich, Daniel, 279, 283

Yes, My Darling Daughter (film), 163

Yezierska, Anzia, 37

Young, Robert, 223

"yo-yos," 271

PERMISSION ACKNOWLEDGMENTS

Grateful acknowledgment is made to the following for permission to reprint previously published material:

Atheneum Publishers Inc.: Excerpt from "Elegy for My Father" in *Selected Poems* by Howard Moss. Copyright © 1971. Reprinted by permission of Atheneum Publishers Inc.

Harper & Row, Publishers, Inc., and *Penguin Books Ltd.:* Excerpt from "Howl" in *Collected Poems, 1947–1980* by Allen Ginsberg. Copyright © 1955, 1984 by Allen Ginsberg. UK rights administered by Penguin Books Ltd. Reprinted by permission of Harper & Row, Publishers, Inc. and Penguin Books Ltd.

Little, Brown and Company: Excerpt from "Father and Son" in *Selected Poems, 1928–1958* by Stanley Kunitz. Copyright 1944 by Stanley Kunitz. Reprinted by permission of Little, Brown and Company in association with the Atlantic Monthly Press.

Macmillan Publishing Company: Excerpt from "Introduction" by Loren Baritz, in *The Culture of the Twenties,* edited by Loren Baritz. Copyright © 1970. Reprinted by permission of Macmillan Publishing Company.

A NOTE ABOUT THE AUTHOR

Loren Baritz was born in Chicago, Illinois, and educated
at Roosevelt University and the University of Wisconsin,
where he earned his Ph.D. in history. He has taught at
Wesleyan University, the University of Rochester, and
the State University of New York at Albany and at Stony
Brook. He has also served as provost for the SUNY system and for the University of Massachusetts at Amherst,
and as Director of the New York Institute for the Hu-
manities. Currently he is Professor of History at the University of Massachusetts at Amherst. His many books
include *Backfire* (1985).

A NOTE ON THE TYPE

This book was set in Baskerville No. 2, a digitized interpretation of a typeface originally designed by John Baskerville (1706-1775). Baskerville, a writing master in
Birmingham, England, began experimenting in about
1750 with type design and punch cutting. His first book,
set throughout in his new types, was a Virgil in royal
quarto, published in 1757, and it was followed by other
famous editions from his press. Baskerville's types, which
are distinctive and elegant in design, were a forerunner
of what we know today as the "modern" faces.